Rekindling Our Cosmic Spark presents an expanded
view of infant and child consciousness. The book suggests an
alternative way of assisting children's development for more
conscious living for everyone. This work is a compelling synthesis of the author's research and that of others that reveals just
how profoundly our essential nature is spiritual. The book offers
tools for parents and their children so that all of us can more fully bring the light of who we are into this world.

-**Dr. Raymond Moody**, best-selling author of *Life After Life*

REKINDLING OUR COSMIC SPARK

A Noussentric Approach to Living and Parenting

Published by Noussentric Press.

© 2017, Geoffrey K. Leigh, Ph.D.

Third printing, November 2017

Noussentric Press, PO Box 3774, Yountville, CA 94599.

For information, visit us at **www.Noussentrism.com** or contact us as info@noussentrism.com

Library of Congress Control Number: 2017900435

ISBN: 978-0-9985966-0-0

General Editor: Morgan Farley

Cover design: Amiel Gervers, Seven Senses Photography and Design

Rumi poems included with the permission of Coleman Barks.

Dedicated to Joan and Henry,
who modeled living their passions,
and to Jen, Greg, David, and Kati,
their spouses, David, Jennifer, Liz, and Dustin,
and their loving children:
Ellie, Owen, Aubrie, Ivy, Autumn, Sienna, and Taylor.
You all are constant teachers and reminders
to love and live from the heart.

"Everyone has been made
for some particular work,
and the desire for that work
has been put in every heart."

- Rumi[1]

ONE ONE ONE

The lamps are different.
But the Light is the same.
So many garish lamps in the dying brain's lamp shop,
Forget about them.
Concentrate on essence, concentrate on Light.
In lucid bliss, calmly smoking off its own holy fire,
The Light streams toward you from all things,
All people, all possible permutations of good,
Evil, thought, passion.
The lamps are different,
But the Light is the same.
One matter, one energy, one Light, one Light-mind,
Endlessly emanating all things.
One turning and burning diamond,
One, one, one.
Ground yourself, strip yourself down,
To blind loving silence.
Stay there, until you see
You are gazing at the Light
With its own ageless eyes.

- Hafiz

TABLE OF CONTENTS

TABLE OF CONTENTS

ACKNOWLEDGMENTS

There are so many people who have helped me and taught me along my path, both through direct and indirect ways, that have lead to this work. Certainly I want to start with my parents, Joan and Henry, who loved me and helped me learn many basic aspects about life, people, questions, curiosity, respect, honor, and integrity. I did not always do well in carrying out the lessons they gave me, and in my own struggle, learning more about myself and what is most important to me in the end. They also gave me a strong heritage from their own parents, Samuel, Catherine, Charles, and Maud, with several European roots, including many English traditions. I also learned about strength and determination in many ways from my older brother, Wynston, who always was pioneering paths for me, some of which helped me find my own freedom. Even when we see things differently, he accepts me as I am today, which touches me deeply. I also learned about caring, connection, and loyalty from my older sister, Soni, who always has been my ally even when we have seen the world from different points of view. She has been a model of support for me. I also have learned to walk my own path, especially with the support of two cousins who learned to walk theirs. Thank you Mike and Lorrie!

I am grateful for my early formal teachers, including Mr. Briscoe, Mr. Jones, Mrs. Stapley, and Mr. Cunningham in my formative high school years. During a time when I was trying to figure out my own direction, they helped me learn skills to deal with the strong atmosphere of conformity that I experienced as I grow up in a conservative culture. I am thankful for both the culture in which I learned to question and hold my own, as well as the skills and support to traverse a fine line of living in that culture and being my own person. In addition, other teachers have had a strong impact on me, including Wes Burr, my major mentor during my doctoral program. In addition, Eli helped me understand the Enneagram from a spiritual path, and Lansing helped me pay attention to subtler energies and learning more self-trust. Finally, I have a deep gratitude to many Buddhist teachers, especially Tibetan Buddhists, who have helped me develop my meditation practice, awareness, and seeing the world from a different perspective.

There also are so many "teachers" in my life because of our connection, friendship, examples, and traits that helped me learn from your lives as a model. Thank you Robert, for modeling strength and trust of self. He has always been an inspiration to me, even when we do not connect for years. I appreciate learning about awareness and projection for my friend, Jan. I am grateful for learning about subtle interactions and control from my friend, Chad, who was very observant and insightful. Gratitude to Gary, who kept everything real and honest, and who also had a deep curiosity about so many things. Thanks to Cynthia for her support and candid observation of my emotionless place when we met and the constant support to be what ever I wanted. Deep gratitude to Collette, who has been a guide, constant support, and explorer of options that have allowed my own expansion over many years. I appreciate David, who helped me allow more options for myself through becoming aware of my patterns and knowing there always are more possible choices when we allow ourselves to see them. I also appreciate Howard for his encouragement of exploring with integrity areas of my life that had been a taboo. Thanks to Patrick, who was such a support in many ways as I was trying to figure out my path, both professionally and personally. Deep gratitude to Leo, who gave me a pioneering model of shifting out of academia to do what feels most important and the loving friendship we enjoyed for a short time. I so appreciate the connection and support I developed from Raymond while in Las Vegas. Your invitations to participate in a class, guest lectures, and informal discussions that included your own personal work and journey was very helpful to my own thinking and the development of a different path. A loving thanks to Lisa, who also helped me open to myself in new ways and facilitated connections to people and aspects of my life that were previously unavailable. Thank you Sterling, a man of vision and strength, who continued to help me stay with this work when I felt weak and unable to complete it. His model and support have been tremendous.

I will always be in debt to Satya and Lyn for helping me journey in ways that have solidified my confidence for these ideas and helped me gain clarity for the central thesis of this work with adults. I would not be able to write some of the most challenging aspects without walking along the paths you have paved. A deep appreciation to Karen and Ruth, who helped me unravel issues of gender and race, allowing me to see the many advantages I experienced as a white male who was given privilege without ever having to ask for it. Your friendship, love, and many gifts of laughter, tears, chocolate, dancing, and long discussions will always be close to my heart and my head. And then there is Celia, my friend, confident, and constant support through the low times as well as any successes I have achieved. She has helped me look at dark places that transformed into blossoms because of the light she shines on them. She also has been such a support in my connections with others, especially my children, that has been a constant source of increased awareness and change because of the trust she has had in her own talents and subtle skills. Thanks also to my dear friends Wanda and Donna, who have been constant sources of support in the development of my energy work, ideas, and writing of this book. Such gratitude for your friendship and encouragement.

At an early point in my life as a young adult, I thought it would be my dear friends who would be my most important guides. Unfortunately at times, I focused more on them and had less of an emphasis on my children. In the end, it has been my children, Jen, Greg, David, and Kati, who have been my greatest teachers. I once told Jen when she was pregnant with her daughter, Ellie, that she would be Jen's greatest teacher. At the time, I thought I was being so insightful about someone else. In the end, it has been these four wonderful children and their spouses who have taught me about love, devotion, strength, resolving differences, and finding your own path that have been an inspiration to me. I also have gained insights about children by watching them and especially how they have been with their children and each others children. Thanks to all that you have given me already Ellie, Owen, Aubrie, Ivy, Autumn, Sienna, and Taylor. I have learned more about love, support, and finding one's own path by observing the people they have brought into their lives to share honest and intimate connection. Thanks to you too David, Jennifer, Liz, and Dustin for being the loving spouses and partners in this exploration of joy and love.

During an early time of my life, I was married to a loving woman, Jayne. We had four great children, which she primarily raised because after our divorce we lived in separate states. She was great at teaching our children to keep their hearts open and care about other people. Jayne and I were not a great couple, in large part because of my internal struggles and lack of ability to resolve differences. Those issues carried on into other relationships, and I have tried to help my children follow a different path.

There were many people in my life who helped my understand different parts of myself, allowing me to shift and live my life differently. Thanks to Kathy and Heidi, who helped me keep my heart open and have more fun in life. My appreciation to Mary, who helped me ask questions and dig deeper into issues, changing the way I teach because my own process transformed. Deep appreciation to Pamela, who helped me bring to conscious awareness my own limiting and strength patterns, which allowed my to make different decisions and see new connections. Gratitude to Brenda, who assisted in my investigation of emotional reactions and learning it is not all about me.

There is a deep gratitude to my current circle of support from the friends and connections I have who are part of the Human Awareness Institute (HAI). Thanks to Collette for introducing me to this larger group and the subgroup of Potluckers, who give me love and friendship on a monthly basis. The Institute has been an important part of my continued change and growth, and I am grateful for the many gifts I have gained from my experiences in those workshops and the opportunity I have to give back.

Then there is Deep Heaven, my dear group of friends, some of whom have shared heartful experiences on the playa, and all of who share the love and support for each group member, as I learn more about living in community in a healthy way. There is so much I gain from our Deep Days, rich and transparent shares, and how to love without expectations of anything more. Thanks to all of you for accepting me as I am and for helping me see more clearly the light inside. I would be remiss not to identify a few particular supports that have been important for this project. To Barbara, you have inspired me to finish my book and supported the learning process of self-publishing. To Richard, I am grateful for your most gracious and loving challenge of my deep self-critical process. To Kurt, I appreciate your connections to a caring pod and the insights it brings as well as the courage to make this all public. To Edgie, I have deep gratitude for your unending exploration of our being and the related universes. To Marci, I am very grateful for your model of love, authenticity, and creativity. To Liz, I forever will be in debt for your encouragement to join Deep Heaven and your unwavering and constant support of me. And to Carolyn, I am grateful for your witnessing and constant encouragement to step out onto the skinny branches. For our conscious explorations, I appreciate our entire group of journeyers and explorers.

I owe deep gratitude to my dear friend, Karen. You always were a model of how to turn things on their head, ask the unasked questions, and expand my outlook way beyond the limited views I held when I met you over 36 years ago. It was from our conversations about children's defenses that I first saw how amazing we were as children, constructing our protections in ways that took decades to unravel. I so wish you and Patrick were here to see the results of our discussions and how they helped form this book. I miss you both so much!

In addition, I want to thank Marianne. She showed up at a time that helped me develop a daily practice to ground my spiritual development and explorations. She helped me expand the questions, methods, and processes, which allowed me to explore myself in a gentle and more loving manner. The soft strength, which she always has shared with me, has been a joy and support in my growth. And now, we come back together after many years on our own journeys to see how we each have expanded our hearts, tempered our skills, and grown in a way that allows us to develop our ally connection. It is a joy to reconnect as heartful allies, feeling the caring and support we enjoy with each other. There also is a way that you carry out your passion for work that continues to inspire me to do the same with mine. I am grateful you encouraged me to explore the Enneagram, which has been such a valued teacher for me in my personal exploration. And thank you for encouraging me take my writing to another level.

This work would not have happened had I not met and began working with my friend and colleague, Jean. We supported each other and immersed ourselves in the topic of energy fields and began a long collaboration that shifted my career and my life. While I am happy with other research and writing pieces over my academic career, the investigations on children, families, and diverse energy fields is the work that makes me most proud. That work lead directly to the paper Jean and I wrote with important contributions from her son, Nate, who added some central ideas and help to lay the foundation for this book (see Appendix A). Thank you does not begin to express my appreciation for entering my life in such a way as to develop a collaboration in many different areas and avenues over time. I will always be in gratitude for our connection and joint exploration in topics that were not common or generally supported in our professions.

I have a deep appreciation for Dr. Morgan Farley, who is a great editor and teacher. She was wonderful with her direction, support, and encouragement, urging me to explore different ways of expressing myself and my ideas. Her insightful questions pushed me to get clearer about my thoughts, own my work, and make it more personal. She helped me make my ideas more available for readers, which is what I needed and wanted. Most of all, she encouraged me to find my own voice, not just learn to write by the book. And in the process, we had fun and could laugh too. I am in deep gratitude for the improvement of my writing and the immense difference it has made with my book. But in the end, any errors or lack of clarity in this writing are my responsibility, as I made the final editing decisions.

I appreciate Morgan introducing me to Amiel Gervers, who created and designed the cover art as well as back cover. I knew this book really was going to be completed when I saw this cover for the first time. I am happy for the final creation you developed and brought to life an underlying aspect to the cover design. Many thanks for your creativity. And gratitude to Coleman Barks for allowing me to reprint several Rumi poems from his wonderful book, A Year With Rumi.

I have focused so far on the people from the past who have helped me come to this point in my life. But finally, I want to thank the readers of this work. It is you who could take these ideas into the future rather than leaving them on a dusty shelf where so many research projects and publications land. If one piece of this journey or one idea from this exploration touches you in such a way that you begin to see yourself, others, or the world a little differently, then all of this effort is worthwhile. Thank you for taking the time to explore these pieces, and I hope you find something of value for your personal life that will be a gift or assistance in your own explorations. If there is anything here that you like or find of value, please share it with someone. If there are ideas that seem inaccurate or convoluted, please add to or sort them out, making them more beneficial to you and others. These ideas are not given as "TRUTH," but rather as possibilities to be tried and explored, elaborated and expanded. This is only a beginning from one person's point of view, building on so many others who have made their own contributions and shared their own gifts. There is much more to be done and developed.

So jump in and add what I did not see and where I did not explore. My deepest hope is that you as readers will find extensions that are beneficial to expanding your hearts, helping your children be more of who they really are, and assisting parents and other professionals support the development of subtler skills and awareness, benefiting all of us as human beings, the quality of our lives, and the health of this earth.

INTRODUCTION

With contributions by Jean A. Metzker, Ph.D.

OUT BEYOND

Out beyond ideas of wrongdoing and rightdoing,
there is a field. I'll meet you there.

When the soul lies down in that grass,
the world is too full to talk about.

Ideas, language, even the phrase each other
doesn't make any sense.

- Rumi[1]

Let me begin by asking you an important question: How do you see children? What is your view of their capabilities when they are born and over the next few years? Do you see them as a "blank slate" or do you see them as having skills and abilities at birth? Over the decades since my four children were born and seven grandchildren were added to our family, my views of children have changed dramatically. Some of that change was brought about by my experience helping to raise our children and guiding them in this life. My graduate work in human development and family studies also shaped my perspectives, particularly discussions with key friends and colleagues along the way. The research I conducted influenced my thinking during the 30 years I spent in academia, as an assistant professor at the University of Iowa, an associate professor at Ohio State, and a professor at the University of Nevada, Reno. But the studies of children's energy fields with my colleague, Jean Metzker, and the investigation of children's abilities in related areas of research have had the greatest impact on my transformed views of infants.

Historical Views of Children

Historically, adults have discounted infants as people, viewing them instead as possessions. When adults define children as their "property" it allows them to treat young people like other types of things they "own." Within this framework, children have been abandoned, sacrificed, abused, sold into slavery, and used for pleasure by those who were older and more powerful, as evidenced by the prevalence of incest and rape.[2,3] In fact, children have been defined as "the absence of adulthood."[4] Whenever grown-ups have characterized young people this way, there was little consequence for the way adults treated them. In fact, it was concern over the treatment of animals, not children, that provided the foundation for changes in child labor laws and other policies oppressing children.[5]

Some adults still continue to view children as property and treat them with violence and abuse, including attempts to "beat the Devil out of them."[6-8] In some parts of the world, young girls have their genitals mutilated by people they trust because of an ancient belief that such brutal surgery will reduce a young woman's libido and increase the likelihood of premarital virginity and marital fidelity, a belief people refuse to abandon. Even when older women who have spoken out about the mutilation describe the physical, emotional, and relationship pain they experience, people do not want to change their belief about this cruelty. The same is true of violence and abuse. We perpetuate pain and brutality with our young people because we believe it is acceptable to use or harm children.[6,9]

There also are many parents who dearly love their children and work hard to furnish what they believe is best for them. They care, nurture, protect, and provide many opportunities in the lives of children, including college educations and sometimes financial support for buying their first car or home. They treat them with respect and attempt to minimize any harm, but they still typically do not include the possibility of enhancing the divine spark and subtle skills.

Within the social sciences, scholars studying infants and young children traditionally focus on their lack of skills, such as the absence of physical, cognitive and verbal abilities. Researchers more recently have investigated early responses to parents, but we basically view children as the absence of adulthood and of the competence that such development brings.

After some years of work within feminism, Berry Thorne asked a key question, "where are the children?"[10] She went on to outline three views of children, all of which focus on their current oppression. She suggested that children are seen as 1) threats to adult society; 2) victims of adult society; or 3) learners of adult culture. In each case, children are viewed as objects of the learning or socialization process, through which they develop skills and abilities as they become adults. Grown-ups generally do not see anything of importance that children bring into this world beyond genetics, reflexes, and potential, as they do not demonstrate any adult physical capabilities, mental processing, or communication abilities. Therefore, children are discounted until they are able to function with more adult attributes.

In the theories and research on infants and preschoolers I have explored, scholars have ignored several unexplained aspects of children. For example, young people develop defense mechanisms during the early years of life, sometimes having a foundation built by ages four to six. If children are born with so few skills, how do they develop such a complex and intricate system of defenses that their more learned parents, teachers, and therapists have difficulty understanding and unweaving later in life? In fact, individuals may spend their entire adult lives and considerable funds attempting to undo what they have constructed as children. So do adults recognize all there is to see in young ones when they view them basically as void of skills? Thorne's question not only begs for an answer, it also calls for an expansion of our perspective of who children are, what they bring to this life, and what they are able to do.

Some indigenous people treat their offspring with dignity, at their birth and during their childhoods, rather than viewing them as property or objects of oppression. A few cultures create celebrations for pregnancy and the birth of a child, generate rites of passage in the lives of young people, and even deify infants and youngsters.[11]

Indigenous people may be acting from the perspective that children embody a "divine spark" or "soul spark."[12] This perspective sees children as "created in the image" of the divine, with a spark of the divine inside each one.[13] But the idea of divine spark has never been developed into a comprehensive approach to raising children. We seem to keep this view of divine spark totally separate from the way we treat young people. If we do not see children as evil or as property, then focusing on the divine or cosmic spark in them takes us in a very different direction and offers us a new approach to understanding and supporting young people, especially if we include investigations of the skills they seem to bring into this life.

From our collaborative research, Jean and I found that infants at three to nine months of age did have a number of skills that could not have been taught to them by adults.[14,15] Such abilities were not found in any of the traditional scientific theories. This led us to expand our view of children, seeing them more in the light of a "spark" that is present at birth. As I have continued to play with and extend these ideas, they have evolved into what I call Noussentrism, the explanation and application of which is the purpose of this book. I will outline the development of these ideas, which expand our understanding of infants and young children, over the next 12 chapters.

Noussentrism: A New Word for a New Perspective

Noussentrism_is a combination of two words: *nous* and *essence*. One definition of nous is: "Neoplasm, the first and purest emanation of the One, regarded as the self-contemplating order of the universe." A common meaning of essence is "the intrinsic nature or indispensable quality of something, the basic nature of a thing." These two ideas combine to signify my view of children. I define **Noussentrism** as "**the basic nature and expression of our purest emanation of the universe, the spark of cosmic consciousness.**" Within this view, children are seen as bringing consciousness, abilities, and skills to this life that develop into the manifestation of their "cosmic spark." Of course, if this is the view of children, it then becomes the view of human beings in general.

We do not see or recognize this spark when extensive defense systems, energy and physical blocks, and disconnections cover it. Transformation from "cosmic spark" to personality can occur through a socialization process that ignores these abilities and skills, which leads to pain, hurt, and closure of the heart. Rather than replacing previous perspectives, the noussentric view expands what we know about children's physical, emotional, and mental development to include aspects ignored in more narrow, traditional concepts.

I have come to believe that we as human beings are born in an expansive state that we call love. In this case, love is not just an emotion of caring and connection, of "loving" others or ourselves, but it is what we are made of, our natural state before increasing levels of fear and contraction take us to a socialized altered state.

One irony of life is that as adults we typically need to be in some "altered state" to know such a feeling, to encounter ourselves as the composition of love. Such an experience is subtle, coming from an open heart, relaxed, and surrendering to a new possibility. Evidence increasingly suggests the infant experiences this state until it is modified by pain, hurt, fear, and other contractions that take us out of our natural state into the altered state we call "life" and "human." From the point of view of an infant, it is this altered state of life that takes us out of our natural state. From the point of view of the socialized adult, it is the altering of our usual state, such as through meditation or a near-death experience, that leads us back into the experience of our natural state of love.

This composition of love is still true of us as adults. Yet we have covered it over so much that we see ourselves more as the personality, or as the Enneagram defines it, as our fixation. But there is a sharp distinction between personality or fixation and essence. An important realization for adults is to know it is possible to rekindle this spark, as some have done. Such a change may be a life's work, but it may also be the most significant work we do. More importantly, this work is not just about ourselves, but also about how we encourage our children as they develop and impact the future of this world.

Infants appear to bring some abilities with them rather than learn them all in this life. They access subtle information from an essence that appears to be more than genetics, reflexes, and what sometimes is referred to as "nature," a catch-all term without any precision. Noussentrism is an expansion of the idea that we as humans have a True Nature.

Infants have a conscious knowing that is more than our current models of development can explain. Young children develop complex defense mechanisms that are challenging to unravel, in part because such basic foundations are often kept in the dark. Yet these defenses develop during a period when children are viewed as having quite simple cognitive functioning. When we expand our view of children to include other aspects of our world, such as energy fields, intuitive knowing, information gathering through subtle means, and the choosing of a primary issue to explore in this life, we have the basics of a noussentric approach.

Shifting Perceptions of Children

The expansion of our view of children to include greater abilities and skills is one contribution of this work. But in order for us to include a new idea such as noussentrism, our current views and beliefs must change. If we want to accept and work with an alternative outlook, we must expand our perspective to include such possibilities. Expanding and transforming our point of view allows us to incorporate something different, move away from a perception that limits how we see children, and include further possibilities. This process is important not only in expanding our outlook of infants, but also in the development of any new idea. I talk about this process as a mechanism for discovering additional ways of viewing and supporting children, especially in Chapters 2-4.

When I began my graduate training in human development, much of the early research on children and families focused on a problem or disease model. This perspective emphasized the problems people exhibit, basically assuming that something was inherently wrong. Later, new perspectives redirected our focus to a resiliency and strengths model. Changes are easier to identify after they have developed, as with this shift from dysfunction, deficit, and problems to resiliency, strengths, and assets. But when we get attached to our beliefs, a different perspective can be difficult to see and even more challenging to accept.

We develop belief systems about ourselves and the world while we are infants and young children, and they are not easily dismantled, even by brilliant therapists. When we allow the ground on which our belief systems are built to shift, turn, and evolve into a new world view, it does not destroy all that we believe, but it does allow us to see our reality from a larger perspective. This shift is important, as we create a vision of what is possible and learn to experience life in a new way. Rather than adopting a completely "new" view with noussentrism, we are reclaiming our own infant perspective that we let go dormant. I am convinced that we can reconnect to inherent and natural abilities we ignored because they were too subtle and not included as a possibility in our construction of reality.

If we embrace a larger outlook, our attitudes and especially our behaviors also shift. When our perspective changes, it allows us to see a different picture and to modify our treatment of others. If we make such changes, shifting our perspective is not just an interesting mental activity. Often it impacts how we treat ourselves and others, especially the people close to us. I have witnessed such changes in my own life and with people I have had the opportunity to know and work. When we crack open a new door in our minds, we crack open a path of possibility in our physical world, stretching the physical and social fabric a little wider.

This book presents an expanded view of infants, children, adolescents, and in the end, ourselves. While we know at one level that children develop physically, emotionally, cognitively and socially, this work includes subtler forms of information, skills, and abilities that are not included in these more traditional perspectives of human development. In the next chapter, I present ideas about children that have not been included in previous theories and most research. These ideas emerged from the work Jean Metzker and I did together, but they also pull from other investigations that extend the outlook on children, an expansion that I believe is past due. With this book, I shine a broader light on children's development and ask questions about skills and abilities that have been ignored by the general population and by the scientific community focused on child development. Fundamentally, I believe the purpose of noussentrism is to create a more expansive, positive approach to the way we care for and nurture our children, and, beyond that, to build a more positive world for ourselves.

As Jean and I developed our research projects on human energy fields in infants, young children, adolescents, and families, we realized how little such a perspective had been incorporated into previous theory and research. In addition, as we observed what skills six-month-old infants have in terms of their utilization of energy fields, we increasingly questioned the deficit model social scientists had been using about children. We recognized that these skills are available to infants and also are manipulated by both adolescents and parents in their interactions.[14-17] Yet most people are not aware of this level of subtle information, nor do they seem to pay attention to what is happening with others. I progressively explored aspects of development that were not included in current theories, especially the ways that infants begin with skills that go dormant when not emphasized or supported by those around them. My views of infants and children, and later of adolescents and adults, shifted again and again as I became more aware of possibilities ignored by others. In the end, these changes in my earlier thinking became the foundation for this book.

The Focus of the Book

In this book, parents will find an expanded view of children and an exploration of how we might support them through adolescence to hold onto more of the core skills they bring into this world. I talk about how we can connect with infants in a broader way, to share our love in a more diverse manner, and thus help them preserve their own core essence and subtle abilities. I also present ways we might communicate as parents and children that would be more congruent and honest, as we pay attention to our own internal separations. Using a more expansive approach, we can encourage children and adolescents to trust and incorporate these skills into their everyday lives. Incorporating such abilities during early development will increase their possibilities as adults to enhance their behaviors and relationships. From my experience, this can then change their relationships with their own children, a benefit which may be passed on for generations.

Teachers will find ways they too can expand their perspective of who children are and what subtle skills they can use in the learning process. They might choose to support an inner trust in children rather than expecting them to be completely focused on an external authority. While this may present a great challenge, it can encourage teachers to expand their own resources fostering the same response in students. Children who pay attention to their intuitive skills, trust their inner voice, and have access to subtle information can be great reminders and even models for teachers, who could expand the same skills in their own lives.

This can be especially true when we as teachers did not grow up paying attention to and trusting our internal assets.

Finally, therapists, physicians, social service workers, and others who work with children may incorporate new ways of accessing information about children or adolescents, as well as supporting their development in a more expansive manner. As I have learned to trust subtler information while interacting with others, I have a sense of whether congruence occurs between what people are saying and what they are holding in their energy fields. I don't always know if they are "being dishonest," but I do have a sense of incongruity that may be about a discrepancy between their feelings and thoughts, or a disagreement in their belief system. This sense of discrepancy can be helpful in leading me to ask more questions or pursue information in various ways to help me understand and clarify the incongruity. Sometimes, the person is not even aware of the conflict, which makes further investigation useful to both of us. I think this has made me a more useful coach in helping people change behaviors, for at times we are not clear what gets in our own way of living our life differently.

In the end, my intention here is to help parents, family members, teachers, therapists, and other professionals try on new attitudes and behaviors in their interactions with children. I am calling for a shift in our perspectives, as well as an expansion in our interactions, which will allow us to view and nurture children in an expanded light.

Outline of the Book

The book is divided into three sections. In the first section, Noussentrism and Children's Gifts, I focus on the aspects of children that we seem to ignore, and describe how viewing them differently could help us all. In Chapter One, I discuss how children might live from essence and their innate abilities, outlining some of the skills that children bring to this life, based on our research as well as on what I have gleaned from other work related to children. I also include information from reports or case studies that suggest a more expansive view. In Chapter Two, I discuss our current socialization process, which encourages children to focus away from their inner strengths to a primarily external view of authority through a game called "Buy My Perspective." Such a shift is not simple but takes place over time, and yet I think a brighter and more dynamic future can occur when we incorporate some important alternatives. In Chapter Three, I describe a process that explains how a shift from inner resources to external priorities takes place over the lifespan. I walk through important phases where we have the choice to diminish or nurture our cosmic spark.

In the second section of the book, Rekindling Our Spark as Adults, I focus more on parents and suggest ways we can recover dormant abilities, increasing our skills as we access subtler forms of information. In Chapter Four, I discuss the opportunities for all of us in shifting our perspectives; this holds true for scientists, researchers, and anyone who is interested in some form of change. Without a shift in outlook, we cannot take a larger view of anything, including children's abilities. I talk in Chapter Five about specific ways to enhance our abilities as adults. We can begin by paying more attention to subtle sources of information, which helps us recover skills we lost as we moved towards adulthood. In Chapter Six, I focus on expanding the heart opening, which seems to be a vital component in allowing us to express greater vulnerability and release some of the many blocks that keep us disconnected from these dormant skills. Here I talk about how to develop an Open Peaceful Heart, a key for our own lives as well as the greatest gift we can both receive from and give to our children. Heart opening gives us balance in our lives when combined with a lively inquiring mind. I dig deeper into love in Chapter Seven, arguing that love is not only an emotion but the fundamental material that constitutes our being, our essence. I also describe the ways that love as an emotion and love as our fabric differ from each other. In Chapter Eight, I talk about sexuality and its relationship to expanding consciousness. I believe this aspect of our being can be utilized in that way, and there is evidence this is happening with some adults already.

In the third section of the book, Adults and Children Learning Together, I focus on modifying our relationships with others, including our children and grandchildren and the young people who are helped by our many professionals. I offer new possibilities for deepening our connections, awareness, and understanding. In Chapter Nine, I discuss the issue of healing our relationships with younger children, for it is never too early to begin this process. In some cases, we may begin while our children or grandchildren are young, with fewer defenses and blocks in the way of our connection and communication. Following that, in Chapter Ten I present ideas for healing our relationships with older, even adult children, for it also is never too late to begin the healing. I keep working on this with my adult children, and encourage others to do the same, for I see the transformation pass down to the relationships with their children. In Chapter Eleven, I suggest ways that teachers, therapists, medical professionals, and others might expand how they work with children, adolescents, and families. We really are connected, and there are so many others outside a family who impact the way we view our world, connect with each other, and share our difficult experiences. The influence of professionals in our communities can be significant, even if only for a short, intensive period of time. Finally, in Chapter Twelve, I describe possibilities for changing our future, envisioning what a different path we could take by expanding our perspective of children, ourselves, and each other, and most of all expanding our heart opening. Within this enlarged perspective, I play with what I believe is possible, given some fundamental transformations of our worldview and the way we treat and communicate with each other.

This book has been a life's work that has included important collaborations, especially with my good colleague and friend, Dr. Jean Metzker. It also builds on many important works that other people have been developing, mostly on the periphery of the scientific community or in the exploration of means for self-discovery. Now is the time to pull these ideas together and see children in a new light, expanding our vision of what they bring to this life.

SECTION ONE

Noussentrism and Children's Gifts

CHAPTER 1

LIVING FROM ESSENCE: CHILDREN'S ABILITIES

With Contributions by Jean A. Metzker, Ph.D.

CHILDSPLAY

There is no one with intelligence
in our town except that man over there
playing with the children.

He has keen, fiery insight
and vast dignity like the nightsky,
but he conceals it in childsplay.

- Rumi[1]

I was 65 years old before I finally became aware of the freeze response in my body. Although I was good at sensing the distance from someone close to me, I was not always able to determine the reason for it. I tended to take any separation personally, assuming the lack of connection was because I had done something wrong. Sometimes I was correct, but often it had nothing to do with me. Still, I would go into this automatic reaction, unable to express my feelings, communicate my thoughts clearly, or assess alternatives that would be useful. Increasingly, it was hindering my life and interfering with my relationships.

I had experienced this response for decades, but I never allowed myself to look at it clearly or pinpoint its impact. In retrospect, I surprise myself for ignoring the clarity of my reaction. At some level, I had been aware of feeling disconnected since I was a little boy; the distance from my mother became apparent when she was sick or upset. Even then I would try to figure out how to "fix it," for I hated the feeling of diminished connection with someone so important to me. This feeling later arose whenever I would feel emotional distance in close relationships.

I had studied psychology, human development, family relationships, sociology, and family therapy, and eventually taught many different theories about change and behavior, including how children develop responses and ways of protecting themselves. As I continued to explore my patterns through long conversations with my dear friend, Karen, I came to see that children develop sophisticated defense mechanisms during infancy and early childhood (birth to age 4 or 5). They developed responses to events, and patterns to protect ourselves. These systems are put into place when children's cognitive abilities and mental processing are quite limited. Yet, none of the traditional theories provided a clear explanation for how different defense patterns emerge during such an early age when they lack complex mental functioning.

Our research work helped me see this issue more clearly. It led me to identify certain skills in infants and young children and to understand how such defenses emerge. I also found evidence of skills others were reporting. In this chapter, I will summarize some important skills very young children have that allow them to access information in a nontraditional manner. In the next two chapters, I will describe how we shift away from these aspects to a more physical worldview, letting go of or covering up subtler skills in the process.

Our Work

When I began my doctoral program in family studies and sociology, I had an important learning experience regarding what was and was not considered "scientific." In one of my courses, an advanced research methods class, each of us had the assignment to develop a research question and the methodology to conduct the proposed investigation. The class was a combination of students from two different departments, so the questions and approaches were diverse. We all developed our proposals, and at the end of the semester we each presented what we would do if we had the funds to conduct our investigation.

One student presented a proposal to investigate the quality of relationships with dating couples where he proposed using traditional surveys about relationship satisfaction. But his most innovative and interesting idea was to use Kirlian photography, an approach developed in Russia in the 1930s, to measure energy fields. This student's hypothesis, as I recall it, was that if you took a Kirlian photograph of the index finger of two people in a relationship, you could measure the energy field between them. Typically, you would see a field that extended beyond the skin of the finger, with a shape similar to but larger than the skin of the finger. If there were a "dent" or pulling away of energy from either person, in contrast to the normally round field surrounding a finger, the two were not emotionally close and might be in conflict. The dent in the field would indicate an emotional distance, illustrated energetically, between them. If you saw the field extending outward, beyond the normal circular pattern, it would indicate an emotional closeness or energetic reaching towards the other person.

The reaction of the class to this proposal was unanimous: "This is not science!" We were not open to using energy fields as a scientific inquiry, even if it might have had greater validity than some of the self-report instruments many of us had incorporated. The embarrassing part is that I was very much a part of discounting this proposal as lacking a scientific foundation. Yet 20 years later, my interest in energy fields had grown tremendously. I wanted to find a machine that could videotape such fields in order to see how they change during parent-adolescent interactions. So began my long investigations into this arena, in collaboration with my colleague, Jean Metzker.

I was amazed when Jean and I reviewed previous research and found the extensive work that had been done during the late nineteenth century and into the twentieth, work that was ignored by all the traditional science theories. For example, a Yale University anatomy professor in the School of Medicine, Harold Burr, began studying the energy fields of plants and later of humans in the 1930s.[2] With support from Filmer Northrup, a philosophy professor at the same institution, they developed a perspective called a Life-Field, or L-Field.[3,4] They believed that this bioelectric field, which both surrounds and is internal to the body, directs the organization of our organism, including our biology. In other words, the energy field controls changes in our biology rather than biology controlling our body reactions. They argued that this field was related to development, healing, mood, and health, impacting the biology itself.[5,6] Burr's student and colleague, Leonard Ravitz, continued this work, studying how L-fields are related to changes in a person's mental and emotional states.[7] What Burr and Ravitz concluded was that the electro-dynamic perspective was the foundation for understanding electro-magnetic human energy fields. A former research scientist for NASA, Barbara Brennan, supported the conclusions of Burr and Ravitz's work, seeing this energy field as important in maintaining health.[8] While others had talked about aspects of the human energy field, these people and others in the area of medicine were doing research about its importance and how its changes impacted health.

As in so many areas of research, children had been left out of these investigations. A British psychotherapist, Ruth White, wrote about the energy fields of humans, including the seven chakras, major energy centers near the body that have a long history in Eastern medicine. White talked about children having more translucent, or more transparent, energy fields than adults.[9] She suggested that energy fields develop over time, like other aspects of development, as children move into adulthood. This theory takes a deficit approach to children, waiting for them to grow into adults in order to have more completely formed human energy fields.

Jean and I became curious about what the energy fields of children actually were like. We began doing some exploratory observations with infants and young children, which led to the development of a coding form. Observational coding is a popular and widely used methodology with children, in part because of their underdeveloped cognitive and verbal skills. In this endeavor, we found two other people who could see and observe energy fields, which allowed us to put together an observational research study of such fields in infants and young children.

After getting approval for conducting this research at a university child development center, we began by randomly picking six children in each of three age groups: 6 months, 30 months, and 54 months of age.[10, 11] We observed and completed an observational form on each child, following up one year and again two years later. In the end, we added another seven infants closest to 6 months in age, so that we had a total of 57 observations with children from 6 to 54 months of age, for most using three observations points one year apart. We then looked at where at least two of the observers agreed on an observation and included those points, weighing them more heavily when all three agreed.

What we found was that the energy fields of older children were denser and smaller than those of the infants in the upper half of the body, but not in other areas. Older children also had more shapes or objects in their fields, which appeared to slow down the energy overall. Infants had not only less density and energy in the field, but also a higher velocity or speed at which the energy was moving. Some might argue that a lower density and higher velocity is a natural developmental pattern in energy fields as they "mature." We argue that this also may be an increased blocking of the field, which would be a part of the defense mechanisms in action. In addition, infant fields were more translucent, as White suggested. But this may have less to do with a lack of development of the field than with the collecting of objects that generate a more solidified field as children get older. These objects are related to emotional events experienced by children, both positive and negative.

What really surprised me and challenged some fundamental assumptions about children was that all of the infants were making energy "rings" with people around them, usually extending from the front of the infant to the back part of the heart on a parent or caregiver. These rings appeared to be an energy connection with the adult initiated by the infant. In addition, the infants made energy connections with objects, sometimes when the object was in their hands while others were at a distance. This connection was most often associated with the sixth chakra, sometimes called the third eye, a concentration of energy found just beyond the middle of the forehead. The infants seemed to be pulling in information about the object. Almost none of the children were making energy rings or energy connections with objects by age 4 or 5; their interactions were almost completely physical.

While the results of the whole project were interesting, I was particularly struck by three things. First, I was surprised and fascinated by the many different things six-month-old infants were doing with their energy fields that no one else had ever described. The fact that they appeared to initiate energy rings with parents or caregivers was astonishing. Second, they initiated energy connections with objects, as if checking out the objects energetically. These findings led me to question the belief that infants are born without any skills, but rather develop them after birth. Third, children's energy fields fill with objects as they get older, making the fields denser and slower. This made me wonder about the process of developing defense mechanisms energetically during this period of development.

Following this research on children, Jean and I looked at the energy fields of adolescents and their parents while they were discussing enjoyable or difficult times as a family.[12,13] We had 52 families where we coded the fields, again using an observational method from videotaped interactions. It was amazing how intense some of the family interactions were in their discussion of difficult times. Each family member also completed a questionnaire that asked about closeness in the parent-adolescent relationship, as well as four standardized questionnaires. Later we analyzed the relationships between the observational coding and the standardized self-report instruments.

We found that aspects of the energy fields were related to the self-reported closeness of mother to adolescent and adolescent to father. In addition, we discovered that fields changed at times during the discussions or when a parent would enter the room while the other parent and adolescent had been talking. In some instances, the fields moved away from a person and appeared to close down, while at other times they would move toward a person entering the room, as if making more of a connection. In some respects, this way of measuring relationships was what the graduate student was suggesting he test some 20 years earlier, when I was unable to appreciate the originality of his proposal.

From this work, I realized that many things going on in the energy fields were similar to what people experienced internally and reported through questionnaires. Yet people did not seem to be aware of what their energy fields were doing with each other. It appeared to me that people were responding with their energy fields, especially in terms of the energy moving towards or away from another family member, apparently in relation to the emotion occurring within them. This reminded me of what we saw infants do with their fields. Although the infants appeared to focus their energy fields on other people and objects more than the adults or adolescents did, we do not seem to lose the ability to have our fields respond to our emotional experiences.

Following the observational work with young children and later with families, I was able to do some research on the energy fields of different age groups using a machine called the GDV instrument.[14] This machine was basically a computerized Kirlian photography instrument developed by a Russian engineer by the name of Konstantin Korotkov using Electrophotonics. The measure was based on the Kirlian photographs proposed by my graduate school colleague in his proposal about relationship closeness. Unfortunately, the machine was not able to measure two fingers at the same time, so I was unable to conduct the interesting research he had proposed. But I was able to compare differences in energy fields by age group and activity.

My youngest daughter, Catherine (Kati), and I gathered data from eight children ages 2-12, 16 adolescents ages 13-19, 16 adults ages 21-54, and 16 adults who participated in a daily program of stretching, meditation, energy releasing, and energy focusing. Using this GDV machine, another colleague, Karen Polonko, and I found the energy fields of children to be the most open and communicative with the environment. In contrast, the energy fields of adults were the most shut down, with adolescents in between those two groups. The energy fields of the adult group participating in the daily energy program was much more like the children and adolescents than the comparison group of adults.

What was most interesting about this project was that the energy fields of the young children proved to be similar to our findings from the observational research, with more open fields and communication with the area around them. While infants may be more open than older children, they seem to shut down the field as they get older, especially from adolescence into adulthood. However, this process is not inevitable. Based on what we found with the adult group doing energy work, there are ways we can change our fields. It may take a fair amount of daily work to do so, but the same is true of keeping in shape mentally and physically. This research helped me to see that the density changes in our energy fields may not be inevitable.

Finally, I conducted a project with another colleague, Jan Cendese, again using the GDV instrument to measure the energy fields of patients with cancer.[15] We had two groups of volunteers, with 10 patients participating in each group. One group received an energy treatment called Integrated Awareness, and the other did not receive any energy sessions, although both groups continued to receive traditional medical care. Integrated Awareness is an approach that assists people to heal the physical, emotional, mental, and spiritual challenges in their lives through increased awareness, movement, and healing touch. We used this approach to see if four 75 to 90-minute sessions might lead to better health and quality of life. The post-test scores of the treatment group showed improvements in several of their reported symptoms. In addition, we found a number of significant changes in energy fields. The treatment group improved significantly in all 39 of the energy measures, such as immune function, physical functioning, and more open chakras. This suggested that these patients experienced a direct impact on their energy fields from this treatment. Again, this would suggest that changes in energy fields are possible with adults, and seem to be related to improved physical functioning.

This series of investigations, in conjunction with relevant research by others, led me to develop what I now call noussentrism. Jean and I saw how sophisticated infants were in their energetic interactions, and these results significantly shifted my thinking about children's abilities in areas we had not previously considered. I also looked at information that is not part of mainstream social science, yet provides insights into both the abilities and skills that infants and young children demonstrate and the information they can access at some level. As I explored this literature, I started to ask more questions and feel even less comfortable with the current theoretical perspectives. Scholars were certainly learning things about children's brain functioning and social communication during infancy that we previously had not known. Yet there still was so much we could not explain. For example, how do children know things about themselves and their families, sometimes from an "altered state," and how do they gain information from re-experiencing their prenatal, birth, or early infancy period? How do children remember information from past lives and report it accurately? While this work is not considered solidly scientific, the contrasting theories that have been produced could not answer these important questions. So I will summarize what I have found about such skills. After outlining the basic elements of noussentrism, I will discuss some of the things I have found children to possess without any previous training or learning from adults.

Noussentrism: An Overview

From a noussentric perspective, the essence is the most significant element of our being, the most conscious aspect of each of us. The essence is the more permanent attribute that exists within each human being, lying within or underneath character structure, fixation, defense mechanisms, or what is commonly called the personality, like a "diamond covered with dirt and tar."[16] I define the essence as "loving, intelligent, energy consciousness." Allison[17] suggests it is separate from the personality, like a guide. I agree the essence is different from personality and guides us as the fundamental aspect of each human being. The essence is who we really are beneath the distortions of energy blocks. It is the consciousness that remains when all the conditioning is removed. In this way, the character structure, fixation, or even personality is simply a set of distortions in physical form covering our cosmic spark.

Brian Weiss, originally a traditional psychiatrist who worked with patients using hypnosis, was interested in identifying the original onset of a problem. Much to his surprise, clients under hypnosis would talk about previous lives, and he could tap into a larger part of the patient that he described this way:

It is as if a large diamond were to be found inside each person. Picture a diamond a foot long. The diamond has a thousand facets, but the facets are covered with dirt and tar. It is the job of the soul to clean each facet until the surface is brilliant and can reflect a rainbow of colors.

Now, some have cleaned many facets and gleam brightly. Others have only managed to clean a few; they do not sparkle so. Yet underneath the dirt, each person possesses within his or her breast a brilliant diamond with a thousand gleaming facets. The diamond is perfect, not one flaw. The only differences among people are the number of facets cleaned. But each diamond is the same, and each is perfect.

When all the facets are cleaned and shining forth in a spectrum of lights, the diamond returns to the pure energy that it was originally. The lights remain. It is as if the process that goes into making the diamond is reversed, all that pressure is released. The pure energy exists in the rainbow of lights, and the lights possess consciousness and knowledge.[16]

Weiss identifies something larger than the personality. His image of the diamond describes what I would call the essence, the cosmic spark of an individual. This element has a larger perspective and can access information beyond the limits we place on ourselves through our personalities.

Within a noussentric framework, people are seen as energy beings, with connected and interacting fields, that include the essence. Energy is viewed as *information* and *consciousness*, as it increasingly is seen in physics[18] and medicine.[19] The essence is a core aspect of the energy or information concentration, yet the connections extend in many directions with different types of fields, all of which are important. In this way, the extensions and connections form an energetic "web of life," as Capra describes it, that sustains individuals in important ways.[18]

I focus on the essence or cosmic spark of children in this book. Although the energy field research is much bigger than this and has been going on for decades, children usually have been ignored in this work, and the particular skills and abilities with which they enter this life have been disregarded. Even in terms of their energy fields, they have been viewed from a deficit model.[9] The essence seems to be an important part of how each of us connects with infants in ways we have not previously identified or seen as important.

From a noussentric perspective, children are energy beings with open, flowing fields that initiate energetic connections to significant people in their lives, such as parents and caregivers. They seem to have within them a capable communication system quite different from the verbal communications we adults hold as important. We do not give much credence to this ability, possibly because it is ignored, disconnected, or atrophied in most adults.

The Basic Ideas or Tenets of Noussentrism

1. *In human beings, the physical body is held in place by the energy field that develops along with the body.*

It is the energy field that holds the physical and chemical elements in place, rather than the reverse. Instead of seeing the physical world as our fundamental reality, noussentrists see the interconnected energy field as the more basic element. A part of this field is the information and consciousness that is contained in the essential nature. Rather than a static aspect of our world, the essence is a part of the dynamic characteristics of energy fields, communication, and consciousness. This perspective integrates of human development research and the energy fieldwork of Burr, Ravitz, and Northrop's electro-dynamic field theory (for a more complete discussion, see Appendix A).

2. *Each of us has an Essence that is more conscious than our brain and body, yet integrated with both.*

Our essence is a "loving, intelligent, energy consciousness" that impacts us in subtle ways. The relationship is so subtle we do not allow ourselves to see its role in our lives or to notice our connection to it. Increasingly, we are finding that children are aware of it and employ skills that seem part of it. Understanding children in this way helps us expand our view of who we are as human beings.

3. *When we focus on the physical plane and take on external perspectives, we use them to replace our internal knowing and accessing of information.*

As we experience pain, hurt, fear, or anger, we cover and protect our vulnerable hearts by creating defense mechanisms, energy blocks, and behavioral patterns that separate us from our own essence or cosmic spark, as well as from each other. We can make choices that allow for conscious skills and abilities to develop and grow stronger or to go dormant over time. We may never recover these skills and abilities, although some do, and such recovery seems possible.

4. *We are interconnected entities, not separate and disconnected from each other and from the world around us.*

Our energy fields keep us connected, interacting and reacting to each other, even when we are not aware of it. We are closely connected physically and even more so energetically, far more than we usually allow ourselves to know. We are energetically connected to the physical world around us. I am fascinated by how people who report near-death experiences have become more aware of themselves as conscious energy beings change and consequently changed the way they interact with each other and the world around them. They typically become more conscious of their interconnections, which impacts how they treat others and the earth.

5. *We are made of love.*

While we as human beings express and experience love as an emotion, we also are composed of love as one form of consciousness. The basic composition of our being is expansive love energy, as children help us see. This relates to the many-faceted diamond found in each person that Weiss describes above. When we open our hearts fully and allow ourselves to experience this core energy without the disconnects of our socialization, energy blocks, and defenses, we can experience our beings in the same way people report from encounters during a near-death experience, deep meditation, altered states, or a deep relaxation into the core spark.

6. *We are born with awareness, consciousness, and abilities.*

Infants demonstrate an ability to initiate energy field connections that could not be taught to them. They also seem able to access information and communicate telepathically without any skill building from adults. These abilities represent the facets of the diamond that are present at birth. They can be reawakened and used more fully when we allow ourselves to expand our vision and understanding. As we remove the defenses and open our hearts, we experience the subtler forms of information and connection while letting go of energy blocks and fears that disconnect us from these sources of information.

7. *We can experience a higher vibrational state through sexual interaction and orgasm.*

Sexual interactions a unique way of connecting energetically as well as physically with another human being. They allow us to open to the greater fields of consciousness, and to experience the energy oscillation just above our current overall energy vibration. This occurrence can provide an experience of what the pulsation of our energy field would be like if we were to raise it to the next level. In this way, sexual orgasm may be a means to help us shift our energetic "set-point," the homeostasis level for our overall energy vibration.

8. *We can reconnect to our own Essence and access our best teacher within.*

This is one of the greatest gifts we can give ourselves and our children. Having a clearer link with our essence allows us to play a more conscious role in our own lives. The essence becomes an important source of inner guidance. It can help us to be more consciously aware, and to encourage our children to maintain their original connection to their inner wisdom as they develop into adults.

The basic tenets of noussentrism could help us focus primarily on the essence of infants and children, see them as energy beings, and assist them in holding onto their cosmic spark connection as a direct guide in the development of their lives. Understanding essence in this way would help children embrace a larger vision in which they are individuals who also are connected to the whole. As they mature, this broader view could help them to maintain subtle ways of accessing information about themselves at a more conscious level, and to look more empathically at how their actions and behaviors impact others. Children still need to develop linguistic, cognitive, and social skills as they move into adolescence and adulthood, but they may be able to hold these skills in a larger and more integrated framework than occurs currently. If children integrated these two worlds, it may help minimize the defense mechanisms that cut them off from their essence connection. Maintaining this core connection would prevent them from becoming so self-protected they might have difficulty remaining aware of their body, emotions, or thoughts without distortion. Of course, as parents and guides, adults may need to regain their own connection to essence before they can truly help others.

With an understanding of early communication processes, parents, teachers, physicians, therapists, and others might influence and enhance a child's immediate post-conception communication through various kinds of responses. Rather than being empty vessels who need to be taught and socialized, children may be "teachers" for adults in connecting to the heart, communicating without words, and of "knowing" beyond the type of mental cognition we seem to value above all else. When infants and children are recognized as having an essence connected to all types of energy fields, including our own, a different type of relationship can be developed between adults and children, where both teach and learn from each other, valuing what each has to offer.

More importantly, this perspective may improve the way adults consider conceiving children, treat children, and work with children. It may shift the current adult role from supporting dependent, separated, and "inferior" children to loving interconnected and respected children who have an essence that interacts with the energy fields of all those around them. This shift may also help us recognize that inner knowing can be nourished and supported as children grow, helping them to balance their inner awareness with the external information all around them.

Seven Aspects of Essence

The Essence not only exists, it is capable of many different things. I have identified key aspects that expand our view of children's capabilities. Some of the skills and characteristics may seem obvious, while others require more explanation and examples. I will discuss each aspect beginning with the overall skill or characteristic, followed by examples to illustrate each point.

So far, I have identified seven basic ways the essence is able to perform. I list them here to provide you with an overview, and to show how different this perspective is from the way we currently see children. In the following sections, I will go into more detail about each one.

1. *The Essence makes energy connections with others.*
2. *The essence gathers information in multiple ways.*
3. *The essence retains and uses information for both growing and healing.*
4. *The essence guides an individual's healing process.*
5. *The essence guides the development of protective mechanisms.*
6. *The essence is able to leave the body and communicate or observe actions.*
7. *The essence can communicate without words.*

Some of these abilities came to light in the research work on infants and young children Jean and I developed. Additional ways are derived from the work of others that fit into the noussentric framework and provide a more elaborate view of what children bring to this life.

1. The Essence Makes Energy Connections with Others

Energy connections, as described in our research work, can be seen in the form of "rings," apparently coming out of the infant and connecting to the parent or other caregivers.[10,11] Such rings do not seem to be just about gathering information, but rather form an energetic connection in a way apparently familiar to infants. Given the lack of "cognitive" and physical development in infant brains, it seems that the essence knows how to form such energy connections in a manner that is natural. As children become focused more and more on language and other aspects of growth, they seem to stop creating such energetic forms by the age of 4 or 5, possibly because such forms are not initiated by others or identified as important parts of their world. It may be that such capabilities are not lost, but simply not used or seen as important. Later in life, energetic connections continue to occur, such as when family members communicate, [12,13,20] and during the development of "love" relationships.[21] While the fields interact, it is less clear that adolescents and adults have any sense of what they are doing. Yet, responses in the fields correspond to the emotions parents and adolescents report feeling about each other.

An important and natural first connection is made between the mother and fetus prior to birth. Gynecologist and obstetrician

David B. Cheek, who investigated the bonds and communications between mothers and their fetuses, posited that fears, both conscious and unconscious, may cause premature contractions.[22] He found that escalating maternal fear initiates a series of events ending in expulsive preterm labor. He came to believe that infants later concluded they are not wanted. Cheek notes an important feature of treatment is the re-establishment of maternal/fetal telepathic communications.

This connection may seem far-fetched from the traditional view of fetuses prior to birth, yet others researchers are supporting these ideas and even moving beyond them. For several decades, David Chamberlain, a founding member and former president of the Association for Prenatal and Perinatal Psychology and Health, has been studying the fetus from conception to birth. He has found solid evidence that fetuses are fully sentient and aware, intelligent beings, impacted by a mother's emotional and physical state. He also stresses the importance of bonding between the two beings.[23] This bonding is not simply the mother connecting to an unconscious fetus, but rather an energetic interaction and relationship.

Cheek and Chamberlain's work supports the notion that the essence makes important connections prior to birth, and suggests that this important relationship may be related to having a purpose here in this life. Others reporting on near-death episodes make the same suggestion. Psychology professor Kenneth Ring has studied the impacts of near-death experiences on many individuals. An important finding from his work is that, after the episode, people believe they are not here randomly but have made a choice and have work to do here.[24] Ring also reports a heightened sense of spiritual (not religious) purpose.[25] Brian Weiss, the psychiatrist who describes the essence as a large diamond inside each person, comes to a similar conclusion.[26-29] The connections we make and maintain have an important role in our lives, even when we are not aware of it on a conscious level.

One interesting insight from the research on near-death experiences has to do with changed perceptions of connection. People often shift their sense of being separate to understanding that we all are connected, impacting each other, and in this world together. Ring found in his research that such experiences greatly expand the spiritual focus of these people. They commonly describe a core being or essence, usually in terms related to light.

[30] This brings to mind Weiss's description of the rainbow light of the diamond.

One of the traditional views of infants gives importance to their learning that they are separate beings. In fact, the infant's not sensing any real separation from a parent may be a more accurate perception of the greater conscious reality, although it is seen as a "lack of development" in traditional frameworks. When we take a "deficit" or "blank slate" view of children, it may be derived from our own disconnection to the larger conscious environment. We then define a more limited view as normal or true, and see the infant as not understanding reality. It may be our infants who teach us about "reality" in the sense of larger energetic and conscious connections. When adults evolve enough to understand the energetic web that connects us all, we may begin to help children work both with the ways we are connected and the ways we are separate.

2. The Essence Gathers Information in Multiple Ways

In our research on energy fields with six-month-old infants, we found they were able to form energy connections to other people and to objects.[10,11] While it may have been the adult who initiated the energetic connection with the infant, I have a harder time believing that the object initiated the energy connection we observed. Infants seem able to create such connections without any training. Given their lack of physical and cognitive development from a traditional point of view, it seems that the essence of the infant is helping to guide such information gathering in a natural way. This ability appears in the child before greater mental structures are formed and may even be working underneath such structures after they are developed.

All of the infants we studied were able to form such energetic connections, apparently checking out the object even if they were holding it in their hands. At other times, they were not in physical contact with the object but still making an energetic connection from a distance, through what people refer to as the third eye or sixth chakra. Infants also made changes in the energy field around the body, or what some call the auric field. In later research, we found that adolescents and adults also shift their auric fields during interactions, incorporating different forms depending on how connecting or separating the interactions were.[12,13] While in some cases a change in the field may be a response to others, it still appears that the field is gathering this response information in some way or a response to current emotions. Such abilities are beyond the current scope of child development studies and cannot be explained with contemporary theories. Yet these field responses can be important information for parents working with their children or adolescents, as well as for professionals.

Stan and Christina Grof developed a healing methodology they called Breathwork.[31-34] They have conducted this work with thousands of people since they developed the technique decades ago. Through deep breathing and strong music, people can move into naturally altered states that allow them to explore many aspects of their being in a non-ordinary manner. These experiences can be both healing and transformative. As I and so many others have experienced through Breathwork methodology, people access information from the fetal period through the birth process. For example, adults often re-experience their birth process and learn about any issues or trauma associated with it. Often the information gained, previously unknown to these individuals, is confirmed by a parent. In some cases, Grof reports, such experiences have even revealed secrets never before shared in the family.[32,33] If we take a traditional view of children and learning, it seems impossible to acquire such information. Yet when we see the essence as loving, intelligent, energy consciousness, accessing all sorts of information becomes feasible.

David Chamberlain's work provides similar findings.[23] He reports parents hearing inner messages about "being ready" and soon getting pregnant, and two-year-old children telling their mothers, "don't you know I picked you?" In talking with young children, he found they revealed experiences prior to conception, were aware of issues around conception, accessed information about parents while still in the womb, and described experiences during birth and shortly after. He shares one revealing story told to her mother by a four-year-old daughter.

"Last time when I was four inches long and in your tummy, Daddy wasn't ready to marry you yet, so I went away. But then I came back." Her eyes lost that faraway look, and she was chatting again about four-year-old matters. Mother was silent. No one but her husband, the doctor, and she knew about this, but she *had* become pregnant about two years before she and her husband were ready to get married. When she was four months pregnant, she decided to have an abortion. She was ready to have a child, but her husband-to-be was not.

When the two of them did get married and were ready to have their first child, the same entity made its appearance. And the little child was saying, in effect, "I don't hold any resentments toward you for having had the abortion. I understood. I knew why it was done, and that's okay. So here I am again. It was an experience. I learned from it, and you learned from it, so now let's get on with the business of life."

Maybe the child didn't have that kind of vocabulary, but that was in essence what was being said, and what was being related to the mother. It does throw a new light on abortion, doesn't it?[35]

Chamberlain says, "For most of a century, birth experiences have been called 'fantasies' and prenatal memories 'impossible.' Actually, it was the false boundaries of science set by psychology and neuroscience that were fantasies."[36] Others scholars are coming to similar conclusions, giving credence to conscious memories of experiences and choices prior to conception and birth, [37,38] as well as experiences or information from previous lives.[39,40]

While we do not know the exact manner in which a being accesses information prior to conception or during pregnancy, the energetic conscious connections are the explanation that makes the most sense so far. This explanation seems particularly accurate when energy is defined as information and consciousness, not just some random vitality existing in our world.

Near-death research also supports this idea of gathering information in multiple ways. What is interesting about this work is that the reports, by adults and children who do not have medical knowledge, contain greater accuracy than one could predict .[41-51] For example, Michael Sabom, a cardiologist who lives in Georgia, describes a woman who went through an extensive surgery that required the blood to be drained from her head, her eyes covered, and her ears plugged.[51] During this operation, she "saw" the instruments that the physicians were using, instruments not familiar to he general public, and could describe them later in accurate detail. She also reported conversations that took place in the surgery room during the operation, which were accurate according to the medical team who talked with Dr. Sabom. Other researchers also report similar information gathering by people whose physical body was not conscious.

3. The Essence Retains and Uses Information for Both Growing and Healing

This concept is supported by several different areas of work. One illustration comes from Stan Grof, who has described how memories and emotional trauma can hold back our growth. They hold us in a restrictive pattern and prevent us from moving forward or achieving outcomes where we want to succeed. When the trauma is released and the pain dissolved, we can continue in the healing process.[32-33] At the same time, such information, once released from the emotional field, can be useful for continued development and understanding. We often gain insights into ourselves through such information, although the understanding may only come after the trauma is released.

A client grew up with an abusive father. She knew that she had "father issues," which seemed to impact her relationships with men. She kept working on this topic with different therapists, but it never seemed to help her change. As she did a series of Breathwork sessions, one key experience revealed how she continued to give up her power to her father as she held on to the pain of past events. This insight made her furious, and part of her session was releasing the rage as well as the pain she held in her body. In subsequent sessions, she increasingly healed her part of the relationship, even understanding that her father's rage was not about her, although it felt personal to her as a child. After releasing the pain, she was able to make additional changes for her growth and health, both within herself and in her relationships with others. This kind of release is important, and it appears that the essence is involved in these healing and growing processes. The essence is wiser than our physical brain about how we make these changes, and it provides information we can access from our subtler field

An example from the near-death research supports the idea that learning and growing are important aspects of our experience, with painful memories holding key information for our learning. Professor Kenneth Ring summarized the case of Gerald, a man in a wheelchair because of crippling diseases as well as challenges from alcoholism and other psychological problems. Gerald suffered an extensive and complex near-death experience (NDE) where he learned a lot about healing. He was able to change his life and heal from many of these difficulties because he put into practice the insights he gained from the experience. Ring summarized Gerald's experience with the Light in the following way:

> ...his remarks sum up the most important lesson the NDE has to teach us about what keeps us locked in the prison of disease in the first place. *It is at bottom the fear to love ourselves unconditionally as the light does.* If the light does not blast away these fears, we need to do it! The light may in some cases, as we have seen, suffice to lift us out of despair or heal us of disease, but when disease remains or occurs, it is well to inquire into its meaning deeply, as Gerald did, because it, too, however unwelcome, may be still another offering from the light, which is meant to show us the very blockages that keep us from realizing fully the light not only in ourselves, but *as* ourselves.[52]

Near-death researchers provide examples of how such events can change a person's life in dramatic ways and help them identify how the experiences can assist their own healing process. These changes primarily seem to follow from what they learned through the experience about death, life, learning, and loving.[25,41,47-49]

Ring summarizes a lot of this work, focusing particularly on lessons learned from the life review process. One very clear expression of insight about our conditioned and higher self from several participants is summarized in a touching manner:

> I have talked about this authentic or true self as something that is the Light's function to disclose to the individual. How does it do that? The answer is, often by

first showing the NDEr (near-death experiencer) his or her false or socially conditioned self.... In other instances, however, the NDEr is given a direct perception into the nature of the false self and is thereby allowed intuitively to understand that the person one has identified with and habitually thought of as one's essential self was nothing more than fiction.... And remember, the NDErs tell us that we are not and are never alone. We each have a source of inner guidance that, once we discover it, can serve us the same way it does the NDEr.[53]

An interesting investigation by Raymond Moody has a similar focus on healing. Moody, who has a background in philosophy as well as medicine, was curious about the Greeks gazing into pools to see people who had passed from this life. To explore this idea, he furnished a small dark room with a chair, a mirror a short distance in front of the chair where people could see into it without seeing their own reflection, and a small light so that people could see faintly.[54] Individuals would sit in the dark room and gaze at the mirror to see if anything would happen. When Moody first tried the experiment himself, he thought he might see the grandmother to whom he felt the closest. In fact, the person who appeared was his other grandmother, the one with whom he felt less connection. After the experience, and man similar reports from others, his sense was that this whole process was about focusing on and healing relationships where there may be distance or an issue that can be resolved.

Another interesting and creative researcher is the psychiatrist, Brian Weiss.[26-29,41] Weiss started out doing traditional therapy with patients and experienced limited success. He began to use hypnosis to help him identify the origin of an emotional problem. As Weiss talked with a patient under hypnosis, he found her responses contrasted starkly with the everyday personality and style she had previously presented. He described it this way:

I would become increasingly frustrated by the uncross-able gulf between Catherine's conscious, awake intellect and her trans-level superconscious mind. While she was hypnotized, I would have fascinating philosophical dialogues with her at the superconscious level. When awake, however, Catherine had no interest in philosophy or related matters. She lived in the world of everyday detail, oblivious of the genius within her.[55]

After the therapy, when this client had found a sense of happiness and contentment she had never experienced before, she felt like life had meaning and purpose for her.

> Now that she is balanced and in harmony with herself, she radiates an inner peace that many wish for but few attain. She feels more spiritual.... She has no interest in pursuing the study of psychic phenomena [which she experienced increasingly during the period of therapy and afterwards], feeling that she 'knows' in a way that cannot be learned from books or lectures.[56]

The implications of such work can be useful, especially when parents tune into this information, or professionals, such as teachers, therapists, or physicians, incorporate this information into the healing process. With such healing information, we can connect with and support children in new and powerful ways.

4. The Essence Guides an Individual's Healing Process

In another interesting area of healing work, a psychiatrist by the name of Ralph Allison was working with patients who had multiple personality disorder.[17] He began like most psychiatrists from a traditional orientation, but his work evolved over several decades, especially with the use of hypnosis. Allison would get in touch with a patient's different personalities. At one point, he identified a personality he first called the inner self-helper, and later, the essence. This aspect of the individual was separate and unique from the alter-personalities. While usually an alter-personality would not know some of the other ones, the essence came forward with complete knowledge of all parts of the individual, as well as a full understanding of the implications of the acts or interactions the individual had experienced. In addition, the essence knew what to do to help the individual heal, more so than Allison, other trained professional colleagues, or the previous research that usually guides a psychiatrist's interventions. In cases of multiple personality disorder, the essence may share information without the direct knowledge of the "personality" of the patient, in part because the communication may not take place on the same plane as the personality.

Eventually, Allison chose to search for the essence of the person, and he could always find it. Then he would follow the essence's guidance to help the individual heal as much as possible. He found, for example, that the essence held important information about learning from difficult experiences, but such experiences were segmented from the personality.[17] With the essence as guide, Allison was able to assist his clients integrate this learning, integrating different pieces back towards some type of whole. This allowed for greater health and growing to a greater extent than before and bring about and sustained improvement. Alison's work is a direct example of how this part of our being guides the healing process without any obvious external training.

Stan Grof also notes that people doing Breathwork seem to know the most important ways to heal at any given moment. I remember the time I agreed to go to my first Breathwork session, conducted by a friend trained through Stan and Christina Grof and their associates. I was curious but not very confident that I would get into an altered state. I had tried to undergo hypnosis in various settings with limited results. I was skeptical, as I have been about so many things, doubting I would be successful in this particular methodology. Yet, as I look back at the experience from a mandala I drew afterwards, I remember feeling energy vigorously flowing through my body. I truly had the opportunity to experience myself as an energy being, but with a mask over my mouth to keep myself from speaking freely. I recently looked back at all the mandalas I created, which reminded me of the many healing experiences I had over that three year period. It felt like I would tap into another part of me during a session, each time allowing for release, insight, and healing. Grof suggests, from his extensive experience, that a part of our transpersonal self guides our healing in this as well as similar work. My experience with this modality corroborates his findings.

5. The Essence Guides the Development
of Protective Mechanisms

One of the more direct descriptions of children's development and protections comes from the work of Alexander Lowen[57,58] and John Pierrakos,[59,60] who built their approach on the theories of Wilhelm Reich. Lowen and Pierrakos expanded Reich's idea of body armor, which is a protective layer around the core of one's being. This core, Lowen suggests, is love and the heart.[58] As children mature, developing layers of body armor increasingly segment and separate the heart, body, mind, and awareness. When this segmentation occurs, it leads to a distortion in our natural energy flow, which is key to healthy living. Muscular contractions around painful or difficult emotional experiences create energy blocks that armor the body. These blocks also shape the physical body. They influence behaviors as well as reactions to the environment, and can eliminate the sensing of information carried through the body. As children continue to armor, they may unwittingly separate the inner, mystical aspect of their being (love energy) from the other physical body. Lowen suggests that such a split separates the feelings at the core from the sensations or outer reactions of the individual. While Lowen and Pierrakos do not directly identify the essence as guiding the work of healing this split, their approach seems consist with this idea. This is especially so in relation to the insight Allison experienced as to how the essence guides the healing processes. It also is consistent with the ability that others have identified of how children are able to respond to the stress of abuse or the crisis of a near-death experience by leaving their bodies rather than enduring severe physical pain.[61,62]

I have not had much direct experience with the approach of Reich, Lowen, and Pierrakos, although I have had some. I also had a good friend who was professionally trained and shared Reich's work with clients, who experienced amazing results in the dis-armoring process. Another friend has extensive experience with this type of healing as a client and applauds its usefulness. Both identify how letting go of the armor begins to change the personality and allow for more freedom and more direct expression of the heart. In my own experience, dis-armoring has come more directly through Breathwork and my inner explorations with the Enneagram.

The Enneagram is a tool to help people identify differences between the socialized self and the essential self or essence. According to the Enneagram, in order to protect ourselves, we develop a distortion of our worldview, which evolves into a fixation, a pattern that warps the energies of the body, emotions, and mind. (For a more complete explanation, see Appendix B.) The distortion is based on a sense of separation, especially from our own essence and the essential lesson of each enneatype. From the point of view of A. H. Almaas, an author and spiritual teacher, we develop the fixation when we lose basic trust through difficult experiences in our environment.[63,64] Yet no one really describes how the loss of trust happens, except to talk about challenges in our family interactions and relationships from a Freudian perspective.

I suggest an alternative explanation as to how this damaging loss happens in Chapters 2 and 3. From my point of view, from infancy we are urged to focus on the physical world while letting go of our subtler domains, including our connection to essence. As we increasingly focus on the physical plane and limit our worldview to physical reality, we create patterns and behaviors that are based on our sense of separation, our socialized self rather than our essence. With this underlying distortion in place, we continue to develop a limited view and sense of who we are as human beings. We may see ourselves either from a deficit model, a belief that there is something wrong with us, or from the position that a "I am fine," and it is the outside world that has the problem. In both cases, we are cut off from the heart, our own essence, and subtle sources of information.

From my experience of working with letting go of the fixation and moving to my essential lesson, I keep coming back to the idea that my own essence has been guiding much of my development, major choices, and intuitive knowing that has occurred in my life, even without my awareness. Of course, when I am deep in my fears and fixation, I have no sense of higher guidance. Yet, when I expand into my heart I continue to embrace this idea of essence guiding my life. I also have an intuitive sense that I have chosen an essential lesson to explore in this incarnation. I have no evidence of that, and yet, when I am more fully in my heart and feel connected to the cosmos, it feels so right. Maybe such a feeling is true only for me. But it does seem accurate for my life, even though I have not had the ongoing gift of such information to assist me in my conscious choices. It would be interesting to know if others have had a sense of such guidance in life. Certainly, some of those who go through a near-death experience report that they do.[24]

6. The Essence is Able to Leave the Body and Communicate or Observe Actions

Reports of near-death experiences, documented by many researchers over the past three decades, clearly demonstrate this ability. In one case, a three-year-old girl had a serious heart condition that would cause her heart to slow down and stop for about a minute. This young girl would share with her mother what she experienced when she was not breathing and unconscious. Her mother reports that she

> floats out to the ceiling and watches her body and us. She has told me exactly what has happened and what I did, said etc. whilst she was 'gone' on many occasions. She tells me that she 'clicks' back into the body. She is 100 percent right in everything that has happened. Amie is very honest and there is no way a child of her age could make up such things. Amie has never been told about OBEs (out of body experiences) or NDEs (near-death experiences), but she has such incredible detail that I am totally convinced... She even tells her mother how it feels when she goes back into her body 'head first - it's not very nice.'[65]

Another case involves a Russian man, thought to be dead, who was placed in a morgue for the weekend.[61] During that time, he visited his family and others in the area. A fascinating element is that just before his "death," he and his wife kept hearing a baby constantly crying near their apartment in the same building. While he was in his body, it must have been difficult to hear the cries day and night. So this man, while out of his body, went to visit the baby to see if he could tell what was happening. The doctors could not find anything wrong with this newborn baby girl. While out of his body and visiting the baby's apartment, the man and infant were able to "communicate," although the newborn was in her body. The infant knew what was wrong and told the man that "her hip had twisted during birth and was broken," although this injury had not been obvious to anyone else. On Monday, when his body was removed from the cooler for an autopsy, the man came back to life, much to the shock of the coroner, I am sure! The man reported what he had learned from the infant, which x-rays proved to be correct, the problem was addressed by the physician, and the child quit crying. The important point here is that the infant knew the man was present without his body, she was able to diagnose the problem with her hip, and she could communicate with him. This example is one of the clearest I have seen of the knowledge and ability infants have without any "learning" from us.[61] In fact, the infant is the one who begins, from birth, to teach us what is possible.

Another relevant incident was reported by a young child named Katie, who was three years old at the time of her near-death experience. As she floated out of her body, she saw her grandfather trying to help remove the cashew nut that was lodged in her windpipe. The ambulance took nearly half an hour to arrive, and her grandfather, who was a fire fighter, pronounced her "dead." During this time, Katie was not interested in her body, but rather moved into the other room where she felt some presence. Later in life she described this presence:

> I went toward this presence, which was within a brilliant, sun[lit], bright, space —not a tunnel, but an area. The presence was unbelievable peace, love, acceptance, calm, and joy. The presence enveloped me, and my joy was indescribable — as I write this I am brought back to the emotion, and it delights me still... Even now, when I recall the experience, it is more real than anything I have experienced in my life. I recall not only the memory, but also the emotion.[66]

In reports of other near-death or out of body experiences by children, scholars find that while the thinking and the language used to describe the experience may be childlike, the deep understanding of their experience goes beyond the questions being asked of them. In addition, age does not seem to impact the content of their experiences or their reports.[47]

Out of body experiences occur in children under extremely stressful situations, such as when they are being physically or sexually abused by adults.[62] Children are not taught how to do this, they simply find a way of removing their consciousness from their bodies. This tactic reduces the pain, since experiencing pain only seems to occur in relation to the body and brain.

Children also seem to be able to shift out of their physical bodies under stress, as do we adults who apparently do not lose this ability, even when we are under less extreme conditions as experiencing a death. Adults, like children, experience leaving the body under torture without ever consciously learning how to do so.[67,68] This seems to be an ability that people have, without understanding the exact process or even knowing that it exists. Under extreme circumstances, we have a natural ability to do this without any conscious learning.

A young actress, Coca Rudolfi, who was part of the resistance to General Pinochet's coup in Chile reported leaving her body. Men showed up one night, searched her place, then took her to a small room at a military barracks, where they made her remove her clothes and strapped her to a bed. For the rest of the night, they touched her and applied electric shocks to her body. At one point, Coca left her body, rose above her bed and, despite the blindfold on her eyes, "felt she could look down and see her own body in the room and the faces of the men who were torturing her."[67] Soldiers also have reported out of body experiences while being tortured. In addition, the Out of Body Experience Research Foundation has a list of 276 people who have reported such experiences under various circumstances.[68]

This, of course, suggests the essence is not synonymous with the body, but can function separately from the body. Such a conclusion would be consistent with the centuries-old spiritual teachings that maintain we are not our bodies, but more than the physical, emotional, and mental functioning we associate with the physical being.[69,70]

7. The Essence Can Communicate without Words

This idea is supported by near-death research. The example of the infant communicating with the man in Russia clearly illustrates this point, where the infant did not know how to talk, but the communication took place anyway.

There are many examples from Raymond Moody's work with psychomanteums,[54] those dimly lit rooms with mirrors in which people would see and communicate with someone no longer living. In most cases, the figure that appeared in the mirror was a relative who had passed, and the person in the chair and the person in the mirror would "communicate," usually nonverbally. It would happen spontaneously, though the person in the chair had not been trained and was not known to be telepathic. The ability appears to come naturally when people do not even think about it. The communication would go back and forth between the person in the chair and the individual appearing in the mirror. While not everyone would see someone in the mirror, when it did happen, communication would take place, and almost all of it occurred without any verbal exchange.

Grof describes working with people in altered states who remembered experiences they had as a fetus or infant, experiences they learned during an altered state not consciously known at the time, whose accuracy was later confirmed by others.[31-34] In a few cases, the person accessed a "family secret," information a parent was actively trying to hide. This power to communicate nonverbally and to gather information seems to be a natural ability, exhibited at many different ages, including infancy, without any need to be taught or trained. When we move into a state where we do not experience or worry about our limitations, we seem to be able to carry on such communications in a very natural manner.

An experience I had during a Breathwork session took me back to a time when I was a newborn infant. While in an altered state, I became aware of the room, of my mother nearby and my father in another part of our home. I felt into my father's energy, the worry and stress he was experiencing. It appeared to me he had been concerned about my mother's health during the pregnancy and birth, and he was still worried about her condition, which seemed rather weak. I sensed financial stress, being the third child in our family with my father as the only producer at the time. As I became increasingly aware of his stress, I felt that the emotional distance I had experienced with him had nothing to do with me, but reflected his concern about more pressing issues of health and finance. As I came out of my altered state, this information stayed with me. Unfortunately, neither of my parents was living at the time I had the experience, so I was unable to verify the information. But it helped me to understand some of my father's behavior. Of course, all of this may have been my imagination, or information I held as a subconscious level. Yet it all felt new and real to me, and I could see that such experiences felt just as real to others when in an altered state. If mine were the only case, I might dismiss it. But when many others confirm it under different circumstances, it is harder to ignore or disregard.

Finally, researchers have found that twins communicate with each other absent any spoken language, even at a distance. [71,72] If that is true for twins, it seems likely that a mother who carries a fetus for nine months would have that same ability, and that fathers who are highly involved and use energy connections to interact with the fetus are likely to incorporate the same communication methods. Mothers certainly "know" things about their infants beyond language and ordinary communications.[73] For example, heart rates between mothers and infants parallel each other during stressful and harmonious interactions, a finding suggestive of physiological attunement.[74] It appears that communications and attunement can occur through a harmonizing of frequencies in the energy fields. Infants seem able to respond and participate to energy information within their field. Just an adult, while outside of his body that was lying in the morgue, was able to "communicate" with an infant and have the infant share important information with him, a "knowing" that occurs and is communicated by an infant only a few days old.

At the end of his latest book, <u>Windows to the Womb</u>, Dr. Chamberlain states:

> Now that it is clear that babies are *not* what we used to think, we must get serious about constructing a new paradigm that will accurately define their multidimensional capacities for out-of-body travel, near-death experiences, past-life recall, and other transpersonal events. The consciousness they demonstrate with or without their brains, their enlarged sensuality and emotionality, and their clear vulnerability to negative learning experiences makes it urgent that we understand the complexity and wonder of babies.

> The resistance of experts who continue to see infants in terms of their incapacities may be the last great obstacle for babies to leap over before being embraced as the intelligent, capable humans they really are. Eventually,

old ideas have a way of dying under the sheer weight of new evidence, but not before millions of babies suffer unnecessarily because their parents and doctors do not yet recognize who they are... Putting together all the bits and pieces of information gathered from around the globe yields a fundamentally different picture of a baby, one with an innate mind, personal yearnings, spunk, spirit, and purpose.[75]

Conclusion

I do not assume that all work cited here is absolutely true without question. Individually, all the work here has raised questions and been somewhat tentative in any conclusions. Hesitancy in adopting results for tentative findings is characteristic of new ways for developing ideas within a new perspective. In addition, there are many more questions than answers raised here and new ideas to be evaluated. Yet the diversity of work, both research and clinical, as well as theoretical contributions made in different fields, all point to seeing children in a new way that is fruitful and important. I simply am suggesting that the collective efforts reviewed here form a picture of children that previous theories and research could not address. This does not discount all the previous work. But it expands our understanding of children and possibilities of how we can interact and nurture them. Certainly each child is different. It may be that each child has a unique essence and energy field interacting in diverse ways with people and the environment around them. Further, children may have ways of knowing and gathering information that we have only begun understand.

I have come to believe that as we continue to wake up, as we continue to grow in consciousness, we will see children in a new light. This allows us to live from a less distorted view of who we and they are, as well as our perception of reality. From this change, we are able to create a more conscious, loving, heartful (a term I use to mean being in and expressing from your heart or full of heart) future. I think this is important to consider, and I think it is an important time for such a change.

As I began my teaching career, a wise mentor told me that a great teacher is not just someone who knows a lot. The greatest teachers learn not only from other scholars but also from their students. While we adults teach children about our reality, infants and children may be our greatest teachers about a world we have lost and a source of information we have forgotten how to use. Shifting our view of children may be a gift to ourselves, opening us to what we ignored or covered up as we were leaving our own childhoods behind. Over the next 11 chapters, I will address how we might rekindle our own spark, so that we can help our children to hold onto theirs.

CHAPTER 2

SOCIALIZING CHILDREN:
"BUY MY PERSPECTIVE"

THERE IS A CANDLE IN YOUR HEART

There is a candle in your heart,
ready to be kindled.
There is a void in your soul.
ready to be filled.

You feel it, don't you?
You feel the separation
from the Beloved.
Invite Him to fill you up,
embrace the fire.

Remind those who tell you otherwise that
Love comes to you of its own accord,
and the yearning for it
cannot be learned in any school.

- Rumi[1]

I recommend two important shifts to anyone involved in children's lives. First, I suggest we expand our view of the capabilities and skills children have when they enter this world. Most adults in our culture do not see these capabilities in themselves, which makes it challenging to recognize them in others. An initial step is to imagine such possibilities in our children, for it sometimes is easier to see magnificence in others. Once we see them in children, we can play with reclaiming or rekindling these aspects in ourselves.

A second shift I recommend is to encourage and trust children's inner guidance throughout their lives. We already give them important information about living and developing successfully in different cultures. These external guidelines are an important part of our social interactions and cooperation. Yet we can also help children balance these external norms and directions with the inner knowing that is the manifestation of the cosmic spark. Human beings can be a combination of socialization and inner guidance, listening to and working with both sources of information. Rather than replacing our childhood connection to subtle sources of information with a highly socialized adult, we can facilitate the integration of these two important types of intelligence. Supporting children's development in these two ways could help to alleviate the difficulty they face when they shift their perspectives away from a holistic sense of the world to the separate, externalized outlook they typically make into their world view.

Honoring and Supporting Children's Capabilities

Adults usually want to help children prepare for the world by identifying what is right and not right, what is acceptable and not acceptable, what is real and what is not real. In most cases, adults teach what they learned from their own development and experience, with a few additions and modification along the way. Parents want to help children not only survive, but also thrive in the world, possibly even doing better than they did. Raising children is not an easy undertaking, and I applaud parents for executing this momentous task. Parenting can be rich, joyful, challenging, exasperating, and fulfilling. I also want to avoid criticizing parents for not doing enough. I know parents who have no time to do any more for their children than they are currently doing. I recommend seeing things differently rather than adding more responsibility. Shifting our focus can change how we see and do the things we do, rather than trying to do more.

Most of us grew up learning in a formal and informal manner what was right and wrong according to the perspective of our parents, family, neighbors, social group, and society. If we grew up in Tibet, Thailand, or Bhutan, we were more likely to believe in the value of daily meditation, desire to be awakened, and work to eliminate the suffering we create in the world with less emphasis on worldly goods. If we were raised in Saudi Arabia, Egypt, Iran, or Indonesia, we focused our beliefs on the Koran, the seven pillars of wisdom, the importance of making a pilgrimage to Mecca, and a conviction that Mohammad was the last great prophet. If we grew up in Western Europe or the United States, we probably put our faith in Jesus Christ as our savior, desired to practice daily prayer, emphasized attendance at church gatherings, and aspired to go to Heaven after death. Or if we were raised in a culture that believed in the Talmud, we would have observed the Sabbath and attended synagogue on Saturday, followed the 13 Principles of Faith, been more concerned about actions than beliefs, and had important cultural traditions that were family priorities. All of these are strong belief systems, handed down to us, we have passed on to our children. We typically hold on to our received system as "correct" and teach this perspective to those who will listen.

In order to help children develop and be successful in life, we share with them our beliefs, judgments, perspectives, and rules. This process begins for infants when parents or caregivers inform them about life. This can be as simple as connecting words with objects or providing information about eating, dressing, and getting around. More often, there are implied judgments with our connections to children. We learn what to eat for breakfast in contrast to dinner, what clothes we should wear for play in contrast to special occasions, and how we should treat our parents and siblings. All of these direct or implied "shoulds" we learn as children form part of the typical socialization process.

In most cases, parental beliefs are not presented as options or suggestions but as facts and truths. For example, we may tell our children they should not play with certain other children because "those children are not nice," are "inferior," or in more extreme cases, such as the Nazis describing the children of Jews, are "not even human." This basically is how whites defined African Americans in the 17th through much of the 19th Centuries in order to use them as slaves, a disrespect that continues for some today. This was the dominant belief that allowed people to massacre and break treaties with the First Americans. We find it easier to treat people without dignity when we close our hearts and see them as less than "us." Generally, we expect children to obey us without question, since parents know best.

I do not blame parents for doing what they think is best. We all try to help our children by giving them a perspective that we believe will assist young people to grow into what we define as healthy and responsible adults. I did that with my children as they were maturing, and now they are passing it along to their kids. There certainly are times when we need to protect children, and we ask them to follow certain rules in order to keep them safe, such as not playing in a busy street and not putting their hand on a hot stove. But issues of safety account for only a small part of our total belief system.

As parents, we teach these things to our children to help them learn to live in the world, learn how to survive and do well within the society in which they grow. This is our justification, our rationale. Yet different parents have conflicting points of view about what is appropriate, what should be done. So which perspective is the best or correct one? The simple answer is "my" or "our perspective," the one that was passed down from our parents and our culture. But that response ignores subtler sources of information and the larger context of learning and knowing. If "my" perspective does not allow for a more inclusive knowing, recognizing the gifts infants bring, then it gives children a limited reality, passing on the limits we learned without allowing for other possibilities.

If we never ask the question, we never look for another possibility. We continue the process that is used to dismiss the cosmic connection we bring to this life and increasingly let go of it as we develop. We focus on others we see as experts for developing our views, guidance, and definitions of reality. We miss seeing and experiencing children as love, with skills in the subtle realm, because we have closed our own hearts and ignored our own skills. If we could step back a little and see this process more clearly, we could participate differently by incorporating subtle views of reality into our own outlook, and then support this knowing in our children as they develop. We are not determined by our early cultural and religious experiences, and when we get enough separation from our belief systems, we can examine them in more detail.

What I want to challenge here is the assumptions that young children know nothing and have no access to other sources of information. I no longer believe that we adults must give them all the answers. Rather than paying attention to who they are at the core and maintaining a connection they bring to this life, we get them to shift their trust to external belief systems, giving up their own inner intuitive guidance. For example, Julia Assante, who has studied near-death experiences and afterlife communications suggests: "Telepathy is your main tool for after-death communication, and you'll find it in that toolbox you were born with."[2]

Because children are not familiar with the human tasks and systems we have developed, we view them as bringing no skills or abilities into interactions. We see children as vacuums to be filled with information from their external world. That is how we have defined children and the greater reality. But what if we simply have buried these inner abilities in ourselves and thus do not recognize them in children? What if children bring skills and abilities that we dismiss, because we are so committed to our own perspective that we are not open to a different understanding of who they are, and, in fact, who we are?

When we push children to focus outside themselves for all their answers of how to live and define the world, we do not take into account their own internal access to subtle information. The major drawback to ignoring their cosmic capabilities is that we do not support children in holding onto an internal perspective. This socialization process begins early and continues throughout our lives, asking us to focus on external authority and accept a physical model of life as our only reality. If we do not allow ourselves to admit the possibility that children bring abilities into this world, especially on a subtle level, then we cannot support them in holding onto these skills. In this way, we do not evaluate the consequences of our decisions and the impacts we have on children during early development. We present the physical world and external perspectives as our only reality.

As an alternative, I propose an interactive process, where we as parents throw out ideas and possibilities for our children to consider, while also supporting their internal decision-making from infancy through adulthood. When we support the combination of external beliefs and internal knowing, children have a better chance of holding on to the cosmic connection they bring into this life. As we nurture our children in this way, we may more easily shift our own perspective.

Games Adults Play

How have we become so engrossed in external views and solutions to our challenges? How have we become so absorbed with the external world that we ignore our own inner spark? Certainly working with the parameters of our world to protect our-selves from extreme elements and utilizing principles to create with physical materials are compelling aspects of our lives. Yet we could incorporate subtle sources if we paid attention to them and believed in their value or contribution. What we define as important is determined by what and how we learn.

One of the ways children learn is through games. For many scholars interested in the development of children, play is con-sidered the "work" of children, and games are one of the many ways children develop skills and understandings of the world. Learning about rules, guidelines, how to interact and play with others, as well as gaining knowledge about numbers, colors, and creativity can all be part of a child's development through game playing. As children gain greater intellectual capacity and com-plexity, they learn about the rules of games and even how to cre-ate new rules. In the process, children explore how they fit into their family, community, and world. During this period, parents, siblings, friends, neighbors, extended family, and community members help children identify what is most important to learn. Reality is defined by the significant people in their lives.

As grown-ups, we do not necessarily quit playing games when we move into adulthood. Many adults play computer games of all types as well as different sports. We also enjoy games and competitions on television, from early game shows such as Hollywood Squares and Wheel of Fortune, to more re-cent reality TV shows such as Survivor. Some people enjoy shows that argue different sides of a topic, including presidential debates, wanting to see who wins.

The most universal game that adults play all over the world is the one I call **Buy My Perspective**. This is a game of compet-ing perspectives, each being presented as the right or best one. Children first experience this game with their parents, who teach them to view the world as they do. The parental view then gets reinforced in schools, places of worship, and neighborhoods. As they learn, children practice this game in the competition be-tween social, racial, ethnic, and economic groups in their subcul-ture. Young people often practice the methods they see their par-ents use to play this game within the larger social context, but the everyday skills are honed in our family, school, and neighbor-hood settings, which prepare adolescents for participation in the larger world competition. They can get so engrossed in the com-petitive aspects of this game that they lose touch with their subtle sources of information. In the end, this game appears to be played at times in order to reinforce adult beliefs, holding on without question as a way of feeling more secure and safe.

As adults, we experience this Buy My Perspective game in groups who support divergent views of the world, such as religions, political parties, economic systems, and countries at war. Every few years in a democratic country, politicians compete for leadership, wanting others to buy their point of view. Sometimes their outlooks are based on experience and facts, while other times they are little more than opinions, generalizations, or even deceptions. Here, people are vying for power, wealth, influence, and fame, and the game is played in earnest.

We also see the game played between religious positions, businesses and related advertising, and best places to go to school or live. While the adult justifications for each view are more sophisticated than in children's games, the processes at times are not all that dissimilar. People representing different points of view may call each other names and react in a defensive manner. Adults may use more diverse tools to convince others their particular point of view is right, yet a similar posture can be seen in children and young adults. As with adolescent gangs, conflicting views can lead to fatal outcomes, including fighting and killing. So we take these attempts to persuade seriously.

While the competition between perspectives can be fierce, positive outcomes can come from the desire to have others adopt our perspective. Some people accumulate wealth and fame, not only for themselves but also for their group. Others compete against those with wealth, wanting more resources for themselves. If we convince key and sufficient numbers of people that our vision is possible and desirable, it often can be manifested. When many believe in an outcome with a strong commitment, it can creates that reality. As Thomas and Thomas said many years ago, "If men define something as real, it is real in its consequences."[3] The result may not be positive for everyone, but negative impacts often are ignored or viewed as irrelevant.

Getting people to Buy My Perspective is how great edifices were built. People developed a vision of a structure and convinced others to participate, or they had the power and money to make it happen, even if those involved were not committed to the vision. The pyramids in Egypt and the Taj Mahal in India were built from great imaginations. We also could include many of the more recent enormous structures now existing around the world because someone or a few had great insight and figured out how to persuade others to support such creativity. The outcomes of this game can be positive: creation and manifestation.

Identifying a unique need and a way to produce it is the foundation for creating an innovative product. A pioneer presents evidence of an outcome that others may support, and the group establishes a reality from that vision. During the past century, creative thinking is how we developed cars, airplanes, computers, cell phones, and many other innovations that have enhanced our lives and brought fortunes to many people. This is the creative process, gaining support from key people to facilitate the production of useful inventions.

Our own interactions can be part of the informal aspect of this Buy My Perspective game. In relationships, we often want our spouse or partner to see things from our point of view, even if they do not agree with it completely. We seek support from close family members or friends, especially if we are going through a crisis or distancing ourselves from someone who has not been nice to us. We often participate in this game by trying to convince someone important to us to adopt the perspective we hold so dearly.

There are drawbacks to playing this game that I think are important to consider. When we get attached to a particular perspective, we do not allow ourselves to see an alternative. We do not open up to benefits or contributions from a different point of view, even defining all others as wrong. We adopt an external authority to follow, remain focused on that perspective and dismiss all others. If we form a strong attachment, we pass this view of the world on to our children without question, excluding what they bring to this life. If our hearts have closed in the process, it becomes even more difficult to expand into a broader, more loving and subtle part of our lives. Holding such narrow and committed views makes it difficult to question the game.

One of the most devastating impacts of the Buy My Perspective game on children is when parents, siblings, or others present a dismissive view that is believed by that child because there is no connection left to the cosmic spark that supports an alternative outlook. This can happen through both direct and indirect communications. Children hear themselves described as dumb, stupid, worthless, unlovable, evil, selfish, valueless, mean, bad, wrong, flawed, unlikeable, useless, disconnected, damaged, and chaotic. While parents or others may make such comments in an attempt to change a child's behavior, negative beliefs can incarcerate the child in a small dark box. Such labels internalized over time become central to children's definitions of themselves. Sometimes a child will let these labels go, or challenge them over time, but this usually happens much later in life and only after considerable intervention from professionals or close friends.

Sometimes parents are not even aware how they are passing on negative views of children. Assante reviews some basic approaches of the five major world religions, including Christianity, Islam, Judaism, Buddhism, and Hinduism. These religions all share a basic belief that "judgment of some kind decides what happens after death. They also share another essential and equally damaging teaching, which is that humans are innately flawed. Each of us born to one of these religions necessarily internalizes judgment as part of the socializing process."[4]

Yet core negative beliefs are not easily modified when a child has hung on to them for a long time. Other parts of the belief system, based on a learned core belief, create a complex web that is not easily modified. The saddest part of this impact is that the beliefs children have about themselves are not true, especially in light of their essence. Yet children hold them as accurate because they have no counterbalance from the internal sources of information that might help them see themselves as cosmic sparks of love.

When adults hide this spark from themselves so deeply, they share this limited view with their children, who trust and accept it as fact. Then these children spend most of their childhood and often their adulthood accepting and acting from these negative core beliefs. I have seen so many adults whose lives are still challenged because of negative views of themselves, even when their parents gave the messages indirectly or inadvertently. This is the saddest and most important reason to begin changing this process we use with children.

A second devastating impact is when the negative belief is delivered by parents who are upset and have closed their hearts towards a child. Such a delivery method amplifies the hurt because the child feels the emotionally disconnected from the parent's heart. Under such circumstances, the negative belief is intensified by the delivery method and increased distance from love. Not only does the message seem to be true, but the child also is now separate and alone. Without the inner connection to the cosmic spark, the child's isolation can be overwhelming. When children do not have an alternative connection to essence, the message and its mode of delivery isolate a child.

When we as parents are in touch with our own spark, not only do we shift the messages we send, but we also maintain the heartful connection to the child so that even inadvertent negative messages have a diminished impact. The energetic connection of the heart between a parent or caregiver and child is key in minimizing the internalization of negative comments or reactions that can come, even unintentionally by adults.

Finding Ways to Maintain the Inner Connection

Sometimes young people do not get caught up with external labels and find a way to access that inner, intuitive source on their own. As I look deeper into this process, what stands out is that a few people seem to pull from somewhere beyond the current external perspective for their creative inspiration. A new artist comes along and sees a different way of painting than others have been doing, and a new method is born. Sometimes it may look crazy, like the Impressionists or Cubists did during the late 19th and early 20th century. And yet, years later their paintings are still enjoyed by many people because they did not go along with what everyone else said was the correct way to paint. The same is true of groundbreaking theories in physics (string theory), family therapy (family systems), changes in communications (smart phones, pads), new approaches in medicine (laser surgery), new ways of doing business (telecommuting or telework), and music (jazz, rock, hip-hop). Through the ages, creative contributions that turn the current perspective on its head or shift something sideways seem to come from an inner source rather than from someone external to the innovator.

I begin to wonder if this aspect of creativity requires getting in touch with that intuitive part of ourselves despite the dominant externally defined reality. I also wonder what our lives would be like if we explored more consciously such sourcing within ourselves and supported the process in children from birth onward. What would our children be like if we encouraged their inner accessing of information rather than demeaning and dismissing such resources? We get so engrossed in the Buy My Perspective game that we seldom step back to question what we are doing or notice the impact our perspectives have on our lives and the world around us. This lack of questioning is of particular concern in relation to what we pass on to children. The most troubling impact I see is the dismissing of the cosmic spark in infants and children, coming from our own burial grounds. Now may be a good time to begin challenging our reliance on external authority as the only useful source of information.

Defining and treating infants' and children's abilities as real can change our interactions and our relationships with them. Supporting internal sources does not mean turning fantasy into reality, but rather incorporating, and strengthening the elements in our lives that can balance external perspectives with profound inner knowing. Focusing on inner, intuitive accessing of information is a key element to creating new ways of building things, new approaches to art and music, and new ideas. We have not incorporated it into our view of children and the world, maybe because we have not paused to examine it closely within ourselves.

We have ignored are the consequences of playing this Buy My Perspective game on other people and the earth, and especially on our children. We have abandoned our responsibility as guides who are willing to look at the consequences of our visions. We have built huge buildings that represent great fortunes without worrying about how this affects others in our own country and around the world. We have perpetuated political parties that seem to be more ensconced with their own survival than in solving the challenges that face the nation. We have fought wars, killed and enslaved people without allowing ourselves to feel the impacts on them, their children, and ourselves. And we have dismissed the knowing that children have shared with us, diminishing them and their cosmic skills in the process.

One of my favorite Mark Twain books is called The War Prayer.[5] In this insightful story, a religious congregation prays for the success of their troops, bringing victory to the war that rages. The minister expresses sincerity in his prayer for victory, and the congregation embraces his efforts. Then a stranger in a long robe walks into the room and steps up to the pulpit, motioning the startled minister aside. The stranger describes himself as a messenger, "bearing a message from the Almighty God." Before answering their fervent prayer for victory over the "enemy," God wants the entire congregation to understand "the full import" of their request, which one often does not realize "except he pause and think."

The messenger proceeds to describe what their victory would cost others. "If you would beseech a blessing upon yourself, beware, lest without intent you would invoke a curse upon a neighbor at the same time." The messenger asks them to hear the second part of the prayer, the unuttered part and yet very much an essential element of a "victory" over others. It is the unuttered piece that most of us ignore, just as the congregation wanted to ignore it in Twain's insightful story of 1905. With victory on one side comes pain, blighted hopes, death, devastation of lives, families, and the Earth. Twain eloquently adds, "We ask it, in the name of Love, of Him who is the source of Love..." If you have never read the entire short story, I highly recommend it.

In war, we pray for victory, just as the other side does, with both prayers carrying the same unuttered consequences for the "enemy." In business, we work diligently for success, even if it destroys lives and the earth in the process. In a political system, we entreat others for our success, without worrying about how "our victory" impacts others. We can get so caught up in perpetuating our perspective that we forget to ask our ourselves and our own hearts what is most important for us, our children, and the world.

As Twain was suggesting over 100 years ago, it is time to begin to look at the consequences or the shadow side of our intentions and actions. I am aware that if we shift our whole paradigm about children and ourselves, others may be impacted negatively by such a change. I do not wish to "destroy" the current paradigm, and yet I believe a change is essential for our survival as well as increased cooperation and joy.

Living from an Inner Guidance System

My whole argument could be framed as just another example of an external influence, another game of Buy My Perspective, but that is not my aim. I want to make the game more conscious, so we can choose a life perspective that is based on our intuitive, cosmic spark knowing. I want to help adults see how we all might play this game differently with each other and especially

71

with our children and grandchildren. We do not need to end this game. We are way too committed to it to give it up entirely, and we can see its positive aspects. Yet, I do think we can modify how we hold this external perspective and learn to incorporate an internal guidance system of our own into a more balanced life.

Here are five brief examples of how parents and children might participate in an alternative process with each other:

1. You can begin with infants, sharing energetic interactions and communications. For example, you could initiate an energetic connection just by imaging your energy flowing from you to a young person. What most people say in this arena is that energy follows intention. So even if you do not see or confidently feel energy in the beginning, practicing would help develop your skills. You can also telepathically communicate your desires and intentions to infants. We apparently have the ability when we do not stop to question or judge the skill. Again, imagine your thought or feeling being sent energetically. Intend it to be shared. We could play with this silent communication and practice it. Neither type of interaction will hurt the infant, and you may feel greater closeness the more you practice them. Finally, you could make energetic connections from a distance, especially if the infant is crying or troubled. Before you arrive physically, you could lead with an energetic response of comfort and love, letting the infant know energetically you are on your way.

2. With our children and grandchildren, we can play this game with more flexibility than we have in the past. We could begin to see that children bring a connection and sometimes a perspective that we have ignored, closed down, or missed, which may help us learn to expand our own point of view, learning from them. We could include the potential of psychic abilities in children[6,7] and reports of past lives,[8] supporting those aspects of a child's perspective that enhance the development of an internal guide, along with the gathering of information from external sources. Assante reports from her research that:

Children's past-life memories can emerge as early as the age of two and generally fade by the age of seven. Occasionally they will resurface at seventeen or eighteen. Parents might hear matter-of-fact statements from their toddlers, such as 'When I died...' or 'When I was big...' A three-year-old might talk about having a wife or husband and not always in the past tense either. Sad to say, parents usually think their children are making it up and either ignore them or scold them.[9]

Another researcher, Dr. Ian Stevenson, collected over 2,000 cases of reported reincarnation from all over the world and examined about 200 of these cases with children.[10] He found that children had birthmarks or birth defects related to the previous life, behaviors, memories, and even predictions of returning to another life. These fascinating results were supported by another researcher in this area, Dr. Jim Tucker, who focused to a greater extent on cases found in the United States.[11,12] Tucker suggested that children report memories of pervious lives more often than most people know. Because of his medical training, he used a very analytical approach to this topic, as did Stevenson. But he also offered advice for parents on how to handle responses and information offered by their children. He suggested that it is important for parents to know that such statements about past lives do not indicate mental illness, that parents remain open to what children are reporting, that parents ask open ended rather than directed questions, write down the statements children make, and that parents not lose sight of the importance of this life. "Overall, parents often find children's claims to remember previous lives more remarkable than do the children, for whom the apparent memories are simply part of their experience of life. The children then move on from the memories to lead typical childhoods."[13]

In his later book, Tucker compares the reports of between life memories by children as similar to those reported in near-death experiences. He argues that some part of us transcends the world we experience, suggesting a larger "self" existing across our lives. While this is a very different perspective for many in the West, there are increasing numbers of people who believe in such possibilities. Tucker goes on to suggest, like William James, that we may be a single train of thought in one large consciousness.

This connection, along with the seamless way in which observations create our holistic world, indicates that a single individual consciousness is only a tiny piece in the act of creation, that all the pieces work in concert as a part of a bigger whole, and just as our physical world grows out of consciousness, so the entirety of existence grows out of this bigger whole, this Ultimate Source. As mere streams of thought from one large Mind, we are not separate; we are all in this together. And just as our experiences in life can enrich our individual minds, if this awareness that we are all part of the Ultimate helps us be a little more patient, a little more accepting, a little more loving, if it helps us to focus more on our shared experiences and less on our differences, then perhaps in some small way, we will be better able to enrich the Ultimate and, with it, all of existence.[14]

Rather than dismissing such abilities, we ask children to reflect on their own inner knowing, their own intuitive information. As we ask them about their inner voice, they turn to it more frequently and with our support. We could help them hone and trust the process as they get better and better at it, as with any skill. We could honor this intuitive way of knowing in them, as they continue to trust the source. We could encourage them to balance inner and outer sources of information from a very early age.

This type of encouragement is what a father did with his son, Magnus Carlsen, the youngest world champion chess player ever.[15] Magnus describes himself as playing from his intuition, which would throw off other players and eventually allowed him to beat the best chess player in the world. Others described his playing as thinking "from another universe." In the end, his intuition was an amazing combination with his mind.

3.   In this process, we could share our own perspectives more flexibly, knowing that we are creating and adapting them as we go, rather than taking them as unchanging "truth" and "reality" all the time. We might include in our discussions and interactions the emotional and feeling elements of our interactions, which underlie them but usually are ignored. We could take the risk of bringing these emotional pieces to the surface, so that our communications and interactions become more honest and comprehensive, even when it makes us feel more vulnerable. While we cannot force others to do the same, our openness to sharing our own emotions may lay the foundation for others to be more open and authentic with us.

4.   One of the most useful elements in our interactions with children young and old is to make sure we hold an open-hearted connection to them as we interact. This is especially important during times of disagreement and conflict. If we can stop and check our heart connection, opening and expanding it towards them, it can change our interactions and the impacts we have on them. It can also alter how we feel from the experience ourselves. It may make our own lives more peaceful, by helping us focus on what is most important to us rather than getting caught up in petty issues. More importantly, it ensures that our children never feel a heartful or energetic disconnection from us, even when we are not happy about their attitudes or behaviors. We can disagree with them or challenge things they are doing without exacerbating the issue by cutting them off from our hearts.

5.   In general, we can become more conscious and expressive when we want others to buy our perspective, knowing that in fact we are asking for something a bit one-sided, especially since we may not be willing to reciprocate. But in the direct asking, we can laugh a little at ourselves and each other for what we are desiring.

The mixture of internal and external support is an important combination in changing the way we nurture children's development. The change begins with us in our interactions with infants and young children. Rather than pushing children to ignore or exclude significant parts of their subtle experience, we can choose to include and incorporate such information, not only through childhood and adolescence, but throughout our entire lives. During sour interactions with children, we can also pay closer attention to when we have a heart-to-heart connection and when we are beginning to disengage our own heart. As we begin to disconnect, we can explore what is driving or triggering it so we can do something about it in the moment rather, than waiting years to figure it out.

The most important measure of "success" is whether or not we look inward for what is the best fit for us, rather than looking solely outward to see what others have done or what others say is most important. It is the inward looking process itself that guides our passion and truth rather than a complete focus on an external opinion. We have used the external perspective, the external authority, as the measure of truth and reality for so many centuries that we have lost our ability to determine how importance and significance are created. Now is the time to develop a better understanding of this game of life, so we can play it more consciously.

CHAPTER 3

COSMIC SPARK CHOICE PHASES OVER THE LIFESPAN

THE BREEZE AT DAWN

The breeze at dawn has secrets to tell you.
Don't go back to sleep.
You must ask for what you really want.
Don't go back to sleep.
People are going back and forth across the door sill
where the two worlds touch.
The door is round and open.
Don't go back to sleep.

- Rumi[1]

If children are born as a manifestation of love, which is a fundamental principle in noussentrism, how do infants become adults cut off from their cosmic spark? How do we transform a baby full of love, happiness, and joy into an adult who is fearful? Environments that focus babies on an external authority, to buy an external perspective, begin this regrettable change. As outlined in the last chapter, many competing forces encourage children to shift away from an internal, intuitive, conscious awareness to an external belief system.

The most devastating external authority comes from parents who, in one way or another, teach children they are defective in some manner. Even if this message comes from an attempt to encourage children or help children be more realistic about their abilities, it reduces their resources and assets. The judgment becomes internalized as their worst fear and shapes the way children learn to view themselves. At the same time, it strengthens the connection children develop to the fear-based physical world and gradually becomes their larger external view, dismissing the subtle love spark that permeates children's early experiences.

When adults focus narrowly on a single perspective, we not only push children into the external domain but also define it as the only reality. For many, the physical world is the only thing that is real. We exclude human energy, intuition, imagination, and dreams, which offer multiple perspectives and multiple realities. We narrow down our world to a single physical reality. This has been one weakness of science, relying only on the five senses to determine what evidence is valid. Even if the external focus is on a set of religious beliefs, they become the primary external reality, excluding internal information and resources.

The gradual substitution of an external framework for internal resources takes place during key choice periods, when children and adults do not see another alternative. In this chapter, I describe seven choice periods children and adults face as they replace subtle sources of information with the dense physical aspects of reality. Fundamentally, these phases describe how we lose the skills we bring into this life as infants, rather than continuing to use them throughout our lives. As we let go of our deep cosmic connection, shame, hurt, pain, and fear create strong defenses that distance us from our spark. Then we create a reality focused solely on the physical world without awareness of how the subtle skills and sources of information could assist us in this life. In the end, we define ourselves primarily as our body and personality, defining ourselves as a socialized being rather than our cosmic spark.

The choices we make along the way alter our course and influence future phases. We can change our mind and shift our perspective at any time, yet modifying our trajectory, as with any habit or pattern, becomes more difficult as we continue along our chosen path. In some cases, a life event such as a near-death experience can shift our view in such a way as to alter our choices. Without such influences, we often tend to commit to our physically defined reality.

At each phase, our choice either maintains the awakened consciousness we experience as infants or inclines us towards less awareness of the energetic and intuitive world. Rumi and others sometimes refer to this loss of awareness as going to "sleep." Our choices take us in one direction or another, but we always maintain our ability to choose. The longer we choose to go down the external perspective pathway, the more distant we become from our initial love spark. Instead, we approach the fear-based physical world with contracted and defended energy fields that hold fear as our socialized reality. Increasing emphasis on the physical world makes it more challenging to shift our focus and see things differently without some additional encouragement or opening of our minds and hearts.

Phase One: Infancy

Choice: To Orient Towards the Physical World
or to Incorporate Energetic Skills

The issue in this first phase is whether early experiences lead to a beginning separation from the larger, more conscious part of the lives of infants, the cosmic spark, or incorporate basic subtle skills into early experiences here. This choice is not a single dichotomy, but rather a continuum of behaviors, both with adults interacting and nurturing young children as well as with older children or even as we mature into adulthood during later phases. These choices are ways of describing our overall behaviors by adults with children and adolescents or as adults when the decisions are increasingly our own. In addition, while the choice is framed as two different options, we do not always act just one way or another over a period of years. What is important here is that the overall focus of parents and others interacting with infants and children occurs more towards one end of the continuum or the other.

Phase One takes place during the first couple of years of life. During this time, infants are connected to their cosmic spark and to the skills they bring into this life. Especially through the first year, infants live in the dual world of the three dimensions we know (eating, sleeping, interacting with caregivers and environments) while also living naturally in their subtle energetic world. They are learning about the physical world around them, spending increasing amounts of time interacting with people and objects in their environment. They are beginning to eat other foods besides breast milk, gain increasing mobility, explore objects in their environment, and increase their interactions with adults and other children. As we observe infants during the first few months of life, they exude love and joy, except of course when something is upsetting their physical experiences (lacking food, needing sleep, having an uncomfortable diaper, or experiencing physical injury).

While infants are developing in the physical realm, they also are comfortable with their cosmic spark and to the skills they bring into this life. For example, all of the approximately 6-month-old infants we observed used their "third eye" to read the energy of objects around them.[2,3] They also manifested energy rings at times, especially while being touched or held, creating an energetic connection to the adult as well as a physical one. People describe them as looking just beyond a person (possibly viewing the energy field of that person), reacting to people differently (even beyond the issue of attachment and stranger reaction), and creating energy connections themselves.[4] Some would argue that children maintain these skills as they get older, especially between a mother and child.[5,6] While adults seem to respond, beyond their typical awareness, to these energy connections, it appears to be the infants who initiate them. It is likely that when adults encourage and respond to such connections, infants experience increased the comfort and support. When adults initiate subtle connections and interactions, they help infants maintain their dual cosmic and physical worlds as equally important parts of their lives.

Rather than being born "blank slates" as Locke suggested centuries ago,[7] we are born into a physical body held in place by a conscious energy field that is expansive and open.[8] This conscious field is consistent with the argument that babies are born with the 'divine spark' or 'soul spark,' suggesting that the cosmic spark resides inside each one of us.[9,10] As an infant's expansive field experiences hurtful and fear-based interactions, it becomes constricted by mistrust of the environment and by armoring of its own being. When infants are supported with expansive, love-based interactions and experience trust in their environment, they have less reason to contract and shut down to protect themselves. With supportive experiences, they hold onto and express their skills during this period, developing a more expansive foundation for their lives.

The challenge for adults and parents during this phase is to expand beyond what we see when we look at infants and their physical dependence. If adults feel into the experiences of infants at the subtler realms where they are connecting and interacting, they can encourage infants to exercise and incorporate such skills. Parents can open to subtler communications and intuitive information in order to understand beyond the physical world what is going on with young children. When adults pay attention to these aspects of an infant's life, it encourages infants to continue and know that subtle skills are an important part of their reality. In this way, parents support and practice more expansive, love based interactions. Infants then experience trust from their environment, with less reason to contract, shut-down, and develop more extensive protections in response to the world around them. Based on supportive experiences, infants hold onto and express their subtle skills during this period, developing a more expansive foundation for their lives.

When parents and caregivers focus solely on the physical world, a "first separation" takes place for the infant. As infants increasingly let go of their cosmic spark or essence, there is a disconnect from the foundation of cosmic love, acceptance, and interconnection that leaves the infant experiencing a sense of being "alone." When the infant later begins to experience a separation from a parent or primary care giver, there is no cosmic foundation to counteract that physical aloneness, which amplifies the sense of being separate. This feeling of being alone also intensifies fear, leading to more protection and defenses and less incorporation of inner skills. First separation is a concept I will discuss in more detail in Chapter 6.

Even if an infant experiences a contracted environment, the constricted path is not inevitable. We can shift our fields along the way. So adults do not have to be "perfect" to be effective. Most of us experience a range of expansions and contractions throughout our lives. The issue during this period is whether as infants we experience more contractive or expansive moments overall, and whether their contractive experiences are extreme. The more extreme the early contractive experiences, the more difficult it may be to open the field and the heart. The more supportive and expansive the early experiences, the easier it will be to maintain our connection with the spark and integrate its subtle abilities into our lives.

Phase Two: Early Childhood

Choice: To Increase Focus on the Physical World or to Expand Understanding of Inner Abilities

The choice during this second period emphasizes the possibility of worldly skills increasingly being added to rather than a replacement for subtle abilities. When the sole focus is on an external perspective, worldly skills usually replace an infant's larger connections and subtle abilities. This focus creates a continued emphasis on the physical reality as a continuation from phase one. The basic question is whether parents, care-givers, and teachers help children to maintain a relationship with their own essence as a part of their continued development.

As children continue to develop in the physical world, their focus broadens to include other aspects into their life. During the approximate ages of 2 to 6, children progress in physical ability, language, mobility, and social interactions. Development occurs at a unique pace with each child. Yet in general, they interact more with parents, siblings, friends, neighbors, and others, including, for some, classmates in a preschool. They learn to use more elaborate language and examine the world around them, often with great curiosity. They typically sleep better, explore larger environments, put together more complex ideas, create longer compound sentences, and develop greater sequencing of objects during play. Their cognition becomes more abstract and logical, although it still is fairly concrete, with a limited perspective of others. Parents encourage children to learn about life, which generally is defined as their physical world, and children navigate their environments in ways that can be challenging to parents.

This was the time when I walked by myself at the age of four about seven blocks to the grocery store in order to find some chocolate, as my mom did not have any. The police apparently found me on a big lawn in front of a church, eating the goods I had helped myself to in the store and thoroughly enjoying life. My mother was in a panic, unable to find me, when the police brought me back home, not understanding the fuss. This was my first real lesson about wandering off by myself and taking things from the store. But we were out of chocolate! What was a boy with a sweet tooth to do?

This is an age group in which children still express great curiosity and imagination during solitary play, as well as play with others. The many possibilities that exist for them are often viewed by experts as a limitation, because they seem to have a difficult time taking the perspective of others. They do not limit their world to the "reality" of the physical plane, which makes for greater imaginative play. These children may still be tuned into the larger world of the energetic universe, where possibilities are enormous. Because they have not accepted our limited view of "reality" and what we define as possible, we see them as unrealistic.

Given the adult focus on the physical world, parents usually do not pay attention to or emphasize energy connections with children. They do not communicate with them beyond verbal exchanges that would emphasize the importance of anything beyond the four-dimensional environment (including time as a dimension). Thus, children increasingly focus on the physical plane and let go of the subtle sources of information. They also seem to rely less on energetic connections and do not incorporate information using their third eye or 6th chakra.[2,3]

An alternative for adults during this phase is to expand their use of subtle types of interactions, meeting children on this plane. Some parents pay attention to the connections and memories reported by young children accessing the subtler realms.[11,12] This type of support would encourage children to maintain subtle connections beyond this early period. Such fortification would strengthen the relationship to a child's inner resources. Adults also could feel into the intuitive and energetic connections, responding to children on this level and encouraging children to reciprocate. This playing in the energetic realm would assist children to claim and incorporate these skills into their whole world view.

During this time, parents work at getting children to develop a physical perspective, teaching them how to exist in this world. But what if it were the children who had the "larger picture" that many spiritual leaders discuss.[13,14] Children certainly are in the present moment much of the time, something many adults spend money and attend classes or workshops to learn to do more effectively. Young children usually are full of passion for what they do, which again is more difficult for adults to identify or describe.[15] They have very few "limiting beliefs," which appears problematic as we view children and their "unrealistic reality."

Yet when we look at how such limits impact our lives and narrow what we as adults see as possible, we often seek help in overcoming these limits.[16] Some of the same characteristics we view as problematic in children we end up paying others to help us recapture as adults. This period is a time where children extend their focus, experience, and skills with the physical world. The fundamental issue at this point is whether they do so as a replacement for their larger connections and skills or as a compliment to them.

This phase also includes children learning about their own "separate" body while not being disconnected in all ways. They learn about their emotional and social connections to others, developing relationships, usually beginning with parents and possibly siblings. The question is whether children also maintain a connection and relationship with their own essence. Part of this energetic connection is expressed through children's abilities to still "know" things about other people, including the apparent viewing of energy fields and the gathering of information that we describe as a psychic process.[5,6]

Traditionally, this has been a time when parents want to help children live more easily in this physical world by discouraging their energetic talents and denying their skills. This seems to happen because parents have lost touch with their own subtle abilities and do not see them as an important part of their lives. In some cases, parents punish the expression of such skills out of fear they or their children will be ridiculed by others. Such a reaction is likely by some adults when children's psychic abilities and other skills have been framed negatively in the world. Frequently, the general population holds these skills as inappropriate, so parents tend to strongly discourage or dismiss both the information and the skills. In strict religious groups, unless the information comes from church elders, it can be seen as emanating from the Devil and therefore suspicious or evil. Yet this time is key time for children to maintain subtle skills and abilities, learn how to incorporate them into their physical lives, and understand the larger view of who they are.

While most children experience some hurt and pain early in life, extreme physical and emotional pain leads them to create greater protections and defense mechanisms, which would further shut down their heart and cut them off from their cosmic spark. It also keeps them more focused on their physical bodies in the world. bIn Chapter 1, I discussed how children even leave their bodies during severe physical or sexual abuse. These traumatic childhood experiences from physical abuse, sexual abuse, or even female genital mutilation move them far from their inner world and subtle skills, especially when they are violated by people they love and trust.

Nevertheless, we parents sometimes hurt our children, even when we know better. I remember hitting my oldest child once when she was very "sassy," in part because I did not know what else to do then as a parent. Even though it only happened that one time, I continue to have remorse. Even worse, I remember spanking a young children my wife and I were tending, especially when he would not hold still while I changed his diaper. I have thought about this many times since, with sadness for my cruelty, and I know my anger was not about him, but anger all the pressure I was experiencing as a married graduate student with a child of my own. This also was true of my behavior with my oldest daughter. It was the frustration I was feeling as a parent, not knowing what to do, that lead to my violent behavior.

We so often take our emotional reactions out on someone else, and children are defenseless. Our reactions are about us, difficulties we are experiencing in life. Now I know that hitting children only teaches them violence, besides confusing them by confounding love with cruelty. How do we trust our world when those who are closest to us are violent with us? Instead, we shut down and armor our bodies to separate ourselves from the painful experiences, and in the process we lose touch with our own cosmic spark. If we want to change this pattern, we must look closely at how we unintentionally teach children to let go of subtle skills they bring into this life and support their continued connection to their own diamond.

Phase Three: Middle Childhood and Early Adolescence

Choice: To Let Go of "All Possibilities" or to Balance the Energetic and Physical Worlds

In this third phase, the choice is whether to encourage children to be more "realistic," which usually involves letting go of alternatives, or to incorporate the world of greater possibilities into the physical world. As we adults cut off from our own inner resources, we often have a limited view of what is an option, and we pass that limited perspective onto our children as if it were reality. When this is done, the external focus increasingly replaces the subtle sources and skills.

This third phase occurs during elementary and middle school. In the physical realm, children expand their physical, intellectual, social, and interactional skills and experiences. In terms of cognitive development, they learn to take additional perspectives, which allows their analysis of objects to become more complex and increasingly abstract.[17] As they learn to be more "logical" in processing information, and less focused on a single perspective, they also become more sophisticated in their moral view, not only looking at an event, but also taking into account the intention of a behavior, a process that is at the foundation of our own legal system.[7]

In addition, children are letting go of what Piaget refers to as egocentric speech. This type of externalized language is exhibited by preschool children when they talk out loud, but not intended as communication, since children that age only view the world from their perspective. Egocentric language appeared to Piaget to have no function, but Vygotsky and Luria argued that it was useful in learning to regulate behavior and therefore an important part of development. Rather than simply disappearing, as Piaget claimed, this language seems to move inward and become an internal manager.[7,18] My concern is that children may internalize the regulating process that they have been learning from others, with its many limiting judgments and beliefs. Such internalized language can include the fundamental fear about themselves, creating the inner critic and judge that so many adults experience.

During this period, children become more "realistic" about their abilities, something Bandura refers to as "self-efficacy."[7] This concept is a combination of their own belief system and their experience in different areas of their lives, such as math, art, or sports. An important component is what children believe about their capabilities and strong desires. Often adults want to help children become more realistic about life in the physical world by providing feedback on what they do well and where they lack skills. Criticism can end up discouraging children about their abilities. While it may be an attempt to help them in the world, critical comments can engender negative core beliefs and devastate young people, limiting their possibilities and discourage talents important to them.

Because I believed, for instance, that my older son, Greg, was not skilled enough to play professional baseball, I did little to find ways that would improve his performance in the sport. Sure enough, he did not play on any institutional teams beyond high school. Fortunately, from my perspective now, Greg is not perpetuating the same limitation with his son. While neither Greg nor my grandson, Owen, know if he is good enough at age 11 to make it into the big leagues, Greg is helping him in every way he can to improve his skills, as long as Owen wants to play and get better. Owen loves many things about baseball, and his father still plays recreational ball, so they enjoy the sport together. Greg does not care if Owen plays professionally, but as long as that is Owen's dream, he finds ways to support it. It will be Owen's decision whether or not to play, and Greg is not trying to protect him from disappointment by imposing some limiting belief. With my son, I unintentionally helped to create a more "realistic" view of his baseball abilities that may have limited what he could and wanted to do. We need to be careful how we help children get realistic when we have such a limited view of possibilities ourselves.

Some children do not pay attention to adult attempts at "realism," and we see examples of astonishing skills in young children when that happens. For example, Kieron Williamson, a six-year-old boy living in England, has skills as an artist well beyond his age, and his work looks more like a mature adult.[19] It is not clear how his artistic skills developed so quickly. What is clear is that his parents supported and encouraged this amazing skill. Kieron has considerable confidence in himself, again well beyond his years. He sent one painting to the Queen and another to Prince Charles. Encouragement by parents also appears to support his self-assurance rather than discouraging possibilities.

Akaine Kramarik began painting at age 4, after experiencing a life-changing spiritual transformation, and writing poetry at age 7. Both her painting and writing would be rather impressive even if produced by an adult.[20] This young woman, now 17, says she says is inspired by God and often includes a spiritual aspect to her work. Her biggest wish is "that everyone would love God and one another." In some manner, her spiritual experiences, along with parental support, appear to have helped Akaine connect to her inner resources and build on her foundation of life as love.

These two examples illustrate extraordinary skills, but even these can be squashed when parents are not aware of what they are doing or demean out of fear of judgment by others. We might have many other examples if children did not accept the typical parental perspective of "get realistic about your abilities" based on their own experiences of limited possibilities. What might happen if parents and teacher were to encourage children to hold onto their own intuition and inner sources of inspiration like these two children did?

We can see some idea of possible outcomes from nine-month old Michael described in chapter 9. In the case of this infant, the parents included energetic connections and presence in their interactions even during the pregnancy. It appears that such encouragement facilitated sophisticated development and outstanding abilities very early in this boy's life. For example, Michael told his father "I love you" at two months old, and never experienced "out of sight, out of mind" as most infants do. Of course, maybe he, like these other two examples, is unusual and not typical of most children. Yet I firmly believe we would have more young people demonstrating amazing skills, especially later in their development, if we did not impose our own limits on them while young.

What is curious about this period is that as children increase their cognitive functioning, they also demonstrate a "decline in make-believe play."[21] Fantasy and creativity in children were a serious interest for Maria Montessori. She wanted children to follow their natural inclinations while also being concerned with their inability to work within adult markers and restricted limits, helping children develop "their powers of discrimination and judgment."[22] She believed that artistic creativity was always tied to reality and was more concerned with the issues of discernment and decision making. I believe creativity is more closely tied with our subtle abilities and intuitive sources of information, more closely alined to the way Rudolf Steiner viewed children's development.[23]

As adults, we clearly define our reality, and we do our best to help our children grow up in the world with our view of how it operates. Yet the way we see the world is not the same as it was 100 or even 50 years ago, let alone 1,000 years ago when so many people in Europe perpetuated the idea that the world was flat and the sun revolved around the earth. When we hold a limited view of our world and ourselves, we try to help our children by having them adopt our restricted view, just as adults did 1,000 years ago. But maybe we limit ourselves too much. Maybe we hold a belief system that does not encourage us to incorporate subtle and energetic abilities, connections, and interactions. If that is true, then we discourage our children from holding onto many of the abilities they display as infants and young children, replacing them with the powers of discrimination and judgment that limit their self-efficacy. We do this with the best of intentions, in part because these abilities are not included in our belief system and increasingly discarded in our world of possibilities.

I would like to see us guide our children's physical and social abilities while also honoring their own intuitive assessments, their ability to find answers inside themselves. Instead, we push children to rely on answers from parents, teachers, religious leaders, police, successful people, or others as the authorities on how to behave in this world. If children have some inner wisdom and know at some level what is best for their own learning, healing, and excitement, then they may be better off with support for balancing that inner wisdom with the demands of a physical world rather than replacing such abilities.

During this third phase, we increasingly exert pressure on children to adopt our view of reality. We ask them to give up their creativity and endless possibilities because we do not believe in them. We do not encourage children to experience and trust these subtle skills as part of their own reality. The choice we face during this period is whether to replace their internal skills and innovation of things possible, or to encourage the type of creativity that Kieron, Akaine, and Michael demonstrate, a creative development well beyond their years. We could support the originality and wisdom, the energetic and intuitive skills infants and younger children employ, even as they grow into adolescence.

I suggest we help young children nurture their inner guidance along with receiving input and ideas from the world around them. To do this, they may need to learn how to balance conflicting views, but in these conflicts, the greatest growth may occur. When children hold multiple and sometimes conflicting notions, they may search not just for an answer but also for an emerging new resolution or perspective.

What is important in this process is that children experience a supportive environment for this exploration, both physically and energetically, one that lets them work through any conflicts at their own pace. In this way, we can provide them with the leadership for seeking balance between their inner guidance and the demands of the external environment, holding onto both aspects of their experience.

Phase Four: Adolescence

Choice: To Replace Inner Wisdom
or to Manifest a Balance of Inner and Outer Worlds

The issue for adolescents, as they work to enter the adult world, is whether to let go of their inner wisdom or try to manifest a balance between their two worlds. At this age, most young people abandon their inner skills in order to embrace a complete emersion into the physical world and society as we define it. We encourage them to let go of any internal skills they have left in order to be totally accepted in the physical domain, when, if we reassured them that it's all right to include their intuition, inner guidance, and energetic connections, our youth could integrate these two worlds in a peaceful and comfortable way. They could learn how to balance these two aspects, and discover how they might work in collaboration rather than in conflict with each other, cut off from the inner voice. They could practice such skills in their personal interactions with others, at home and at school, figuring out how to respond with greater honesty and presence, the hallmarks of true embodiment of being.

As children move into adolescence, they experience more change and skill development. Centuries ago, young people were taking on full adult roles, even becoming pharaohs or monarchs, during their teen years. Many began adult careers after serving years as an apprentice or learning skills at home to take over work and family responsibilities.[24,25] Now, we place greater emphasis on education, from high school to trade schools and universities, which were not common for the majority of teens even decades ago. Remaining in school for longer periods of time has created considerable change for adolescents in many parts of the world. It places them in a dependent state while they prepare for gainful employment and incomes that will provide a good standard of living for themselves, partners, and families, if they choose to have children.

Young people also begin more serious dating and socializing that will lead to long-term relationships, marriage, sexual connections, and communication patterns that influence many parts of their lives. Adolescents are going through puberty, which impacts their hormonal balance, changes their bodies, and influences their behaviors. Their brains continue to develop, with greater abstractness[17] and increased specialization of the prefrontal cortex, an important element in good planning, considering risks and outcomes, and impulse control.[26]

Erikson described this period as a time of identity development vs. role confusion.[27] He argued that young people experience a type of crisis regarding how they define themselves, what they want to be as adults, and how they make commitments and sustain freely pledged loyalties. For adolescents, this of sorting out how they define themselves is focused on the social aspects of life, but Erikson sees it as a long-term exploration that includes our accomplishments, social commitments, and a sense of who we are as adults. The strain of having to make important individual and social decisions during this period can produce a type of crisis. Of course, not all adolescents experience this period as an extremity. But for many it is a challenging time, as they learn to take on adult roles and fit into the larger social context. The great challenge that is not addressed in this approach is that without their inner core resources, adolescents are making decisions about external perspectives and social values with no inner wisdom to assist them.

I believe two critical changes take place during this phase that have not been previously discussed. The first could be called a "final separation" from their internal voice with its wisdom, the final silencing of our cosmic spark. If adolescents experience some difficulty during this phase, I think, at some level, it develops from a subtle discomfort in the final disconnect from the inner voice, not trusting it because we focus so heavily on the external assessments, expectations, and judgments. Without this inner intuitive voice and subtle source of information, young people can only concentrate on external authorities, vying to win in the game of Buy My Perspective.

A second and related change is the complete internalization of the "inner critic". This hypercritical voice appears to be inside most of us as human beings, not just adolescents. But it is during this period that it becomes a key informant. An inner judgmental voice adjudicates us based on our definitions and discernments of what is beautiful, acceptable, and successful in the physical world. This inner voice of self-criticism finds some way we fail to meet its extreme standards of physical size, beauty, intelligence, resources, skills, knowledge, power, and financial accumulation. For most of us, there is some aspect that does not measure up to these external standards, and without an internal voice of wisdom, we tend to encapsulate these harsh judgments that begin with others.

It is during this time that we figure out how to hide these self-critical assessments from the world, though we seem to have some difficulty hiding them from ourselves. We hold back and shield certain aspects of ourselves as we enter into interactions and relationships, whether with friends, family, or colleagues. These secrets make us feel fraudulent and distance us from others, preventing us from developing the closer connections we seek. If they really knew who we were, we think, they would not like or accept us. We want to bring our full selves into relationships, and yet we are afraid to expose ourselves completely, even though we know we cannot be fully present or authentic when we feel like an imposter. Our desire for connection is hindered by our own hiding of the parts we have come to believe are flawed. The paradox is that we yearn for connection, and yet we employ strategies that create disconnection.[28] We feel broken and not totally present even in our closest relationships.

When we hold these self-criticisms as adults, we cannot help our adolescents develop any differently because we model what we have experienced and pass along the same process. As adult examples for adolescents, we cling to the same type of judgments, shame, and world view. We hide parts of ourselves and create this same disconnect in relationships. If we do not heal this "split" from our own cosmic spark, which begins in infancy and gets amplified during adolescence, how can we help our children avoid it?

Parents and other adults can change this pattern by providing leadership and support for adolescents to expand their experiences and trust their inner skills and guidance. Young people experience plenty of pressure to collaborate with the external world, and while some have developed a clear vision of the path they want to take, many wrestle with a sense of purpose. These subtle skills would create a stronger foundation for being present and embodied when adolescents and young adults get into close intimate relationships and become parents. Adults could model the authenticity and honesty that allows adolescents to feel whole. Some argue that this type of full, energetic presence and embodiment is the greatest skill we could possess as partners and parents.[29] In addition, adolescents' sense of self and self-efficacy would be more balanced and less dependent on the perspectives of others if the internal voice and wisdom were an essential part of the "self" equation.

At times, the differences between the inner wisdom and external reality may create conflicts between these contrasting outlooks. Yet, divergent views are not always negative. The holding of opposing perspectives can be useful to sort out priorities and help adolescents discover what aspects or paths are most important. Such experiences help adolescents step back and evaluate a belief, view, or conflict by allowing enough distance to explore it on several different dimensions, as Kegan suggests.[30] This also can be a significant exercise in holding complex ideas that can facilitate the growth of more sophisticated thinking with young people, a skill that can assist adolescents as they move into adulthood, facing many conflicting issues and views in their lives.

Phase Five: Young Adulthood

Choice: To Focus on Physical Plane Success or to Integrate Inner Guidance with External Work

In this phase, most of us become socialized adults working for success on the physical plane as many of us have done, without the assistance of our inner resources. Here, the choice becomes more of the individual adult, and even more so in the next two phases, rather than a parent guiding and socializing a child or an adolescent, although parents often continue to have influence into adulthood. What we have forgotten about this choice is another option that would incorporate our inner resources to guide their work on the physical plane and follow life passions from an early age. This alternative approach would include more possibilities, using our intuition, and applying our inner wisdom and creativity to the tasks we undertake in the world.

As young adults begin to move into the world of work, family, consumption, and responsibility, they experience increased pressure to focus on living, surviving, and thriving in the physical world. For most of us, figuring out how to earn an income in order to experience a comfortable place to live, purchase items that bring ease and pleasure, and be able to do enjoyable things like recreation and travel is a constant stress. This is a time when some young people begin families, experience pressure for making a sustainable living, and purchase the necessary goods and services to enjoy relationships with friends and/or as a family.

At times, plans do not unfold or go well for earning a living wage to support yourself, let alone a family. Some young people plan careers that do not provide sufficient income, or find themselves replaced by technology. Others are disappointed by a career that was not a good fit or did not provide the happiness expected from such work. Businesses or institutions fail, jobs are lost with cut backs, and workers who were planning on a long career are laid off. When difficult things happen, what resources can we draw on to make our lives better? If we turn to our creativity and inner wisdom as assets, we may create more interesting and passionate possibilities for ourselves, ideas and projects that may enhance our chances of success in the outer world.

Even when career development does not take a lot of our time and energy, either because it comes easily or does not develop well, most people focus the remainder of their energy on friend and/or family activities and interactions, challenging recreational activities, traveling, or exploring new adventures. Many find ways to obtain the many physical items they love to enjoy in their lives and often make living easier. In other words, the focus seems to be on the physical world and ways to be successful at what ever a person wants to achieve in that arena. In this process, little encouragement or modeling occurs to incorporate subtle information and listen to the inner voice, reclaiming the subtler guidance. In this process, such wisdom and inner resources gets buried deeper and becomes less available for use. The one exception to unavailability of inner resources is when people feel pressure to figure out a problem for which there is no apparent solution, such as losing a job or facing a challenge at work. Yet even such circumstances may not prove useful if the individual has completely shut off the inner guide, the trusted intuitive voice.

Phase five is a time we either speak our truth to the world or close down and become silent. For some, the social or organizational pressures silence their truth, suppressing their communications in order to get along and "succeed" within the larger organization or society. Rather than experiencing support in the expression of views and insights, young people silence yet another part of ourselves to fit into the limited, physical model we have created and continue to support. For others, they speak their truths, but they are not necessarily shared from an open heart with caring for others. Their opinions can be very strong, but they may have little empathy for how such expression is experienced by others or the reactions they create. In this way, sharing information may not be well received.

Yet another possibility exists. Despite the strong value we place on doing well in our physical environments, we see some young people who appear to have an inner focus along with the external drives. They examine what brings them joy as part of their exploration. They use their intuitive side to guide them in their work and family life. This kind of balance keeps alive the inner skills, fostering their growth and trusting their intuition. They also speak from a more open heart, which is connected to the inner voice, for the heart has not been shut down. This kind of balance can keep alive the inner skills, fostering their growth and deepening trust in their utility. It can be nurtured by family, friends, and others important in young people's lives. Finding a balance between the two worlds helps young people to become fully functioning, successful, joyful adults, sound not just financially but emotionally as well.

Phase Six: Middle Adulthood

Choice: To Extinguish or Expand Inner Passion

During the middle adult years, people may not discover the meaning in their work and family life they were seeking and thought they would find. They realize their jobs have little passion and value, and they have had to give up much of themselves in order to achieve success. The choice that faces them is whether to extinguish the fervor that brings joy to life or hang onto and enlarge the inner wisdom that provides life's passion. There also is an element of expanding such enthusiasm to aspects of life beyond a socialized job and even family life in the physical domain. When the inner resources remain active, they continue to contribute to a deeper understanding of a person's purpose and passion in life, and this understanding can be applied to the opportunities that become available as financial and family responsibilities lessen.

As adults move into the middle years (40s and 50s), they have usually developed a career and figured out how to provide financially for themselves, and in many cases for their families. If children have entered into their lives, these young people are getting older, becoming more independent, and even beginning to leave home. Now that they have more free time and options, feel the lessening of financial burdens, parents can begin to focus on what aspects of their lives they want to change, including sometimes shifting jobs, careers, living locations, and leisure activities.

This period Jung[7] describes as a "midlife crisis," where men and women begin to question the dominant focus on the outer world, feeling like something is missing. During this time, adults may begin to focus inwardly, looking for more balance and wholeness. Yet for others, changes in perspective seem to remain on other aspects of the physical plane rather than an expansion of their inner vision.

Levinson found that most of his subjects reported a type of crisis during this period of life.[31] Even before external circumstances or transitions pushed individuals to challenge their perspective, Neugarten, and Havighurst found that both men and women in their research were dissatisfied with their outer roles and focused on a more internal perspective or inner self.[32,33] Even with a push, many people ignore the signal, instead maintaining a focus on the security of an externally defined reality. Crain suggests that people studying development in middle age "have long been concerned with how we seem to lose so much of ourselves and our potentials as we become socialized, as we become adjusted to the external world."[34]

During this period, adults experience increased challenges with health, lose people close to them, and question their own mortality. Such issues can encourage people to consider questions previously ignored, while also inquiring into the deeper meaning of life. These increasingly relevant concerns may inspire people to investigate alternative ways of living, explore spiritual avenues, and seek methods for finding peace. All of these means may facilitate a turning inward, promoting a reconnection with subtle sources of information.

While this search for meaning occurs for many people later in life, as Jung suggested, there also seems to be some who attempt to tune into internal guidance from an earlier age, or at least earlier in life than the middle years. The difficulty, as I see it, is that such an option is available from birth. But parents and others do not encourage its development with children and adolescents in conjunction with the physical plane focusing that is important for living in this world. When people do hold on to this facet of their lives, say during early adulthood, it can play an increasingly important role during this period of greater exploration.

People have options, as outlined in the first five phases, to incorporate this subtle aspect of life along with the physical world when adults encourage it with children and adolescents, or such skills can be recognized and incorporated during young adulthood. Some people have their own inner strength, which is maintained despite the lack of nurturing by parents and society. When people do hold on to this facet of their lives, I suspect there is less need for a "crisis" to turn them inward, for they have been developing and nurturing their own connection with their essence or spark, along the way. Thus, as Crain points out, when adults get to this part of their life span, they have less need to "take stock, to resist the pressures of conventional roles, and to concern themselves with the neglected and unrealized aspects of the personality."[35] When adults have been integrating a balance of these two worlds throughout their lives, they have less need to recreate one later in life.

Phase Seven: Older Adults

Choice: To Solidify Limits or
to Share Subtle Aspects and Wisdom

In this seventh phase, people can choose to maintain their hold on the external reality of the physical domain or share a renewed connection to the more expansive energetic world. If they choose the latter, they also can share the greater wisdom they have rediscovered or even been developing along the way.

In the aging process, Erikson argues that people begin to make a larger shift as the possibility of death becomes more real and looming more closely in our inevitable future.[7] They ask bigger questions, including those that take them beyond the physical world where they have been so focused. For many, this is a time of transition from long work hours and the pressures of "survival" to an inclusion of other aspects of their lives that they may well have ignored while being so focused on "living in the world." But even when people focus on religion and giving more service to others, the conversation seems to emphasize how they can be "better people" in the socialized world, how they can help others on the physical plane, rather than what they might do to prepare for death and whatever comes after that final transition. For many, there appears to be little discussion about an inner life, intuitive resources, or inner guidance.

Jung[8] suggests that people often try to make meaning of their lives during this period, turning to contemplation and reflection to understand the nature of life. They want to know what gives life meaning and makes it whole, especially as they face death. In this process, people may do a type of life review, looking at what their lives were about and what meaning their life has had for themselves.

The life review process of life review is a version of the episode many go through as they experience a near-death. During these incidents, people not only go through a review of their life, but they also experience the impact their actions had on others, even when children go through such a process.[36-43] But Ring argues that a life review is a valuable experience prior to death, helping us see the larger picture our actions have painted on this physical landscape and taking responsibility for the impact we have had on others.[44] The individuals he studied recommended that people undertake a full-fledged review while still alive, not only looking at their behavior, but also experiencing empathically its impact on others.

> I wish everyone could have one (life review) — it would change the world! Everyone would understand each other, and there wouldn't be conflict, and there wouldn't be

chaos, and there wouldn't be greed and war... The life review is the ultimate teaching tool.

Everyone is loved infinitely, and with incredible compassion. There is a plan, or one might say, a kind of blueprint for everyone's life, and, while we each are free to embrace or reject it, the Light is there to help us find it. If we can open ourselves to the Light, invoke it into our lives, we will, in time, be shown our own way — and we will recognize it as ours unmistakably because it will give us joy. Joy in living is the truest sign that we are living right.

What kills is judgment; what heals is love. The Light itself is only love, and it never judges; instead, it gently *nudges* you toward your essential self. It wants you to realize that your core being is the Light — it is not something external to you. When you become identified with this Light, you will have only love and compassion for yourself — and for everything — and you will be able to let go of all judgment. Self-condemnation, guilt, and other forms of self-laceration likewise are vanquished. When judgment — that ruthless sower of division — falls away, there is only acceptance — of everything. And that is called love.[45]

For people who are connected to their inner resources, the life review may be as impactful as it is for those going through a near-death experience. Their connection to inner wisdom and intuition may help them have a deeper understanding of the impacts they have had on other people through their actions. They may also be more loving in letting old traumas dissolve and less judgmental of their actions once they have made amends for them.

This final phase may include a reconnection to the larger energetic world and the energies of the universe. A focus on the subtle realm helps us with a life review from a larger, more conscious perspective and the accessing of greater wisdom during this phase of our lives. Such wisdom can help individuals focus more on love than judgment, more on compassion than self condemnation and guilt. Enhancing our wisdom in this way takes a person back to the cosmic spark itself, experiencing the connection they may have been missing and seeking at some level their entire lives. As our wisdom is expanded, we may share it with family members and friends, encouraging them to access their own subtle skills and sources of information. Sometimes older adults can share information in such a way that is more easily heard by young people, helping them tune into their cosmic spark and intuitive knowing.

For some, this phase may include a basic rekindling to our larger perspective by attempting to redevelop a connection to the more expansive energetic world. For others who have been including the energetic skills along their path in the physical world, this focus may be a manifesting of the greater wisdom they have been developing along the way. In either case, this phase could incorporate a greater emphasis on our connection to the larger, energetic plane of our cosmic spark.

The only thing better than the gaining of this wisdom during this final phase would be to carry it and the spark with us throughout our entire lives. Connecting more to our spark of love allows us to be more compassionate with ourselves and share that with others from childhood rather than reconnecting with it at older ages. In the end, the sharing of this wisdom of love, light, compassion and cosmic connection is the important contribution people can make with family, friends, and the larger community around them. The fundamental question is when we want to access and incorporate such elements into our lives and support this inclusion with others.

Conclusion

I have described seven phases of life that present choices to shift the focus of children towards the physical world either as a substitution for, or as an addition to, the inner wisdom they bring to this life. These phases included key choices in our life that determine whether we will move away from and diminish our subtle skills or nurture and incorporate the cosmic spark as an important part of our life here.

These proposed phases and choice periods allow us to develop a view and experience of the world on a purely physical plane or to include a larger, more expansive and conscious perspective of the world, incorporating skills and abilities that are evident from our birth. These phases are cumulative, as all our experiences tend to be in our lives, helping us create the model we use to view, experience, and interact with the people and environment around us. The choices we make at early ages impact our experience later. Yet it is possible to revisit those choices and take a different perspective at any point in our lives. In this way, we can rekindle our spark at any time, if we have lost the connection at some point along our path. The biggest challenge often is knowing that such a possibility exists and finding ways to enhance it when we have disconnected from it so early in life.

In the focusing of a single reality, we emphasize and trust only one set of beliefs, whether scientific, religious, or some combination. When we rely on a single perspective, we let go of the possibility of multiple realities, multiple perspectives, which can provide more than one option. This focus on a single option is what I experience when I am in deep fear, as I described in the last chapter. Such a focus is part of the limitation we put on ourselves when we move away from a more expansive view of who we are at the core.

While we know a table is solid, we also now know there is more space than actual density in a table, a chair, or a planet. When we trust only a single reality, fearing other views, we have difficulty allowing other possibilities. Out of our own fear, we teach our children to focus on a single perspective. When we step back, evaluate our beliefs and views, and hold more options in our mind, we can see more possibilities and create different choices.

In some cases, a shift in our perspective comes from a transformative event, such as a near-death experience. Yet even in such experiences, people sometimes feel anxiety when they first leave their body and move into an unknown greater than the physical world in which they have learned to put their trust.[46] When we attach ourselves to a single physical reality, it becomes a challenge to let go, and yet in the letting go we find such freedom. In Long's research of people going through such experiences, one participant said this: "To overcome our fears, we need to love and accept ourselves and each other. The actions and choices we make can either be from love or fear — love is golden light, fear is darkness."[47]

Oftentimes, the accessing of subtle sources and intuition is not necessarily difficult at occasional times in our lives. We seem to find ways to use some of the abilities and obtain information. The greater challenge we may experience is to trust the information we gain in the process. When the connection is infrequent, we do not have a clear sense of confidence or reassurance about either the information or our skills. Trust is gained by use on a regular basis. An important aspect of nurturing the skills from infancy is the development of conviction children gain as they incorporate both abilities and information over the years.

Sometimes we go through these phases in a particular fashion because of the way we have grown up and been taught to view the world. The support we experience for certain choices from those around us strongly impacts our views. Later in life, we may want to make a shift in perspective. We may question what we have been doing, find out what is most important to us, and alter priorities in our lives. We might even begin to increase our focus on more intuitive information and guidance for our decisions. This particular kind of questioning is central to the direction we take during the fifth, sixth, and seventh phases outlined above. But if we do want to make a shift in our perspective, how do we go about doing that? What methods are most useful in helping us change our belief systems, values, priorities, and most of all our behaviors? The next two chapters will address these questions.

Section Two:

Rekindling our Spark as Adults

CHAPTER 4

NEW OPPORTUNITIES IN SHIFTING PERSPECTIVES

With Contributions by Jean A. Metzker, Ph.D.

ONE SONG

Every war and every conflict
between human beings has happened
because of some disagreement about names.

It is such an unnecessary foolishness,
because just beyond the arguing
there is a long table of companionship
set and waiting for us to sit down.

What is praised is one, so the praise is one too,
many jugs being poured into a huge basin.
All religions, all this singing, one song.

The differences are just illusion and vanity.
Sunlight looks a little different
on this wall than it does on that wall
and a lot different on this other one,
but it is still one light.

We have borrowed these clothes,
these time-and-space personalities,
from a light, and when we praise,
we are pouring them back in.

- Rumi[1]

In the first section of this book, I described basic skills and abilities infants bring into this life and the ways we lose connection to subtle sources of information. In this second section, I want to focus on ways adults can rekindle our spark to assist and encourage the integration of such resources in children as they learn about the physical world in a more effective way. We can reconnect to our spark in different ways, and I will describe several processes I find useful. An initial step in such a transformation is to allow a larger view of possibilities to enter our reality. As we reshape our outlook, new opportunities become available to us in the process.

Oftentimes the greatest challenge for adults, (parents, teachers, medical personnel, counselors, and friends) is to allow ourselves to see things from a different point of view. In this process, we usually have to step back far enough to examine our beliefs and systems more like objects, using an awareness that has some distance from our fears. If we are unable to shift our perspective, we cannot see a path to support children's inner resources and skills, for we typically do not allow such a possibility to exist in our world.

This book is about adjusting our view to see children in a new light, with skills and abilities that we have not been included by most of us. In order to experience a different option, we must alter our current limits to include a new possibility, a different way of how we see young people. Without stretching what we include in our worldview, we could not include the potential that our very being is composed of a cosmic spark.

Robert Kegan[2] describes the holding of our values and beliefs as either "subject" or "object." I find this distinction very useful. In this case, when our mental structures are so close and intertwined with our being, it is difficult to examine and evaluate them. They are subject in that they are interwoven aspects of how we define ourselves. He talks about a belief being such an intimate part of ourselves that we have difficulty getting any distance or space from it to scrutinize it clearly. Something that is subject is an intimate, non-discriminating part of us.

When we have hold values and beliefs at some distance, we can see them as elements we have incorporated into our life, existing with enough space to investigate just what they are to us and know they are things we have rather than who we are. Once we create a sufficient gap to look at a belief as an object, then we can truly examine it. Even with this small expanse, the relationship changes. We are able to scrutinize our convictions or opinions, treating them like other objects in our environment. We can turn beliefs around, feel them, smell them, evaluate them, do all sorts of things to inspect these objects. When we have such a space for analyzing, we then are able to view a conviction or belief system in a new way or new light.

In some cases, we feel greater appreciation for the system we have examined closely and keep holding it, as we find it useful, even if for different reasons than when we began. At other times, we find pieces that do not fit for us, or we begin to question a part of it, eventually even allowing the whole system to transform. We may find a system too confining, or we find a larger and different perspective more useful or expansive, one that allows us to move in a different direction. A belief system is not inherently bad or wrong, but we find something else more helpful and integrative of other parts of our lives that do not fit into our current and possibly more limited set of beliefs.

I often have wondered how people generate a new idea, an innovative invention, or a whole new perspective on things. How do they shift their way of thinking about something in order to see it differently? I have been impressed with people who could do that. Some individuals make it appear easy to create an unusual idea or product. I can change my view once it has been delineated by others. But I have never felt very creative in my life. So when others present something new, very different, or unique, I am taken back by their ability to invent. As I reflect back on some of the ideas I have developed, I even began to wonder how I constructed something new to offer. Without deliberation regarding my own path, examining my perspective more as object, I was not immediately clear how I ended up with this result.

It has taken a long time, a professional lifetime really, to put together these ideas I call noussentrism. The concepts presented here were not difficult to see once I became available to see them, but I had to shift my perspective in order to allow them to enter my radar over time. Otherwise, I simply would have disregarded or never envisioned such notions, unable to consider them within my limited realm. Great friends and colleagues have assisted me along the way, people who have challenged my thinking or offered new points of view that expanded my own perspective. But without opening up to a different possibility, a different outlook, I would not have been able to see and incorporate an alternative perception. When I held a narrow view of how I defined myself as a human being, I did not allow my perspective to include subtle sources of information or a cosmic spark.

These changes did not come quickly for me or all at one time. Rather, they were slow modifications as to how I viewed children and development. Now that I see these creative ideas, I more easily look back and see the trail I followed to get here. But as I moved in this direction, I had difficulty to seeing what was ahead, not always understanding which trail to pursue, or knowing the direction that eventually would pull me.

Along this path, I kept encountering a question or topic that called to me in an intuitive sense, or a type of intuitive pull, one after another. Each time, I simply would investigate the issue as long as there was some attraction to it. Over time, I would let one go as another aspect would rise up and catch my attention. While not all ideas or perspectives are illustrated in this conceptual framework of noussentrism, each made a contribution towards shifting my vision of children and the world, allowing me to see a larger picture.

I will illustrate how such shifts can be important in our lives, allowing us to see new ways of being and doing things. Sometimes these changes enable us to be happier or more at peace. At other times, we see something that is missing in the larger scope of things, stimulating us to create a unique product or service. In each case, the intuitive draw helps us develop a broader vision, something that can be a modification or expansion in the way we see or define things.

Early Experiences with Shifting Perspectives

I grew up in a conservative religion that dominated politics in my state, as it can do in other locations. In the fall of 1960, I was in Mr. McGuire's 6th grade class at Stoker Elementary. Our teacher decided we should hold a mock presidential debate. That September, Senator John F. Kennedy was going to debate Vice President Richard Nixon during the first televised debate in history. My denomination had a negative view of Democrats and Catholics. There was a deep fear in our state that the Pope would be the real influence and making all the important decisions for a puppet president. Based on that bias, my family did not like then

Senator Kennedy and was rather suspicious about a Catholic being elected as president.

I was happy and proud when I was chosen to represent the Republican candidate in that 6th grade moment. As the other boy, who sadly had to represent Senator Kennedy, was standing in front of class with me, we both spoke about the issues as we understood them. I had studied for several days, and my mother helped me strengthen a few points. I remember being very nervous, and yet there was a force in me because I knew I was "right." In the end, after much anxiety in explaining what I knew about the general topics, I won the debate. Coming out on top was not too difficult, as most class members belonged to the same sect and did not like the Democratic candidate. Buying our parent's perspectives can be well ensconced by 6th grade.

I found it quite ironic much later that people felt great about a member of "our" religion, the "correct" religion, being president. In fact, church leaders in that denomination hold a belief that leaders from the church will step in and "save the nation." If the president of our sect would give advice or direction to a US president, that would be fine, because that was God leading the country. But if leaders from other churches had any influence, that was all wrong. This was a clear, black and white issue to members of the "right" church. This is an example of enfolding opinions so closely they are held as subject, making it difficult to analyze or investigate them in any significant manner. It was part of how I defined myself.

By the end of high school and even more in college, my interest in politics increased. I no interest in becoming a politician, as I am not a great public speaker and have never felt comfortable with my oratory skills. But I wanted to go to the state convention and had begun to shift my political identity from Republican to Democrat. Part of the transition may have been a way of differentiating from my parents, both of whom were Republicans. In my county, it also made it easy to attend a state convention as a Democrat because the competition was minimal. It also was the 1960s, and personal views were under scrutiny and beginning to shift for many in my cohort of Baby Boomers.

One of the other things I learned early from my parents, as with other churches, is that all other religions were "wrong." They not only were wrong, a few were seen as so fallacious they were described as "of the devil." I wanted God to love me, and devoting myself to the correct religion felt like the only way for that to happen. When someone grows up with such strong views, they have a significant impact on young people, making such a perspective difficult to investigate. We become so immersed and committed to these views that it is challenging to be able to examine them in any objective way.

As we gain enough distance to begin an examination, we may let go of one piece within a set of beliefs and add another in a way that the system transforms slowly over time rather than experiencing a sudden dissolution. We sometimes change an assumption, expectation, or view that shifts the system in dramatic ways over a long period of time, as I have done, and yet the process feels quite natural as we make a slow and steady transformation. There may be some small jolts along the way, or new lights shining on a piece of the puzzle that allows other parts to dissipate in a manner we hardly notice in the moment. Alternatively, we may make dramatic shifts, throwing off or transforming whole belief systems in a brief time as some did in the 1960s. This may happen when an enormous metamorphosis occurs in our belief system or from dramatic experiences such as a near-death. Such experiences can permanently and quickly change lives.

Kegan also suggests that we may expand our mental processing to include more complex ways of holding ideas and the interrelationship between them. For example, we might move from a view that religions are either right or wrong to a perspective of how each makes a contribution and has some drawbacks or limitations. An example of this larger picture is Hanh's comparison of Buddha and Christ.[3] In this case, Hanh examines the commonalities and spiritual truths underlying two very different religious approaches rather than focusing on differences. Holding opposing points of view until a larger picture arises is a useful way to help our children develop more complex thinking as they develop.

It took me a long time to be able to treat my religious belief system more as "object" than "subject." I was so close, so committed, and so involved in the organization that I could not examine the tenets objectively, even when I began to question ideas or rebel from them. I still was very attached to the ideology in the resistance, as happens with conformity, still too close to examine and decide for myself.

When I finally walked away from the church, I tried to delete the belief system from my "hard drive." Unfortunately, we cannot simply hit some button and have a set of beliefs disappear from our neural pathways. It took time exploring other views and creating more space before I could objectively examine my old views and the larger system. I felt like I had to leave the doctrine in order to explore my spirituality in a broader context.

While still in high school, I began to wonder if people who were able to tell something about the future or the unseen simply were accessing subtle information that was available to us all, whether or not they were in the "right" church. I was very intrigued with this idea and was surprised when it did not go over well with other church members. I also began exploring diverse spiritual traditions that seemed to offer valuable insights and intrigued me.

I had an increasingly difficult time believing that everyone else was wrong when there appeared to be many different spiritual gifts offered to the world by good people. I began to read about Buddhist ideas and practices, stimulating my interest in meditation. This practice has been especially useful for my busy, chattering mind, which had a challenging time ever stopping and resting. It also has helped me rest in an open heart. As I continued to develop a meditation practice, it has allowed me to myself to subtler aspects of living and information, slowing down the mind to access subtler resources, which have been invaluable to me along this path.

Professional Shifts in Perspective

As an undergraduate, I studied child development within the discipline of Psychology, which was intriguing and exciting. And yet, when I began to have children, I realized I was not well informed about normative change, as I had been so heavily focused on abnormal issues at the time. I decided I wanted to know more about the nature of development and typical change with children.

I began to explore new ideas in my graduate training, which turned older concepts "on their head." For example, many of the developmental theories were constructed by men, particularly white men, who had not integrated either feminist or multicultural perspectives. When I investigated these alternatives to traditional male views, I could see an inherent bias that did not incorporate a broader view of women or non-white experiences and issues. I enjoyed learning new approaches and appreciating how I could expand my outlook to include more diversity in the way I understood and worked with people. I realized how gender and ethnicity impact our experiences and interactions with each other, even how we treat children differently at an early age based on their sex or race. This reminded me of how people were treated differently in my denomination based on gender and ethnicity. While I was not supported by my professors in some of these areas of investigation, I found these revisions fit some of my deeper values of equality. I also found a deep peace in these new spiritual shifts that opened a broader view of people and solidified my challenge to discrimination in my religious background. These expansions in my outlook were important keys in the transformation of my larger world view, both personally and professionally.

During this intense time of graduate work and the onset of my academic career, new views were introduced into the field of human development, which impacted several different disciplines. Social scientists investigated challenges children and adolescents experienced, trying to figure out how to "prevent" choices that created defeatist long-term outcomes. Researchers and practitioners were investigating ways to guide young people away from problematic behaviors, such as drug abuse and delinquency, which negatively affected them as adults. As I increasingly focused on adolescents and families,[4] I became fascinated with this literature, especially in terms of children's maladaptation and incompetence as adults.[5]

About this time, scholars began to ask a whole different set of questions, developed from a contrasting way of looking at these same issues. A few investigators began to notice that in certain environments where we would expect negative outcomes, many children and adolescents were thriving. At the same time, in environments where we would expect children to do well, some were developing serious challenges. These scholars began to identify "protective" factors with children and adolescents who grew up in places where you and I would not expect them to succeed, and yet they did.[6] This research expanded to develop the concept of "resiliency," with a focus on the strengths of children, their families, and the larger environment rather than a primary focus on problems and pathologies.[7-9] This shift in view dramatically changed the literature, looking at how children who are nurtured and supported by family, friends, or teachers grow up to do well in life, sometimes even becoming heads of agencies, companies, or countries when we may not predict positive outcomes. It also helped us look at our own stereotypes and how that influenced the way we saw and judged diverse groups of people and impacted our expectations about them.

According to Anthony, this work on resiliency developed because researchers began to look beyond the concepts and frameworks from which they had been working to see what had been in front of them the entire time, "illuminating presences that simply had no form before the light fell on them and lit up the entire intellectual landscape."[10] New ideas and perspectives develop when scholars allow themselves to look beyond the assumptions, concepts, frameworks, and language used previously in their research.

I think the concept of resiliency with children, adolescents, and later families, illustrates how such a shift in our view influences our thinking and framework once we allow ourselves to see something in a new light. It really helped social scientists alter approaches from a problem prevention to a strengths enhancement, focusing on positive aspects of people and how they might be fortified and supported to a greater extent.

Further Expansion of My Perspective

In his book, <u>The Tibetan Book of Living and Dying</u>, Sogyal Rinpoche suggests we sometimes limit our perspective, which makes it difficult to see something new. "Confined in the dark, narrow cage of our own making, which we take for the whole universe, very few of us can even begin to imagine another dimension of reality."[11] After Jean introduced this idea to me, it motivated me further. I have never wanted to feel "confined." I am the kind of person who likes to feel as though I am free and have options, even within a system or institution. So Sogyal Rinpoche's description has had a strong impetus on me to continue moving beyond my "dark, narrow cage" to see what else may be a possibility and another dimension of reality.

I have always enjoyed the freedom I feel from flying. I enjoy seeing birds and butterflies move about with ease in the air. One of my favorite examples from science while growing up was the metamorphosis of a caterpillar turning into a butterfly. What is most important about this transformation, as I understand it, is that you cannot really help this creature in the emergent process. If you provide too much assistance as the caterpillar works its way out of the cocoon, it apparently does not have the strength to fly. I understood the concept of this mentally while I was young, but I did not fully feel the truth and implications of this idea deep inside me until much later. Even today I still am learning to understand the subtleties of breaking out of my own "cocoon."

What has become increasingly clear about emerging out of my "dark, narrow" cage is that I needed to do the work myself if my perspective were to change. Teachers and friends could offer ideas and provide support, all of which were immensely helpful. I doubt I could have made the shift as easily without such encouragement, and yet I needed to choose how my way of seeing the world would transform. No one could do the work for me. I needed to learn about my own inner strength and experience its importance to modify any trappings. I needed to make the decisions, the choices of which direction to take.

I could attach myself to other views and other perspectives, and at times I did so in order to examine the fit for me. I would try on different ideas and points of view, identifying aspects that were comfortable and those that felt foreign. These views were helpful in my own "perspective taking exercise," building strength in the process by working with different ways of looking at the world. But if I had simply replaced one perspective for another without learning to go inside and see what felt most useful or appropriate for me, I would not have learned to trust my instincts and inner voice along the way. I also would not have learned to hold contrasting ideas in more complex ways. These, for me, were the most valuable outcomes. I found my inner voice, learning to trust it completely, through the deep explorations that became my exercises in this transformation process. I began to embrace my world in a more complex fashion, moving away from black and white to a whole rainbow of options.

When I adopted the definition of what is science in the research methods class I described in Chapter 1, I embraced a perspective without really examining it. At the time, I held a narrow view of what was included as "scientific research" and what was excluded. Not only did I dismiss the possibility of testing relationship strength utilizing human energy field measures, but I also focused primarily on information sources that came from experiments or other kinds of quantitative methodology (techniques that can be measured based on objectivity and numbers). Interviews with people or case studies was not considered by many as solid research at the time, although I have expanded my view to include both as well as other types of what is referred to a "qualitative" data collection.

Once I became interested in energetic interactions some 18 years later, Jean and I developed an observational study of children's fields. In this case, we relied on people who could see energy, as no instruments were readily available to do this work. Including these uncommon skills, we were able to conduct work in a whole new area. In the end, I also was able to contribute unique and creative work that I value as the most vital contribution during my academic career. When I expanded my world of possibilities, I was able to guide the innovative research we created as well as other investigations of energy fields that laid the foundation for noussentrism and this book.

As I opened myself to explore energy work, I expanded my interests in other areas of non-traditional work. I began to investigate research on near death experiences, Breathwork, psychomateums, and hands on energy work. In workshops offered by the Human Awareness Institute, I examined how my judgments, a core part of my defense mechanism, create separation between myself and others, even those close to me. I explored how I could do tasks while keeping my heart open and expanded at the same time. Finally, I focused on more ways that I could open my heart and live from more expansive states. These explorations not only broadened my outlook, they also have allowed me to experience greater peace and joy in my life.

I was driving home from a workshop a couple of years ago feeling particularly aware and noticed there was little fear and little to no judgment accompanying my mindfulness. The lack of fear had become increasingly more common, but the lack of judgment was rare. These two closely related siblings have been pervasive in my life. I had increased my mindfulness following some early training with a friend and Gestalt therapist, Jan, many years ago. As I still had some time to complete my familiar freeway driving, I began to consider the difference between awareness and information that is based on fear in contrast to awareness and information in the absence of fear.

As I continued my drive, I realized how different I felt without fear and judgment, two very close companions who show up in my life as a powerful duet. During my drive and at times since then, the inner voice seems stronger, calmer, and clearer when fear and judgment do no permeate my being. I do not believe I would have experienced this peaceful place without all the personal work to emerge from my own "cocoon." But I realized is how fear and judgment keep me in a narrow, more limited framework. I hold on tighter to my point of view when I am in fear, defending it with great stringency and verbosity. My judgments also strengthen, even getting expressed in more defended ways. Rather than being open and vulnerable, I am more closed and protected, seldom open to new outlooks.

When I want to shift away from fear and judgment, I find it helpful if I allow my whole-body to relax, trusting my inner voice to guide my choices, and open up to new possibilities along the way. In that process, I allow my judgments to soften, in some cases even to momentarily disappear. As with my drive home, I have found more peace, joy, and gratitude to fill my life during those times.

A related way of relaxing my judgments is to increase the openness of my heart. When I allow myself to focus on and feel my heart expand, I can ease both my judgments and my feeling of separation from others. The more I can expand my heart opening, the easier it is to loosen my judgments. I will talk more about this process in Chapters 6 and 7. You also might begin to play with this idea simply by focusing and feeling into your heart, noticing how your body and being change when you do so. This is a place where I feel more at peace and relaxed. More and more, this feels like being at "home" within myself.

Creating Change from Expanded Views

Many people want some type of change, as evidenced by the assistance individuals seek from different professionals, both personally and through books. The amount of modification and the way we go about releasing fear, judgments, and protective layers is different for each of us. Our paths and issues are diverse, and we have unique pieces and gifts to explore.

In that process, I do not believe that increasing the density of a "cocoon" facilitates the creation of greater strength when one emerges. We certainly do not need to pile more "stuff" on children to generate more exercise by them working through it. The importance of an expanded view is to create an environment that encourages more positive outcomes, expanded possibilities, and encompassing abilities with less armoring struggle. The work of noussentrism is helping people see a different way of supporting children to access more resources for working out of what ever cocoon they have in life with fewer defended layers in the process. As we broaden our view and include greater possibilities, we are better able to facilitate such outcomes in children and adolescents.

While breaking out of the cocoon is important for each of us, I believe we can help our children unfold from family environments with greater clarity and consciousness along with fewer defenses. How well we facilitate this process depends on the resources we incorporate to assist and nurture children in their growth as they emerge into adulthood. I believe this collaboration with children increasingly is the general direction we are headed as a world, and such support is what children and adolescents are desiring in order for them to grow beyond us, a primary task of parenting.

As I look at my four adult offspring, I am pleased in the abilities they have developed to raise their own children and support each other's offspring. I was relatively young when I became a parent and was not really prepared to be one. I made a lot of mistakes along the way, often not practicing or sometimes doing the opposite of what I propose in this book. So these suggestions are not ideas I have developed from my great expertise as a perfect parent. The big, loving heart of their mother was an important influence in the way these kids have moved into their adult lives. At the same time, I see them making better choices than I did, growing beyond me in the process. I have learned how to maintain support for their maturation and choices as adults, partners, and parents, helping them do better than me. I am extremely proud of them for such growth. At times, I think I have done a better job as a grandparent, especially as my own views and perspectives have continued to expand. I feel like I give better suggestions or possibilities than when I was so worried about their outcomes as adults and was in fear as a parent. These shifts in my perspective and the development of the noussentric ideas have helped me in this way.

117

Shifting Perspectives in Other Sciences

Major shifts in perspective are not limited to the social sciences. For example, medicine is expanding its heavy reliance on pharmaceutical interventions and incorporating more wholistic approaches. A prime example of recent alterations in scientific outlooks also comes from the work done by Robert Lanza and Bob Berman in the area of physics.[12] For a long time, this basic branch of science focused on a fundamental cause and effect model, referred to as classical mechanics. That dominant view was challenged in the early 20th Century when Albert Einstein and others began to suggest alternative perspectives and explanations that developed into Quantum Mechanics and String theory. More recently, another shift in this physical science has been proposed that further transforms current views of our physical reality, how life is formed, and how we explain the way our world works.

Rather than supporting string theory or quantum mechanics in physics, Lanza and Berman expand these ideas into what they call biocentrism as a new, more comprehensive framework to explain our physical world. They propose several basic principles, which incorporate the ideas that reality includes our consciousness, external and internal perceptions are inextricably intertwined, behavior of subatomic particles is linked to the presence of an observer, the universe is fine-tuned for life and consciousness, and both time and space do not have real existence outside of perceptions. These are not simple changes, but appear to be substantive transformations of basic world views.

Given that I am a real novice at physics, although I love the topic, I have difficulty even attempting to challenge their principles. Yet Lanza and Berman seem to have at least some support in the larger academic community. I find their ideas intriguing and a major transformation from the way we viewed our world a century ago. Lanza and Berman even propose the question, "Is consciousness synonymous with everything"?[13]

In the end, these authors do not support nor exclude the possibility raised by this question, for suggestions of consciousness occur in almost every discipline. Yet they argue that objects and entangled particle phenomena vastly far apart remain intimately connected. They also suggest a "theory of everything" that does not account for life or consciousness will ultimately lead to a dead-end. This certainly is not an attempt to infuse religion into science, as they clearly demonstrate. But the challenge of developing an exact definition of consciousness remains. One significant conclusion from this work which relates to the ideas of noussentrism is that if people are more than their body, then consciousness cannot die, for it is ultimately unconfined.

> "..one of the surest axioms of science is that energy can never die, ever. Energy is known with scientific certainty to be deathless; it can neither be created or destroyed. It merely changes form. Because absolutely everything has an energy-identity, nothing is exempt from this immortality.... Incorporating the living universe, or consciousness, or allowing the observer into the equation, as John Wheeler insists is necessary, would at a minimum produce a fascinating amalgam of the living and non-living in a sway that might make everything work better."[14]

New Opportunities by Shifting Perspectives

When I teach classes about modifying our outlook, I enjoy showing optical illusions[15] to my students. One well known example is called the Dali Illusion. This illustration is a picture showing the left side of a young woman holding a book in a room or a picture of the right side of Dali's face. The young woman's head becomes Dali's eyes, her upper torso his nose, her arms and book his mustache and mouth, and her lower body his beard. For some, they see the young woman first, then can shift to the other image right away. For others, I have to point out "Dali's face" or the young woman with a book. Still, some struggle for quite a while and may never see the other perspective. Once we see a picture in a new way, it can appear so easily. It can be a simple alteration in our focus. But we can get so attuned to observing something from a single point of view that a shift takes a major effort before it can happen. A basic belief sometimes is modified just by seeing a new view. Other times, it may take years of work and many alterations to transform a belief system.

Altering our outlook can provide new opportunities that were not available with our previous view of the world. For one thing, we begin to develop an idea that we could not allow into our outlook before, even a piece that is missing from the larger picture. For example, we may begin to see a service that is needed in the community, or we may identify a way we have withheld support for an adolescent wanting to develop a new skill. We may see how our communications are based on fear with a desire to explore what it might be like if we expressed ourselves from a place of love and gratitude. When we expand our way of looking at something, we can begin to see a piece that previously was not available to us.

Another example is provided by Assante in discussing social responses to people who have nontraditional experiences. She identifies the importance of expanding our view not only for ourselves, but for family and friends we otherwise would not be available to support when challenging experiences occur in their life and social norms direct us not to discuss such matters.

> The percentage of people reporting contact with the dead in surveys range from 42 to 72 percent. Widows having contact with their deceased husbands can go as high as 92 percent. If the surveys had included children and deathbed encounters, which are extremely common, the percentages would have been heftier. A whopping 75 percent of parents who lost a child had an encounter within a year of the child's death. But a sad 75 percent of all those who had encounters reported not mentioning them to anyone for fear of ridicule. It's hard to believe that a society can deny the validity of an experience shared by such a large proportion of its population. But we do. Many organized and not-so-organized religions go so far as to condemn communication with the dead, a position that at least admits contact is possible. Until recently, near-death experiencers have suffered great distress from dis-belief and derision, silenced by those they were expected to trust most, their families and physicians. The same holds true for people on the verge of death, since the phenomena they typically experience, such as visits from the dead and visions of the other side, are treated as symptoms of dementia.

As you become more familiar with the phenomenal world, you are bound to notice more within your own circle of family and friends, dead or alive. Then you too will be faced with risking your credibility if you dare to speak about your experiences. The more of us who openly pioneer the last frontier and take that risk, the more we, together, add to the sum total of knowledge of the afterlife and the nature of reality itself. When that total grows large enough, it will cause an unprecedented sea change in our collective worldview.[16]

Assante reinforces the importance in allowing ourselves to include possibilities we previously have excluded, especially when they occur with our own family members and close friends. When they may need us the most, we would not permit such discussions or acknowledge these possibilities. When we open to a broader view, we enable our connections to sustain those close to us and offer the acceptance and love they want most under stressful circumstances.

When we shift our perspective, we expand the possibilities of our creativity. We allow ourselves to play with a new idea that may be useful but not developed or provided in our culture. We see an alternative way of cooking something, a different way of using an instrument, or a radical way to treat a disease that might be better than the current methods being used. In order for this to happen, we must expand our scope of what is possible, including aspects that we have not allowed ourselves to view as an option.

In order to create, we need to be very familiar with the physical tools in our area of exploration so that we know how we might manifest an idea. At the same time, we also must tune into that intuitive, creative spark that facilitates seeing an option in a new way, including solutions that have been ignored before. When we combine our knowledge of our tools or methodologies with an expanded outlook that incorporates new possibilities, we can be in the height of creativity.

When encouraging children, we incorporate our knowledge of the world with our intuitive access to resources combined with the subtle abilities and sources of information introduced by them. Then we create a magical connection, allowing ourselves to see ways we can integrate the spark and skills children bring with the wisdom we have acquired on this earth.

Changing our behaviors is difficult without altering our sense of what is possible for ourselves and what we might prefer in contrast to our current habits and patterns. When we allow ourselves to see other options or new ways of acting, our path is more straight forward. I certainly have experienced times when I felt deep in fear and my view of the future was very narrow. At those times, I could only see one or two possible paths, and neither one looked good to me or would take me out of the hole I had dug for myself. Only when I began to open my view to a larger outlook and new path could I see something positive and bring myself to significantly shift what I was doing.

The only way to generate a new way of supporting children's subtle skills and abilities is to expand how we view them and change how we support their development. Once we initiate alternative questions and enlarge our outlook on children, we can alter how we encourage them. Without amplifying the parameters of how we see them and ourselves, we maintain the current trajectory of our fear based protections. Yet the knowledge about subtle sources of information and energetic skills lies directly in front of us, waiting to be explored further. My hope is that we allow other possibilities to enter the garden of our beliefs and water them not only to survive, but to thrive, especially those that bring us peace, joy, and the experience of cosmic love.

CHAPTER 5

REKINDLING ABILITIES AS ADULTS

EVOLUTIONARY INTELLIGENCE

This groggy time we live, this is what it is like.
A man goes to sleep in the town
where he has always lived, and he dreams
he is living in another town.
He believes the reality of the dream town.

The world is that kind of sleep.
The dust of many crumbled cities
settles over us like a forgetful doze,
but we are older than those cities.

We begin as a mineral. We emerged into plant life
and into the animal state. Then into being human,
and always we have forgotten our former states,
except in early spring when we almost
remember being green again.

Humankind is being led along an evolving course,
through this migration of intelligences,
and though we seem to be sleeping,
there is an inner wakefulness that directs the dream.

It will eventually startle us back
to the truth of who we are.

- Rumi[1]

When people talk about altering some aspect of their life,
many different approaches can be utilized to assist in a change of
one's perceptions, behaviors, thinking, intentions, and interactions. Elaborate and effective methods have been developed

within psychology, psychiatry, social work, marriage and family therapy, and counseling over the past few decades to support alterations for people of all ages. Researchers in the medical community have created medications that help people create significant modifications to the chemical challenges some experience in their bodies, and people in alternative medicine continue to develop other important approaches to increasing health. Innovators within spiritual traditions, self-help advocates, as well as personal coaches have assisted people in making effective life changes. We also have models outside the main stream of these fields, such as the work by Alexander Lowen or Myers and Briggs, giving people insight into their motivations, actions, and patterns that have helped people shift the way they view and do things, making their lives easier and happier.

When we talk about change, we often focus on the things we do not like about ourselves, wanting to "fix" them, attempting to eliminate those aspects we judge as inadequate, wrong, or broken. At the same time, we have those parts of our being where we have performed tasks very effectively, have developed strong skills, and have made significant contributions to others and the world. But how do we recapture a part of our lives with which we have little familiarity? How do we access, expand, and trust attributes we have ignored so well they generally do not fall within our scope of possibilities? How do we rekindle a spark we are not even aware remains in us, especially if we question its very existence? Such an adaptation can be challenging or even impossible to imagine.

A first step in this process is the willingness to explore our internal environment. Some people are quite comfortable with this, having spent lots of time digging into their inner workings. For others, their focus is so external that the inner environment may be a whole new domain that is unfamiliar to them, an uncharted frontier. Most of us have spent some time looking inward, even if only to critical assess all the things wrong with us. But that is only one part of the exploration, and judgments do not assist us with an objective examination or loving transformation of our inner landscape. As we investigate the internal environment, incorporating all the diverse elements within that setting is crucial to any thorough investigation. Seeing the entire scope, both the "broken" and the "outstanding" pieces, allows us to embrace the whole.

Approaching Internal Change

Several people have provided useful concepts for exploring our inner environments. One example is the work by Dr. Bruce Lipton on human cells. In his ground-breaking book, <u>The Biology of Belief</u>, Lipton discusses the process of how we came to see the nucleus as the "brains" of a cell.[3] In about 1955, a hypothesis was developed that cells were run by the nucleus, in large part because the DNA was contained within it, which determined how cells formed and replicated. By the mid 1960s, more and more biologists believed that this idea was accurate, and by the 1970s it had become accepted as a "truth," even though scientists had no empirical research supporting this conclusion, according to Dr. Lipton.

As a cell biologist, Lipton began to look closely at the evidence of this theory. He would remove the nucleus, and a cell could live for months. How could such an organism live for months without a "brain?" What Lipton discovered is that scientists had confused different parts of the cell. He realized it was the membrane that really functioned as the "brain" of the cell, while the nucleus was truly comparable to the human reproductive organs. We had an idea that made a lot of sense in the beginning, and everything was interpreted consistently with that belief. When the view was put to the test, the theory fell apart completely. This is the way beliefs influence what we see as possibilities and what we ignore or dismiss, even sometimes defining our reality with no evidence to support it.

One other critical point made by Lipton is that cells tend to be in one of two states. They can be in a "protective," contractive state, where they tend to be closed down to their environment, letting little to nothing enter from the external territory or attach to the cell. Alternatively, cells can be in a "learning," expanded state, where they are openly exchanging with their environment, allowing certain things to enter or attach to it.

The same contractive or expansive states could be described for the cells making up our entire body. Lipton goes on to suggest that we as human beings have a similar approach to life, experiencing existence from a closed down, protective state or living in a more open, learning mode. In that way, we, as a human organism composed of cells, could be in one approach or another. Of course, some cells may be in a protective state while others are in a learning state. We often have conflicting elements going on inside of us, including one view from our mental state and another from our emotional system. But as a general idea, we have these two modes where we fundamentally can be in one or the other as we approach life.

Goldschmidt[2] identifies a similar dichotomy, which she called our Limiting Patterns and our Strength Patterns. A limiting pattern is a response to an emotional trigger that brings up our protective, fear-based approach to life that is developed in order to avoid feeling our core fear, our most negative belief about ourselves. As this fear pattern arises, we continue to interpret information according to that belief, which reinforces at some level this core fear and our basic negative view of ourselves. It tends to be an automatic response coming from that initial emotional reaction, and it is difficult to change the response once we have moved into the pattern itself, triggered by the emotion. We end up reacting and responding in the same old way and getting the same old outcome, which typically is what we are wanting to avoid in our lives or the opposite of what we want most.

I know a woman whom I will call her Mary. As she began to investigate her fear based limiting pattern, she discovered her worst fear was the belief that she was "evil." This view of herself was reinforced when she focused on times she was not nice to people. She could be very angry and hurtful to her friends. She did not care about how other people felt when she was in protective mode. When she closed her heart, she did not care how her words and actions could wound others. Any contrary evidence of being nice to people, helping her friends, giving things to people who needed them without thought for herself, and really being present with her friends when they needed her help would be ignored or disregarded as superfluous data when she was in the belief system about herself as "evil." When Mary was in her fear, she could not even see or remember such conflicting evidence. Everything would point to the conclusion that her worst fear must be true. What is most interesting about this woman is that when she shifts to an open heart, she is loved and admired by so many, for she connects easily to others and is a place of helping them in many different ways.

In another example, Stacey would only be able to see how people treat her consistent with her fear belief system. If there were presents on the guest bed when she would visit a friend, they must be for someone else. If someone would do something nice for her, there must be some underlying motivation of wanting something from her. They would not do this just because they cared about her. While people can have very different underlying motivations, the pattern we see when we are in our fear based response allows only a very limited, single vision that confirms our worst fear about ourselves. We distort the information and make it consistent with our belief system based on our worst fear, without allowing any divergent data to rebut it.

In contrast to the limiting pattern, Goldschmidt also identifies what she calls our strength pattern. This is a behavioral pattern, or a set of behaviors, that we have developed typically as a mirror to our limiting pattern. A strength pattern includes our positive behaviors, our many gifts, even if it is a challenge to see or acknowledge them. Instead of being driven by fear or making decisions based on a belief that we are lacking something, the strength pattern is a set of behaviors that we have developed and utilize when we are expressing ourselves from a more expansive place, love and the heart. In this response, we exhibit what we really want to have and be in life, rather than fearing it does not exist. In addition, our strength pattern helps us get what we have always wanted, which is the opposite outcome of our limiting pattern.

Where the limiting patterns provides evidence again and again that our worst fear is true and gives us the opposite of what you are seeking (for example, separation when we are wanting connection), the strength pattern gives you what we always have been desiring. My fear pattern, for example, is based on doubting myself and demonstrates that I am not enough or have no real value, no essence. In contrast, my strength pattern gives me the feeling of clarity without any doubt, allowing me to act with confidence and strength that is not available when I am in my limiting pattern. One of the greatest difficulties when we are not clear about our strength pattern is that is shows up more by chance than choice. Once we get clear about the patterns, we more often can choose which patterns we want to exhibit and where we want to focus our energy.

Here is one example based on my strength pattern from an event that occurred a few years ago. After several years of training with a group and conducing some research, I had the opportunity to go overseas and present the results of our work. One of the presentations was at a conference attended by people who were interested in the topic of working with energetics and children. I had given longer presentations before at large conferences, often with more complicated results. Although there is always some anxiety before a presentation, this one was in a more unusual setting. The actual speaking engagement was relatively brief (a ten minute overview of what I had learned from this work) in contrast to others I had presented for 20-60 minutes. But this talk was to be given in front of about 40,000 people at a large soccer stadium. Not only was it more difficult to get to the essence of my remarks down to ten minutes, but the thought of the crowd and setting were a bit daunting. I did a lot of preparation in order to speak from my heart and share what ever wisdom I had learned with passion and conviction. Afterwards, I realized I was in a place of strength that included no doubts, regrets, or fears. As I got up to the podium, I was able to get into my heart and speak without fear. While the rehearsing had helped, it was being in my heart and speaking from that place which, I believe, created the opportunity to share my best self and what I was able to offer others. This is an example of choosing and then exhibiting my strength pattern.

We all have gifts and contributions, and they come out or are demonstrated from time to time. One challenge some people experience is that they have such strong negative views and beliefs about themselves that they often ignore, minimize, or even dismiss their strengths. I have worked with lots of people over the years. Just as each one has been able to identify the behaviors that get in their way, each also has been able to identify some of their gifts and behaviors that generate the outcomes they want. The model is more complex than what I am describing here, but this basic difference I believe is very useful to understand and has been helpful to me personally. By becoming aware of our patterns and what drives them, it also allows choice to be more available to us.

The Enneagram Approach

The dichotomy about cells presented by Lipton and the distinction between limiting and strength patterns described by Goldschmidt are similar in many ways to opposing ends of the continuum included in each of the nine points of the Enneagram (for a more complete review of this approach, see Appendix B).

This model includes nine contracted responses people develop because of a distortion in their view of the world and a basic negative belief about themselves. Each pattern is described as a fixation at one end of the continuum, a way of believing and acting from a contracted emotional wound. When we are functioning in fixation, we are constricted, closed down, responding from a basic emotion (fear, anger, desiring love) and not putting our best skills and insights into play. We are being protective, as Lipton suggests, or in our limiting pattern, as Goldschmidt describes, not letting in expansive views or sharing positive expressions as we defend ourselves or even get aggressive with others. This usually is the worst of our behaviors, the things we do not like about ourselves, behaviors that drive others away or put them into a defensive stance.

In contrast to the fixation, each Enneatype also includes an expansive Holy Idea or what I call the Essential Lesson at the other end of the continuum. When we are expressing our essential lesson, an expansive place, we usually are calm, strong, moving ahead with a clear vision of what we should do or have in mind. We act from a place of heartful confidence, applying our best skills and insight to a situation. We are caring about others, the impact we have on them, and choosing from an open heart. In fact, in my experience and as I watch others, an open heart tends to take us more regularly into our essential lesson patterns. Many of us spend much of our time in the fixation side of the continuum, based on my own life and people who have come for therapy or coaching. Being in our heart takes to an expansive place.

One challenge some people face is that it can be more difficult to identify their gifts and strengths because of the strong internalized judge. Essential lesson patterns often feel like they occur less by choice, but show up as a "random" event that appears by chance. Sometimes they occur in a time of crisis, especially a difficult situation other people are experiencing and you have the opportunity or responsibility of helping. I find this particularly true when helping others is an important part of your "mix" of issues. The down side for most of us is that we do not seem to know how to elect bringing out our strengths related to our essential lesson.

Knowing such differences can be useful and conceptually interesting, but what happens when you feel like you end up primarily on one ends of the continuum? How do we develop options and choices? When we fall continually into our protective state, our limiting pattern, our fixation, it usually feels like we are in a place where we have little choice. We seem to slip into that place, unaware even how we ended up there. Such contractive, fear based places keep our protections in place and make it more difficult to feel into the subtle realm and reclaim our abilities. These states also create a greater challenge in becoming aware of our cosmic spark and rekindling our connection. The important piece here is discovering ways for us to have more choice in moving from fixation to essential lesson, a process Jaxon-Bear calls true freedom.[4]

There are three important aspects to enhance our becoming a steward of our responses rather than a slave to our patterns. A first step is increasing our awareness of both what we do and what is driving our behaviors. We often have a basic fear that we do not acknowledge but impacts how we react to things. Becoming aware of that fear, shining a light on it, gives us a different option that our typical response. This is not an easy task or one for the faint of heart, but it also can change a repetitive pattern when one is aware and therefore can nurture an alternative view and belief.

A second element to change is the development of other alternatives, which then gives one more choice in the matter. We often focus on modifying what is "wrong" with us. An alternative is to change our view of the flawed and judging process itself. Sometimes what we view as undesirable has been part of the development of a mirrored strength. Seeing such a gift in the emergent talent helps us transform the critical assessment of ourselves and gives us other options and therefore choice. When we recognize our gifts, we often begin to find ways to put those into play rather than the part we defined as defective. When we recognize and own our strengths, we provide ourselves with more choices and options.

One of the most useful ideas, I find, from a behavior approach to therapy is to focus on a "replacement" behavior, a behavior you desire which substitutes for the action you do not wish to continue. They become competing behaviors, so if you do one you cannot do the other. This would be true for being in the learning state in contrast to the protective approach in relation to our cells (Lipton), for strength pattern over limiting pattern (Goldschmidt), and for essential lesson over fixation (Enneagram). When we are at a point where we face the option to move either into our fixation or essential lesson, we more easily can make the choice we truly desire.

A third and most essential part of the shift is the focus on and opening of the heart. This seems to be an essential way to shift our patterns. With an open heart, we more easily can see our fear, we open to more alternatives for choice, and we can loosen the self-judgments that keep us in the fixation end of the continuum. We are able to allow greater compassion and forgiveness of ourselves, which softens and expands our whole being. Relaxing into and expanding the heart towards ourselves and others provides more expansive views and possibilities, more choices of how we see and respond to life.

Shifting from fixation to essential lesson is not always an easy process, especially since the responses from protection/fixation are such well worn groves in our brains. Yet as we keep making a different choice, we also create new neural pathways that make the options to live in the essential lesson part of the continuum easier to choose. Instead of watering the weeds, as Thich Nhat Hahn talks about, we water the flowers, those things we want to nourish and develop within ourselves. As we begin to see this point as a choice, the old belief systems about ourselves become more and more dissipated and fragile.

Playing with Physical and Subtle
Ends of a Continuum

In many ways, the physical/subtle continuum is much like the protective and learning states, limiting and strength patterns, and fixation and essential lesson continuum. The physical realm is denser, which makes it easier to feel, easier to pay attention to, and easier be aware of this territory. Contracted energies also work that way. It often is easier to feel a knot in a muscle, a contracted intestinal area that is cramping and sore from intense anger. It helps us pay more attention to such physical and emotional constrictions, just as it is simple to pay attention to a table or wall when we hit it in contrast to the air that is passing by us. It is easier to feel the anger when it is very strong than the subtle love we feel for a baby.

In contrast to these contracted energies, expanded states, such as the excitement of learning, feeling good about something we have done for another person, feeling in touch with a life purpose, or experiencing deep love for a dear friend are subtler and less obvious. We have to pay closer attention to fully experience expansive states. When you are in the middle of a wind storm, the air is obvious. When the wind is a slight breeze just caressing you face, you may have to pay more attention to be aware of this gentle motion.

Knowing these expansive states makes it easier to pay attention to or clearly access subtler realms and abilities, even at times when feeling that spark inside that connects us all. The heart opens, subtler feelings arise, and our expansion includes so much more beyond our bodies. These are ways to begin accessing more of the subtle parts of our lives and feel more at ease with ourselves and the world if we have not been in touch with them previously. One way we are able to practice differences that help us increase our awareness and choices for reclaiming the subtler parts of our world is by paying close attention to contracted and expanded ends of a continuum. Noticing these differences also helps us make choices of where we want to focus our intentions and what is available for us to choose. It brings us a more joyful life and increases our ability to recapture subtle sources of information and skills. When we more clearly see the subtle, expansive option, we more often can choose to be in that place.

As I work with people, a key to expanding joy in their lives is to focus on living from their hearts, in particular open hearts. I realize it is much more easily said than done, and that is why I have emphasized this process in order to help others rest in an expanded heart and live from this place more frequently. As a result of shifting from a closed, protective heart to an open one, you are likely to experience more peace and joy in your everyday life.

Of course, if joy and peace do not interest you, feel free to put down this book or give it away to someone for whom that is a strong interest. We all have choices when we see them and take responsibility for them. Not changing also is a choice that is available to you, and the choice is not wrong. We often learn a lot from our fixation and related patterns.

Sometimes we have other things going on in our lives that overwhelm us. Or we are not ready to let go of our fixation, to create a dramatic change in our life. You may believe that it is not possible right now for some reason.

I believe there is no judgment around a choice of keeping things as they are. We all have a time for change and a time we may not be comfortable with doing things differently. There certainly were times when modifying aspects of my life not only appeared impossible but did not seem all that desirable. One thing I strongly suggest is that you avoid self-criticism for not wanting to change in the present moment.

Maybe you will feel like changing tomorrow, next month, or next year. Or maybe you will never want to make this change. I recommend you do what is best for you without any judgment of yourself. You may have another way of creating change that appears more appropriate to you for whatever reason right now. Deciding what is best for yourself without self-criticism could be an example of coming from your essential lesson, using your intuition and accessing subtle sources of information. Keeping things as they are may be the best thing for you in this moment, and only you will know. Choose it and go with it, with my support and best wishes, especially if it is not harmful to yourself or others. This is a way all of us can begin to incorporate our subtle skills to benefit ourselves.

Maybe you have learned enough from that contractive, limited exploration and would like to take a new road. Perhaps you would like to experience more of your strengths and see those develop. You may begin to see how such a contractive approach is harmful to yourself or others around you. If so, I recommend you explore what an open heart can do for you and the development of your own choice points, how it might move you into your essential lesson, or how you might utilize your own subtle sources of information.

Opening of the Heart

After years and years of work, I have learned to open my heart more often, allowing myself to hear the positive things my friends and others tell me, not deflecting or dismissing the feedback and discrediting their encouraging experiences of me. While it may not be the complete picture, it also is a valid part of what is going on in the total view. The more I open my heart, the less my worst fear and fixation run my life and the more effectively I access subtle skills and information.

Heart opening can be a daily practice, and there are many ways to explore such an experience. One approach is to try the following exercise. For this process, I suggest that after reading through the exercise, you get into a comfortable position and close your eyes. You could do this exercise standing or lying on the floor, but I would suggest either of those options rather than sitting in a chair, if the other two options are available to you. If not, a chair will work. But ewer movements are available to you when sitting, which is why I suggest either standing or lying on the floor.

Begin by recalling an experience when you did something you later judged as wrong or hurtful. Pay attention to your contractive response as it was running large and dominant in your life. Feel into that part of your body that most closely is associated with or where the emotion feels strongest when thinking about that event or your response. Spend a little time until you feel it pretty solidly in your body. You might even amplify the contraction momentarily in order to increase your awareness and the memory of it. Let it grow stronger, paying attention to where in your body you feel it the most. Get to know the feeling and let it intensify.

After you spend some time with your awareness of the contraction, shift your focus to your chest, and particularly your heart. Imagine the shape of the heart, the beat of it on a regular basis, and the blood being pumped to all parts of the body. In this way, the blood is an extension of the heart to your entire body, carrying oxygen and other important elements in order to keep the body alive and healthy. Pay attention to how the heart connects to all parts of your body and supports the rest of the body without ever asking for something special or complaining. Imagine the energy of the heart encouraging the surrounding muscles to relax and expand. Allow the muscles in the chest to loosen around the heart so it can extend further into the chest cavity with more ease. Just imagine the energy of the heart extending further in the front, expressing caring about someone you love in your life, someone important to you. Also imagine the energy of the heart expanding in the back, as the rear muscles relax, and the energy reaches out as an expression of caring for yourself, or self love. Even if you are not feeling a lot of love for yourself at this moment, just imagine that it can happen and allow the possibility right now.

Maybe it seems like you cannot feel your heart. Just pay attention to it and imagine what it might feel like if you could. Pretend like it is happening for a few minutes. Spend a little time just imagining and exploring this possibility.

Next, begin to find a slow, small movement somewhere in your body that expands what you are feeling in your heart. It may be a movement of a finger, a slow slight movement of an arm or a leg. It could be a movement of the head or shoulders. For me, taking a deep breath and letting the shoulders relax and move back slightly, opening the chest slightly, expands this feeling. Take some time to explore a few movements and see which helps consistently expand what you are feeling or imagining in your heart to other parts of your body. Take some time to explore this. You may even find more than one movement that is helpful.

Remember the feeling in your body related to your contraction that you were feeling a few minutes ago? How is it now? For most people, they forgot about the fear and feel much more connected to their heart and closer to the experience that occurs when you are expressing your essential lesson. If the contraction is still available, hold both feelings simultaneously. Feel into both of them without trying to make any change at all. Embrace the contraction and the expansion, knowing both are important parts of your life. Keep relaxing and see if one begins to diminish. If it does, is it the one you want to lesson? If so, let it continue to diminish. If not, see if you can support it to expand, allowing it to grow and spread.

If you did not experience an expansion of the heart with this exercise, you might keep playing with it to see if you can develop a movement that will take you to your heart. For almost everyone with whom I have worked, the fear and physiology of the contractive pattern lessons, providing the individual with greater choice. In place of the contractive state, there is more peace, joy, and a feeling of strength. I hope you have felt these expansions with this exercise too.

As you continue to focus on your heart, allow or encourage it to open, and express your gifts from this place. When you do so, it is much more likely to feel as if you have a choice when fear presents itself and the old contractive pattern appears. If you are deeper in your heart, it seems to provide a type of mutually exclusive experience for the essential lesson over the fixation, learning over protecting. In this case, you do not have to worry so much about "getting rid" of the contractive responses as simply focusing and moving your focus to the heart and expansive pattern.

I know from my own experiences as well as working with many other people that such a switch is not easy. Yet when I do move to an open heart, the contractive pattern does not find room or good reception in my body to continue growing, developing, and manifesting in my life. This seems to be the most significant key to the change process I desire.

I also find that when I am focused on an open heart, my intuition is much better and I have a stronger sense of presence and connection with others. I am much better at problem solving, listening to others without taking things personally, and hearing their issues without the need to find a solution unless they actually are asking for such help. I believe this process is key in recapturing the abilities we have let atrophy from lack of use since our infancy. If there is any credence to a noussentric perspective, and we enter this life with some skills, the process of reconnecting to and expanding our hearts seems to be an important part of strengthening these skills and utilizing them with both ourselves and our children. As we increase our awareness of the fears that limit what we see and feel, we increase our ability to make different choices, including the movement into more expansive views and behaviors. This shift also provides ourselves with more choices and opportunities to live from this more expanded place.

This is the process I use to help me write when I feel like I have nothing to say, nor have any good ideas to express. Getting into my heart at least helps me have a broader sense of what to share and how to express myself in the most effective manner. It may not be completely articulate, clear, or interesting to others.

Yet it is my voice and a collection of ideas I want to communicate in the best way possible. When I relax into my heart, I feel like I am putting forward my best expression. I would love to hear whether it works for others too.

Conclusion

There are several reasons to play with and experience more expansive states and patterns. For one thing, expansive and subtle sources often contribute to a greater sense of peace and joy in our lives. When we spend less time in contractive experiences, we can pay attention to parts of our lives we often do not access on a continual basis. These feelings remain available to us, as they do not just go away. But when we are focused on more contractive and physical aspects to our lives, the subtler parts may elude our awareness and attention.

A second contribution of more expansive states is to increase your ability to access intuitive and other subtle sources of information. This is a skill we all seem to possess but often do not utilize or trust. Sometimes more extreme experiences help us bring such skills to awareness. For example, Parti learned from his near-death experience that he always had and at times used this ability to access information, which he then would use to teach himself. "I realized I had always received valuable guidance through my own intuition.... But you must teach yourself; all people must teach themselves. Finding your own knowledge inside you is the best way to learn. If you don't learn for yourself, you will not learn completely."[5]

In some ways, a near-death experience is an extreme case of accessing subtle information. In most cases, such experiences change a person's life. Parti put it this way:

It is clear that having a near-death experience has a profound effect on the rest of a person's life. Many researchers have noticed the transformation that takes place and have identified its elements: a changed self-image that allows them to take a long view of life, increased compassion for others, an appreciation of life that leaves them with a sense that they still have something to accomplish here on earth, a diminished fear of death coupled with a belief in life after death, a decline in religious affiliation while at the same time an increase in spirituality, a sense of greater intuitive sensitivity and heightened sensitivity to the five physical senses (sight, sound, taste, touch, and smell).[6]

In addition, exploring expansive places along with contractive states allows you to hold contrasting experiences and ideas at the same time. Such occurrences increase the ability for more complex thought, which can increase problem solving ability, integration of ideas, and development of additional alternatives. When we hold conflicting views or opposing perspectives at the same time, we may find a new alternative or synthesis that emerges from the endeavor. This not only helps us as individuals, but it also strengthens our ability to teach others, such as children and adolescents in our lives, a process that can be very fruitful for them as well.

Finally, I have noticed a very interesting paradox regarding the physical and subtle states, especially when these less dense places include a connection to our inner spark. We often hold on to and rely on the physical world for a sense of security, a place where we feel safe and protected. Yet, in my experience, the connection at the core to our own spark gives me greater fortitude and resilience than anything in my physical world. I laugh, sometimes, when I feel the shift from the physical to the subtle realm increases my comfort and solidity in a very different and significant manner. My spark and open heart allows for a relaxation into peace and well-being, a sanctuary like no other.

I will talk more about love and an open heart in the next two chapters. But I would like to end this chapter with some words of wisdom from Hafiz, another brilliant Sufi poet.

ALL THE HEMISPHERES

Leave the familiar for a while. Let your senses
and bodies stretch out

like a welcomed season onto meadows and
shores and hills.

Open up to the roof. Make a new watermark

138

on your excitement and love.

Like a blooming night flower, bestow your vital
fragrance of happiness and giving upon your
intimate assembly.

Change rooms in your mind for a day. All the
hemispheres in existence lie beside an equator
in your soul.

Greet yourself in your thousand other forms as
you mount the hidden tide and travel back home.

All the hemispheres in heaven are sitting around
a campfire chatting, while

stitching themselves together into the *great circle*
inside of you.

- Hafiz[7]

CHAPTER 6

EXPANDING THE HEART OPENING

THE BRIGHT CORE OF FAILURE

Sometimes you enter the heart.
Sometimes you are born from the soul.
Sometimes you weep a song of separation.
It is all the same glory.

You live in beautiful forms,
and you are the energy that breaks form.
All light, neither this nor that.

Human beings go places on foot.
Angels, with wings.

Even if they find nothing but ruins
and failure, you are the bright core of that.

- Rumi[1]

When I first see a new born baby, I typically am fascinated by their tiny fingernails and toenails. That is one of the first places I look, after their adorable face, because I find these "miniature" nails so interesting. They are not as much fun to cut when they are so small, but to this day I still find them amazing. Small children usually are so cute and adorable.

Children are not as much fun when they are crying or distressed, especially with very well developed lungs that can carry a cry right through your bones. But when they are sleeping, eating, giggling, or just gazing at you, and especially a smile that emerges from their whole-body, they are fascinating, picturesque beings that can cuddle your core. At the same time, they are so physically dependent, so in need of our protection and support for their survival. When infants are born, they need so much care for feeding, changing diapers, keeping warm, helping them when sick, and getting them from one place to another. One of the big challenges during the first year of life is when children are uncomfortable or sick and are unable to express what is wrong. It can be challenging and frustrating to figure out at times how to help a distressed infant.

Our oldest child had colic when she was a baby. Her mother and I did not have a lot of experience with children, and it was frustrating trying to figure out how to help her. She also had difficulty going to sleep and staying asleep while we put her down. So we would go for car rides just to help her get to sleep. Of course now, as an adult, she still falls asleep easily when riding in a car. We begin lots of patterns as infants that may not change as we grow into adults.

We also begin feeling strong pains in our bodies that must get our full attention as an infant and young child. Some of these occur internally from hunger and discomfort over a full diaper to accidents, diseases, or experiences in our lives, such as trauma.

When I was a small child, I attended a preschool just down the block from our house where my mother taught part-time. She was trained and began her career as a teacher, like her older sister, and really liked working with children, although her greatest passion was writing and directing plays. But her teaching focus was evident again after our children were born, and mom would enjoy those times when she could instruct them about colors, words, or other skills.

One day my mother, who also liked to get away once in a while by herself to go shopping, dropped me off at preschool and left. I could not believe it. I was stunned. It was not like it was the first time she ever had left me, but it seemed like the first time she had abandoned me at this school. Instead of putting out puzzles and games as we would gather in the mornings, she took me in the door and said goodbye.

Our preschool had big windows in the front so that we could see out into the street, as our big room was the front of a converted double car garage. I could look out the window and watch her walk away as I began to sob, tears running down my cheeks as I realized mom would not take me with her. Sure, my legs were shorter than hers, and I had a hard time keeping up with her during those first few years. Of course, all that changed much later, as I grew to be almost a foot taller than her. But at the time, it was a challenge to keep track of me (yes, I did have a tendency to wander off and explore when we were in shops, usually looking for candy) along with bags of things she would purchase.

That day, my heart felt broken as she walked away alone. Mrs. Arbon, the owner of the school, tried to comfort me at first, telling me she would be back. Later, as the sobbing just continued, the teacher got irritated that I would not be quiet, upsetting some of the other kids. It was a tough day, knowing that my mom could just leave me. My mother and I were pretty close, as I was the youngest, with an older brother and sister in school and a father who worked in the city as well as traveling a lot for his chosen vocation. But it was a sad day when I first remember my mother walking away and being gone for what seemed like an eternity. At least, that is how I remember it, and stressful times often are remembered when marked by an intense emotion. In this case, it was the first long separation I remember from my mother. I survived it, of course, and was not nearly the trauma faced by many children. But it felt intense at the time, and it taught me about separation from someone very close to me.

As I got older, during adolescence, I became aware of a deep wound that felt like a "dark, endless pit." It sometimes would appear in my chest, but most times it showed up in the bottom of my stomach. This was an endless pit that could never be filled, a type of black hole, or at least dark gray, that could consume all the positive feelings and happy experiences that had occurred in my life. I do not know when it developed or I first noticed it. Certainly by early adolescence, it appeared and could devour all the love I felt from my parents, brother, sister, and good friends, leaving me with this internal emptiness.

In fact, the dark pit could take me to such a discouraging place that nothing looked or felt good in my life. It reminded me of the empty feeling I felt when my mom left, and I was there all alone among friends and teachers who cared about me and yet could not console the grief and pain I felt from being "abandoned." I do not know if these two feelings were related, but certainly some connection must exist between my broken heart as a child and the empty pit that I felt as an adolescent and later experienced at significant times through my adulthood. Even as I write about this black hole now, I can sink down into it if I am not careful. The only thing that can consistently prevent such a slippage is the uncovering, opening up, and feeling into my own heart.

When we feel pain, we tend to contract physically, emotionally, and/or mentally. We usually go into a place of fear, hurt, grief, and/or sadness that may include other emotions, like anger, rage, and even a sense of hopelessness. We also may develop a sense of abandonment, loss, and isolation in our world. These feelings we hold in our emotional and mental fields, but we also seem to hold these contractions in our bodies, limiting our movements and the flow of energies.[2,3]

From Experience into World Views

From our experiences, we develop belief systems within ourselves that begin to create a picture of who we are and how we see the world. These tenets are powerful and often difficult to break or shift, as I mentioned in the last chapter. When they primarily are based on fear, these types of contractions take us into our Fixations, to use the language of the Enneagram. Such constrictions are dependent on our perceptions and how we interpret the things that go on around us, for we experience some of the same events with different interpretations of those occurrences.

Some time ago, I was feeling grief about the loss of my latest relationship. We had experienced many conflicts, and they were difficult for me to handle. On the one hand, I was happy to forego the ongoing challenges that could occur on a daily basis. On the other hand, I really missed the physical, emotional, and spiritual closeness that were the gifts from our connection. For several days, I felt distant from what was going on in my life, doing more observation than interaction with people around me. As I woke up early one morning, I focused on a dream that had just ended. In that dream, I was sitting in the driver's seat of an old truck, looking out the window to something going on just behind me. I saw the woman with whom I had been in relationship, standing in the road with her furniture and big boxes all over in the road, as if they had all fallen out of a big truck. I felt bad for her, and yet there was no movement to help her. I felt as if dealing with her "stuff" was over for me. As I woke further, I began to ask myself why I was still so heavy into the grief? I certainly had felt this off and on for several months. And yet, everything else in my life was so sweet, so pleasant, so joyful. I had just completed some remodeling of three rooms in my house, and I loved the way they looked. My life felt fresh, and yet this one part of it was sad. I realized that this was a very old pattern and belief of mine, that I could not be happy if one thing was "wrong" in my life. I would get so focused on one negative that I ignore or let go of 99 wonderful things in my life. In that moment, I let go of the sadness. As I focused on my heart, letting it expand, keeping my eyes on all the joy and happiness in my life. I loved my home, I really enjoyed the town where I lived, having lots of friends around and doing well with my work. How much of the joy of life I had missed because one thing was not defined as going well.

First Separation

We begin developing these responses, reactions, and patterns as young children. As a child, we use all the skills available to us to figure out how to protect ourselves from these hurts. Some of the psychological literature focusing on the development of children discusses the issue of infant separation and how young children first understand the basic issue of being separated from people with whom they have a strong emotional attachment. These ideas have been developed by people like Bowlby, Ainsworth, and their followers,[4] and the concept has come to be known as Separation Anxiety Disorder. Some theorists have talked about how these patterns that develop as infants and young children can impact our connections and emotional relationships as adults, especially in romantic interactions and marriage. Some support has been found for such pattern continuation and influences.

An issue that has been ignored by current developmental theories and research has to do with a separation that occurs prior to experiencing the distinction from "other." This "first separation" takes place when we distance ourselves from our Higher Self, our connection to the larger cosmic connection which I refer to as essence. This separation from essence seems to be the first significant separation experience that amplifies or make possible the separation from other. For without this initial separation we would not move to such a strong, fundamental experience of "separation" or "being separate" from others without also knowing the connection too. Once we experience separation

144

from the larger cosmic connection, separation in many forms is possible and makes more sense. When we feel no separation from the larger cosmos, we see and understand the illusion of "separation" as individuals. We learn that we are both "separate" people and connected at the same time, especially energetically. When people go through a near-death episode, for example, they experience the underlying connection and see more clearly how the separation rather than connection is the real illusion in this life.[5]

No empirical evidence exists for this initial separation from Higher Self beyond my own experience retrospectively and from altered state experiences, such as through Grof's Holotropic Breathwork.[6-8] This separation from essence also may be more of a process over time than a single experience, and yet the impact is significant in that we feel more "alone." We also may experience the greatest sense of "separation" from significant others when it occurs as an infant because we have no alternative perspective to hold on to at that time. Parents typically do not maintain an energetic connection or reconnect as we get older, for we as adults have lost this connection ourselves. I even wonder if clear separation from others is possible to encounter so extensively without first experiencing some prior type of separation from essence. At the same time, I find that as I reconnect more strongly with my own Higher, more expansive Self, I am less likely to feel separate from others or anyone.

Some time ago, I was in a workshop doing some work with a mirror. We were requested to look into the mirror and inquire of ourselves how we keep ourselves separate from ourselves, how do we hold ourselves apart from our larger, wiser, more expansive Self. As I looked into the mirror and kept asking this question, I realized that a major way I keep myself separate is through judgments and criticism. I am very well developed in this arena, having honed some of my very best skills to use against myself and then generously apply to others. As I began to feel these judgments in my body and how they hold me separate from my larger, loving and wiser Self, there was a deep sadness for all the time I have spent in this place. The sorrow was followed by gratitude for having such a rich experience in this area, knowing the idea of splitting off from the more expansive part of me. But mostly the sadness showed up. Then, I realized that as I developed such immense judgments of myself, I shared these criticisms with others by judging them, also separating myself from others that I loved. And more sadness showed up for how I have kept others away from the closeness that I wanted and sought to experience with them. In my experience, judgment can be one of the big facilitators for separation from Self as well as others. When I am connected to a higher more expansive Self, I see the illusion of separation and have less of an issue with distance from others.

Later, I read Ring's summary of the importance of love and judgment. Summarizing his research of those who have experienced a near-death, he suggests we expand our vision, especially in understanding love, the greatest teaching of all. But the question rises, how do we not feel free to bask in love? How are we separated from it?

> But, you may fairly ask, what is binding us? From what do we need to be freed? The answer, of course, has already been hinted at: It is simply how we tend to think of ourselves and especially the *judgments* we continually make about ourselves that wall us off from the love of the Light. We have created our own prison through self-judgment, and every judgment immures us even more deeply. But remember, the Light *does not judge*. It loves....When we learn to see ourselves as the Light sees us, we will finally be free to experience ourselves as we really are and perhaps come to love ourselves truly for the first time.[9]

Of course, these judgments are not the only separating issue that starts in infancy. The severance from Self seems to occur as infants get more and more focused on the physical world without any support to retain such a connection to our more expansive Self. Later, as we develop greater cognitive capacity, we develop more elaborate belief systems supporting our separation, not only from our Higher Self but also from others. I am not clear that feeling separate and the accompanying belief systems are really necessary in this life. We may do it more out of tradition and habit than incorporating an inherent concept of this life.

Certainly we can see ourselves as discrete human beings, making choices for ourselves based on the idea that we are distinct individuals. And yet, as Kirtana so aptly puts it in her song, "I Am" from her album <u>This Embrace</u>, she "cannot find a boundary in consciousness."[10] In some ways, we can see this even with social roles in our dichotomous world view. What is a "teacher" without a "student?" What is a "doctor" without a "patient?" What is a "real estate agent" without a "client?" We often use these as examples of "opposites" in a dichotomy. But even in a dichotomy, connection inevitably exists. We don't even move into a role such as "parent" without a "child," and the two are inseparably connected, as are all dichotomies. For too long we have focused on the separation at the expense of the connection, when in fact both are true.

While we can see the world of discrete people, we also may see the larger picture where there really is no separation between us. We talk about the US economy, but how does that system exist without the people and economies of Europe, Latin American, Africa, the Middle East, and the Far East? Especially today, we are so interconnected, and that may be the greater focus as we get beyond this traditional illusion of separation.

In the developmental literature, we often talk about "individuation," meaning a separation that takes place between a healthy adolescent and her/his family. Yet this concept more recently has been challenged from a Feminist Perspective. Comstock and Qin, for example, argue that rather than separating, we really are trying to find a balance between ourselves as developing people and more complex connection with the group.[11] Again, the process is about maintaining a connection while developing our own perspective at the same time.

I was having dinner with a friend not long ago, getting to know each other and sharing some of our early experiences. She talked about her father leaving their family when she was age four, and the sense of abandonment that keeps showing up as an issue in her current relationships. Early the next morning, I was thinking about our sweet conversation the night before and reminiscing about this issue of the first separation from Self. If we begin to experience that and feel less whole or solid with ourselves, then a major separation like a father leaving would amplify the sense that we may have less value, that we are not important, or that people do not care about us enough to stay. Then we continue elaborating a belief system of lower value, no importance. We expect that people we really care about do not stay in our lives. Then we play out this theme over and over. It develops into a structure we can hold for life.

As I laid in bed pondering this issue, I began a light meditation about my feeling of separation. I then began to explore a reconnection to a larger, more expanded Self, feeling more whole within myself. This also is a belief system, I thought. As I experienced this feeling of connection, in contrast to the former sentiment of something wrong with me, something broken, I began to ask myself why I do not hang on to this framework of being whole and connected. Both systems are possible. Both beliefs are options. Yet the latter one feels so much better in me, a sensation that helps me write this book in contrast to all the times that I feel like I have nothing to say or that no one will give any credence to these words. When I feel whole and connected to my expansive Self, I see myself as having something of value to share, whether or not any one agrees with me or cares about what I have to say. The feeling itself is so much better, and I am so much more comfortable with myself and my world when I embrace this experience and outlook. I keep working with the reconnection and the shift in my beliefs in order to hold a larger, more expansive view of my essence, my spark, expressed through my connection to the world around me.

As we experiment with reconnecting to our spark, we can explore how we this association modifies and permeates our lives. We can learn to strengthen and remain in this place as we adapt to a new foundation and express ourselves from that place. At the same time, there is another important step in this process. While we expand our view of essence and spark, we can stretch our perspective further with the exploration of love itself.

Expressing Love as an Emotion

One way we get to see the patterns we have developed, if we are open to shedding light on them and recognizing them, is to get into close, interpersonal relationships. We "fall in love."

I really enjoy the word "fall" here, for sometimes that so accurately describes the experience. It seems like we relax into some automatic patterns that just take over and lead us into ways of interacting with an intimate partner or spouse that brings up ways of behaving and belief systems we did not even know existed. We respond in a manner that express our caring or love for another, stimulating our oxytocin and thrill of being in love.

One thing that happens in these interpersonal circumstances is we experience the emotion of love that often times seems challenging to access without some object on which to focus it. In this case, we have some person, activity, passion, or object on which we can feel and express our love. Many wonderful love songs and poems exist that convey this idea in a beautiful and touching manner. I have a playlist of over 175 love songs that I have collected just to hear and do some analysis of this concept.

At another weekend workshop on love and intimacy, I was awakened in the middle of the night from three people near me all snoring and in a different frequency or style. It was difficult to sleep, so I decided to take out my earphones and iPod, which I had with me. I was feeling very sad that night because I was not in a romantic relationship, having no object on which to focus my love. A number of people in the workshop were there with spouses and partners, which amplified my lack of "someone to love me." As I turned on my music and began to listen to my love song collection, I realized that I could focus my love on myself, that I could be the object of my love, as others have suggested. When I listened to the songs from this perspective, my whole feeling and attitude transformed, allowing me to feel love and loved. An interesting outcome to that experience is that I also felt more expansive, more connected to the larger cosmos when I made such a shift. My heart felt more open to everything around me in contrast to just that one person, object, or activity in which I was engaged. I felt like I could be more caring to everyone when my heart was more open. At that point, the songs sounded and felt very different. It was an enjoyable and transformative experience that I lucked into because of not being able to sleep.

Musicians have created many great love songs. Here are three of my favorites. The first one I heard and was made famous by Etta James. The second one was sung by Bonnie Raitt and used as a part of a love scene in the movie, <u>Michael.</u> The third one was sung by Collin Raye, but I heard it first from Israel Kamakawiwo'ole, a version that touched me deeply. The lyrics to all of these songs are available on the Internet.

At Last

At last
My love has come along

My lonely days are over
And life is like a song

Oh yeah, yeah
At last
The skies above are blue
My heart was wrapped up in clover
The night I looked at you

I found a dream, that I could speak to
A dream that I can call my own
I found a thrill to press my cheek to
A thrill that I have never known

Oh yeah, yeah
You smiled, you smiled
Oh and then the spell was cast
And here we are in heaven
for you are mine…
At Last.

Feels Like Home

Something in your eyes, makes me want to lose myself,
Makes me want to lose myself, in your arms.
There's something in your voice, makes my heart beat fast.
Hope this feeling lasts, the rest of my life.
If you knew how lonely my life has been,
And how low I've felt so long.
If you knew how I wanted someone to come along,
And change my life the way you've done.

Feels like home to me, feels like home to me,
Feels like I'm on my way back where I come from.
Feels like home to me, feels like home to me,
Feels like I'm on my way back where I belong.

A window breaks down a long dark street,
And a siren wails in the night.
But I'm all right, 'cause I have you here with me.

Heart Opening

And I can almost see through the dark there's light.
If you knew how much this moment means to me,
And how long I've waited for your touch.
If you knew how happy you are making me --
I've never thought I'd love anyone so much.

Feels like home to me, feels like home to me,
Feels like I'm on my way back where I come from.
Feels like home to me, feels like home to me,
Feels like I'm on my way back where I belong.
Feels like I'm on my way back where I belong.

In This Life

For all I've been blessed with in my life
There was an emptiness in me
I was imprisoned by the power of gold
With one kind touch, you've set me free

Let the world stop turning, let the sun stop burning
Let them tell me, love's not worth going through
If it all falls apart, I will know deep in my heart
The only dream that mattered had come true
In this life, I was loved by you

For every mountain I have climbed
Every raging river crossed
You were the treasure that I longed to find
Without your love I would be lost

Let the world stop turning, let the sun stop burning
Let them tell me, love's not worth going through
If it all falls apart, I will know deep in my heart
The only dream that mattered had come true
In this life, I was loved by you

I know that I won't live forever
But forever I'll be loving you
Let the world stop turning, let the sun stop burning
Let them tell me love's not worth going through
If it all falls apart, I will know deep in my heart

The only dream that mattered had come true
In this life, I was loved by you
In this life, I was loved by you.

These are just three songs out of hundreds or probably thousands that have been written expressing the joy and pain of loving someone else. They are beautiful songs with great melodies and touching lyrics that express how important loving others has been in our lives. Listen to these or maybe a few of your own favorites and get a sense of how deeply they often touch us, especially if we have a "special" song about a person you love or have loved in our life.

For something a little different, try changing the focus of love from another person to yourself. Find even one part of yourself that you like, about which you care, and let that expand a little so that you are able to sing that same song or two to yourself. Listen to that song or even sing along with it, focusing on loving yourself instead of another person. It is you, or at least that part of you, that is the focus of your love, the exchange of a loving feeling between different parts of yourself. You might try singing from your personality to your Higher Self, your essence, your cosmic spark. As you do this, notice the feelings inside when the focus is turned to you. Share love between the socialized self and your essence, as this also can bring out the feeling.

For some, this may be no easy task. For others, a switch in focus is simple and common. While I was a senior in high school, I quit playing football and wrestling in order to be in our school play in the fall and our musical in the spring. That year, our drama director chose to produce the musical, "How to Succeed in Business Without Really Trying." The play was made into a movie in 1967 starring Robert Morse as the man who was trying to succeed. One of my favorite songs from that musical is when Robert sings a beautiful love type song, "I Believe in You." Here are the lyrics from that song, not that well known by many.

I Believe in You

Now there you are, there's that face
That face that somehow I trust
It may embarrass you to say it

152

But say it I must, say it I must

You have the cool, clear
Eyes of a seeker of wisdom and truth
Yet there's that upturned chin
And the grin of impetuous youth
Oh I believe in you, I believe in you

I hear the sound of
Good, solid judgment whenever you talk
Yet there's the bold, brave
Spring of the tiger that quickens your walk
Oh I believe in you, I believe in you

And when my faith in my fellow man
All but falls apart
I've but to feel your hand grasping mine
And I take heart

I take heart to see the cool, clear
Eyes of a seeker of wisdom and truth
Yet there's that slam, bang, tang
Reminiscent of gin and vermouth
Oh I believe in you, oh I believe in you.

What is fun and most interesting about this song is that
Robert sings this song to himself in a mirror. When I first saw
the movie and did the play, I had such a pessimistic view of myself that is was hard to fathom people actually singing any love
songs to themselves. And yet now, I am suggesting that you and I
both do it, that we both include the Self in the love that we experience. Can that love focus on ourselves as well as others? Of
course, I am not suggesting that love is only for oneself. That
could lead us to an egocentric or narcissistic life. At the same
time, I think it also is important to not limit love completely to
others. This love arises from within us, no matter what the reason
for it, and the focus of such feelings does not have to be focused
solely on something external to us.

As we expand our object of love from others to include ourselves, an important shift can happen in our being. We begin to
expand our hearts, opening them to ourselves, which, from my
experience, opens them more to everything around me. In this

way, we begin to be more loving in general and come from our larger, more expansive selves. Sharing our hearts with others begins by expanding and opening our hearts to ourselves. Such an expansion takes us into our Essential Lesson from the Enneagram perspective.

A shift also opens us in ways to being and seeing the lover we seek inside of ourselves, not just in others. This provides greater love to share because the experience is not completely dependent on another person to feel love. The experience comes from more from our core and at the same time universal source that never stops or has any limits on the amount of love we can access and extend to others. This expansion is not just a defended sense of I am great, but rather a true opening and expansion of the heart.

As we open our hearts, we shift our reference of loving from the outside in to loving from the inside out. When we love others and feel loved by others, we then feel more love inside ourselves and for ourselves, including the love from that person. This allows us to be in the feeling of love. But when we focus love on some object only and lose that object of love, we also lose the sense of being loved and often may feel not only less loved, but sometimes even less lovable. When we love ourselves first and then share that love for someone else, our love of self and sense of lovability is not dependent on another person.

Losing this feeling of being loved is why people feel so hurt and angry at the end of a relationship. The loss is not just about that person going away, but also the depletion of feeling love, loved, and lovable. Of course we are sad when we lose that connection and intimacy with someone important and close to us, either through death, divorce, or upset. Yet we lose less when that connection to love has not totally disappeared with the absence of that person because love becomes part of our being rather than dependent on having someone close to us in our life. The bond is always there and available, even if it does not feel present in us at the moment. In order for that to happen, however, it seems important to have our hearts more fully open.

Expanding our Hearts

One cannot talk about the issue of love and opening our hearts without some inclusion of the work by "the Love Doctor," Leo Buscaglia.[12-15] Leo began teaching and writing about love and how to incorporate it more into our lives before most people even considered it in the academic community. Increasing numbers of people have been exploring this area, developing ideas and tools for opening our hearts, helping us live in a less defended way.[16-24] I certainly am not an expert in this, and yet I have been exploring this idea of living from a more expanded heart for several years now. I have a few ideas to add to the contributions that others are making on this topic. I have outlined a few suggestions below for living a more heartful and noussentric life.

One of the most useful and simple way for me to relax into my heart is to focus my energy and attention there for a period of time. If you find it helpful, you can image the 4th chakra. I allow my body to relax, taking some slow deep breaths, which also allows my heart to relax. I pay attention to the heart and the slow, relaxing process that emerges from this. I energetically encourage my heart to open, first in the front part of the heart, followed by the back part of the heart. I find it easier if I begin in front. But you may find just the reverse. Start with the front one time, then try it by beginning with the back part of the heart. I keep focusing my attention there, allowing my heart to soften a little more with each breath, relax and expand. I maintain my focus, paying attention to how it feels and what I experience as it softens and enlarges. I may spend three to five minutes just paying attention, like a "heart meditation." You may find you want to spend even more time at this after some practice.

As I continue to do this, I also feel more peace and joy in my heart, which slowly expands to my entire chest. Experiencing such changes did not happen in the beginning. But the more I do this practice and spend time softening my heart, the more I feel the joy of life able to reside there. This little exercise does not take a long time. The nice thing is, you can do it anywhere, even while standing in line, driving, or waiting for an appointment. The more I practice it, the easier it seems to happen for me, especially if I am in a pretty good place when I begin. If I am in a place of discouragement, pessimism, or depression, it takes me much longer to feel my heart and experience the expansion. But even from these places, if I spend enough time at it, I can feel some joy return to my heart.

Heartful Communications

Another way to experience an opening of the heart relates to how we interact with others, especially when one is sharing a sincere apology. Think about the last time that someone close to you shared a very sincere "I'm sorry." If that is difficult to remember, you might reflect on a time when you told someone important to you how sorry you were for something you said or did. In either case, I usually feel my heart soften, when I pay attention to it. I feel closer to the person and more relaxed in both my chest and my heart. I do not always feel a lot closer or a softer heart if I am not as close to the person or if the apology does not seem totally sincere. But when both are the case, I feel a heart opening, more connected, and often tears come to my eyes. That is the kind of heart expansion I am describing here.

I remember a time when a dear friend was hurting because I had a tendency to get focused on tasks and be less emotionally available to her. After one incident, she was in a place of deep sadness, feeling like I did not care about her, nor was I connecting or even available to her emotionally. I liked into her eyes and could sense the pain inside from this. While her hurt was not just about my behavior, for most of our deep wounds, especially as we are older, did not begin at this point in our lives. We simply are hitting triggers of early wounds that have not been healed. I knew this at one level, as did she, when we both were feeling the pain. Still, I honestly could say that I was very sorry for not being more available to her and connecting energetically with her heart. As I looked deeply into her eyes and shared my apology, both of hearts softened and expanded. I felt good about connecting to my heart and sharing that connection with her through my words and energetics. At the same time, she felt understood, really felt heard, and loved in that moment. No only did our own hearts both expand, but they also opened more to each other, allowing ourselves to feel the love we had for each other, the love coming from deep inside us to be shared with that person who is the focus of our loving expression.

Another way I have experienced the opening of my heart is through the sharing of appreciations. Much like the sharing of an apology, again especially from someone who is important to us or where we have a lot of caring, an appreciation is another way to help our hearts soften, expand, and connect with another person. And these appreciations are not limited to others. As our hearts soften, sharing appreciations with ourselves can be an additional healing process beyond diminishing the self-criticism and judgments.

I have attended several workshops offered by the Human Awareness Institute, where the sharing of appreciations is a common element of their work. One of the very useful things about the approach they use, I think, is that you first ask if the other person is available to hear an appreciation. Not only does such a request respect for the other person, it also allows them to be or shift to a place where they are able to allow an appreciation pass through the normal defenses. While this idea may sound silly to some, I do not think this is the case at all, especially for people who have a more challenging time accepting positive statements about ourselves. I, for one, sometimes have a difficulty really letting in a compliment. To do so would mean oftentimes that I would have to shift my belief system and self-judgments. That has not been an easy process, especially in the past. So I can hear the words, but I would not let the truth and weight of them really sink into my body and soul.

This gets back to Marianne Williamson's statement about our fear of being so magnificent.[24] With such a basic core fear, we do not let in compliments or appreciations. By asking if we are ready to hear it, we may take a minute or even a few minutes to connect and expand our hearts a little in order to create a small crack in the armoring, allowing something positive to slip through. Of course, some individuals have such a positive view of themselves that creating such an opening is not a challenge. And yet, for them, it simply may be a different type of defense mechanism (see Appendix B on the Enneagram).

After we have asked the person if they are willing to hear an appreciation, we then share something that we admire or treasure about that person in the most heartful way possible. I find it useful to connect through our eyes, allowing my heart to open and connect to their hearts, then verbally sharing my sense of what I value about them. Some therapists recommend this effective tool in couple's counseling. They suggest this way of connecting be a part of a daily practice for two people wanting to build and maintain a close, loving, relationship. They have seen the results of such a practice on relationships because when we share sincere apologies and appreciations, it helps our hearts stay more open and available to share the love people want to feel in a close relationship. When I hear such gratitude that is said from the heart, I feel my heart expand, open more, and be more available for loving that person, that friend, that lover. I do not think we can ever hear to many loving, sincere appreciations. Well, OK, I do not think I can hear too many. And for others I have asked about this, they have responded the same way.

We probably all have had experiences where some real communication from the heart had to take place before a change and healing could occur. Such a communication is much more than just words or even the tone of the voice. You may well know of similar examples in your own life, your own family, or with close friends, where people are communicating more than simply through words. A feeling gets expressed as people truly share when their hearts are open, when they are in a vulnerable state, and when their energy, body and words are all congruent. It may not be something that we know how to create on a conscious level, but I would bet that you can feel such an expression in your own body when you pay close attention to such an occurrence from others. Try experiencing that very sincere, loving, "heartful" communication. When you pay close attention, you probably know when you are expressing it in yourself or when you experience it from others. I think the connection is most noticeable when both are communicating from such a place.

Think back for a moment when a parent, a sibling, a close friend, a spouse or partner, or someone else close to you gave you a very sincere apology or appreciation. Maybe they simply said the words, "I am sorry," "I so appreciate how you care for others," but the message was much larger and louder than just the words. You could feel it in your own heart and knew the sincerity of what they were saying because their whole being was consistent with the words being expressed. Yet that often is not the way we share communication, the way we express ourselves to others.

More often, we may say something that is not completely what we mean. For example, as a child we often are told to say we are sorry when that is not the way we feel. We may not be remorseful, but we say the words out loud. The words are expressed, but we do not feel the congruence in our bodies. Sometimes a spouse or friend may say they are sorry just to move on, but some part of the person holds information back because the situation is more complex than was expressed. In such cases, the words are not consistent or completely congruent with the feelings. We may hold some anger, resentment, or some other way have not let go of the situation or experience. We may not be able to tell this in every situation, but often we may have a feeling of it, even if we do not say anything or even pay attention to the incongruent message in our own body. In some cases, we find out later that the "sorry" was only half the story, and we may recall that feeling which said there was more than the words that were being expressed. At other times, we learn to pay more attention to our body responses and the information that it can tell us about ourselves as well as others. What is very interesting to me is that often children report having a sense of whether someone's words are congruent or not as others speak. As we access more of our subtle skills, our awareness and the information we gain gets stronger in such situations.

You may be able to speak quite well from an open heart already, at least when you are feeling comfortable and safe. As we increase our skills in this area, we may learn to speak and listen this way even when they do not feel very safe. The decision to share no matter the circumstances comes from the strength within, the strength of connection to our spark. This practice I continue to do for myself as well. I also work to help people establish environments that invite such heartfelt and caring communications that can occur beyond words, encouraging others to respond in like during such interactions.

Conclusion

I think the way we see, experience, interact, and respond to children from an open heart are the most important interactions we can have with young people, not just our own but with all children. Our heartful response is not only about loving them, but it also is about helping them hold on to the larger connection they seem to experience from birth. When we help them see and access this connection as they mature, we will help them maintain this connection, knowing they too have a relationship to a larger source and support that experience in them. Then, they will have less difficulty creating such a connection as an adult or having to reopen their hearts rather than living from that place throughout their lives.

Our job as adults is less about teaching our children this process, but rather supporting a connection that already exists, helping them keep hold of it rather than letting it fade away because we have not focused on it with them. Sometimes we may even ridicule and punish such connections when children reflect on them or talk about things that are beyond our belief system. As we follow their lead in areas we may not be as experienced, not discouraging it or focusing them away from their abilities, which then atrophy. When we pay close attention, we learn from our children, letting them be our teachers about love, connection, and a larger view of ourselves and each other.

One final comment on this topic. I have a friend whose soul name is Earthwhale. He is tuned into the whales of this earth and receives guidance from Grandmother Whale, who speaks for the pod. He often is inspired about different issues and sometimes asks questions. When we were together some time ago, he asked if I had a question for the whales. I thought for a minute, and then I asked: "How do we open our hearts?" He slept on the question and felt inspired by an answer the next morning. This is the answer he received, and I asked his permission to relate the information here. He knew I was working on this book, but he had not read any of it beforehand.

Question from my friend Geoffrey: How Do We Open our Hearts?

Grand Mother Whale: Gracious Earthwhale, please keep writing. We miss your connection.

Human matter arrives on earth in different stages of evolution, without clear awareness of themselves or others. There is a common conscious awareness that all humans share, but there is also a deeper awareness that others may experience that is more evolved.

To open your hearts, one must first connect to one's innate intelligence and the pulse that allows that intelligence to thrive and grow.

Man made fears, greed, and self absorbed thoughts are barriers to deep connection to Self.

When humans are awakened on our water sphere, human matter is quickly reminded of past fears that lead to previous deaths from past lifetimes and sometimes open hearts close.

To re-open a closed heart, you may ask any spirit guide for assistance. This simple invitation will vibrate with truth, and your inner spirit will easily accept and integrate into your conscious and unconscious awareness.

Keep the invitation present even in the event of dark and limiting thoughts, as the light of the vibration will crack open all barriers to opening your heart.

End[25]

Thanks, Earthwhale and the pod that inspires you. While not all may be open to such information, I find it both interesting and very useful. My appreciation for any assistance such inspiration might provide that helps us open our hearts to ourselves and each other.

One final thought from Rumi:[26]

> Your task is not to seek for love,
> but merely to seek and find
> all the barriers within yourself
> that you have built against it.

CHAPTER 7

LOVE AS ESSENCE

BEYOND LOVE STORIES (1)

Love comes with a knife,
not some shy question,
and not with fears for its reputation.

I say these things disinterestedly.
Accept them in kind.

Love is a madman,
working his wild schemes,
tearing off his clothes,
drinking poison, and now quietly
choosing annihilation.

A tiny spider tries to wrap
an enormous wasp. Think of the spiderweb
woven across the cave where Muhammed slept.

There are love stories,
and there is obliteration into love.

You have been walking the ocean's edge
holding up your robes to keep them dry.

You must dive deeper under,
a thousand times deeper.

- Rumi[1]

In chapter 6, I talk about love as an emotion, which is the general consensus by most of love's definition. Love is an intense feeling of deep affection, or a strong feeling we have for someone; a person or thing for whom we have a strong affection. The Urban Dictionary goes on to suggest a definition of "nature's way of tricking people into reproducing." So for some, it is not even a strong affection, but rather a trick or maneuver into making something happen. There are others, however, who suggest that love is not just an emotion but the basic composition of our being, the obliteration into love as Rumi describes. Love is not just a feeling or a part of what we experience in our bodies when we fall in love, but our essence as human beings.[2,3]

Love also is the essential lesson of Enneatype 9 (see Appendix B), the most fundamental of all the essential lessons and "heart of the truth."[4] In this place, we see existence without distortion that makes our entire existence lovable. We view objective reality as having an intrinsic quality of being wonderful and pleasing, that it is intrinsically lovable. Our understanding is that everything around us and in us is composed of love, that love is the basic reality of the universe. So rather than an emotion of feeling love, we see reality as composed of love, such that there is a sense of lovability for all aspects of our reality. When we see and understand this basic view of reality, it takes us into action that is based on love and expresses that through all we do.[4] It is our composition, which we then cover over with defenses, hurts, contractions, and protections from pain, abuse, and other challenging experiences. Ruiz reminds us that "Humans use fear to domesticate humans, and our fear increases with each experience of injustice."[5] As these fears and pains increase, we lose touch with our own essence made of love.

Many years ago, I was talking about love with my dear friend, Jean. I kept referring to love as the basic, expansive emotion and how important it was when we as human beings wanted to be more expansive. Then Jean responded that love is not just an emotion but the basic composition of who we are as human beings. I stopped talking, stunned, and kept chewing on this idea that at some level I knew and kept ignoring. The more I sat with this idea, the more I knew she was right. Yes, we access it as an emotion, and it is much more than that. At the same time, I thought I only knew it as an emotion and an idea, not an experience of being love.

Experiencing Love as Composition

One day a few years ago, I was in a very deep, intensive meditation. In an instant, I was out in a feeling of expansive space on the outer edges of what seemed like such a powerful light and feeling of love that I thought my body might explode from it. In my fear, I did not steep forward, later regretting that once again I was living my life from some fear, as I had done so many times previously. In a later meditation, I was further in this light/love atmosphere, even dissolving some as a personality. Rumi, of course, would have suggested I jump into the fire. On other occasions, I continue to move closer, letting more fall away and still experiencing fear. But it keeps drawing me back to this amazing place where all of my being, except of course the fear to which I seem to be attached, is composed of overwhelming light, love, and conscious knowing.

Even in times of less intense meditations, I can feel this connection, which allows my being to be more expansive, open, and feeling the existence of love rather than love as simply an emotion. Of course, I do not know if this is true for everyone, and some likely would suggest it may be my imagination. But the whole feeling that permeates my being during those times suggests something otherwise to me. And this seems to be the understanding of others who talk about the experience of satori, a Zen Buddhist term for when one experiences one's own true nature. I also suspect this experience is true of infants when they come into this world before covering this up with the contracted defense mechanisms, the socialization process that we put into place from our hurts, pains, and traumas. We as adults might learn this from infants and regain our own experiences of it.

Many children and adults who go through near-death experiences have encounters with this light and love, and they often are impacted by it for the rest of their lives. In summarizing the extensive research Ring has done in this area, he says this:

> Of all the teachings in the world, the greatest is love. And of all the lessons of the NDE (near-death experience), none is greater than the importance, indeed the primacy, of love. And what the NDE teaches about love is that everything *is* love, and is made of love, and comes from love.

"The Light told me everything was Love, and I mean everything! I had always felt love was just a human emotion people felt from time to time, never in my wildest dreams thinking it was literally EVERYTHING!"

Since we are part of everything, we, too, are conceived in and by love. Love, therefore, is our true nature. And yet, why do so many of us fail to experience this love in our lives and even come to feel so unlovingly toward ourselves at time? Why do we have such difficulty connecting to this molten core of love or even believing that it exists within us? What keeps us so estranged from the essence of what we are?

If we accept the truth of the NDE's chief revelation, it can only be that we have lost touch with the Source. For us moderns, this is the Fall. Existentially, we have fallen out of Love, like babes thrust from the womb into the cold world, and have forgotten our true home. But the teachings of the NDE now come to remind us, to reconnect us to the Source, and to restore us into the arms of Love. And more than that: Since Love is the essential truth of the NDE, it can also set us free.[6]

Parti experienced similar insights from his near-death. He summarized it this way:

Yes, communicated Michael, *this pure love is the source of all that makes the universe. It is contained in everything imaginable yet somehow ignored by so many. Enlightenment comes when a person realizes that love is everywhere and is the only thing that matters. Yet most don't reach that realization until they leave the earth. The ones who come back remember the purpose and presence of love in everything. And they remember it the rest of their lives.*

Love is the underlying true nature of all things, including "even humans" as archangel Michael put it. Science has revealed this, showing that the further we humans move away from feeling love, the more resentful, unforgiving, isolated, and negative we become, and the more rapid our degeneration toward disease. On the other hand, the more we cultivate compassion, love, and forgiveness, the more we experience healing and well-being.[7]

Long presents what he describes as one of the most profound reports given to the professional association collecting experiences about near-death by a respondent named Amy.

I also had this knowing that the essence or spark of the Highest is in everything — every mineral, vegetable, animal, and human. I knew that the Highest waited within everything to expand and create and grow and experience. I lost all desire to analyze everything in life, to judge everything as being either "good" or "bad." I wasn't concerned. We are all just consciousness experiencing life and learning how to love, create, and develop to the highest we can be.[8]

Long goes on to summarize the messages many experiencers reported from their near-death this way:

They describe this love as being the very essence of God. Hence, it is the very essence of all reality, the cosmos, life, all things. It is our essence. The light, or energy, behind all creation is or consists of love. That is what NDErs are describing when they talk about the universal love and unity that takes place during their experience, and it is why they often feel as though they have inadequately expressed themselves. Words aren't big enough.[9]

While some gurus proposed this possibility centuries ago, few have incorporated such a possibility into their everyday lives and views of others. Among the Hindu, the term Namaste, is used as a greeting to others. It technically means "I bow to you," but also for many incorporates the meaning of recognizing and acknowledging the soul or divine spark in the other person. While this greeting is a touching when one takes the time to recognize what is being said here, it has not changed the harm and damage we still perpetuate on other people and groups when we forget this idea and quite integrating it into our lives. We may reflect on our divine spark at times, which is lovely and touching. And we still do not treat children, women, or people of a different group with that same kind of open heart and connection in love.

More importantly, so many of us do not treat ourselves with such a reverence. But those who go through more extreme experiences do tend to change their lives and the way they treat themselves, others, and the earth. They also begin to notice that love is not just about a focus on another person, that lover we want in our lives, but it also is about each of us and everyone.

While we may spend time searching for our "true love" in some other person, we are and have constant access internally to the "love" we seek. When we remain connected to our more expanded Self, we never lose that lover. We may lose many other things in our lives, including a person who is loved dearly. Yet the essence as lover is ever present, except when we leave that knowing of ourselves, disconnect, when we separate from our own essence. When we maintain or reconnect such an experience or feeling, we are never out of love or separated from it. We are that and always have it with us. This lover never leaves. It never abandons. We, as personality, are always the leaver. And, as we become both clearer and more aware, the responsibility for staying or leaving the connection with the inner lover is completely our own.

This may be more responsibility than people want to take on in their lives. It may be too much for which to be responsible when we see and experience this aspect of ourselves so clearly. And yet, when we do, as Rumi says, why not "dive deeper under, a thousand times deeper."

Are we really afraid of ourselves? Are we, as Marianne Williamson so famously has suggested, afraid that we are powerful beyond measure?[10] Is it our light, our being so full of love that frightens ourselves, that makes us shy away from our inner essence? I am in deep gratitude for her suggestion that playing small does not serve either ourselves or others. Yet shifting our view is not easy, to take on such magnificence when we are so accustomed to being in a small, defended place, full of belief systems that limit how we see ourselves, our abilities, our light, our internal divine. When we open our hearts, release our limiting belief systems, and liberate our own fears, we emancipate ourselves and help others do the same.

If the idea presented by many people experiencing a near-death, sages, Williams, and other are saying is accurate, how amazing it would be if we could find a way to help children keep in touch with their hearts, not taking on such restrictive belief systems, and allow them to incorporate and utilize intuitive and knowing skills they seem to bring into this world. Such an approach would allow adults to keep passing on these gifts to their children and others to expand the consciousness and awareness of the world. Yet first, it is important to expand and open our own hearts, allowing ourselves to feel the larger aspects of our own being.

Living from Love Daily

An important question is: how do we expand and hold open our hearts in a world full of pain and hurt? Will it not create more hurt for ourselves and our children? This is what my fear kept telling me, which is one reason it has taken me so long to write this book. My fears keep showing up, and I seem to keep giving them great authority and influence in my life. Now is the time to change that within me, and, if this feels true for you, I suggest it is time to shift it in yourself and your life as well. As we do so, it makes it easier for our children and others to do the same, no matter who else chooses to hold on to the fear and restrictive belief systems.

After I have such powerful meditations or even experience an open-hearted connection with someone close to me, I often ask myself why I do not live this way all the time? Why do I ever leave this place of love? At first, my response to this question was to berate myself for doing so, judging myself as "bad" or belittling myself in some way for shifting into fear. Increasingly, I notice this shift and ask myself whether I want to live in a place of fear along with judgment of myself and others, or would I rather connect to that place of experiencing unconditional love, acceptance, and peace? The more I practice moving back into love, of making this conscious choice, the easier it gets. At times, it also remains a challenge. And then I ask myself, am I simply moving into the emotion of love or the essence of who I am, which is composed of love? This is a more challenging question to answer. But if we do not consider such a question, we never are open to the possibility.

The more I allow myself to expand deeply into my heart and experience love, the more it fills my entire body. Grof[11] argues that emotions are a whole-body experience, not just located in some specific place, and I agree with him. When I feel anger, sadness, joy, or even fear, they tend to permeate my body, especially when the emotion is strong, although I may notice the beginning of them in one specific place. At the same time, when I experience the amazing expansiveness of love, it feels more like it is in every cell of my body and being as well as everywhere around me. During these times, it begins to feel like the composition of the universe. So when I feel love for someone else, does it begin with them or is it simply accessing aspects of my own being? Increasingly, I believe we are accessing our own being and sharing that with others. We are getting in touch with what is inside of us, that of which we are composed, and experiencing that more fully when we use others as the reason for doing so. But the love is inside us, part of us, and our basic composition. So we access that aspect inside ourselves, uncomfortable seeing and claiming it, then "projecting" it onto other people in our lives.

Projection is an interesting concept. This idea was made famous by Sigmund Freud as part of Psychoanalytic Theory.[12,13] The idea, Freud argued, was that we develop ways of defending ourselves and use tools to avoid looking at issues that make us uncomfortable or we do not want to own. One such tool is projection, which is to attribute our own feelings and characteristics onto others, especially when we have difficulty taking responsibility for them. We can project "negative" characteristics, such as aggression, rage, or prejudice. When we do not want to see our own anger, we can describe other people as angry or aggressive in their behavior. We can easily identify people who are prejudiced while we deny that we have any prejudice within us.

But we also can project more "positive" feelings or characteristics, such as charisma or brilliance. Similar to the "negative" projection, we may see how wonderful another person is when we have difficulty seeing such good things in ourselves. Or we see others as smarter in part because we do not view ourselves as that bright. In this case, I believe we project the characteristic of love onto others. "You make me feel so lovable." "I feel so much love with you!" "Finally, because of you, I feel love!"

One of the interesting aspects of the near-death research is the impact that such experiences have on children and adults as well as those researchers who study this phenomenon. Moody suggests several areas where the transforming power impacts people going through the experience.[14] First, they tend not to fear death any longer. While they are not longing to die, they also have a sense that death is more of a transition than "the end" of experiencing. Second, they also have a sense that love is very important in our lives. "Upon their return, almost all of them say that love is the most important thing in life. Many say it is why we are here. Most find it the hallmark of happiness and fulfillment, with other values paling beside it."[15] Third, people who return from this experience have a sense that "everything in the universe is connected."[15] While many have difficulty describing this sense, one put it as "we are all part of one big, living universe. If we think we can hurt another person or another living thing without hurting ourselves, we are sadly mistaken.... If we send love along those connections, then we are happy."[16] There also is an increased appreciation of learning, a new feeling of control and sense of responsibility for the course of their lives, and a sense of shortness and fragility of life. This notion of love and connection seems to be the foundation of this impact, which may be impotent insights for all of us to learn.

One individual, Peggy, became very clear about who we are from her near-death experience. She reported it this way:

> In fact, the more I looked at it, the more mesmerized I became with peacefulness. The light was extremely soothing and joyful to "take in..." I clearly and instantly knew the light was not just a Light but was ALIVE! It had a personality and was intelligence beyond comprehension.... I KNEW completely without any shadow of a doubt that it was the strongest force in existence. It was the Energy of Pure Love....

> I was shown how much all people are loved. It was overwhelmingly evident that the light loved everyone equally without any conditions! I really want to stress this, because it made me so happy to know we didn't have to believe or do certain things to be loved. WE ALREADY WERE AND ARE, NO MATTER WHAT! The light was extremely concerned and loving toward all people. I can remember looking at the people together and the light asking me to "love the people." I wanted to cry, I felt so deeply for them.... I thought, "if they could only know

how much they're loved, maybe they wouldn't feel so scared or lonely anymore."

I vividly recall the part where the light did what felt like switch on a current of pure, undiluted, concentrated, unconditional LOVE. This love I experienced in the light was so powerful it can't be compared to earthly love, even though earthly love is a much milder version. It like knowing that the very best love you feel on earth is diluted to about one part per million of the real thing. As this stream of pure love went through me, I felt as if the light was saying simultaneously, "I love you COMPLETELY and ENTIRELY as you are, BECAUSE YOU ARE.

One of the many beliefs I have formed from the experience is that whenever unconditional love is bestowed upon an individual, no matter what the strength or from what source (a person or a light), it causes a purging of "unloving energy" or self-hating energy (which are all illusions) to come into the consciousness of the individual to be examined and discharged. Thus, the individual's level of consciousness is raised every time this is done.[17]

Even as people describe their experiences, it appears as if they are encountering love as an external presence. But what if that love simply is stimulating and enhancing our love composition inside of us? What if, like the people in the psychomanteums who suddenly are able to communicate telepathically when the inner skill is stimulated, we are able to access our inner love composition when exposed to the love intensity external to us? Our experience may not be as strong internally when we are not used to such an experience. But what if the difference were acceptance and practice? One challenge may be the tremendous change such awareness and experience creates in our lives, just as it does with so many near-death experiencers.

When we feel this connection and experience the love inside of us, we no longer can ignore how we hurt other people or the planet so easily. We are less likely to judge others as dissimilar and inferior because of the color of their skin, how they look, their gender or orientation, the religion they practice or different beliefs, physical abilities or challenges, or where they were born. And this may shift our perspectives and lives radically. It also challenges how we go along with other perspectives who have convinced us that hurting others, ourselves, and the earth is fine and "natural" for us. This is one of the reasons, I think, changing our perspective is so difficult, seeing all the impacts we are having on ourselves and everything around us. The responsibility or impact of this view is enormous and bigger than most of us want to embrace.

Yet the flip side of not wanting to take responsibility for our expansive selves is that we miss the larger, more amazing picture of who we and the possibilities we truly hold and have in our capacity. This view seems to be expanded often through a near-death experience. But what about those of us who have never had such an experience? How do we expand our perspective?

Even as I write this, it often is challenging to keep such an open view of myself and others. Expansion and contraction are natural phenomenon in our universe. But the contraction internally does not always feel so great. For me at times, it feels like my world is caving in on myself, and there is even some sadness and a feeling of darkness around that. I feel as though the light goes out of my world, and I am left in this place that feels dark.

Yet the practice is to continue monitoring and making a shift whenever possible. I find it works best when I first notice the contraction, or that feeling of fear, pain, hurt, or sadness inside. If I can catch it early in the process, I have a much better chance of shifting it, making a different choice. The more I have practiced this, like any skill, the easier it has become over the years to choose a different path in that moment. And it has taken a long time to develop such a skill and practice, even a noticing of the shift as it is happening.

Ruiz suggests that the love inside each of us is what is most important. "The whole world can love you, but that love will not make you happy. What will make you happy is the love coming out of you. That is the love that will make a difference, not the love everyone has for you."[18] Although Ruiz talks about love as both an emotion and as our essence, fundamentally he is talking about focusing on the love inside each of us. This can be a basic way we share love between each other, by loving from the "inside out," rather than feeling that love comes because someone else stimulates us to feel that way, or loving from the "outside in." This shift is a fundamental difference in how we see the source of love as coming from our deepest, most basic composition, which of course is all part of the universe, not something separate.

Thus, I and others are arguing that we simply are sharing who we are in our most basic composition. And this composition is not separate from the love all around us, the love that is the basic composition of the universe. The difference is that love is not just coming from others, but rather it get shared from the inside out.

This loving from the inside out also is consistent with the view of helping children keep the inner connection to essence, which is another way of saying our inner connection to love as essence, our composition. In both cases, we are strengthening the inner core, our essence, our being as love. They simply are two ways of working on the same connection and outcome, or should I say our basic "income."

Distinction of These Two Aspects

While we all are pretty familiar or have had some experience of love as an emotion, the fundamental question that comes up is how to distinguish between love as an emotion and love as essence or the composition of our existence. I have wrestled with this question, and it has taken me some time to feel like I have any idea what so ever as to this distinction. Still, this difference is not easy for me to describe to others. I will attempt to explain what I experience with love as composition in the hopes that it gives you some idea of what is possible beyond the emotional experience. It may even put to words what you have felt at different times when you pay attention to the subtler aspects of our being.

1. First, I want to go back to this idea about emotions themselves. When people experience an emotion, it often may feel isolated to one area of the body. When I feel fear or rage or even love, it may be focused in one part of the body, such as experiencing anxiety in the chest or anger in the gut. When the emotion is intense or very strong, it is more of a full body sensation or experience as Grof has suggested.[11] This is how emotions tend to organize experiences and memories into emotional constellations that allow emotions to be an organizing energy of in-

terconnections for the human psyche. As we work with them, it also helps us identify the issue or belief that is being held in the emotional field for healing.

As emotions may organize memories and experiences, the energy field itself seems to organize and hold in place all aspects of the human form on a subtler level.[19,20] Again, this is a whole-body aspect rather than relating to just one part of the body. People who see or feel energy fields can focus on one part of the body, such as a foot, arm, or chest. One may focus on the heart, feeling the loving energy, and then spread such energy throughout the entire body. Yet the energy field permeates the whole-body, whether we focus on one part, another part, or the whole. But this subtler energy is important when focusing on the distinction between love as an emotion and love as our essence or basic existence.

When we begin to pay attention to the subtler aspects of our being, it too may be an over-powering experience. In the beginning, most people seem to focus on one part of love as existence and move outward from there. In some cases, as when one is in deep meditation or some type of altered state, one can fall into the full bodied, even over whelming experience of one's essence of love.

2. In an early Breathwork, I dropped into a full body energetic being experience. It began even then as a feeling of love all around me, followed by a flowing or becoming aware of the love inside of my being. After a while, no distinction occurred between the love that was noticed external to one's being and that which is felt inside oneself. At times, this experience is accompanied by a sense of emptiness, which can even be frightening for people when it first occurs. It is a feeling like everything is full and present while also feeling at the subtle level a sense of emptiness or nothingness, without any kind of solid structure, nothing to "hold onto." So this sense of emptiness or nothingness is a second way to distinguish emotional love and compositional love.

The first time I felt this, it was completely unnerving because I had come to rely on the physical solid sense of my world as a place of security. And yet this occurs primarily because we have left the more etheric places as an infant, focusing increasingly on the physical plane and our senses of the world being solid, secure. And as people spend more and more time experiencing once again the subtler realms, there is an increasing comfort in the spaciousness of the emptiness. Rumi addresses this in the following poem.

BUOYANCY

I saw you and became empty.
This emptiness, more beautiful than existence,
it obliterates existence, and yet when it comes,
existence thrives and creates more existence.

To praise is to praise
how one surrenders to the emptiness.

To praise the sun is to praise your own eyes.
Praise, the ocean. What we say, a little ship.

So the sea-journey goes on, and who knows where?
Just to be held by the ocean is the best luck
we could have. It is a total waking-up.

Why should we grieve that we have been sleeping?
It does not matter how long we've been unconscious.
We are groggy, but let the guilt go.

Feel the motions of tenderness
around you, the buoyancy.

- Rumi[21]

As we gain more experience in the subtle world, we more easily can rest or even fall into the emptiness and fullness at the same time, of love and aliveness as existence. It may happen in mediation, or simply allowing it at times during the day. Sometimes it seems to creep up on you or will suddenly happen in a particular circumstance.

A dear friend of mine, Marianne, was in Israel for a week doing some intensive Breathwork with a large group of people being led by Stan Grof, introducing his work there. After several days of the workshop, a small group of the facilitators had an opportunity to go to the Wailing Wall in Jerusalem. Suddenly, as she was standing before the wall, she fell into this place, this aliveness and emptiness at the same time, feeling at peace and the connection to the whole world. In this place, we feel the essence of who we are that is beyond the emotion of love, but rather a total loving acceptance of oneself, others around us, of life.

Sometimes the feeling subtle, and other times it is an overwhelming experience. And it can shift our "reality," what we think and believe is real, to include a subtler and pervasive sense of reality as love. If we were to compare emotions being subtler than our physical body, and thoughts being subtler than emotions, then this knowing in general is subtler than thought. Yet it feels as real in the same way emotions are as real as our physical bodies. But because most of us have not paid much attention to this level of awareness since our infancy, it may not a familiar aspect of our life. At the same time, if these ideas about infants have any reality to them, then this also is not a brand new area for us to explore. It is simply coming back to where we existed in so many ways without the more concrete memory and brain pathways to bring it into our field of thought as easily as other parts of our life. Still, it may well be there, and a deep remembering may be what is happening rather than a brand new exploration.

3. A third distinction between love as an emotion and love as essence is that the latter tends to be accompanied by an amazing sense of peacefulness and serenity, which usually relaxes into trust. With love as an emotion, we want to feel trust for ourselves or other people, but trust does not always occur. In this subtler state or place as one begins to spend more time there, it is an increasing sense that everything just is, and there is little judgment about it. It includes a sense of serenity, peacefulness, and acceptance of myself as well as everything around me, allowing me to trust what is happening and see things in a place of trust. I experience less judgment occurring, less of a sense of black and white, right and wrong. While we still care about what we do or how it affects others, there simply is less focus on judgments about people and life, along with more peace and trust of life and our living process.

4. A fourth way to understand and experience love as essence is that when we are in that place or state, the sense of love does not end at the skin or with our body. Rather, it tends to extend beyond the body, connecting us to things beyond us and eventually to life all around us.

Of course, when we feel an emotional connection with someone else, as when we are in love with someone, it certainly extends to that person. When we are feeling love for someone and the oxytocin which accompanies such feeling is flowing, we often feel more love for the world and experience a lot of happiness in general. But the subtler feeling of love as essence naturally connects us to all life without any particular person and place being the object of our focus.

Related to the third aspect described above, there can be a "meeting" of love that seems to occur where we begin to connect with the love all around us at a subtle level. As we feel our love extending beyond the skin, further than our body, it can feel like no ending occurs to this feeling, easily extending on indefinitely. In this place, we experience no clear boundaries, where all is connected and interconnected. One can sense differences in density with things all around. But one experiences no distinct beginning and end to "objects" or even yourself.

Even numbering these aspects or characteristics about love as essence makes no sense in this state, for none of these things exist without the other. These in fact are not distinct and unique aspects of this experience, but rather they are simply an attempt to describe what is an integrated state and process of our existence that also helps us understand a distinction of sorts between who we are and what we may feel when attracted to another person.

5. A fifth aspect of love as existence is that at this level, we experience a place of choice, options, and possibilities within an atmosphere of love and acceptance. Things in the world around you do not feel as distinct and independent of each other. There is less of a dichotomy in the world, less black and white about things and more a sense of gradation and simple preferences, options, and possibilities all around. At the same time, more possibilities feel like choices and options for us, even expanding what feels like a possibility.

6.   In this place of love as existence, there is no "object" of our love. It simply is and occurs all around us. Nothing outside of ourselves feels like it is stimulating this experience. Life is simply love as it composes our bodies, our beings, and the world in which we live. This feeling does not rest on someone or something else, a person, a location, or an experience we have that fades or disappears. Love just is, existing inside us and connecting to all around us. As it feels stronger inside our being, it also is stronger outside our body, for there is little distinction between the two. We may focus our attention more strongly in one area or another. But it is the focus that changes our awareness rather than the existence or stronger sense of love in one place or another.

7.   As I experience it, the feeling of love as composition may not be as intense, especially in the beginning of our awareness as "loving" someone or something. When we really "fall in love," the emotion can be very strong and palpable. When we are in a place of experiencing love as existence, there may be less focused intensity initially. But one notices more spaciousness and calm in the experience. The more we live in this place, the stronger the feeling that one experiences while also expanding the calm and intensity at the same time. We find greater love to share with those around us, with less distinction between those we have "judged as deserving of our love" and simply experiencing love for all. Our judgments often may get in the way of experiencing this state or place, keeping us focused on the dichotomies, the black and white of the world we have come to know.

8.   When we focus on love as essence, we experience a fundamental acceptance of who we are, even if there still remain areas where we want change. There is a resting in a place of peace and acceptance of ourselves as a being. With all the flaws and judgments about ourselves, there remains love and acceptance that is not dismissed by what we notice about ourselves, what we define as our "weaknesses" or our "strengths." We have skills and drawbacks, places where we have developed great abilities and places where we still may want to grow and change. We neither dismiss ourselves or have to exaggerate what we can do to feel good about ourselves. It is a given, a fact, a basic aspect of our being that takes us to a place of simply seeing what

is. And in that seeing, we feel peace and loving acceptance in all of our flaws and strengths.

In this place, we connect more with ourselves and have greater love to share. For the love that we "give" to others is simply an extension of the universe that comes through us, from us, because that is who we are, that is our basic composition. When people close to us make a decision to go away to follow their path, it still may hurt, there still may be sadness. But love has not gone, for love is always in us. We miss them, we miss the sweet connections and fun times. And still we love from the inside out because love in this way is never ending. It never fades or leaves except when we let go of this connection, experience, and understanding.

9. One final distinction I would like to make again has to do with judgments. When we love someone else, we can do so even if there are things we do not like, things we judge as inappropriate, irritating, or even wrong. Both feelings can exist, our love for them and our irritation or judgment of them. When we move into a place of universal or love as existence, it increasingly seems to loosen or dissolve the judgments that separate us. It also feels like or judgments prevent us from moving into such a state, or they become less important when we do experience such a pervasive unconditional love. For love cannot be unconditional when we put conditions on things and people with our judgments of them.

I am not suggesting that we lose all sense of preference, but increasingly I think we choose to impose less painful experiences and feelings both on ourselves and on others. At the same time, we are more open, relaxed, and loving with ourselves and others. We care more about us as people and connection than belief systems. We are more open and accepting while also more sensitive to how we can hurt others and desire to do less of things that hurt. We see the bigger picture rather than the minute details that can stimulate our judgments of separation.

Conclusion

What if we greeted children into this world by joy, congratu-lations, whispering how welcome they are and how long we have been waiting for them to join us? What if each adult and older child first got into a place of an open heart before we ever con-sidered holding a new infant, and then showered them with feel-ings and words of love and welcoming? What if we kept this feeling of welcoming a new member through the first years of life, even when they throw food on the floor, want to walk out in the snow just in their diapers and cowboy boots, or cannot get to sleep unless you drive them around in the car or held them in your arms? What if they felt for the first five years that there was nothing but love and acceptance of who they were, even when we were going through our own difficulties which do not get taken out on them? What if we deeply apologized for the fear we had of being able to afford such a child and so we were not sure we even wanted to have this baby? What if every time we began to get upset with an infant or young child we realized how much of that is about us or something else going on in our life rather than focusing the blame on them for what may go wrong, even if they are involved in the act in some way? How much might it change how infants and children grow up feeling about them-selves, knowing they are love because we help them feel that inside themselves every day, constantly in early life? How much would it change us as well, being in a place of love as composi-tion ourselves, and extending the love from the inside out, open-ing our hearts, and sharing that with our children?

And would all of this come easy for adults, shifting how we do things to this kind of possibility? I think it would not be so easy, and I am not suggesting it would be. I am only suggesting that it may be an important part of this life changing process where children begin to hang on to this notion of love as compo-sition because they are born with it, and we find a way to lay claim to this shift in our perspective and support it in them.

I will talk more about some of these ideas further along with suggested ways of healing our connections that did not develop this way in the last four chapters of this book. But first, I would like to talk about in the next chapter how we as adults can ex-pand our abilities through our sexual explorations and experi-ences.

In summarizing this perspective, I would like to turn to Hafiz for the final word about the impact of our heart to heart connection:

CAN ANY BEAUTY MATCH THIS?

When the sun within speaks, when love
reaches out its hand and places it upon another,

any power the stars and planets might
have upon us,

any fears you can muster can become so
rightfully insignificant.

When one heart can do for another heart,
is there any beauty in the world that can match this?

Brotherhood, sisterhood, humanity becomes
the joy and the emancipation.

- Hafiz[22]

CHAPTER 8

SEXUALITY AND
EXPANDING CONSCIOUSNESS

YOUR TRUE LIFE

As you start to walk out on the way,
the way appears.

As you cease to be,
true life begins.

As you grow smaller,
this world cannot contain you.

You will be shown a being
that has no *you* in it.

- Rumi[1]

For much of my life, these two aspects of our existence, sexuality and consciousness, were worlds apart, an opposing dichotomy. This was especially true if the concept of consciousness was replaced with the term spirituality. Then these two ideas truly were opposite ends of a continuum. For many of the people in my world during the first half of my life, they also tended to see these as contrasting polarities. One could not be spiritual if they were focused on sexuality, for sex fundamentally was "bad," especially if you enjoyed it or participated in it for pleasure. It is amazing as I look at it now, examining an act that sometimes results in the most amazing creation. Yet if done for pleasure, it was defined in such negative terms or seen as good only through abstinence. The only positive rationale for sex was conception.

What was even more interesting to me as I began to question my religion was that within the organization, there were two ways men (and in this case I use the masculine case completely on purpose) could act in God's name. The first manner was through the use of the priesthood, which, of course, only men could hold. When men used the priesthood, they were doing things through God's power and in His name. The second act was procreation, to participate in the creating of an infant. This is the other way humans come closest to acting in a divine manner.

In that church, boys were given the priesthood typically at age 12, if they were found "worthy" by men who already held that authority. Then they would begin attending meetings for an hour each week to learn about the priesthood, how it should be honored, and how it should be used appropriately. If a boy received this priesthood at that age and continued to attend regular meetings most weeks until they died at say, age 75, they basically would earn the equivalent of a bachelor's degree from a university having put in so much time. On the other hand, if there were an hour in the same church spent directly discussing the other manner in which we come closest to a divine act, it would be rather unusual. Talking directly about sexuality, how fertility occurs, different sexual interactions, or ways people might pleasure their partner were topics completely missing from church manuals and classroom teachings. It was as if sex was necessary and even divine, but it was not a spiritual practice or something to be honored unless it was experienced for the procreation of children.

I do not blame my previous religion for this polarity. Such an approach has been going on for centuries, emphasized by most Christian religions and even cultural norms that go along with them. And this view of sexuality is not limited to Christianity. Many other religions ignore the discussion of sex, especially beyond the basic importance of procreation. Yet keeping these two important elements of our life separate and oppositional makes less and less sense to me, especially as I expand my view of the power and sacredness of sexuality.

There are, of course, a few groups who have honored sexual interactions, even discussing ways partners could pleasure each other, stimulate and delight in sexual interactions and unions. In some cases, there were teachings about ways to connect more deeply with each other, with the universe,[2-4] and expand intimacy through sexual unions.[5-7] These traditions tend to come from the East, included in Taoist, Hindu, and Tibetan traditions. Yet, even there, such traditions as Tantra often were kept more secret and saved for more advanced students along the spiritual path.

Diversity of Sexual Experiences

Wilhelm Reich addressed this issue of sexuality and the ways we suppress ourselves and our bodies that limit our orgasmic experience and in that way our life energy.[8] From his point of view, releasing the tensions we hold in our bodies allow us to breathe more completely, relax our bodies, and enjoy the pleasure of a full body orgasm.

Reich's students, who carried on his work, further talked about the connection between sexuality and spirituality. Alexander Lowen states:

> The problem most people face is that the tensions in their body are so deeply structured that orgasmic release rarely occurs. The pleasurable convulsive movements are too frightening, surrender too threatening. Regardless of what they say, most people are afraid and unable to give in to strong sexual feelings.[9]

Lowen[10] also talks about research studies involving both women and men that suggests a relationship between lack of sexual satisfaction and heart problems, an interesting correlation. While the nature of this research is association and not causation, it still raises questions that would be useful to address more directly. He also looked at the relationship between sexual behavior and spirituality.

> When our spirit enters fully into any act, that act takes on a spiritual quality due to the transcendence of the self. This transcendence can be expressed most vividly in the sexual act if it leads to the merger of two people in the dance of life. When this merger occurs, lovers transcend the boundaries of the self to become one with the larger forces in the universe. Love is the key to such a merger.[11]

Another student and colleague of Reich, John Pierrakos, who also collaborated with Lowen, put it this way.

The sexual force manifests itself at all levels of our existence: physical, emotional, mental, and spiritual. This force is the expression of both consciousness and energy as it reaches for fusion — unification. Although sexuality exists in all life forms, from protozoa to mammals, for us it has the power, through orgasm, to bring a transcendence of time, space, and duality. When it is unified with love and truth, it brings a fulfillment that sours beyond the limits of personal reality. To achieve full self-realization we must connect our sexuality physically, emotionally, mentally, and spiritually.[12]

Of course, Reich, Lowen, and Pierrakos were talking primarily from personal and clinical experience with clients. This can be a biased segment of the general population.

An interesting study conducted by Jenny Wade[13] focused on the transcendent experiences of a purposive sample of 53 women and 38 men ranging in age from 26-70. She recruited participants who could articulate altered state experiences through personal and professional contacts as well as word of mouth. While the majority lived in California (44), the remainder lived across the United States. They primarily were Caucasian (88%), the others were African American, Latino, Asian American and Native American.

Wade asked them to report on their transcendent experiences during sexual interactions and the impact it had on their lives. While classifying complex human encounters can be challenging, she tried to distinguish different incidents after participants had shared their experiences. She found that people reported merging with their partner, feeling Kundalini flowing, having the sense of a third presence, being transported to a past life, having out-of-body experiences, feeling one with nature, experiencing visions, experiencing clairsentience (a sudden knowledge of truth), experiencing uni mystica (the non-dual dissolution of time, space, and agency), experiencing telepathy, falling into the Void, shapeshifting, being able to channel, feeling they were transported, experiencing a magical connection to nature, experiencing trespasso ("an involuntary, here-and-now vision of another head, or a succession of heads superimposed on the lover's head"), and experiencing Deity possession.[14] What is even more interesting in some ways are the impacts these people reported from such experiences. The outcomes included spiritual awakening, personal growth, enhanced relationships, comprehending a greater reality, sacralized sex, and healing.[15]

While most people do not report such experiences or impacts from sexual interaction, it is noteworthy that a number of people have done so without any previous suggestions or readings that would lead to such reports. At this point, we have no idea how many other people have experienced such an incident or impact yet have never reported it. Until we begin looking at such possibilities and asking these questions, as Wade has done, we will never know. The same is true of many areas of sexuality, because it has been identified as a topic not to be discussed, not unlike my early experience in the church, which seems to be typical for young people in many religions around the world.

Most Westerners had little information about sexual experiences of people in general until people like Alfred Kinsey[16,17] as well as Masters and Johnson[18] began asking such questions and doing investigations regarding human sexual behavior and responses, despite the reactions in the general population and many people in power. For most people in the West, we also did not discuss or teach the power of energetic and sexual union, as was done by some groups in the East.[5-7] Until we expand our questions, report more about such unique experiences, and share these ideas more freely, sexuality will remain a hidden and even somewhat unknown topic for many. Yet it seems as if there are greater possibilities regarding sexual experiences and their impact than we have inquired, experienced, and really explored as a general population.

While all of the experiences reported by people in Wade's investigation are very interesting and diverse, one that jumped out for me were those 12 people who reported sacralized sex. In this case, people described an experience that convinced them:

> that the act of sex was holy in and of itself. This finding was usually associated with people who said their enculturation about sex had been repressive and negative, but it also included those with previously promiscuous attitudes about sex who determined to limit their relationships out of respect for what the act came to represent to them.[19]

This shift is rather sudden by those reporting this perspective about sexuality, which also seems to have altered their lives. They came to see sexuality not just as an act of pleasure and connection, but as a sacred and holy interaction, even when done for pleasure. This is a stark contrast to the way sexuality has been held by so many religious and spiritual leaders who have focused on the abstinence of sexuality as sacred or that sexual pleasuring was evil and dirty.

One of my energy teachers, Lansing, often would talk about an idea of how to hide an important principle or something that people did not want others to see. He referred to this hiding as "lie by reversal."[20] If you want someone to avoid seeing the power and sacredness of an act like sexuality, you reverse it by calling it the opposite. So you lie by calling something such as sacred sex as bad or evil, thus hiding the truth of it in a reversed perspective. Then people never see the sacred and powerful energy such an act contains, whether with one's self or with someone else. This happens because we build such views into our belief systems, which then only allows us to view sex in a particular way, limiting our perspective and experience.

Interconnecting Sexuality and Sacred

Increasingly, I have come to believe that we lie by reversal about sexuality being sacred, just as those 12 people discovered during their transcendent experiences. Rather than holding such a belief and never talking about it, as my former church leaders did, I think it is important increasingly to inquire about the sacred aspects of this connection, both as procreation and pleasure. While sexuality is not treated or even intended to be held as a sacred act by many, such a belief does not discount the possibility for others. Many places, objects, buildings, and rituals are held as sacred by some people, even when others disregard them all as benign or even foolish.

How we hold ideas or objects and the meaning we place on them influences their impact. W. I. Thomas discussed this idea and developed what he described as "self-fulfilling prophecies."[21] When people define things as real, they are real in their consequences. For example, the fear about scarcity of toilet paper because of the oil crisis in 1973 in fact produced a scarcity of such paper, even though there was no other reason to create a run on this product. In some ways, the run on the banks in 1929 also amplified the problem of banks not surviving because of the lack of trust in them at the time. Banks never have enough money on hand for all of it customers to withdraw their funds at the same time. So if we were to lose trust in a bank, the run on it would make it fold, even though otherwise it is a sound financial institution. If we fear there is not enough of any product and we all go after it at the same time, there will in fact be a scarcity of that product, although no scarcity occurred prior to the fear. This is one way people make large amounts of money, by creating a sense of scarcity, causing people to react in such a way as to create at least a temporary scarcity in that product, making it temporarily more valuable in the process.

Yet the belief that sexuality is sacred does not always produce such an impact as experienced by those 12 participants in Wade's study. If we were to continue to inquire about how such an act is sacred, it may increase our awareness about it, even giving us a greater understanding of how important it is in our relationship and spiritual growth. We also may begin to see other, subtler aspects that previously have been ignored when we change our perspective about sex. For example, some argue that orgasm opens our energy fields, even taking on some of our partner's energy or creating specific energetic connections, when two people engage in orgasm together.[6,22] In addition, it opens ourselves in ways that no other act or behavior seems to do. This seems especially true when we have released a lot of restrictions we hold in our bodies from contracted belief systems and negative experiences, especially involving the sexual organs.

This is one reason that sexual abuse and female genital mutilation, especially when done by relatives and people close to them and trusted by the victims, are such betrayals to the victims,[23-25] holding such pain and violence deep in their physical systems. Even the suppression of sexuality and "lie by reversal" approach holds contracted belief systems in our bodies. In this way, Reich, Lowen, and Pierrakos argue such a suppression of life energy and sexual expression do not allow ourselves to experience sex as a sacred act. Rather than helping us as humans become more spiritual beings, holding sexuality as dirty, bad, and evil keeps us from understanding the beautiful power and growth that can come from such experiences.

Sex and Gender Orientation

If the sexual act with one's self or with another person is sacred, what about the issue of our own orientation as humans? This is another area where we have held clear dichotomies about both sex (physical anatomy as female or male) and gender (the identification one has as male or female). Yet we know at birth that infants do not always clear male or female genitalia. Kinsey also reported from his work that people really fall along a continuum from heterosexual to homosexual orientation for both men and women.[16,17] Yet some young people today report even greater fluidity in orientation, feeling one way one morning and differently another morning. Friends of mine have a young adolescent who is going through the process of shifting her identity from male to female. She is particularly lucky because she receives support from her parents, teachers, class mates, and school administration for the transition, which also is happening with a few others in her school and all over the country. When people are full of fear and define such things as wrong and evil, they may suggest that the school personnel are "spreading" this tendency by supporting it. More likely, from what I know of these kids, there simply is an atmosphere where kids can be honest and reveal what really is going on inside of themselves.

In other cases, young people, especially in high schools and colleges, are finding support from others to get clear about the gay identity they have known at least in some fashion since they were young and either not yet clear or not sufficiently comfortable to share it with others until this time period. For others, it took many more years to get both clear and sufficiently courageous to come out to family and friends. Over 20 years ago, a close friend came out as gay when he was in his 40s, having lived with the discrepancy in his life for many years. Later in his life, he in fact wondered if he were bisexual, a group that in the past has lacked support from both the gay and straight community. As they release the blocks to both sexual and gender orientation, they are freer to experience a more full-bodied orgasm and any spiritual component to their interaction.

As a bisexual man myself, I know the challenges it takes to come out without being made wrong by both the straight and gay communities. It took me 20 years to admit to myself that in fact I had a gay side. Having grown up in such a conservative religious community that declared gays as a sin in God's eyes, it was not an easy process, even after leaving the church. I could see the hurt and pain of many gay friends who wanted to live within the church. But from their experience and the belief system around them, their lives and choices were sinful and evil. And yet being gay is who they are. They did not feel like it was a choice. Their sense of attraction was way too clear and strong to simply be a choice, especially when it occurs at a very young age.

Even the attractions of straight people are not simply about choice. Attraction in many ways runs much more in our unconscious levels. What kind of people do we find attractive and enticing, and what type of individuals do we like yet find no physical or sexual appeal. For me, it took a long time getting to know that I was bisexual, understanding the concept in my head compared to feeling it my body as a physical knowing. And once it did, both the straight and gay community labeled me a "traitor." The straight community labeled my sinful and evil, wrong for accepting that part of me. For the gay community, at least at that time, they saw me as lacking sufficient courage to admit that I simply was gay trying to hide within the "straight community." But my attractions and sexual responses to certain women we just as clear and strong as my reactions and attractions to certain men. It took me even longer to be clear and confident enough with myself and my orientation to be up front about who I am when developing relationships, even willing to let one go if they could not be supportive of my orientation. It may appear to be a choice from the outside, but from the inside is was accepting the whole of me. And if we are to see ourselves as love, that our essence and manifestations of self come from that place, then our sexual orientations and attractions also are part of that same aspect of being.

Sexuality and Increased Vibrational Frequency

We certainly can treat sexuality, intercourse, and attractions without much sense of the sacred. And we can do the same thing with our bodies, churches, temples, synagogues, mosques, and other holy sites. At the same time, we can treat all of these things or see all of these elements as sacred and respect them as a part of our divine connection. Much has to do with the way we define and treat ourselves as well as objects, expanding both our belief systems and our hearts. In this way, all of our sexuality can be an extension of the sacred or can continue to be treated as bad and evil.

Increasingly, I not only believe that sexuality is sacred, but that it also can have a specific contribution to our evolving consciousness in a way no one seems to be discussing, except indirectly by Wade and Tantric teachers. I do not have a lot of data and support for this idea beyond my own experience. But I think there is a potential for conscious and energetic growth through sexuality like no other physical act I have experienced, similar to the respondents in Wade's study.

I have been very fortunate, as have many other people, to experience some amazing meditations and altered state awarenesses. Some of these have been particularly helpful in understanding love as essence, for example. But none of these altered states or meditations, or even other life experiences, have had an impact on my awareness of increasing the vibration of my energy fields like sexual orgasm. In this way, I believe that not only is sexual behavior sacred when we treat it that way, but that it can be one of the best experiences to have a sense of how the body is transitioning into a higher vibrational frequency overall. Just as some have argued for a "set point" with our weight or other aspects of our body,[26] I think that orgasm can help us raise the set point for the overall energy of our field, which, as Burr[27] argues, holds together the physical form. If we want to increase our vibration, there seems to be many ways to assist such a transition, including releasing belief systems that hold us, letting go of contractive pains, releasing our muscles and relaxing our bodies, deep and relaxing breathing, eating better foods, and exercise. But what sexual orgasm can do that none of these other things seem capable of achieving is to help us actually temporarily experience this next vibrational step or level.

As we raise our energy vibration, the orgasm also seems to become more intense, showing us or allowing us to experience the next step or level. We do not always maintain that level of our vibration, just as we do not always maintain exactly the same weight. But the variation averages or the set point may increase so that the average variation is higher when we do things to change and maintain it. Sexual orgasm is just a temporary experience of what is possible, where we are headed energetically if we want to create such a change in our lives. It may be the pre-

view, the foreshadowing of where we could go if we pay attention and do things to allow ourselves to make the shift. Brennan[22,28] and Chia & Chia,[6] for example, talk about ways to shift
our energy and work with things that block our way. If you want
a preview of how that would feel energetically, it is my guess,
pay attention to your next powerful sacred orgasm. Then watch
what happens with your orgasm as you release blocks in your
body and field, release limitations in your beliefs, and relax into
love as existence.

This idea is simply another possibility to be considered as
we expand our view of us as humans, what is possible for us, and
how we might create a larger perspective around human consciousness and our progression. Maybe this is just another crazy
idea, or maybe this idea is one like Sogyal Rinpoche described
about how we limit our realities of the universe. This also is what
Anthony described about the concept of resiliency, which had
been in front of researchers the whole time, "illuminating presences that simply had no form before the light fell on them and
lit up the entire intellectual landscape."[29]

Conclusion

I am not asking you or anyone to take these ideas as fact or
truth. Rather, I am trying to present a collection of ideas that may
help us expand our view of children, as well as us as adults, and
of some of the ways we might expand our own consciousness if
we allow ourselves to relax and enlarge the way we view our
world. I think in the long run, sexuality is another way for us as
adults to recapture our abilities we have ignored since we were
infants. When I look at the diverse aspects Wade[13] describes in
terms of both experiences and impacts of the participants in her
research, these all point to the kind of skills that relate to children's abilities and ways that we can increase the subtle realms
we all as humans are capable of experiencing and expressing.

One of the reasons I so love Rumi's work is that he has
helped me see things in a different way and expresses it so subtly
and eloquently. The same is true as I became familiar with Feminist Thought, helping me turn ideas on their heads.[30] As I have
expanded my view of life and what I define as reality, Rumi's
work has touched me even more deeply, as he often slips in

through a side or back door, giving me a piece to chew on I have not seen before. Then I do not view things in the same way as I have previously. While there have been many great writers about expanding our consciousness, Rumi has a way of saying things so beautifully with so few words. I wish I could do the same, and yet it seems to take me much longer to express the ideas I want to share. My hope is that you will see his words differently as you read these passages I have offered as well as many other writers about human behavior.

In the next section that includes the last four chapters of this book, I will attempt to outline some possible implications of this perspective I call Noussentrism. I will talk about some examples of how we might do things differently with younger and older children, how parents and professionals might integrate some of these ideas in their interactions and support of children, and what I see as the implications of such changes in terms of our future.

Section Three:

Adults and Children Learning Together

CHAPTER 9

HEALING RELATIONSHIPS
WITH YOUNGER CHILDREN

With Contributions by Jean A. Metzker, Ph.D.
and Nate Metzker, B.A.

QUIETNESS

Inside this new love, die.
Your way begins on the other side.
Become the sky.
Take an axe to the prison wall.
Escape.
Walk out like someone suddenly born into color.
Do it now.
You are covered with thick cloud.
Slide out the side. Die,
and be quiet. Quietness is the surest sign
that you have died.
Your old life was a frantic
running from silence.

The speechless full moon
comes out now.

- Rumi[1]

If infants have the skills proposed by noussentrism, then beginning early is important when working with children so they incorporate and apply these skills in their daily lives. But how is that done? What do we as parents, siblings, grandparents, and professionals support children's subtle skill enhancement and trust? How can we nurture their maturation as they integrate their inner voice with their physical learning through childhood and adolescence as they move into adulthood? At what age to we start to help and assist them in this process?

I think the last question is the easiest to answer. The age we begin is what ever age they are right now. This moment is the time to begin, as it is never too early to initiate such support. We cannot begin too early or love too much from an open heart, which is different from enabling difficulties and self-destructing habits. In fact, I believe the research on interaction and stimuli with the fetus suggests increasingly that we have an impact prior to their birth.[2,3]

The daughter of a close friend used to tap on her belly as the fetus was getting older, doing a variation in the number of times she would do this. For a while prior to birth, she would initiate the tapping, feeling the mirroring of her tap by the fetus. If she would tap once, her baby would tap once. If she would tap three times, her baby would tap three times. This would go on quite consistently, mirroring the number of taps the mother would make. Given this awareness prior to birth, it seems quite likely that infants also are aware of many things after their birth, even when they do not register in a traditional cognitive manner.

I would like to provide one case example of how such a change in perspective might impact the way we interact and work with children. The following is a true example of two conscious parents who knew of this work and applied it to their interactions with their first child. The names and any identifying information have been changed, but nothing about the interactions have been modified. In this case, the interactions were described by a professional psychologist who worked with the infant followed by the father's observations.

Case Example

The following is a summary given to me by a psychologist close to the family:

While watching this tiny newborn human baby (I will call him Michael), I was mesmerized by the focusing and attending that went on between parents and infant. I have had several children myself, and I have worked professionally with many parents and very young children. In this case, these clients intended that the infant be conceived in conscious awareness. During the pregnancy, they both energetically connected to their fetus, sang to him, talked to him out load, touched and generally sent loving energy to him from conception to birth.

At birth, the newborn was immediately drawn to the parents' voices and light from the window—natural light even though the room lights were on. Michael was a particularly focused newborn, more so than any infant I have ever seen. Although the judgment was made to perform a C-section, the parents were given equal participation in making the decision. It was a disappointment to them because the pregnancy was monitored by a midwife, where the parents were expecting to participate in a *natural* birth. However, the inference from this decision is that the baby's awareness was not affected since both parents 'talked' him through the invasive birth. The father talked from a distance and connected energetically while the mother was open to being with the infant and focusing on him in the birth process rather than on her own discomfort or body invasion.

At the time of this report, Michael is 9.5 months old. Since the day of his birth, the parents attend to this infant with eye contact, genuine positive regard, and, while observing small frustrations with learning, are constantly addressing him in clear verbal communications, using sign language and including body language. They offer to help in learning particular skills and often sing with him. What all this has done is allow the child to experience apparently only slight anxiety concerning learning tasks and to give him the ability to attempt more complex tasks, more so than any baby I have ever witnessed.

When attempting to mediate debilitating frustrations, the father especially has made connections at a core level, which is observed by psychic awareness and felt by the father. From his report, the baby is a willing participant energetically, and he seems to notice the energetic connections of the father. The connections seem to sooth Michael and help him relax. It also seems to encourage

him in greater exploration at the time and respond energetically during the exploration. From my professional
observation, the baby is more peaceful, alert, aware, and
courageous when such connections are made between
Michael and his father.

Here are additional descriptions written by Michael's father:

When Michael was a couple of months old, I read a book
called Nurture Shock that talked about how children learn
to talk. Basically, it said that babies learned to talk when
parents responded to the babies sounds, not just the parents talking to the babies. I raced back through the last
weeks to see if we had been doing that, and we had, not
so Michael would talk more, but because he's a person
and we love him, so we listen and we respond.

When he was two months old, he said, "I love you," one
night in the bedroom. I called my wife in from the other
end of the apartment, and he said it again before she got
there. Then when she arrived, he said it three more times.
We really celebrated it and we listened. When Michael
was four and a half months old, there was a period of
about three weeks where every morning he would wake
up, look through the bars of his crib and said, "Hi Dad."
He said the word sock and cat when he was five months
old, and also started doing downward dog (the yoga
pose). When he was almost three months old, he was
kicking a ball up into his own hands and catching it in his
little sheep crib. I think Michael's incredible, but also,
how many parents miss their babies' miracles because
they can't get past what is "possible" and "impossible".

As far as his sleeping, he usually slept through the night
until he was three months old and we had to move him to
his crib. Then he was up every hour or two for three
months. When we moved him into his own room at six
months, he slept through the night. I don't really get that
one, except it seems he was very particular about how he
liked things.

When Michael was 3 days old, the pediatrician came in to do the tests to check him out. When she tried to make him bend his legs, he held them straight. She pushed with all her might, but Michael wouldn't budge. "I've never seen this before!" the doctor laughed. (He finally bent his legs.) Don't forget that he walked when he was 8.5 months old.

That little boy is so smart. I have never experienced, "out of sight, out of mind" with this boy. If he's interested, he remains focused and you can't trick him, though you can reason with him. He outsmarts us all the time. His sense of humor is extraordinary. Seeing other people suffering upsets him. His communication and cognitive abilities are amazing.

Also, Michael's energy is felt by all different sorts of people who happen to be in his vicinity. Of course, it's partly because he's a baby, but he has a special effect on people. Defying any boundaries of age, gender, skin color, nationality, socioeconomic status or cognitive ability, his presence brings out the smiles and good energy of strangers everywhere we go. I've never seen anything like it.

My wife's pregnancy was really an extraordinary time, and she was very tuned in to her body, and subsequently Michael's. We did talk and sing to him, but she also avoided any possible contaminant or disruptive substance. She studied nutrition and made certain to take DHA and flax oil and eat organically whenever possible. She had a great deal of energy throughout the pregnancy and did yoga consistently. There's also a certain silent attentiveness that she has but doesn't talk about, just does it.

When my wife and I met ten years ago, we both had a feeling that we were supposed to have a child together. Though many of the next years had a lot of turmoil and difficulties and even questions of whether we would have children at all, the listening, remembering and trusting in our feelings and intuition were part of the process of Michael's birth. When a teacher said that we shouldn't wait until our children are born, or even until we're pregnant, to begin taking care of them, we both took note, just in case. We both quit using any intoxicants years before she got pregnant.

Here's a few more things about Micheal:

He smiled when he was one day old.
He pursed his lips at one day old (a developmental milestone, I'm told) and continued to give kisses like that until 8 months old.
He raised one eyebrow at one day old.
He laughed at three days old.
At one week old, he began to cover his face with a blanket when he slept and to remove it when he awoke.
He doubled his birth weight in one month.
He could stand while leaning on me at two months old.
He watched, laughed and reacted with concern at story events at two months old.
He refused to sit down in his car seat at two and a half months.
He could catch a ball that was thrown to him at five months.

This example is intended to help parents and professionals understand how they might participate with infants and young children from a different point of view, moving beyond what we believe is "possible." In this case, parents and professionals not only are working with children on the physical level, but they also are including the energetic level. In this way, physical changes and development occurs in addition to rather than instead of the energetics that infants seem to bring into the world.

Any boundaries between parents and children work more like cell membranes, which allows for an ongoing exchange, knowing what is best to allow into the organism and what should remain outside of it.[4] This seems like a much more useful metaphor, especially when we begin to see the cell membrane as the "brain" of the cell, rather than the nucleus, which apparently functions more like the reproductive organs.[5] In this way, we again begin to move into a larger perspective that allows for more spontaneous evolution.[6] It allows for more exploration with children physically, emotionally, energetically, and consciously. If we do not allow ourselves to see such examples as possible, we will not observe them, even when they happen right before our eyes.

A Broader Scope of Possibilities

We do not yet fully understand the developmental process that children go through as they mature into more protected, defended adults. I have described a logical method from infancy through adolescence and adulthood in Chapters 2 and 3. It appears as if parents, siblings, and teachers, help children focus increasingly on the more concrete, physical plane without supporting and encouraging the connections they have with subtler energies and skills. In addition, when pain and hurt occurs, there is a natural protection, contraction, shutting down process that takes place. If we do not support maintaining connections on subtler and energetic planes, children let go of these skills and sources of information. Children then increasingly focus on the "physical" world without incorporating the energetic links to the intuitive and subtler ways of gathering or accessing information. Yet these skills could help them understand and utilize a larger scope of information, including possibly the motivations of people initiating the hurt or a larger view of the situation.

In some cases, children seem to have been actively discouraged from sourcing more intuitive or energetic information, such as focusing on the energetic fields. With the intuitive resources fading, children increasingly focus only on information that is gained through the basic physical senses and pay less and less attention to subtler energetic information. This process would be consistent with our findings, where children had quit using the 6th chakra or 3rd eye pretty much by age 4.[7,8]

Some adults have described accessing physic skills that were present when they were children at ages 3-5. But parents and others in their environment discouraged or even punished the sharing of such skills and awareness.[9] This seems to be a consistent reporting, although without more exploration it is difficult to determine whether such skills are present for all children or just some with special abilities. These skills do not seem to appear for the first time as an adult without some extraordinary event occurring when older, such as a near-death experience.[10]

One way to begin healing this relationship with children is simply to listen to what they are experiencing without automatically assuming that children do not know or are making up the perceptions or awareness. In the case of one mother, nurturing her child's report not only changed her life, but it also changed her profession. Both parents listened to the awareness of their two children and supported what they said, even if it did not feel easy or comfortable at the time. In this case, both children reported memories of past lives. Rather than shrugging off the reports as crazy and make believe, they listened closely and paid attention to all their two children described. Later, the parents reported outcomes that were quite astonishing. The mother shared this with Bowman, an investigator of such incidents and abilities in children.

> Both of my children are creative and full of curiosity, which I attribute, in part, to their experiences with past life memories. They know that Steve and I accept their non-ordinary experiences, and I believe that has encouraged them to push the limits of what is possible or normal. Most importantly, they learned to trust their own intuition and inspiration, keeping their channels open to the source of creativity..... Now I see my story as more than a personal tale, but as an example of what can happen when you open to those greater forces in general. And in particular, what can happen when you listen to your children — *really* listen with all your heart and all your soul.[11]

The parents of James Leininger also listened to their son, who started having nightmares at age 2 and continued to provide amazing details of a past life.[12] While his parents initially did not believe him, they began to investigate the information and found amazing details that any 2-year-old child could not know from the physical world. The more the parents researched the comments, the more they realized that their son was reliving experiences in his nightmares from a fighter pilot who was killed in the battle of Iwo Jima over 60 years before. Rather than dismissing or punishing their son, the parents listened authentically and expanded their view of what was possible, taught to them by their young child.

In another example, a woman by the name of Asia remembered having different beliefs than her conservative parents at age 3. She would communicate with angels, animals, and spirit guides. As she looked at people, she noticed their faces change, at times making it difficult to recognize them. She also has a strong impression of past lives, a belief that was in stark contrast to her parents' Christian heritage.[13] She later had a near-death experience at age 23, where she met three Ascended Masters who were there to teach her about her life and guide her "back to love."

"Your spiritually connected childhood has been forgotten and your adult years have so far been marked by fear," said the elder male Ascended Master. I nodded.

"We have teachings for you about regaining that oneness. We will show you your other lifetimes to assist you."

"When you say 'other lifetimes.' do you mean past lives? I was raised in the Christian faith," I stammered. "My minister professed that there is only one life, and then heaven or hell."

"That's not true." ….."In a moment, you will see and feel how similar lives, one lived in fear and one lived in love, profoundly influenced you and those with whom you had contact. This experience will guide you out of fear and toward the deliberate choosing of love, thus transforming your life."….

"Circumstances outside you do not have to lead your heart. Instead, allow your heart to lead in all circumstances….We are all connected. The well-being of the individual is woven into the well-being of all things. Whether we give love or fear, everyone and everything is affected."[14]

Another way for us to help heal our relationship with younger children is to simply slow down, be more patient, and keep our priorities on our children rather than worrying about what we might look like as parents and adults, worrying how others might perceive or judge us. Our relationship with our children is more important than the views and judgements of others, even if it does not seem so or we forget in the moment. To do this, we may need to do more of our own personal work around any insecurities as a parent. It may be important to ask what is going on inside us when we start getting upset and strongly reacting to a response, especially a simple, innocent response. We can begin to be more aware of our feelings and internal triggers when they arise. Even facing the fact that we may have such insecurity is an important first step.

My Own Evolution as a Parent

In the arrogance of my youth when my first child was born, I felt like I had so many answers and knew what I was doing. To make matters even more complex, I was in graduate school studying child development and family relations. So not only was I dealing with the personal issues, but I also had my professional face I was developing and portraying to the world. This made it even more difficult to be wrong and pushed me to look at how I could be doing things better with my children. To further complicate the situation, my wife at the time also had studied child development and had some professional experience. While she was a very good mother in so many ways, we had a hard time talking through areas where we disagreed about how to work with our children. On many things we agreed and did quite well. But for me, at least, it was difficult to find a way to express my fears and insecurities around parenting in a manner that made me feel internally at ease and comfortable. It was not my wife's fault, for I had a difficult time allowing myself to be in such a vulnerable place with her. Still, if I had been willing to look at my own issues of insecurity, I know I would have been both more energetically present and patient with my children, especially my oldest, listening more to her rather than thinking I knew what to do. In addition, I knew very little about energy fields and connections, creating a larger discrepancy between my confidence and my competence. I tried to look like I knew what I was doing and acting like a good parent. Yet there were so many areas I was not comfortable and so many times I was not really in my heart.

While I present alternative ideas and possibilities to parents, both in this chapter and chapter 10, it is not because I believe that the way parents currently are working with or treating their children is "wrong." So many parents deeply love their children and work hard at being the best parent possible. Rather, I simply am trying to present an expanded perspective and options to make some different choices that can be useful, to provide additional possibilities. As parents gain more experience, they often change their parenting techniques. This certainly was true for me as I gained experience with the first child, altering how I did things with my children who came later. The way I acted as a parent was not totally wrong, as I did many things well. At the same time, I was not very conscious or emotionally comfortable within myself. As a parent, I simply found a different way of doing things over time that seemed more useful and I liked better. I developed more patience and learned to be less reactive when something went wrong. This is particularly true now with grandchildren.

When my oldest granddaughter dropped a favorite bowl and broke it a couple of years ago, I knew in an instant that my response to her, avoidance of belittling her, was so much more important than any bowl I possessed. But that has taken time to develop, wanting more to help her clean up the mess that tear into her psyche for the same thing I had done with a bowl from the same set. When I was a young father, I would have gone to my anger about the broken bowl. With my granddaughter, I could see the bigger picture and take the more compassionate approach. Berating her would not have helped her develop greater coordination or avoid accidents. I still break things from time to time.

More experienced parents have different ideas of what may be useful and begin implementing other ways of doing things with their children. Parenting a "fourth" child was very different than the way I behaved and responded with my first child. This can occur because the child is very different, but I also had changed from the earlier experiences and the learning along my path. Fortunately for my grandchildren, my experience helps me see them as more important than objects and our connection more significant than my judgement about their behavior. I still care about how they respond, especially in terms of how they treat each other. I think it is easier to see the bigger picture now in contrast to being caught up in the details or even how I might look as a parent to others. Such responses not only develop from experience, but they also emerge when I begin to focus more on the larger view of both them and the world. More importantly, as I pay attention to our energetic connection and the opening of my heart, other options appear that I would not have allowed into my awareness when I was so closed down.

Parents also may change as they gather more information about themselves as people and in the role of parenting. They may learn things from friends, neighbors, parents, grandparents, siblings, as well as their own children. This can change the way they parent, as new ideas about themselves provide alternative methods for being with or working with children. Here is a report from my friend, Lisa, as she reflected back on the way she parented her daughter.

> I have so struggled with many issues you address here as both a child and a mother. As I mentioned to you in person, my knee jerk response as a mother was to hide away my soulfulness and overcompensate by immersing my daughter in the real world, hoping she would gain facility and comfort living in the physical world. At that time, I had such a split between essence and action...I wish back then I had a working model and reference about how a balanced life is possible as mother and child.
>
> Instead, I pushed my daughter as I pushed myself to be a high achiever, becoming a figure skater, musician, la la la la. I was not entirely soulless in the process....but there was always the feeling that essence was a liability, something to accommodate rather than express.

From Lisa's reflection, I think it is most important for parents to model their own soulfulness, creativity, intuition, and heartful expression. When parents talk about and live from that perspective, it becomes an important example for children, supporting their own exploration of a path that includes the skills children seem to bring to this world. In this way, parents are not just talking about but living such a life. They can model this behavior and provide support for children to do the same. This is s significant way parents can nurture subtle skills in their children.

Additional Suggestions

There are a few other ideas and suggestions to help parents and other adults maintain and heal these connections with younger children. First, I would recommend that we let go of the typical limits we have about who children are and what they can do. We do not have to have some magical idea or goal we are pushing. Rather, it is more about being in a place of possibility and wonder, exploring areas we might normally ignore and paying close attention to what comes up from our experience and interactions with young ones. Sometimes it provides amazing responses, as the parents found when their children reported past lives as described previously. At other times, it simply provides an enjoyable interaction.

Recently, I had an opportunity to put my 3-year-old grandchild to bed. As we were walking upstairs, she mentioned a time that "she died." Given my reading about children's near-death experiences, I was fascinated with her comment and could not wait to talk with her about it. Her mother got her ready for bed and asked if she wanted G-pa (my name as Grandfather) to read her a story or if she wanted to tell him a story. She chose the latter, which excited me even more. So she got into bed, told her mother good night, and proceeded to tell me a story about when she died. I was on the edge of my seat, so excited that such a story would happen for me, not just others. Then she proceeded to talk about when she died, "and the zombies came, and dad killed them all. And then he got me and we ran away, and then....." I chuckled to myself. It was a great story, but not what I was anticipating. So then I tried another possibility. I asked her if she remembered being born. She replied that she did remember. Again, the excitement rose inside me. I asked her to describe what she remembered. She looked at me for a minute, then looked down at her soft greet blanket. "I got this blanket for Christmas, and it is really soft." Again, it was a great story, not what I expected, and it was all fine. The fun conversations and connections were the most important aspects for us to share.

Some kids remember things, and others do not. Or they remember them at different times and not just when asked. Actually, the same is true of some of my memories today! And the two of us had a wonderful conversation, listening to her story telling, until her mom and dad had returned from the ice cream shop with dessert. So we all said good night and went down stairs. While our story telling went in a very different direction than I anticipated, it was a delight to experience this precious time together. These times are not always about "magical" interactions, but such events are a joy when they happen, and it seems to touch the heart when we pay attention to them.

As parents, you might keep an image or possibility of greater tasks and abilities with young children. Try seeing things from their point of view without the normal limitations we place on them as adults. Then, when a child presents something different or new, play and explore it in order to understand where they are going with it rather than dismissing or minimizing it because "he or she is only a child." Just stay open and explore new things, always trying to understand them from the child's perspective, as the parents did with Michael, the case study presented earlier, and the children's report of past lives.[11] In addition, hold open the possibility that there is more or something else that might come from this early exploration. Sometimes they turn out like the interactions with my grandchild. And all can be precious moments and connections.

Another suggestion for both healing and maintaining is to continue to make energetic connections with children, while both very young and as they grow older, even if you believe you do not know how to work with energy or know how to create such connections. Just imagine in your mind that the energy is going from you heart to their heart, or from your hand to their hand without touching them, or even when you are touching their body.

When I was working with both children and adults in terms of how to make such energetic connections, I would have them begin by clapping their hands several times, then rubbing them together vigorously for 15-20 seconds. You may want to try this, then slowly hold your hands close to each other and feel into your experience. At first you feel the heat of the hands. As you pay closer attention, moving them further apart and closer together without physically touching, people often begin to feel some tingling or sensation. As you focus on this area more, it sometimes can feel stronger. Energy follows intention. So even if you do not "know" how to make energetic connections, you may well do so just from your intention. Play with this over time, sensing or even just imagining an energy flow moving from you to a child. Then pay attention to see if you feel anything in return.

People doing an initial exploration in this area may not feel energy in the beginning, but over time your sensitivity can increase. Even if you never feel it, it would not do any harm to continue imagining such connections could occur, especially from the heart. And the child may feel something even if you do not have any awareness of it. In addition, if the child does feel something, just being open to it and playing with it could encourage the child to continue working with it. Talking about it and playing with it also lets a child know that these things are not only acceptable but encouraged in your world.

As a parent, you also could inquire about things such as whether a child remembers his/her birth, whether she/he remembers anything about past lives or having lived before, whether he/she sees things in subtler realms, or whether she/he feels anything energetically. Again, children may or may not remember, see, or feel any of these things. Their view may be quite different from what you image it is, as with my 3-year-old granddaughter. How much they do or do not know, or whether they remember things, is not most important. Even the asking and conversations about these things allows children to feel OK if or when any of these things happen with them or with others around them. It tells children that you are open to discussion of such possibilities, even if other adults are uncomfortable with these topics and skills. In this case, children do not have to hide or repress either their experiences or their skills, but rather they feel some acceptance and support for who they are and what they can do, even when it does not fit into the world view of others.

Finally, it can be very useful for parents to grow in these areas themselves. It can be useful to learn about energy, read about children's past-life reports, read and discuss children's near-death experiences, and learn about things where children have a difficult time talking about them or sharing their experiences for fear of being shamed, dismissed, ignored, or even punished. We do not have to accepting everything at face value, but it is important to avoid dismissing them because they do not fit into the "normal" experiences of life. What we describe as "normal" in most cases is simply a statistical average. But that does not allow for people who do have unusual experiences and yet are not strange, bad, or crazy. This is especially true in terms of young children who often are tying to describe their experiences and seeking support for understanding them. If we put such experiences into a context that helps them, they can see a broader range of who and what we are as human beings. If we hold a narrow perspective of ourselves, then we force children into that same point of view. If you hold a view of greater possibility, it allows children to hold on to, maintain, and even expand skills that could be critical in their own expansive and conscious development as an adult.

One of the most interesting books written by Grof[15] is a review of the thousands of experiences reported by people who have utilized the methodology he developed for people to move naturally into non-ordinary states of consciousness. People report all sorts of "impossible" things happening, impossible at least from our mechanical view of this world. Yet they happened, and people keep reporting them, at times with verification or support from others. Such reports included remembering birth and prenatal life, reports of lives of ancestors who lived long before them, reincarnation and past-life experiences, along with extra sensory perceptions and other paranormal experiences. Do these skills emerge in adults because of increased development and advanced cognition? Grof doubts it, and so do I. Such experiences have helped to change his whole world view, as it has done for those going through such experiences. In addition, he also reports his discovery of an inner healing intelligence in humans. He concludes that such holotropic states show us examples of the "mobilization of deep inner intelligence of the clients that guides the process of healing and transformation."[16] This is very similar to the finding by Allison[17] with the healing process guided by the person's essence of multiple personality disorder. Such findings again suggest that this intelligence is present from birth and could be supported and strengthened by parents, family, friends, and professionals working with children.

I attended a workshop not long ago where the participants were put through a simulation of death and rebirth. The process itself was quite powerful for many of those attending, including myself. But what followed was for me even more potent than the first two pieces of the exercise. The participants formed a long double line. Then we each had an opportunity to walk down the line as a welcoming into our new life, a birth where we were celebrated for being here, being alive, being part of this loving community. As I walked down the line and listened to the heartful and accepting words that were said to me, at times even whispered into my ears, tears came to my eyes. I could not help but cry from joy at the acceptance I felt for being there, for being alive. "Welcome, welcome, welcome," they would say. "I am so glad you are here." "We have been waiting so long for you!" "Look how beautiful you are." "I am so happy to get to know you." "It is a joy to have you here." People on each side of me were so loving in their welcoming of me to my new life. As I continued to walk and listen, tears of joy ran down my face, feeling such acceptance for my presence. I wondered afterwards how babies would feel if those were the first words they heard and felt after their birth into this world and for the next years of her/his life. What would a young child feel if we continued to say such things to them, connecting from our hearts to their hearts at the same time?

After walking through the double line with my eyes closed, listening to their loving comments, I had the opportunity to welcome others as I joined the end of the line. Several other people came through, and I too was able to greet them as they passed, offering my own words of appreciation for their presence. Afterwards, I noticed how such an offering to others was so good at expanding my own heart and sharing love and acceptance from a place of caring and support. Not only was the experience beneficial for the newborns, but also for the adults doing the welcoming.

Being very present with our children, heartfully listening to what they say, holding and touching them in a loving manner whenever we get the chance is a gift we forget to give them at times. It also can be a gift we forget to give ourselves by the offering. When they talk about the presence of those who have passed before us, reporting something from a past-life, having a precognition of something happening or something wrong, making energetic connections to them, even when we are not talking, these are the ways we begin to heal and maintain the kind of energetic connections that are important for young children. We can help them preserve energetic connections and skills that otherwise seem to fade away and go dormant and hold onto the deep inner intelligence that Grof describes.

Conclusion

Children often respond to what they experience in like manner. When they experience hurt, pain, fear, and other contractive interactions, they will create a similar reaction. When children experience spanking and violence, they often perpetuate it in some form. When children experience love, appreciation, being really seen, and caring connection, they again will give back a response that mirrors their experiences.

Some time ago, Dr. Alexander and associates[18,19] did work with delinquent and non-delinquent families. They found quite consistently that parents who respond to their children by criticizing, controlling, name calling, blaming, and judging were more likely to have difficult, less effective communications and interactions while also having more problematic outcomes with their children, such as greater delinquent behaviors. Families who were more supportive, spontaneous, involved children in solving problems, provided genuine information, sought empathic understanding, and exhibited greater equity had fewer problems with their adolescents, were better at problem solving, and experienced more positive outcomes in the family. They also found that children mirrored the patterns of their parents. At the same time, when families got into negative response and interaction patterns, they were more difficult to change. Families with more supportive and caring communications and interactions also tended to carry on these patterns. The question for parents really is what type of relationship, communication, and interactions do you want to pass on to your children and possibly even grandchildren? What patterns do you want to model and experience with your children? How do we invite and treat children to join us in this earthy exploration? How do we open our hearts and share our best selves with them?

My hope here is that we adults will continue to expand our world view, our belief systems, and the opening of our hearts. I invite you to be fully in your body, energetically present, and open-hearted as often as possible with your children. Even when they are upset, sad, discouraged, or angry, you begin your interaction with a heart to heart energetic connection. They may be closed in the beginning. But with awareness and desire, we can change these patterns. As we practice, we can choose to remain open-hearted, even in the face of their difficulties as well as our own. Especially with infants and young children, this is the foundation for healing that can occur on many levels when we allow ourselves to be more fully open and present with them, no matter what is occurring in the moment. This can create a different foundation than most of us experienced as we matured, and allows for a more conscious parent, friend, and partner when they become adults.

CHAPTER 10

HEALING RELATIONSHIPS
WITH OLDER CHILDREN

OUT IN EMPTY SKY

If you catch a fragrance of the unseen,
like that, you will not be able
to be contained.
You will be out in empty sky.

Any beauty the world had, any desire,
will easily be yours.

As you live deeper in the heart,
the mirror gets clearer and cleaner.

Shams of Tabriz realized God in himself.
When that happens,
you have no anxieties about losing anyone
or anything. You break the spells
that human difficulties cause.

Interpretations come, hundreds,
from all the religious symbols
and parables and prayers.

You know what they mean,
when the presence lives through you.

- Rumi[1]

To begin this chapter, I would like to present two examples of working with older children in the healing process. While we sometimes learn to do things differently with more experience, there is no time like the present to use new insights to improve our interactions with others, especially our children. The following are true examples of people wanting to improve relationships with their adolescent and adult children, healing possible hurts and having a more heartful connection to them.

Case #1

David believed he was a pretty good father. Since the divorce 10 years ago, he had tried to stay involved in the lives of his children. Even though he lived in the Midwest and his children lived out west, he would visit at least two times a year and call them every Sunday he was available. It certainly was not the same as living with them daily, and he tried to put aside his guilt in order to focus on the things he could do well with them. When he was visiting with or calling them, he focused on what they were doing and saying. He attempted to leave his business matters to his associates and assistants, wanting to concentrate his time and attention on his kids.

Sometimes he would take his children on vacations, for those were some of the fondest memories David had with his own father. He wanted to help create similar happy memories for his children. He also wanted them to experience other parts of the world, starting with different places in the Western United States. Eventually, he would take them to other places, sometimes together, sometimes one or two at a time, to create special memories.

Still, he struggled with the guilt. Vacations and phone calls from seventeen hundred miles away did not compensate for being present when they fell down, picking them up and caressing them, telling them they will be OK. Yes, he paid his child support consistently, but would money buy their love and affection? His youngest child, Meg, was only two years old when they had separated, and she had no apparent memory of ever living with him on a daily basis. How would he be connected with her? How would they have any relationship except for the "visiting dad?"

There also was the nagging, underlying truth. He had come to realize that at the time of her birth, he had not wanted another child. What if, somehow, Meg sensed that in him and took it personally? What if babies do sense emotions? What if she had the

216

impression of not being wanted by him, encapsulating that into her sense of self and her relationships with others? Her mother clearly wanted another baby, and Meg and her mother were very close. But what if she still held that sense of "rejection" in her body, a piece of "I'm not wanted here?" It wasn't really about Meg at all, of course. It was about being overwhelmed with the responsibility of providing for a wife and three children on his meager manager's salary. Sure, he believed he eventually would make more money, but it was not coming as fast as he had hoped. The bills certainly were piling up more abruptly than the income. So the shock of another pregnancy, another person to be responsible for was not the best news he had experienced that year. In fact, it just added to the depression.

David had read about babies feeling things and sensing what is going on around them. He hoped it wasn't true. And besides, there was not much real "scientific" evidence for any of that. In fact, many physicians kept saying that babies do not hold memories, which was one justification for not worrying about pain around circumcision. Yet, David was increasingly concerned that we do not understand all that goes on in a baby's mind and body.

As David now was sorting through and working on lots of "issues" in therapy and other modes of exploration, he began to experience some of his own awareness of information as a new infant while experiencing an altered state. In one case, he had a sense of a difficult birth and being "pulled" from the birth canal before he was ready, which he related to his sense of feeling rushed by others faster than he wanted to go at times throughout his life. So he asked his mother about the birth, and she verified that the doctor had used forceps to help because he was worried about the birth "taking too long." His mother was in quite a bit of pain, but she also felt like the doctor was rushing things. She later found out that he had two other deliveries and wanted to get through this one in order to get to the next. But David didn't remember talking about this before, and in fact his mother did not remember it until he asked. Still, they might have talked about it. How did he know for sure?

During a session of Holotropic Breathwork, David got in touch with the feeling that his father also had not wanted another child when David was born. As David explored this issue, it was not that David's father did not like or want children. He had three older siblings, and he always felt like his father had cared about him. David's parents also were not doing well, given the stress about his father's job change and the conflicts that created. During the pregnancy, David's father must have worried about their relationship and the added stress on an already fragile marriage. David also had the sense that his father worried about the additional financial strain, not unlike David himself when Meg was born. So apparently, there was a pattern developing that David did not want to extend into the future. He would try to heal the hurt he felt, whether or not it was true, and certainly he would try to heal what he had been experiencing when Meg was born, given the possibility that any such experience could affect his daughter, whom he now loved very much.

What he worried about presently, however, was the impact his attitude might have had on his daughter. One day, while visiting him at his home, Meg had a very serious headache. She experienced these from time to time, but she had not had such a strong one with David before. He called her mother and asked what she would do during those times. She suggested some pain medication that worked for Meg, and then she said she would sometimes just hold her. David had the medication in his cupboard, and he gave some to Meg. Then he just suggested that they lie down on the couch, and he would just hold her in his arms. He cradled her and even began a small rocking motion. He began to discuss things he liked about her and some fond times he would remember that they did together. He began talking about some early times when she was quite young, including a summer trip to the Midwest to visit him with the other kids for several weeks. One experience he was very fond of was a day when David took Meg and her older brother to play at a local park. They would swing, slide or play in the sand, what ever the two of them wanted to do. He realized this was such a fond memory because he had been so present, concentrating just on them. He had taken his camera and also had fun photographing their laughs and smiles, loving to see them so happy that day. They were photographs he loved to show others, the twinkle in her eyes, the smile on her brother's face, holding hands and really enjoying just being in the park experience. He later hung those pictures along with other fond memories on his "family wall."

As he talked, David remembered the possibility of another awareness Meg might have about his attitude of not wanting another child in his life at the time of her birth. It felt like this was a great opportunity to discuss how his attitude and feelings had changed, even including an apology to her for his early reaction.

He talked about the time when she was born and all the things going on in his life. His work was demanding, he and her mother were not very close, and he was very unhappy with life. This was the environment into which she was born. This was the context of the beginning of her life. It was not one he would have wanted to have for her, especially knowing her as he does now, 12 years later. He went on to share many of his feelings, talking to her as if she might know this already at some level of her being. Meg was lying very still. David was not sure if she were just listening very intently or dozing off. It did not matter to him now. He was there, at the point of saying, "I am sorry," and he would neither wake her nor put it off any longer. He tried several different ways to be clear that whatever overwhelm he was feeling, any depression, conflict, stress, that none of it was about her personally. None of it had anything to do with dismissing her, but rather it was about not being very good at handling all the challenges and stresses he was facing at that time in his life. If there was any sense of rejection that she might have experienced, please forgive him and know that he loved her very much and wanted her in his life now and forever!

David talked for some time, then just let her rest. She was asleep now, so he let her continue while he just held her and tried to let his arms and emotions tell her silent, still body how much he loved her. Later, when she awoke, she felt better, and the headache had disappeared. He felt like the medication and relaxation had helped her get rid of her severe headache. He would never really know if what he said had made any difference in her headache or her life for sure. But in some way, their relationship changed, from his perspective at least, from that time forward.

The next day, during their drive back to her home, Meg seemed more talkative and cheerful than usual. They talked about a project that they wanted to do together, and made plans for her next visit. Maybe it was just a coincidence, but she seemed more open and shared more about herself that she ever had in the past. Over the next few months and years, this increased openness and sharing continued. Maybe it was because she was getting older. Maybe it was because they were able to spend more time together now that he now lived in a neighboring state. Maybe they were just strengthening their relationship with their visits and spending more time together. Maybe just holding her and letting her feel the love that he felt for her made the difference. Or maybe it was because David helped clear something out of their way, energetically if nothing else, in order for them to connect at multiple levels more clearly and deeply. He never knew for sure, and it would be difficult to tell just what had changed and why. It could have been a combination of several things or all of them. What David did know was that after the discussion on his couch, their relationship deepened, they grew closer, and there was a transition, at least from his point of view, that would connect them as closely as any of the relationships he had with his children. In some ways, it did not matter for certain. In another way, he felt like the discussion and energetic connection helped create a transformation that thrilled him. In the end, he was grateful for what he shared with her that day.

Years later, when David asked Meg if she remembered the event, she had some faint memory of it, and she too didn't know if it changed things between them. And yet, there was a feeling that it might have been a very positive thing from her point of view too.

Case #2

Miguel also was a single father, having been divorced for almost 24 years now. Both his children were grown, and they seemed to be doing very well. Although he did not live in the same state as his children, he was close enough to visit from time to time, and he would arrange times where they could stay at his home and spend more daily time with him. Yet, both his daughter and his son developed their own lives with their friends at school, and he was not able to see all their activities or be with them on a daily basis.

As do many children with an active part-time parent, Miguel's kids had a pretty good relationship with him, at least it seemed that way. His daughter, Sophia, now 30, enjoyed her time with her dad and seemed to be quite like him. His son, Jose, almost 27, had been closer to his mother, yet still seemed to like his father and enjoyed visiting from time to time. But he also had grown up with some anger, and he had been in many fights as an adolescent. While he was not a really tall young man, he was very strong and acted like he was afraid of nothing. Miguel knew he was not as close to Jose as he was to Sophia, yet he still felt like he had developed a pretty good relationship with his son.

Recently, his son has been offered a job in the same town where Miguel lived. Miguel had invited Sophia to live with him earlier while she was going to school in town, and although they had had a few disagreements, he was very happy she had spent the time with him. So he invited to Jose to live there for a while too. Neither Miguel nor Jose knew how it would be living in the same household, and by now Jose was married and had a child. So it also meant having the three of them move in, and Miguel did not know Jose's wife all that well. Jose was a bit nervous about it all, but he also thought it was important to try it at least, and Miguel certainly did not want to show favoritism towards his daughter, especially since they had some greater closeness already. He was determined to give it a try and let Jose and his wife save some money by staying with him, only sharing the cost of the utilities. Miguel had the room, so it all made sense to him, and he wanted to increase the closeness with his son.

Jose and his family moved in that September, finding enough space to feel comfortable and putting the rest of their things in a near-by storage unit. It was not a large house, as Miguel was not rich, but it was adequate for the four of them. There was enough space between the two extra bedrooms for the three of them to have some separate space of their own, somewhat away from Miguel's bedroom area. Miguel actually worried more about Jose's wife, Maria, feeling comfortable at first, as they had not spent a lot of time together. Miguel kept checking in with them the first few months to make sure things were going OK with them and that Maria felt comfortable. According to Jose, Maria was doing quite well. She felt like she had enough space as well as privacy to feel at home, and they seemed to settle in well under the circumstances.

What Miguel did not know was the level of anger that Jose had towards him. Jose was both hurt and angry that Miguel had not been there for his football and basketball games, for the times when he would beat up another elementary school child because the other kid was making fun of Jose being from a divorced family. While it was the early 90s, Jose lived in a small, conservative town where there still was not a lot of divorce, and Jose stood out as an "oddball" because his father had left his mother and caused the divorce to take place. Jose also was angry that his mother had been hurt, that he did not have a father at home to "protect" them, to take hikes or do the "father and son" sporting activities that other boys his age had. He was angry that

Miguel was not there to watch out for his older sister when she was dating or to meet his girlfriends in high school. He was not there to help him learn how to drive or shoot a bow and arrow as his best friend's father did. At times, he was embarrassed to be from a "divorced family," having to explain to his friends and girlfriends why he was not around. He was tired of such explanations, hurt that his father did not care enough about him to "stay," and angry about the deal he had been handed in life. Yet Jose didn't show any of this to Miguel. He had learned to hide his feelings, especially when he was responding to a situation that may call for physical action. While he shared a lot with his mother, he could turn it off and hide it from his father, who did not really want to see it either. In retrospect, Miguel knew enough to realize what many of the fights Jose had as a youth might be about, but he also tended to avoid conflict, making it easier not to notice his son's anger.

After spending a few months living with Miguel, things began to change for Jose. It was not like there was some big fight or even a specific breakthrough. Miguel had changed over the years. He was more open, more aware of his own feelings and actions, and he was much more comfortable taking responsibility for his actions. He could apologize for not being there for his son without going deeply into hurt or anger. During the discussions, Miguel would have with his son, he could empathize how difficult it was for Jose without going into heavy guilt and reactivity. He simply could listen to Jose the few times he would talk about these things with his father. Fortunately, Miguel had a good enough relationship with his ex-wife that she could tell him, at this point in life, of Jose's anger towards him, and he could simply take it in as useful information. There were times Miguel had been defensive with his older daughter when she raised issues with him, and it had not been useful at all for them. Having settled things with his older daughter, he knew better than to go there again. He simply would have an opportunity to apologize for his defensiveness later to Jose, for it was Miguel's own pain and guilt that helped create a defensive posture. Being much clearer about this now allowed Miguel to make a different choice when he began feeling any defensiveness with Jose. He could make a different choice based on what he had learned from his interactions with his daughter and his own personal growth, and that seemed to help the situation too.

Years later, when it was clear to Jose that he simply had let go of much of the anger with his father, Miguel asked his son what, if anything, made the difference. Jose could not really point to any one thing that Miguel or anyone else had done. But he felt like lots of the anger and hurt had melted away through the discussion, empathic listening, and his father's apologies. He also was happy to be there living with his father, finally spending some close daily time with him. If anything, the apologies Miguel made to Jose touched him the most. Feeling the sorrow in his dad's heart helped him open his own heart and let things go.

Miguel also could not identify any single significant event, process, or interaction that was directly related to this change. He could not help but wonder, however, whether the changes he had been making in his own life were not influencing the positive changes and more loving responses he was experiencing with his son. They may not be the "cause" of the change. Who would ever know what that was, or even if there was a "cause" for such an effect?

There were several things that Miguel felt were important, however. For one thing, Miguel simply was less reactive and better at listening to what people had to say, including his children, without taking everything personally. He could keep his heart open in the face of hearing about his son's hurt and anger, and that seemed to help him listen empathically. He had been working on being more aware of multiple influences occurring rather than looking for single issues or causes, realizing that things often are more complex than how they first appear. Even more importantly, he felt like he had more choice in his responses, able to not get caught up in defensiveness, hurt, anger, guilt, and resentment. This allowed him to hear more of what his son was saying and feel the difficulty his son might have been experiencing without wrapping it all up in his own feelings and reactions. He also could be more present and loving with his son, even knowing that his son had some anger. Miguel knew he could feel both love and anger, even at the same time. So it was no longer an either/or situation when someone was not happy with him in his life. While such reactions from his children may have been the most challenging, given that they were very important in Miguel's life, he had been working with others to create such change. Now he seemed better able to carry that out in his closest relationships.

Miguel, who had committed to spend more time with Jose when he first moved in with him, now reached out even more to enjoy the activities that were most important to his son. That did not mean that there were no more conflicts or hurts. Later, when family and friends were around, Miguel did some care-taking with his daughter, which ended up impacting an activity Jose had planned. Jose was both angry and hurt. But now, both of them could process it directly without as much old hurt interfering in their communications. Miguel, who realized what he had done, could go to Jose and apologize immediately. Jose also then could see that there was no real intentional hurt by his dad, and he could trust and believe in his dad's sincerity without going to a place of, "Oh, here we go again!" Of course, it was important for Miguel not to keep doing the same things over and over again. And it was important for Jose to let things go, rather than holding onto old pains. They could be more in the present moment without carrying around the old hurts from 20 years ago.

People began to notice the difference. Sophie and Joseph's mother both commented independently on the changes they saw and felt without anything being said out loud. Both Jose and Miguel, when they later talked about the change, were able to express the joy both felt with the transformation. They also talked about feeling lighter, happier, and more alive, which is what others had been noticing too. They both knew that given their strong personalities, they may have another disagreement or hurt. But they also knew they would figure out a way to resolve it and that both cared enough about the relationship and each other to find some resolution. After Jose and his family moved back to their former state, Miguel continued to visit and talk with him. And when Jose had a difficulty with Maria's family, it was Miguel he called first to discuss it.

Healing Older Relationships

The above cases are reports about actual relationships, although some details have been changed to protect the people involved. These are not intended to be models or ideal ways of healing in relationships, but simply examples of ways two parents have tried to explore a method of creating change that at the core they knew was important. They did not have a lot to guide them except their intuition and desire for healing, key elements, I believe, in mending relationships with children. It is listening, trusting, and following such information that is key.

A third element that I also think is central is the willingness to really hear the other person without moving into a defensive, protective posture. We can keep love central to the conversations and interactions, caring as much about the other person as the process and the impact on yourself, while maintaining a connection between the two hearts.

In the last chapter, I mentioned that it is never too early to begin the healing process in relationships with young children. At the same time, I suggest that it is never too late to work at healing a relationship with older children either. David worked with his 14-year-old daughter, while Miguel changed the relationship with his 27-year-old son. I know of adult children who have experienced healing with a parent who was on their death bed. And that process was beneficial, seemingly to both participants, even later in life.

When this healing happens, no matter at what stage it occurs in life, it seems to release contractions and a heaviness in the body that allows for a greater lightness of being, a freer state. People can experience an expansiveness of their bodies that can create a feeling like they literally weigh less in this gravitation pull of the earth. I have worked with my own children to do this, and it still comes up at times, even in to their 30s and 40s. As far as I know, there is no statute of limitations on apologies and telling someone you are sorry, speaking directly from the heart. The importance here is about opening the heart, working from your intuitive sense of how to connect and move hurts out of the way while avoiding the disconnect through a defensive posture. This is the essence, it seems to me, for healing relationships at any time in our lives.

One thing that can help is for us, as adults, to continue our own work and take responsibility for our choices. When we increasingly see and understand that our reactions are about us, not someone else, then we can explore what is or was going on that led to our choices and reactions, especially with children. I think both David and Miguel point this out in their descriptions of healing the relationships with their children.

At the same time, we as children also take on issues or information from our parents and families, often making it personal in our lives. When David became aware of his father's stress and overwhelm when he was born, he took that on as a child, developing a belief that he was not wanted. Then he seemed to pass that pattern on with his daughter. This issue was about David's father, not him. The issue was with David, not Meg. Separating that out and letting parents experience their difficulties and own their hurts rather than passing them along is an important part of the healing process. When they do transfer to others, finding ways to make an apology and any amends also is important in healing relationships.

What is important is not taking things personally, as Ruiz points out.[2] We can take responsibility for our stuff, our hurts, our pains, and our contractions, which lead to our reactions with others, even when they are the ones so lovingly pointing out our issues by triggering them. Other people may be the triggers, but, as adults, the pains we feel are things we still are holding onto inside us from early experiences. There triggers typically do not begin with us as adults. These things are about us, our own hurts and history, the things we have not yet healed inside our own being. When we get triggered by someone and go looking for the issue and hurt we still are holding, we are more likely to be able to release it and heal in the process. As we do this, we are better able to help our children do the same thing, whether they are younger or older. It brings us closer to others, and it lessens the likelihood of being triggered the same way in the future.

As our hurts and triggers belong to us, other people's reactions are about their own hurts as well. This is why Ruiz encourages us to not taking things personally. While people may project such issues on to us whenever they have a difficulty seeing them, that does not make them our issue. Even if we trigger hurts in others, those pains are still not something that typically began with our stimulating the response. This is why two people can have the same interaction with someone else but have very different reactions in the process.

Let me give you an example. After moving to Napa Valley, I joined with a group of people who would get together to work on projects, have social gatherings, and spend time consciously connecting with one another. There was one man in our group that I found particularly irritating to me. Given that I am so good with my judgments, I could see all sorts of things that were "wrong" about him and that I did not like. Yet he was liked by many in our group. I kept wanting him to change so that I could like him better. I really liked his wife, who loved him dearly.

But it was a challenge for me to see what she so loved about him, and yet I trusted her own assessment of people to such an extent that I knew I was missing something. And yet, I kept finding things from my own interactions and observations that keep me from ever enjoying him or at times even liking him. At the same time, we both had attended workshops at the Human Relations Institute, where they teach a process of clearing. If something is in the way from opening our hearts to another person, we keep working to let go of it in order to experience more love and closeness with another person. I had used this process with other people and found it valuable, but with him it seemed impossible, especially since I did not "trust" his response.

Early one morning, I woke up and realized that the judgments, pain, and upset I was holding on to with this man were only hurting me, as I kept holding these contractions in my body. I knew they were not doing me any good. I committed to get clear what was going on inside me that I was not seeing, what he was triggering in *me*. We had a mutual friend who also would get upset with him at times, but at the same time she loved and admired many things he did. Most of the time, I was unable to see very little that I viewed as positive about him. Increasingly, I was clear that there was something I was not seeing in me, a piece that was difficult for me to identify and love about myself. I started spending lots of time meditating and processing this question, looking into internal hiding places I apparently did not want to see before now. The challenge sometimes is that we hide such information so deeply that it can be difficult to find later.

It took me quite a while to get clear about my projections on to this man, and it came in pieces rather than all at once. Eventually, I saw what I had been hiding, not wanting to see about myself. This man sometimes would lead groups, and I kept judging him as not highly competent in this area. I kept looking for what he was doing wrong. Over time, I realized that he was in a position of teaching that I had wanted all my life and had experienced for only a short time. I realized I was jealous of his situation, and it was something I wanted to have for myself. Once I got clear about that, I sat down with him and a mutual friend, for I was not sure I would be able to own my stuff sufficiently to avoid getting into a defensive posture with him. Just having the friend there, someone I admired and trusted, helped me stay in my heart. I shared with this man "my stuff," my jealousy and judgments (not all the specifics about judgments, but just that I had them). Then I looked him in the eyes, opened my heart even more, and apologized for projecting this stuff onto him. And he thanked me for my apology.

At a later date, he ended up apologizing for a part he played in it too. Afterwards, I felt lighter and more at peace. I was happy for letting go of the projections and getting clear what I was hiding, seeing what I wanted in my life that he represented, and had resented for having it. As our connection has continued, we have increased are enjoyment and ease with each other.

At another gathering when he was in charge once again, I was able to watch him make a magical decision with a participant and following the energy in the room. I never would have suspected he could have done that before, and I probably would not have allowed myself see it as positively. At that point, I was able to complement him honestly on the process afterwards. It feels so much better not to hold the bitterness and criticism, but rather be lighter with him and in myself.

This man triggered my jealousy, but he did not generate it. Such a feeling was inside long before I met him, especially my desire to have a teaching situation that he had developed for himself. He only shined the light on my issue and let me look at it in such a way as to lessen it inside myself. Once I realized what I was feeling and projecting, I could let go of that desire. By this point in my life, my major priorities and shifted. This was a left- over desire that I did not even realize I still was holding so strongly.

Conclusion

When we increase our awareness to see, work on, and release these pains, that is a central part of our healing process. When we apologize to children for not helping them understand that our issues are about us, it helps them not take them on or to release these contractions if they have internalized them already. Children want to help and sometimes they take these issues on as if such aspects are about them. They can use this as a type of loyalty towards a parent when a child, even unasked, adopts such issues.

When we can apologize and heal the connection, these internal contractions and pains are less likely to interfere in our relationships. Loosening those contractions and removing the energetic blocks seems to be a key in the healing process. And we keep working here, for children sometimes need help understanding what is theirs and what is ours. This is where a healing relationship can be so central to them, whether they are very young or old, even grown adults. For the cognitive process and the egocentric period of young children can imagine all sorts of power and possibilities. They can use our support in clearing these out early in life, separating and clarifying ownership by loving adults who help them see who they are without taking on the baggage and pains of their parents.

If we can help them do this while they are young, that is great. If we can help them do it when they are older, it also is useful and still very healing, especially in relation to their children, literally, symbolically, and metaphorically. For we all are in this together. Whether it is my own biological or adopted children I am helping, or the children of those close to me or in my community, healing affects us all. I believe there are no time and space limits on healing, which may be part of the new physics argument by Lanza and Berman.[3] It just may be that time and space do not have real existence outside of our perceptions. And thus, our perceptions, and the changing of those in ourselves and in our children, become a major factor in our well-being and the healing processes of our relationships.

CHAPTER 11

A NOUSSENTRIC APPROACH
TO OTHER SETTINGS

With Contributions by Jean A. Metzker, Ph.D.

YOUR EYES FIRST

A lover has four streams inside,
of water, wine, honey, and milk.

Find those in yourself and pay no attention
to what so-and-so says about such-and-such.

The rose does not care
if someone calls it a thorn, or a jasmine.

Ordinary eyes categorize human beings.
That one is a Zoroastrian, that one a Muslim.

Walk instead with the other vision given you,
your eyes first. Bow to the essence
in a human being. Do not be content
with judging people good and bad.
Grow out of that.

The great blessing is that Shams
has poured a strength into the ground
that lets us wait and trust the waiting.

- Rumi[1]

    I have talked about how parents might assist children in holding onto and encouraging their gifts as well as healing relationships in order for all involved to experience more peace and allow love to flourish in their lives. While parents and close family members often are the first to touch a child's life in an ongoing way, they certainly are not the only ones to impact their futures. Teachers can have a strong influence as they work with children from preschool through college. In addition, neighbors, counselors, therapists, social workers, and medical personnel also can have a strong impact on the lives of children and adolescents, especially when they become involved in state or local agencies working with children's issues or have medical challenges over an extended period of time. In this chapter, I want to talk about some possible means that other professionals might utilize to expand the ways they could positively influence the lives of young people.

The suggestions I make here are not just random ideas pulled out of the blue. They are based in part on the observational research I began working on with Jean Metzker nearly 20 years ago, following a sample of infants and young children over a period of two years.[2,3] These suggestions also are based on our later observational work with parents and adolescents.[4,5] In addition, these ideas continues to build upon the work by many others in relation to children's hypothesized skills, energy fields, and the subtler ways we impact each other.

All Professionals

Some time ago, I was having a conversation with one of my teachers, Lansing Barrett Gresham, about what characteristics were most important for new parents. Without any hesitation, he said "presence."[6] I was aware of many attributes of good parenting from the literature I had both studied and where I had down some writing.[7] But that was not one that had been introduced much into the scientific literature about quality parenting. As I thought about it more and more, focusing on my own experiences of when I felt close to others and when others talked about feeling close to me, I realized I agreed with him. The issue of presence is very important, although difficult to measure in scientific work. But again, until we ask the questions and begin to look beyond those elements that we can more easily measure, we will not develop measures, instruments, or observation techniques to detect important characteristics.

As you think back, how many times have you have been interacting with others when they did not really feel present in their bodies? People often notice a discomfort with such a situation, even when they are not clear or cannot describe the exact reason for the uneasy feeling they experience. They may not put their experience into words. Another important question is how often have you been interacting with others when you have not really been present with them? I do not know of any scientific investigations addressing this issue, but I suspect, and you might agree, that interaction when people are energetically and emotionally present is much more comfortable and enjoyable than when they are not, when their body and energy are incongruent. If you are aware of energy and/or presence, begin to notice how often people are fully present with you. See if you feel congruence with their physical body and energetics in contrast to when their physical body is there, but they are not really present energetically. Notice when you are fully occupying your body or not present in your own interactions, and see which you prefer.

One way to pay attention is experiencing the difference when you are feeling in love with someone, fully in your body and aware of what is going on from head to toe. At times when you are with someone and don't want to be there, you are bored, or you are thinking about some other place, you most likely are not really energetically present in your body.

Often people prefer not to be present during conflicts, which is one reason we may go away energetically. Not being energetically present is a good way to defend ourselves, especially from the discomfort and pain that can occur during these interactions, which is one reason we like to avoid them. Such a defense of not being fully present may be useful for our own protection, but they tend not to be useful in solving a conflict or disagreement with a child or other loved ones. Such absence may add to or fuel the conflict without really intending to do so, for presence, from my experience, has a way of calming a situation for myself and others.

In our research with families, we would observe people shifting their energy backwards away from others when there was conflict or when they would appear upset. Again, they may not even be aware of a change, but such a shift still happens. This shift may affect others during an interaction and seems to impact their reports of feeling close.[4,5] Being present also seems to help us access resources and options that may facilitate resolving conflicts rather than continuing or escalating it. For when we are fully present and congruent, we may access information within ourselves or create ideas that we otherwise may not be able to retrieve. In addition, our feelings may change and both people may talk more from their heart, shifting the interactions.

Again, from my experience at least, I have much more difficulty being in my heart and speaking from there when I am not energetically present with myself. I find it easier to access other options and possibilities to resolve a difference when I am present and in my heart. We also begin to teach our children the same pattern of defense, and so they too learn to not be present and be more defended, wondering why we have difficulties solving family differences.

What is particularly important in this context is our energetic presence with children, especially new born infants and young children. It is the sharing of energy/information that is easier for infants, as described by the man in Russia who communicated with a newborn during his near-death experience. And the easiest way to tell when people are energetically present is by paying attention to the subtler levels of consciousness. At subtler levels, we can access other information, including the qualities of energetic presence.

Infants do not have the verbal language to communicate with us, although most infants begin to pick up word meanings as well as gestures and intonation rather quickly, especially with sign language. But some of their first reliance may well be on information at subtler levels, where they seem to be more experienced, focused, and living in the present moment. While we are versed in language and the physical plane, they seem to be versed in picking up information using the "3rd eye" or 6th Chakra.[2,3] Which skills are more likely to pick up the energetic presence of another person? It seems increasingly difficult to argue that infants cannot determine when people are energetically present. And how do you think you might feel as an infant going through dramatic changes with adults who are energetically present compared to those who are not, especially if infants are feeling any stress and are more sensitive? Do you think babies would feel more comfortable and reassured, feeling more "trust and support" from people who are not even aware that energetically they are not home in their body?

This is not meant to make anyone feel bad or wrong about what we probably all have done at times in the past with infants and adults. But rather, these issues are to point out and empha-size the importance of parents, other caregivers, and other pro-fessionals paying more attention to being present and making such a choice, especially when we are with infants (as well as before birth) where language is less central. For as energy moves by intention, then being present, once we become aware of ener-getic absence, becomes a choice. We stay committed, especially when we are around and touching infants, to make ourselves present in our interactions with them. This allows us not only to express the trust and support we want them to feel, but also to access information about them and their needs in order to help them more completely. It also allows the infant to feel constant support, both physically and energetically.

In other cultures, for example, parents are more likely to know the timing of bodily functions of infants, including urina-tion. In these cases, "accidents" are less likely to happy. Such awareness probably is not that critical when infants are in dia-pers. The significant issue here is the ability of parents to know what is happening with infants when it is not obvious, which seems to happen most often when parents who are closely bond-ed with infants and accessing information at a different level.

In this case, it really is the parent who is the "expert" about what is happening with their infant, at least in terms of symp-toms and issues, rather than the "professional." Parents still need help to find solutions and alternatives from others, but their intu-itive sense of what is going on may well be pivotal in finding appropriate solutions when they are paying close attention to it. Holding on to such information also may be important for par-ents to do, even when dismissed by a professional, which some-times can happen. As professionals, we also may need to treat parents as informed, just as parents may not want to dismiss their infant's own "knowing" and consciousness.

This feeling of being present not only is pleasant to experi-ence from others, but as people become more comfortable and it becomes more common in our lives, most people report that it feels good to do for themselves. For an infant, presence provides a supportive environment for development and encourages chil-dren to follow the same process, being present all the time. Ba-bies seem to do that naturally, until they have encountered ex-tremes of stress, fear, and/or violence. Pay attention and feel how present babies are, excited about exploring their bodies and envi-ronment. At the same time, babies typically learn from what they see and experience in their environment. So if children experience adults who typically are not really present with them, they typically will learn to do the same. They also will learn to carry out their life using a vacant body that just acts and does things rather than being fully present in their body energetically and in their experience. They will learn to interact and develop relationships where they are present physically but not present emotionally or energetically.

More importantly, most people create some meaning to the experience of another's being absent energetically. For example, we may begin to feel unloved, unimportant, not worthy of love, insignificant, or even unlovable. What are the feelings or meanings that came up or that you experience in your body when another person withdraws their energy? These and other meanings are what people report when they re-experience such times in their lives. But what ever the label or meaning applied to the experience, we have never had someone report anything "positive" from such an experience. They primarily report on judgments of being "bad," often combined with a feeling of rejection. So when the infant's physical cognition develops and begins to combine with the conscious experiences, such meanings are placed retroactively on these experiences. And as we are increasingly aware, such experiences have impacts on our bodies and physical health. It can increase our stress, which can affect our immune system and other physical aspects, such as restrictions in our blood vessels. In this way, starting our lives with higher stress can reduce our health and quality of life from the beginning. In addition, it can assist in the creation of negative views and belief systems of ourselves, even when there is no intention to do so. For intention is only a small piece of how such meanings affect our lives.

Parents and Teachers

Another important aspect of presence is for parents and teachers to be aware of when children are energetically present with them. This is especially important when parents or teachers are tying to teach some idea or concept to a child. When children are not totally present, in the moment, it can be difficult for them to pay attention and learn. Having a negative reaction may not be the best way to get them to pay attention or be more present. But a loving touch, a smile, or doing some relaxing, physical activity may help them get back into the present moment and their bodies energetically in order to pay closer attention. Again, it may be important for parents and teachers to make sure they are present first, inviting a child to follow suite and do the same rather than trying to get them to do what we do not do.

Paying attention to the energetic interactions between children is an important source of information for parents and teachers, whether with siblings at home, friends visiting, or children in a classroom. Noticing and stopping any energetic "bullying," or aggressive energetics can be as important as verbal and behavioral aggression. In fact, the energetics may be a preview of what is happening at other times verbally or behaviorally. This would be especially important with young children, who may be even more sensitive to the energetic dynamics of older children and adolescents. This period also is a time when interaction patterns develop with young children. Learning to withdraw from energetic as well as physical bullying can create patterns that stimulate less personal and environmental trust, which is not helpful to healthy development. Thus, recognizing such interactions and being aware of energy interactions going on between children can be essential for providing support, especially when children may not be as forth coming with verbal revelations of their actions. This is a way to have a better sense of what is occurring, especially at the energetic level.

While some suggest we can learn to see energy fields quite easily,[8,9] it is not always a simple process for all of us to learn such skills. At the same time, we know that the same frequencies can be assessed through either sight or feeling, basically obtaining the same information.[10] Energy fields are vibrational information that is subtler than the physical, yet one can "feel" the same vibrational information that others "see." For those who do not "see" these fields, we can access them by becoming more sensitive to feeling what is occurring. For example, I have not been able to learn to see the different colors and clear dynamics in energy fields. So I have learned to rely more on the feelings I get about fields. When I compare them to what people see in the field, we essentially access the same information, including colors surrounding a person.

Paying attention to the energy fields is not just about seeing colors or auras, but more importantly paying attention to the dynamics of the field. When people communicate and interact with others, our fields often respond to such verbal and emotional exchanges if not lead them.[4,5] If a teacher is talking with a parent and child, for example, one may get a sense of closeness by paying attention to the interactions and responses in the field, both in relation to the professional as well as between the two family members. This can provide useful clues and information as another way to know what is going on within and between people. Learning to trust what we pick up may be the critical aspect to practice for many of us.

When one begins to pay attention to energy field dynamics, I find it useful to see how connections are made between children in a family or a classroom. In this way, parents and teachers can have another source of understanding the family or class dynamics and what relationships are like. Teachers also get can another sense of what is going on between children and when the energetics and language are not congruent. Children, for example, may say they like another person when their energetics are saying they are not as close or that there is some conflict with another child. Again, this is a way to access additional sources of information to get a more complete picture of relationships and interactions between people.

Counselors and Therapists

In addition to parents and teachers, energetic presence is essential when counselors, therapists, psychologists, or psychiatrists are conducting work with a client or patient. I know from experience how easy it is to have so much energy focused in the head and brain, in order to observe, process, and pay attention to details in a session. I can easy avoid being totally present in my body and especially in my heart. On the other hand, the connection and relationship with the counselor or therapist is a key ingredient of success in the therapeutic treatment.[11] I find it hard to imagine that the relationship is as good if the therapist is not energetically present in the body and heart with a client during that process. Like other professionals, it could be interesting to look back at when one has been as energetically present or not as present, seeing if the process of therapy was more successful when fully present in contrast to instances when the counselor is not energetically available. One's impact may be as strong, but it is hard for me to conceive of it, having experienced therapy both as a therapist and a client.

In a recent session with one of the best therapists I have experienced as a client, one of the things I noticed about him was his strong energetic presence and tracking. He not only focused strongly on the words, but he also paid close attention to what was going on beneath them and what felt like was occurring energetically between my partner and myself. I think the quality of his work was directly related to his apparent energetic presence and tracking.

When one is working with more than one family member or in a group process, it also seems important to identify the energetic reactions that occur when family members make comments, even pulling away or reaching out energetically to another family or group member. While language, physical, and nonverbal information is all very important in understanding what occurs in groups and families, the energy field dynamic provides another important source of information typically not accessed consciously or intentionally by most professionals, including family therapists and other counselors or psychologists. Many professionals get a "feel" for some things going on in families or groups, which may well be a part of the energy field dynamic. But they may not be accessing the information in a more conscious or intentional manner. Thus, it is quite likely that therapists could increase these abilities, like other therapeutic skills, such as paying closer attention to nonverbal communication and underlying meanings in communication, common skills developed in the family therapeutic training process. The accessing and incorporating energetic dynamics may be a useful element for therapists to begin accessing in a more systematic way.

In addition to elements of energy fields dynamics, there are other related aspects that may have direct application to the therapeutic process. Such elements include understanding when and under what therapeutic circumstances people go away or leave the setting energetically, even when remaining there physically. Such information could be especially useful during conflictual interactions. It also could be useful to pay attention to what people are doing energetically that may be different or even in conflict with what they are saying and doing physically. Just as words and behaviors often are not always congruent, both of these aspects of our lives can be incongruent with our energetic responses. Looking at these areas of congruence or incongruence also could be an important source of additional therapeutic information.

Finally, it may be useful to begin to see where people are holding energetic experiences, contractions, or hurts in the field or body. While we may not be able to know everything about a contraction or hurt in the field, it may be an important topic of conversation, something the individual is not even aware of in the present moment. Thus, some exploration around the issue may not only be helpful for the client, but it also may help release an aspect of their past that is not in their conscious awareness, possibly healing relationships with others in the family. Discussing such topics in groups or families also may assist in sharing past hurts, experiences, or interactions that could lead to healing not just in the individual but with others who share such experiences or were part of the interaction within a family setting.

Medical Professionals

Similar to therapists, it may be useful for medical professionals to pay attention to energetic presence, both their own and that of their patients. When a patient is in fear about a medical procedure already, it may undermine any verbal reassurance if professionals are not very present in their own bodies. It may have more of a reassuring impact when a professional is trying to support and assure a patient that everything will be fine when they are both present and in their own hearts during difficult interactions. This is not only important for physicians doing the medical procedure, but also for nurses and staff in assisting or when giving the ongoing care and comfort that is important in the healing process. Like therapists, relationships with clients are an important part of trust and healing, and presence enhances such connections.

Life threatening situations are very difficult times for patients as well as medical professionals, for many times these can include life and death discussions. It can be a real challenge to stay present during the many intense discussions that can occur during a day. And yet, at least for a short time when the issue is critical, it may be helpful for professionals to take a minute and be totally present for these interactions to help a patient feel their full support, especially during very sensitive discussions. It may even be interesting for medical professionals to pay attention to how conversations go when they are totally present in contrast to when they realized that they had not been present. Notice if there may be a different impact on patients when professionals bring their full presence to a very difficult interaction rather than tending to protect themselves by absenting themselves from the energetic intensity.

Again, like parents and teachers, it also may be useful for medical personnel to have a sense of the energy dynamics of a patient. It may help professionals have more information about how a patient is doing or when they are having difficulty, even if not verbally reported by the patient. This process can gather information at another level and a different source so that they have as much diverse information as possible to assess all they can about a patient. I realize this is not a common area of assessment, but it also may be an important one that is overlooked by professionals because we simply have ignored or dismissed the whole area of energetics.

Another area particularly relevant for medical professionals is to be open to and even ask some of the avoided questions or listen to clues of other things that may be or have been going on with patients that may be difficult for patients to share, especially children. Such things as near-death experiences or even experiences patients are having when in an altered state may be an important part of the conversation with medical staff that have been discouraged or discounted in the past. These are important, sometimes life altering experiences for people, and it can be very helpful for people to be open to listening and understanding these events, knowing the impact they may have in a patient's life.[12,13]

The possibilities suggested here are not necessarily easy, especially when professionals have so many other things to consider. I realize that "yet one more thing" may be challenging to consider and accept. Still, I think it is important to begin the discussion and identify aspects of our connections and interactions that may influence clients and patients already. These ideas also may facilitate more comprehensive information gathering and more positive outcomes if they are included in the mix. I point these out for consideration by professionals who may want to expand the way they work with children and families in the future.

CHAPTER 12

DEVELOPING A NOUSSENTRIC FUTURE

THE LOVE RELIGION

The inner space inside
that we call the heart
has become many different
living scenes and stories.

A pasture for sleek gazelles,
a monastery for Christian monks,
a temple with Shiva dancing,
a kaaba for pilgrimage.

The tablets of Moses are there,
the Qur'an, the Vedas,
the sutras, and the gospels.

Love is the religion in me.
Whichever way love's camel goes,
that way becomes my faith,
the source of beauty, and a light
of sacredness over everything.

- Ibn Arabi[1]

Imagine moving to a new country, one that is not familiar at all to you. The people there speak a "foreign" language, so you do not understand the words. Envision the possibility that you are unable to move your own body for whatever reason. You are totally dependent on these people with whom you do not share the ability to express your thoughts through words. At the same time, what if you really had nowhere to go and nothing you needed to do? You were not hungry and did not have to go to the bathroom. You were adequately warm and feeling quite comfortable. Add to that a sense of curiosity, of wonderment about who these people are and what they are doing. You might have a general sense or could feel that they care about you, even if they cannot express that idea through language. At times, you might even find them interesting or fun to watch. You may try to interact with them, despite you not being able to share words with them. If you have a sense of caring from these "strange" people, you may not worry or even feel some connection to them. At the same time, such huge changes also can be exhausting, and you may find yourself sleeping more just to recover from the transition.

In many ways, this is how infants enter the lives of parents, grandparents, friends, and professionals. Adults provide support during this time of transition, but the verbal interactions are limited. How should we respond to this kind of event? What are our desires as we enter this new phase of life, in many cases being so responsible for another living being? What are the essential pieces we want to incorporate as a newborn infant begins this journey of life with us?

The Future is Present

After reading the previous 11 chapters, would you see infants and children in a different way or be curious about how you might interact with an infant that you had not considered previously? How would you gather information about this new one, using any senses beyond your sight and sound? Do you feel any connection to them beyond the physical holding in your arms? Is there any more going on with the infant beyond what you experience from your five basic senses? Have you begun exploring other ways to connect and interact with young children that you have not used previously?

One of the things you might try is to initiate an energy connection with this infant. This is something I now play with whenever I have a chance to hold a newborn child, or even as they get older. Again, energy follows intention. So you do not have to be an "expert" in working with energy to create such links. Just intend or even pretend to make a loving connection, possibly extending from your heart to theirs. And if infants or

243

young children do experience such connections, they might enjoy such a loving energetic embrace.

While you are making such an energetic relationship, it also might be fun to try including a loving "hello" and "welcome" as a part of your interaction. Imagine how it might feel if you were a stranger in a new land and you were able to understand that people were so pleased to see you and welcoming you to this new environment. It may be an interesting and creative way to interact with this newborn or young child who does not yet understand the verbal interactions that we share with them. They may, however, understand the intention and energetic communications we share. You might play with making infants as welcoming and loving as you can imagine, even if you think they may not understand it. You could pretend that they do understand and treat them that way. Would there really be any harm in that? And it might be fun for you too as well as expanding your own heart opening.

If you want to take it a little further, you might pretend you could communicate without words, paying attention to what thoughts you are sharing with infants and what they might be communicating back to you. You could consider how you would want an infant or young child to experience your energy field if they could do so. What is your field like, and how would others experience it? Are there things in your field you would not want to pass along to others that you might consider removing? There is a fair amount of evidence supporting the idea of energy fields, including fairly sophisticated devices to measure them and identify differences. We used a machine to compare younger children and older adults, including those who work with their energy and fields in a systematic way.[2]

If you want to go a little deeper, you might also make a connection from your essence to theirs. Again, you do not have to know or agree with these ideas to play with them. You could explore or pretend that they are true and just experiment with them, paying attention to what you feel like as you do it and whether you have any sense of reciprocity from the infant or young child when you investigate these skills. If you could communicate, what would you want to say and what would you want to know from them?

If the infant is uncomfortable, what would the infant want to communicate with you about her or his problem? If you could use some telepathic communication, if you both were able to do it, how might that occur, and what would be the most important messages that would be shared? You might just use your imagination as to the kind of communication that would take place and play with that, finding out what would be most important for you to share as well as learn from the infant or child. It also might be informative to pay attention to your heart after such interactions and see if there is a positive impact on yourself from such interactions.

Could you go beyond the basic question of how they are feeling or what they need? What would the essence of an infant want to share with you and you with her or him? You might try to connect more with their intention for being here. Do they have a life purpose? If so, what things might you do to support their lesson, action, and manifestations?

While these abilities seem quite foreign to most of us, scholars are finding increasing numbers of people who describe this ability, especially when in an altered state. Weiss and Weiss report many different clients describing these abilities in different ways, all suggesting that we have had this ability inside us all along.

> Every one of us possesses intuitional abilities and powers far beyond what we know....If we do not follow our intuition we create obstacles and opposition, and oftentimes this can be dangerous. But if we follow our heart, we flow with the process, we do not force or block, much like the Taoist principle of *wu wei*. Spiritual beings strive to understand and flow with the process not struggle with it....When in doubt, choose from the heart, not from the head....We actually are all psychics and mediums. We all possess incredible extrasensory talents that our ego and logical mind keep hidden from us....We are capable of using channels far beyond the usual five senses. We are designed to connect with each other at levels much deeper and more detailed that we can begin to imagine....Spiritual messages can transcend the usual senses and be received in many ways. They do not require words or language.[3]

It would be a very difficult challenge not to play the game of Buy My Perspective with children. Yet, it may be helpful to children if you kept checking in with their own intuitive knowing and sense of purpose along the way. We could help them pay attention to what they know inside, supporting them to check in about an issue or decision they face, even with less important situations while they are young. Rather than simply directing them to do as they are told, which is usually much easier for us, we could investigate what they are sensing and feeling. And when they present us things out of the ordinary, try to avoid dismissing them.

We cannot always give choices to them, especially when a decision would be dangerous or deadly. Yet I know from experience with my own children, I certainly could have given them many more options and supported their process of choosing more than I did. My adult offspring and their spouses give their children a lot of choices, even when they are not always comfortable with them. One in particular will live with very divergent choices of what her youngest daughter wants to wear, even if it may be create judgment by others when taking her out in public.

One day, I took one granddaughter who had a particularly interesting choice of clothing to the bank with me. She had on colors that would clash, socks that did not match, and, as I recall, a tutu. At age 3, that was her choice. I hesitated at first, thinking "this is a bank, a fairly conservative business." Then I decided if that is what she wanted to wear and her mother did not care, why should I? It was amazing not only the number of smiles I saw at the bank from different customers and employees, but the number of compliments she and I both received for our choices. Sometimes children and grandchildren really do help us get out of our own way, learning important lessons we forgot along the way of what is most important to us.

I continue to practice this focusing on their inner guidance with my grandchildren, still learning this process myself. I know how challenging it is to be patient with children when we are rushed or pressured to make choices quickly and efficiently with so much going on in our lives. But as a daughter-in-law recently pointed out to me, is not this time with children some of our most important? We never want to lose someone close to us, and the loss of a child or grandchild can be devastating. Such loss is one of the most difficult, sad, and stressful times in people's lives. So I want to take every opportunity possible to savor these moments with children, living more in the present as they are able to do so well.

I have been very lucky so far not having to experience the death of a child myself, luckier than both my sister and brother. Having experienced death close to me, as well as friends and clients around me, I have a sense of how hard it is. Would we not want to live with as few regrets as possible? If such a tragedy did happen, would we not want to live in a way that would give us the most peace and joy for what ever time they lived? And if we were never to lose a child or grandchild, would we not want to live in such a way that they look back and cherish the times we supported and spent loving time with them, creating fond memories with them?

I tried to provide tender memories with my children by taking them on trips to different places. But I was not so patient in my everyday life with them when they were young. And, as one daughter-in-law reminded me so lovingly not long ago, I have another chance to do it differently with my grandchildren. My kids are very capable at guiding them and setting up any rules they feel necessary. I get to play and have fun with them, giving them some cherished moments that they can remember when they think of me after I am gone. That is more joyful than worrying about appropriate behavior, other than to look out for danger while they are with me, and whether they are wearing clothes that others would find appropriate. Such playful times are more enjoyable moments for me too now, including my support of their own intuitive actions and opportunities to make choices in their everyday lives.

Opening to New Opportunities

I found a very interesting book recently just by "chance," one I purchased because of an intuitive hit. It is a book by Matthew MacKay entitled <u>Finding Jordan</u>.[4] This is the story about the author who lost his 23-year-old son, a young man killed suddenly. Matthew is a psychologist and had been focused on both science and reason. Yet the pain of his son's death pushed him to explore alternative communications. He needed to know his son was all right. He did not really believe in intuition or automatic writing. But as he began to explore subtler means of connection, ways appeared that allowed him not only to communicate, but to hold conversations with his son that later turned into this book. Once again, even without believing in the process or having a sense that he could intuitively retrieve information this way, he found that he was able to converse just by allowing himself to access subtler sources of communication. This did not get rid of all his doubt. And yet he persisted, and his skill improved as he learned to trust it more. In the process, as well as from hypnotic regressions he did himself and with others, he learned much about life, other lives, and the time between lives.

> The only thing now standing between us is my own doubt. The doubt visits often, whispering that my conversations with Jordan are wishes rather than truth, and that all he has taught me is a fabrication, my own thoughts attributed to him. When in doubt, I withdraw. I seek him less. I feel frightened that I'll discover something false in what he says, which will destroy my faith in us..... I've learned one more thing about doubt. My need to send Jordan love and feel his love in return is bigger than doubt, bigger than the uncertainty and loneliness of living here without being able to hug my boy.[5]

I so applaud Matthew for following his intuition, especially since accessing subtle information was not a skill on which he relied heavily in his life before his son's death. I also appreciate the vast information about life he shares in the book, reaffirming what others have related in this area, especially the reports from near-death experiences.

Beyond the issue of trusting subtle skills, I have opportunities as a grandparent to consider major choice phases with my children and grandchildren, wanting to expand the possible options in their lives. Parents, teachers, friends, neighbors, and other professionals experience different situations where they can support expanded possibilities for children and adolescents to include subtle choices not normally a part of our everyday living. Any of us can expand the opportunity to exercise the skills infants seem to bring with them, interacting on energetic levels or learning to trust and connect intuitively. This can happen whether in physical proximity to them or not. It even occurs even when they are not on this physical plane, as MacKay found with his son.

I think early choice points are a critical time for supporting such skills, playing with them, whether or not we include verbal

248

interactions along with energetic play. Of course, if we do talk about and verbalize the energetic communications, it also helps to keep such interactions and connections more present and obvious as we nurture these skills. A verbal emphasis can be an added bonus to the energetic connections themselves. Playing with possibilities rather than dismissing or ridiculing them in children also makes our support more clear and obvious.

As infants begin to be able to move on their own and develop language, they also begin to demonstrate their own styles and personality. Good friends of mine found it very helpful to understand the Myers-Briggs description of styles in order to better work with their two boys with much less effort and greater compassion.[6] I also have found that understanding those styles have been helpful working with my own children, although I did not learn that approach until my children were much older.

One approach I did learn while they were younger was the explanation of the Nine types in the Enneagram. This helped me understand possible ways my children approached the world and how I could help them focus more on their essential lesson rather than live from fixation. As I became aware of key challenges they faced, I would suggest ways they could work with these challenges to shift away from their fixated and defended approach and expand their more open-hearted skills. Another way, of course, that also seems to work is simply to help them expand their heart opening, no matter what personality style they had.

My understanding of their particular Enneatype also helped me focus on other suggestions that could facilitate a similar outcome. For example, one of my children whose primary Enneatype is Nine, typically would approach stressful or conflictual situations with humor and direct conflict avoidance. At the same time, his chosen spouse wanted to deal with conflicts directly and wanted him to step up and discuss disagreements. Early in their relationship, he and I talked about my own inability to share what was on my mind and the similarity I saw with his behavior. Because he also was very close to his mother, I also told him that I thought it was one of the reasons that our marriage did not work, and I hoped he would do a better job speaking his mind and talking directly about conflicts than I did with his mother. It took him a while to find his voice. But he has learned to hold his own and speak his truth with his wife, which has helped them both in their relationship. His wife, of course, does not always agree with him. But she is happier about him talking and sharing his point of view, even at times changing her own opinion because he has held his ground, with her own perspective changing to match his at times. He still may use humor with conflict, but he also is more direct at sharing what he is doing rather than keeping everything indirect, the more common pattern of the Nine fixation. Paying attention to his inner discomfort and making a change in how my son deals with it has brought him more peace and happiness in his life and his family.

From my own experience observing others, when adults are happy and peaceful with themselves, it is easier to live from a more open heart. When this happens, it also is much easier to keep the heart open with children. If parents can keep their hearts open under those circumstances, at least the majority of the time, I believe it creates a much more magical and positive relationship with kids. I could give you more examples of this from watching my children with their kids, friends, clients, and others I know as they interact with young people. More importantly, you might look at your own life. Take a few minutes to remember times when your own heart was more open. During those periods, even if they were brief, what was your interactions with others like from your own point of view? Did you enjoy your interactions and yourself more during those times? Were you more relaxed and in the present moment?

One of the places I have a challenge keeping my heart open is while I am driving. I find all sorts of judgements coming out about the way people are driving and how it is wrong! Even when I am in a pretty open place prior to getting into my car, I have a habit of shifting and criticizing people for the choices they make behind the wheel, especially if it interferes with me.

I came home the other day from visiting family who lived out of town and was in a very open-hearted, peaceful place, reflecting on the lovely times I had enjoyed while away. The plane landed, and I quickly found the shuttle, getting back to my care in no time. Everything was going peacefully, and then I turned onto the road to begin driving home. Within minutes, it seems, I was getting upset at one driver after the other. I began looking at myself and how I had experienced what felt like a 180 degree shift in my mood.

Then I remembered a drive I had while I was in Nepal several years ago. The driver was taking me to the airport, with busy traffic all around. I had done sitting, walking, and eating meditations, and so I was familiar with different forms of meditation.

But what I recognized here was a driving meditation he was doing. I knew a little bit about him and knew he was Buddhist. So I asked him, "how long have you been doing driving meditations?" He chuckled for a minute and said, "I have to, otherwise I would just be upset all the time." So while driving on the freeway coming home from he airport, I began to shift back into my own practice of a driving meditation. After a short time, because I try to do this whenever I notice myself getting upset while driving, I was able to shift back towards that peaceful place and let people do what they do on the road. I cannot change their behaviors, and I like my mood so much better as well as the time driving when I make a different choice of how I respond. When I get back into my heart and simply enjoying my own company, I can experience a relaxing drive home. I find it so much easier when I can keep my heart more open and let that be my experience, making a choice of my inner environment. It is particularly helpful when I then come in contact with others important to me, especially my children and dear friends, having a very different interaction with them than when I bring frustration to our conversations. While I cannot choose other people's responses, increasingly I can choose my own, despite choices they make.

Being Love

The biggest challenge I face with others is finding ways to help them see themselves as not just loving but love itself. In fact, this is the most challenging piece I face myself many times. Like any skill and intention, the more we practice, the easier it becomes. When I open my heart and speak from there, I am more likely to find the words to express what I most want to share in the moment. I find I use fewer words and communicate as much from my energetic connections. For speaking from the heart is not just a mental concept, but much more of an emotional and experiential challenge. If I take a minute or even prepare through my driving meditation on the way to an appointment, I show up in a much more open place. I then have a more heartful conversation and connection.

Living from love is an ongoing challenge to even understand, let alone incorporating such an experience into our very being. Yet I believe love is a fundamental aspect of who we are as humans. I remember an incident at age 16 when I had an overpowering experience of love, but I had no context to really understand it until more recently. At that time, I had heard of other people who had prayed and experienced or saw God. I too wanted a personal relationship, a special connection to know that I was loved by Him. So I knelt down and prayed to see God too. I prayed and prayed, and nothing happened for quite some time. I stayed with it, and suddenly I overwhelmed by this powerful energy inside me. I slowly crawled onto my bed and lay there for some time, this loving energy filling my body. I did not "see" anything, so I had no framework or a belief system to help me understand this experience. Because it had some similarity to a sexual orgasm, I did not know how to describe it to anyone. So I chose not to speak about until decades later, and then I have shared it with only a couple of people. It felt like something came to me from externally. After my experience with the altered state and the strong feeling of the love and light energy, I now feel like it was a stimulation of something inside me. As I move back into a very open heart and feel myself as love, there are similarities to that early experience at age 16.

I think it will take some time and continued exploration of this issue for many of us to feel into it more completely and make it a central piece of how we see ourselves. It continues to be a challenge for me at times, especially when I act as if it is not true. Still, I work with the feeling and feel more inner peace when it occurs. I believe that living from this place will fundamentally change our lives and the way we interact with each other when it is a part of how we experience each other and is the foundation of our humanity.

As I continue my own work and develop more skills as an adult, especially in terms of opening my heart and attempting to live more from a place of love, I find ways to interact and share with others that feel more positive and expansive to me. Sometimes I laugh at myself as I see patterns emerging again, and I love the challenge of "playing" with changes rather than always "working" at them. We do not have to take ourselves seriously, and I am learning to laugh at myself when a good friend points out issues I have been ignoring. At times, there also is "relief" when I see something that allows me to change and quit doing the same old thing.

At a gathering of one group of friends I hang out with a lot, we were spending some time going around the circle sharing something about each one in the group where we have been holding back information or a judgment. As it was approaching my turn, I kept thinking about one person in the group that was particularly irritating to be around for me. He was very sure of himself, very big in his energy and his expression, both verbally and physically. And he was usually so damn happy! It had to be fake, and it certainly was irritating to my depressive, self-critical state. I kept thinking about what I was going to say about him when it was my turn. Was I going to tell the truth? And what was my truth about him? I was listening to others and at the same time chewing on this issue. What was it that really bothered me about him?

Suddenly, I realized that I was irritated with him because he felt so comfortable being energetically big and so full of life, a place where I really hold myself back and do not like that about myself. In that moment, everything shifted with him. I realized that instead of being irritated by him, I could use him as a model for letting myself be bigger and more expressive. I did share the truth with him and the others in the circle, apologizing to him for my projections and judgements, even if he was not aware of them. From that moment on, I have enjoyed my interactions with him and often chuckle when around him, figuring out another way I can be more expressive and full in my life, not to mention happier.

Such insights and instantaneous changes used to be rare for me, yet they can happen when we stay with the question and are open to answers. In my experience, it is especially important when asking such questions that we pay attention to the subtle information that comes to us. At those times, I experience both relief and humor rather than work and difficulty. Those are the times that can help us enjoy change and insights, making our life easier rather than more difficult. Yet these moments are just as important at increasing our skills and creating positive changes in our lives as the difficult and challenging times.

Another area that is more challenging still to talk about with my children and others is the topic of sexuality connected to spirituality and consciousness. Even though I feel much freer to discuss such topics, especially after my participation with the Human Awareness Institute (HAI), I continue to find it challenging to find a way to discuss how sexuality can expand our own consciousness. Some of that awkwardness most likely stems from the conservative environment in which I was raised, both culturally and religiously. Yet even with my education in this area, teaching classes, and lots of workshops, I find less opportunity to discuss the connection between these two topics than other aspects. I am quite comfortable in discussions of sexuality itself, but the connection to consciousness or spirituality is somewhat more challenging. When I first thought about writing a chapter for this book on the issue, I immediately felt like that would be crazy. After writing it, I feel better and clearer from the process. I hope such awkwardness is less true for you, and I would love to hear how you or others find ways of connecting and integrating these two central aspects of our lives.

Healing Our Relationships

One of the most important things I believe we can do in exploring this idea of noussentrism is to experiment with ways of healing relationships with children. I mentioned in Chapter 9 ways of trying this with young children energetically, and I find the process fun to do with my youngest grandchildren. I think the energetic and behavioral ways are most useful, although apologizing for things we have done and not done also can be a useful aspect in any relationship. I find this especially true as children get older. When I realized I was being harsh or critical of these loving kids when I was upset about other things, I have tried to sincerely tell them how sorry I was as soon as I realized what I was doing. Unfortunately, some of my insights came when I was not around them, and then there would be extended periods of time if I wanted to do it personally. Fortunately, the phone, Face Time, emails, or a card is another way we can share when not physically present. And there is no statute of limitations on apologies. That is the beauty of healing any relationship at any time. But I think modeling this is important for our young people, both in terms of our apologies and taking responsibility for our actions. We often are quick to push young people to take responsibility for their actions, but sometimes we are not as swift to do it ourselves. I suggest we are clear about asking children to do what we do, not just what we say to them. Such modeling is a much stronger impact on their choices, especially as they get older. But I think it is an important model for children of all ages.

There are several challenges in our work with older children. For one thing, they can see where our words and our behaviors are not congruent. I remember during my own adolescence how I sometimes had no difficulty in pointing that discrepancy out to an adult, not something that usually went over well, especially when I threw in the word, "hypocrite." The positive thing about such observations is that adolescents are looking at this issue, even if it is more often directed at others. Another issue with adolescents is that they can develop strong argumentative skills. Such a skill served me well when I was on the high school debate team, but it was not seen as positively when I used it with my parents! Both of these skills can be very important to young adults, but we often do not appreciate them when we are on the other end of either ability.

One of the things I do with my oldest grandchild (at the time age 14) that I think can be important is to listen to her views of life and people without challenging them directly. First, I find such views both interesting and insightful for understanding how she is looking at important life issues, even when I strongly disagree with them. I also think that her explorations of such things as how relationships work, the problem with politics, religious ideas, and how people stay healthy are important. Instead of "straightening" her out, at least from my point of view, I would raise questions for her to consider. This, I think, is one way for young people to trust our connection, that I will not make her wrong, and that I will listen to and honor her thinking. Talking about it now also gives her some time to express and explore different opinions without staying committed to just one point of view. When I give her some things to think about, to consider, she continues to explore. Yet the final judgment really is hers, especially as she gets older. At the same time, I have watched how her views have evolved, even without my questions. So I do not worry about the current "truth" too much in any one moment.

Luckily, she and her mom also have a very good relationship. Yet we can have some good conversations about things that are not focused on everyday living, on more general topics. These are enjoyable to me, and I get to see the evolution in her thinking as she takes in new information. I think this is one way to have a close connection, and I can support her trust in her own sense of self and her own intuitive processing. We talk about how she makes decisions, and I raise questions that may lead to new perspectives. Her points of view may not be the ones I had in mind, but she still will think about it, in part, I think, because I honor her process.

At the same time, she has ideas I never even considered when I was her age. When I was about 13, a friend and I became very interested in how we might travel through time. We even tried to read some of Einstein's theories, an endeavor that did not last long for me. Even with my former attempted exploration, I was not ready for my granddaughter's observation. As my granddaughter turned 14, she talked about "what if our dreams were our real life, and what we know as our real life was really a dream?" I was shocked when she shared that statement with me. After my initial surprise, I tried to jump into her conversation, loving where her creativity was taking her. In this way, we continue to learn from young people, even if we do not know it as truth or if it is possible. At the same time, I always try to honor her exploration. In that way, I think we support our children being the most that they can be without holding them back with the limits we have developed.

I understand that not all topics of discussion are positive and there are lots of challenges we must address with older children too, especially as they begin to explore aspects of life that are not healthy for them or dangerous in terms of their life choices. What I am suggesting, even then, is that we might keep the ideas presented here as possibilities, even under more challenging circumstances. When children have challenges with anorexia, drugs, alcohol, or fighting, it is important to help them shift their behaviors and patterns. At the same time, honoring aspects of their lives and choices can still may be a very important part of this change process.

I am not dismissing or ignoring all the things infants, children, and adolescents need to learn in order to live well in our societies and in this world. As parents, neighbors, and teachers, we try our best to help them gather information, develop skills, and embark on trainings and professions that will provide them with all they will need to be happy in this life. At the same time, we can expand our own view and enhance their learning to incorporate abilities they bring with them to enlarge the many ways they interact with others and their environment. We can build on some basic elements within themselves to be more expansive with their own interactions and utilize subtle aspects of their lives more consistently. First, we need to know they exist but lie dormant because we do not allow for such possibilities in our own view. We may find it easier and more congruent when we rekindle our own spark in order to nurture the connection they have with their own essence. This is the possibility I am suggesting, not as a fact or truth, but as potential abilities we could incorporate into our model for living if we explore what infants and young children seem to do so easily.

The Giving Game

One way to play with keeping our heart open is to try different experiential exercises. Here is a fun little game that you can play, illustrating how we have been living on this earth in more recent societies. I have shared this game with strangers, but it also could be played with friends or even at an extended family event. It works best if you have at least 10 people to play, and get a bag of a favorite little goodie that can be shared easily. A collection of inexpensive bracelets or trinkets, bags of little candies, such as those on sale for Halloween, or other similar collection of objects that people like and have a little value. If people like the object that you are going to share, it makes the game more interesting. You will need at least 5 pieces per person for this to work well, especially in the third round.

During the first round, have the people number off from 1 to the highest number in the group (i.e., if you have 10 people, number off from 1-10). The numbers should be on a sticky paper or some other object so others can see each person's number easily. Then pass around 5 pieces of the object or goodie you are using for this game, whether it is trinkets, lollypops, or even glow sticks. Each person should start with the same number. Have the people mingle around the group, greeting each other and sharing a short conversation. In this round, the person who meets another person during the interactions who has a higher number then their own must give them one of their objects. If the number is more than half again greater (for example, out of 10 people, a number 1 meets a number 6 or 7), they give them two of their objects. If they meet a person with a lower number than their own, they do not give them anything. After about 5-10 minutes, see how many objects each of the people have in their possession. Then you can spend a little time talking about their experience and how each person feels from their interactions and the gaining or losing of objects.

Then you can start the second round. First, divide the number of objects equally again so that each person has the same number of objects. In this round, people again interact and are free to give or not give any of their objects. If they like the person and feel like this person is "worthy" of receiving an object, then give them one or even possibly two objects. If they are not feeling very close to the person or they do not feel like this person is worthy, then they do not have to give them any of their objects. Again, after about 5-10 minutes, see how many objects each of the people have in their possession. Following the interactions, you again can spend a little time talking about each person's experience in the gaining or losing of objects. Was it similar or different from the first round?

In the third round of this game, once again begin with an equal number of objects for each person. In this round, the objective is to get rid of all of your objects. The winner is the first one to give all of their objects to others (rather than obtaining as many as possible). When each person comes up to another, look them in the eyes and connect with your hearts, then offer this person an object. The other person looks the first one in the eyes and says thank you from the heart. Then they move on to another person, as only one person shares during an interaction. If you started with five objects and the person has three or less, you can offer them two of your objects. Each time, give of yourself as well as the object by connecting and loving that person energetically. After 10 minutes, see how many objects each person has in their possession. Talk again about their experiences with this round, especially in relation to the first two rounds.

When I play this game with people, no one in the third round ever gets rid of their objects because everyone is sharing and getting more than they can give away. In this case, no one can win, and no one can lose. It is in stark contrast to the top of the hierarchy getting more and more while the bottom has nothing (round 1) or the hoarding that can take place in the second round while again, those that are more generous have much less and only those you judge worthy or you like get something from you. With the third round, everyone gains and no one loses everything.

In the past, we primarily have played by the rules of rounds 1 and 2. It is an interesting shift if we were to begin moving from being what Quinn[7,8] described as "Takers" to being more "Leavers." Another way to look at this is a contrast would be between Takers (those that want to collect as much as possible, even hoarding what they have) and Givers (those who want to share what they have with others, focusing much less on the collection of things). This last round of the game is the experience of moving more towards the Giving approach.

I do not set up this contrast as a right and wrong way of being in this world. There is an interesting experience that happens, however, when we move from the first two rounds of this game to the third one. I believe something impacts our hearts with that shift, both with the giving and the receiving in that third round. Try it and see what your experiences are in this game. Last time I organized this game, there were tears in people's eyes from the experience of receiving and giving so much in the third round in contrast to the hurt many experienced in the first two rounds.

Choosing Our Future

I have proposed an expanded idea of infants and young children that begins to shift the way we view them and how they come into this life. I have presented some evidence for these skills, which also may change some of what we know about ourselves as adults. This idea is not entirely new, as many aspects of this perspective have been proposed previously by others in separate descriptions. I am simply putting it together into what I call noussentrism, based on our own previous work[9-12] as well as the work of many, many others. Like most ideas, this work builds on scholars and sages before us as well, including these ideas of who we are as human beings. The fundamental question here is, if we were to follow this approach and implement it in our lives, what might the future look like as a result of such changes?

The changes suggested by many and integrated into noussentrism would begin to create a new world, I believe, and one that is important in our current state of the earth. In this place, we would nurture children's connection to an inner essence, a Higher Self. We would encourage the accessing and integrating of subtle skills and sources of information. We would stimulate more choices being made with the guidance of our intuitive skills, and be more conscious of our energetic interactions. When this happens, we create a world where we shift from separation to connection, from intellect to heartelect, from ideologue to empathologue, and from hurtful to heartful.

One of the things that I believe would happen as an outcome from living this approach is a closer, caring connection with our children free of physical, emotional, mental, and spiritual abuse. We can help them learn about living in the physical environment while also incorporating and trusting the internal gifts we possess. We would hold space for their growth, suggesting guidelines and possibilities, and at times providing limits when that feel necessary. But even the limits would come from the heart rather than the heat of anger and be for their benefit rather than just our ease.

I believe the greatest gift we can give our children is to provide them with a model of love rather than a world of fear, living from our essential lessons rather than our contracted fixations. When we hold this expansive model of love as essence for ourselves, living our lives from that place, it could not help but be experienced and typically chosen by our children. It then becomes their way of living in this world, based on their magnificence rather than smallness, their open hearts and intuition instead of their defenses and greatest fear about themselves. Being examples of loving from the inside out and trusting our own subtle skills will give our young people a whole different way of being and interacting, spreading to others and making choices about friends and spouses that enhance such a way of living.

We might incorporate into this model playing the sharing game, even if only a little. Watch what happens to your heart when you play. Watch what happens to others when you play. Is there anything more important that being the love that we are and at peace with ourselves? And if we were to do that, would the collection of things bring more peace and happiness than the experience itself? Yes, I love nice things and new things. I love a nice place to live, a nice car to drive, good food, and even good wine. At the same time, nothing makes me happier than seeing the happiness and laughter of my children and grandchildren, my friends and neighbors. Nothing makes me happier than a very open heart when I feel at peace with myself and my world.

I do not think such choices have to be mutually exclusive, especially when we get more creative and collaborative in developing ways of experiencing both an open heart and beautiful things in our lives. That, I think, is the most positive aspect of such a future. That is what our children and grandchildren will be able to achieve, even if we are a little more stuck and limited in the options we can see. I have the greatest hope in their future. I want to share what ever positive aspects might emerge from this view of who we are as children and adults, along with other possibilities this perspective offers for the children.

We keep shifting what we know, how we see our environment, and how we see our world. Lanza and Berman add a new perspective of our reality in raising the question of consciousness, the issue of energy never dying but changing forms, and shifting the way we see our reality.[13] These alternative views allow us to change how we interpret the world, just as my judgement of my friend who was living so boldly allowed me to shift my relationship with him as well as within myself. Now he is an example of how I might larger, be more expansive in the world rather than a source of irritation, a joy instead of anger.

From Weiss and Weiss, we also gain a different way of looking at our experience here in this life. From the many clients in their work, they summarize the experiences this way.

> The glimpses that such other worldly experiences provide us are extremely valuable, for they offer insight into the true nature of mind and of being. Such insights show the permanence of existence beyond the body, beyond the brain. They allow us to reach enlightenment. They show the beauty and the wisdom of the process (or the Tao, or the flow), which is always there, which is always right....yet all the roads lead back to the same place: a life-transforming recognition of our soul's essence....Circumstances outside you do not have to lead your heart. Instead, allow your heart to lead in all circumstances....We are all connected. The well-being of the individual is woven into the well-being of all things. Whether we give love or fear, everyone and everything is affected. [14]

When we change the ways we hold and see things, we open to new possibilities, and new possibilities allow for new behaviors, interactions, and different connections with both ourselves and others. This is the reason I think Lanza and Berman offer

261

their model of biocentrism and this is the reason I have outlined noussentrism. And yet if no one allows themselves to see a different point of view, we do not change, we do not grow. At the same time, I think it is important to remember the quote that is attributed to have been said by Margret Mead and very important to remember. "Never doubt that a small group of thoughtful, committed citizens can change the world. Indeed, it is the only thing that ever has." There is no known source for this famous quote and currently is disputed.[15] But there seems to be much truth in the saying, where ever it originated.

One final point made by MacKay is the suggestion that we begin to join science and spirituality. Such a connection would require that we expand our definition of science, as I had to do to begin exploring human energy fields. Certainly the entire Transpersonal Psychology movement has pioneered the way for this and has been a significant contribution. And we can take it further. We have works shared with us by MacKay, Grof, Chamberlain, Moody and all the near-death researchers, Weiss and the past life investigators, and many more exploring consciousness that do not fall easily into the scientific method. They do, as MacKay's son suggests however, provide a "science of *multiple, independent observations of phenomena,*"[16] as do many others cited in this work. I agree with this suggestion and hope we can expand our perspective further to make our explorations more integrative.

I would like to end with a final Rumi poem. This one encourages us to continue along this amazing path. I would like Rumi to have the last word here, for he expresses himself and his conscious insights much more eloquently than I do, as does Hafiz and Ibn Arabi.

RESPONSE TO YOUR QUESTION

Why ask about behavior
when you are soul-essence
and a way of seeing into presence?
Plus you are with us. How could you worry?

You may as well free a few words
from your vocabulary: *why* and *how* and *impossible.*

Open the mouth-cage and let those fly away.

We were all born by accident,
but still this wandering caravan
will make camp in perfection.

Forget the nonsense categories
of *there* and *here*.
Race and nation and religious.
Starting-point and destination.

You are soul and you are love,
not a spirit or an angel or a human being.
You are a Godman-womanGod-manGod-Godwoman.

No more questions now
as to what it is we are doing here.

- Rumi[17]

EPILOGUE

4 March 2017

Dear Parents,

We have not met yet, but I am writing this letter while I still am able and before you make decisions that begin to impact me. I am still in my current incarnation, which for me is the present and for you the past. I know this may seem a bit odd, but I have this very strong inclination to write this letter to you and share it at the end of this book.

You see, during my investigations, I have come to believe that all my work leads me to this moment and the hope of making a connection across "time" into a dimension where I will get to experience the model I am proposing in this book. The basic purpose for writing about these ideas is to share it with people who might rekindle their own spark and then support it in children and others. But I also write it for you, as my new "parents." I am hoping you will read this and use it to support me as your new child. I am asking you to help me remember things while growing up that have taken me 60+ years to incorporate into my current life. I would like a chance to experience this possibility, to grow up knowing and trusting my inner wisdom and higher Self as a part of my development in this world. I imagine a possibility where I build on what I bring as an infant rather than losing it and trying to recapture it late in life. It is a desire to explore life from a foundation of trusting and utilizing my inner guide as I explore this physical domain and learn experiences of life in this world.

I do not even know if you are my biological parents, my adopted parents, a single parent, two men, two women, or some other combination. The configuration is not as important to me as is the way you help me see myself and learn to trust myself, helping me pay attention to the skills I have from birth. While all of the opinions of others can be useful, please help me balance my own natural skills and abilities rather than ignoring and losing them. Please help me pay attention to my own inner knowing and connection to All as a balance to the external opinions that bombard us every day. Please help me feel, see, know, and hear that aspect of myself from the moment of conception to the moment I step into adulthood. With that foundation and support, I believe my life as an adult in this world will be unlike I have ever experienced. And I would love to have that kind of opportunity at least once in this amazing Earth "school."

My parents in this incarnation were very good parents, and they tried very hard. They both cared for me, loved me, and gave me so much. I have had an amazing life in many ways, with many gifts and learning opportunities along the way. And now I would like to build on these in a more conscious manner to have a new, more conscious life experience.

If this letter touches you in any way as a possible model for raising your child, then please practice this to the best of your ability. I am not asking for perfection or for you do to it "just right." I am only asking for you to try and give it your best shot. Then I will do the same as a new being on this planet. I also will not be perfect, and we will continue to struggle at times. But I keep coming back to this idea, this feeling that such a way of helping children is not only possible, but that it will make a difference in how children learn and grow from a more conscious beginning. And I want to experience this myself.

So I am asking for your help in carrying this out in the way that makes most sense to you and your own inner knowing, your own divine guidance as parents. Then, please, just help me grow up doing the same. I think we both will gain useful lessons in the process and have an amazing life, even more than my life has been this time.

> In deep love and gratitude,
> Your future child

APPENDIX A

ESSENCE THEORY:

RECONCEPTUALIZING OUR VIEW OF CHILDREN

Geoffrey K. Leigh, Ph.D. *

Jean A. Metzker, Ph.D. **

Nate Metzker, B.A.***

This work was supported in part by the Nevada Agricultural Experiment Station and the Nevada Cooperative Extension System. Appreciation is expressed to Karen A. Polonko, Deborah Bechtold, Dionne Maxwell, and Mara Duncan for providing assistance early in the development of this project.

* Private Practice, Napa Valley, CA.

** Bereavement Counselor, Visiting Nurse Service of New York, Hospice, and Private Practice, New York City, NY

*** Private Practice, New York City, NY: Teacher of autism and music, author, musician.

Overview

While much of the early work on children and families focused on a problem or disease model, later perspectives began to redirect our focus to a resiliency and strengths model. In the area of child development, for example, there was considerable work on the development of children and how adults might learn better to manage their behavior. Yet much of the early research was directed towards the problems and factors associated with outcomes viewed as problematic and negative, especially in terms of children's maladaptation and incompetence as adults (Garmezy, 1983). In contrast to this research, especially on children's stress and dysfunction, a pattern arose around children who seemed to have "protective" aspects of themselves and their environments, which allowed for the unexpected outcome of success when the prediction was for failure (Rutter, 1979). This research expanded to develop the concept of "resiliency," with a focus on the strengths of children, their families, and the larger environment rather than the primary focus on problems and pathologies (Barnard, 1994; Jessor, 1993; McCubbin, 1997; Rutter, 1990; Werner & Smith, 1992).

According to Anthony (1987), this work on resiliency developed because researchers began to look beyond the concepts and frameworks from which they had been working to see what had been in front of them the entire time, "illuminating presences that simply had no form before the light fell on them and lit up the entire intellectual landscape" (p. 3). Such new ideas and perspectives develop when scholars change some of the assumptions, concepts, frameworks, and language used previously in their work. The concept of resiliency with children illustrates how such a changing view influences our thinking and framework.

It is easy to identify the changes after they have developed, as with the shift from dysfunction to resiliency and strength or assets (Benson, 1997), although it is not always easy to see them at the time. Scholars also simply may be "rediscovering" ideas people have suggested some time ago. This paper is a summary and integration of a wide range of theory and research, expanding the way children have been viewed in the past with an extended perspective. The challenges derived in this paper are not so much a dismissal of previous work, but rather additional information, which modifies current assumptions and provides more specific explanations to expand the view of children and reframe our relationships to them. The connections outlined in this paper, although based on investigations, are more conceptual and theoretical in nature, certainly requiring additional research. We have tried to explicate this framework so that key questions could be addressed by future work. Without such a framework, we often do not ask the questions from which the research and measures are derived.

Theoretical Views of Children

Over the past century, theories about children and different aspects of their development have continued to expand. Freud (1949), in many ways, set a foundation about children, although contrasting points of view developed very quickly and simultaneously (Bretherton, 1993). It is not possible to review adequately any of the theories in this paper, and there are excellent reviews done elsewhere (Crain, 2011; Miller, 2010). The present interest is in identifying some key issues and questions, as well as some unexplainable aspects, which may be addressed appropriately by an alternative point of view. What will be introduced here are key issues and aspects from the theories most relevant to the current topic.

Freud's legacy in the study of personality development underscores the extremely important relationship between mother and infant (Noam, Higgins, Goethals, 1982), which is related to the development of the influential attachment theory (Bowlby, 1969, 1973), unconscious determination of behavior, and the development of defense mechanisms (Lowen, 1985; Noam, Higgins, Goethals, 1982). These concepts have been important in both the developmental as well as the therapeutic literature, such as the long-term impacts related to the development of attachment, including the impact on other relationships as adults. Yet it is difficult to actually explain the development of this connection between mothers and infants (Bretherton, 1993). While there is considerable discussion of both the unconscious and defense mechanisms, again, there lacks an adequate explanation of either concept. Many continue to ask just what is the unconscious mind, especially as the concept of mind expands (Hunt, 1996;

269

Pert, 1997; Schwartz & Begley, 2002; Schwartz & Russek, 2001). How do defense mechanisms actually develop, and what specific impacts do they have on our lives? At the same time, people often have begun to take such concepts for granted because they seem to be an essential aspect of human behavior (Lerner & Ehrlich, 1992).

Other theories contain critical concepts about children's growth and development, and yet many specifics are missing from the explanations. For example, behaviorists focus on development from the experiences and learning of children (Benson, Messer, & Gross, 1992). From this point of view, children primarily are absorbers of information and responders to experiences, which then create complex behavior patterns and demonstration of skills (O'Donohue & Krasner, 1995), yet what holds the consequences of repetition, or the molded behavior, in place? In addition, it is difficult from this framework to explain outcomes and behaviors demonstrated between twins in terms of communication and connections they demonstrate (Bates, O'-Connell, & Shore, 1987; Playfair, 2002). From the symbolic interaction framework, children are seen as 'active agents' who play an important role in constructing their world as well as taking in information and responding to their environment (Burr, Leigh, Day, & Constantine, 1979). While the environment presents critical stimuli that influence growth and development of skills, it is the child who creates meaning to these experiences and learns to construct a reality of his/her own. As Searle (1995) asks, "How does a mental reality, a world of consciousness, intentionality, and other mental phenomena, fit into a world consisting entirely of physical particles in fields of force" (p. xi)? While assumptions are made about children, explanations about being an 'actor,' creating meaning, and constructing realities are more difficult to describe. From a systems perspective, behavior and development are viewed as understandable only within the context in which they are embedded (Bretherton, 1993). From this point of view, meaning arises from the interplay between subsystems or individuals and systems, and the interconnections and intersystem influences are key aspects in the transmission of values and information, but the explanation for such transmissions are still being sought (Leigh, 1986). In addition, as Bretherton (1993) points out, "How can the interplay of multiple individual, familial, and societal factors explain the observed variations in parent-child relationships and how are these relationships experienced and interpreted by participants in this and other cultures" (p. 290)?

While the theoretical explanations around children and development have continued to expand, they still have remained primarily Western in their focus. Yet there are many contributions to explaining development, behavior, health, and interaction, which are based in Eastern traditions and perspectives. For example, 'physical development' takes on a different meaning from an Eastern perspective, even varying from culture to culture (Kasulis, Ames, & Dissanayake, 1993). The mind also takes a very different meaning from an Eastern point of view (Guenther & Kawamura, 1975), which has sparked interesting discussions with scholars from Western traditions (Goleman & Thurman, 1991). What is particularly interesting about the Eastern view of mind is that this long tradition seems to be consistent with some of the latest research findings about the interrelationship between the body and mind, and an expanded view of mind within Western science (Hunt, 1996; Myss, 1996; Pert, 1997; Schwartz & Russek, 2002; Schwartz & Begley, 2003). There also are long traditions of developmental stages, although in some cases they focus more on such things as the chakra centers and energy fields (Chogyam, 1986; Judith, 1996; White, 1993) rather than segmented aspects of our being, such as physical or cognitive development. In addition, there are Eastern traditions related to other aspects of Western science, including physics and the mind (Schwartz & Russek, 2002; Walker, 2000; Wallace, 1996) and healing (Benor, 2002, 2004; Gresham & Nichols, 2002; Rapgay, 1996). In contrast to Western frameworks, a central concept of Eastern perspectives has to do with energy flow, energy centers, and, in general, the human energy field (Chodron, 1990; Chogyam, 1986; Judith, 1996; Kasulis et al., 1993; Myss, 1996; Rapgay, 1996; Wallace, 1996). While this contribution has been dismissed by most scholars in Western paradigms, there has been on-going work in this area by some researchers for some time (Becker & Seldon, 1985; Brennen, 1987; Burr, 1972a; Davis, 1978; Krippner & Rubin, 1975; Moss, 1979; Schwarz, 1979), and the work continues and expands (Bache, 1995; Becker, 1990; Brown, 1999; Colinge, 1998; Gerber, 1988; Hunt, 1996; Karagulla & Kunz, 1989; Korotkov, 1998, 1999, 2002; Lee, 2002; Leigh & Cendese, 2008; Leigh, Metzker, & Pierce, 2010a, 2010b; Motoyama, 1982, 1993; Northrup, 1994; Pierrakos, 1990; Popp, 1994; Yasuo, 1993).

With the incorporation of ideas from Eastern perspectives, many questions that previously have been difficult to address find new plausible explanations that are expansive and exciting. In addition, new questions arise, which allow further explanations to develop and new research ideas to emerge. These new perspectives also begin to challenge some basic assumptions about children and development. For example, the possibility exists that there is a conscious connection between the mother and fetus/infant at a different level of communication and within a different band or frequency by which information transfer can exist (Burr, 1972b; Hunt, 1996; Leigh, 2004; Wilber, 1993). In addition, it is possible that the human energy field has a similar dynamic along developmental stages as are manifested in other aspects of development, such as the physical body or cognition (Leigh, Metzker, & Hilton, 1999; Metzker & Leigh, 2004). Further, with more recent developments in this area, the emanation of energy from living organisms is measurable and therefore can be researched and analyzed along developmental lines (Hunt, 1996; Leigh, 2004; Leigh et al., 1999, Leigh, Polonko, & Leigh, 2003; Metzker & Leigh, 2004). Thus, the questions now being asked also can begin to be researched through a scientific methodology.

Essence and Character Structure

In contrast to many traditional theoretical views of children, almost every therapeutic approach to human behavior deals with the development of defense mechanisms and what Lowen (1975) calls character structures (structures providing protection for the self or some type of essence of who we are). Some defenses, it is argued, develop from drives or other "innate" aspects of the being, while others argue they are a result of learning or reinforcement patterns. Although these structures may continue to develop over a lifetime, the foundation is characterized often as being in place during the first five to seven years of life (Lerner & Ehrlich, 1992).

Character Structures

One of the basic questions about children has to do with how they enter the world and what attributes or characteristics are key in their development. People often have asked about the nature of children and whether an essence exits at birth. One approach that addresses this question by identifying a vision of who we are and what health may be about is the bioenergetic model of behavior, body, and personality developed by Lowen (1967, 1971, 1975, 1988, 1990, 1995, 1997, 2003) and Pierrakos (1990, 1997). This approach, which developed out of Reich's (1961) notion of body armor, suggests that people develop protective layers around the core of one's being, which Lowen (1988) suggests is love and the heart. These layers are defense mechanisms that protect the heart and include the emotional layer, the muscular layer, and the ego layer (in order from inner to outer layers of the body). These increasing layers of defenses, however, also increasingly segment and separate the heart, body, mind, and awareness. Such segmentation leads to a "betrayal" of the body and a separation of the mind, spirit, and soul (Lowen, 1975, p. 43). In addition, such segmentation also leads to a distortion of the natural energy flow of the body, which is a key to health and healthy living (Pierrakos, 1990). The segmentation occurs from muscular contraction around emotional experiences that are difficult to handle and unpleasant or painful. Such muscular contractions of emotions and memory develop "blocks" to the energy flow and a literal armoring of the body. In addition, these blocks begin to shape the human body and influence behaviors and reactions to the environment. These blocks also eliminate the sensing of the body and distort energy flows and the related information carried through the body, such as our emotional experiences. Thus, separation between mind and body increases.

A central concept within bioenergetics is the integration of the inner, mystical aspect of one's being with the outer, objective physical body. Lowen (1975) suggests that such a split exists because of the "armoring," which separates the feelings of one's core of existence and the sensations or outer reactions of the individual. Such a wall exists because of the conflicts between mind and body. The only way to integrate the two aspects is to tear the wall down by removing the armoring and relieving the tensions, which allows one to connect both to duality and the underlying unity. Such a process involves both bodywork and language (or words), since both are related to their respective worlds and frame or structure the worlds of body and mind. In order to develop both body consciousness and mind consciousness, as well as an integration of the two, one must connect the sensations of the body ("dearmoring") as well as consciousness framing of the mind (words).

In order to create healthy living, Lowen (1975) also suggests that a balance must exist in our lives, such as occurs naturally in bodies, what might be called "balance in movement" (p. 332). Such principles occur from internal development rather than external pressures. The intent is to remove the ego defenses, the muscular and emotional blocks in order to get to the core, which is love and the heart. In this way, Lowen sees people essentially being "love" energy, which becomes distorted by emotional blocks, physical blocks, and ego blocks or defenses. When these layers and blocks are pealed away, one then gets in touch with undistorted essence energy that flows freely within the body and connects to such energy outside the body as well. From this perspective, energy attracts like energy (Hunt, 1996).

While Lowen (1975, 1988, 1990) discusses the concept of character structure in terms of energy flow, as did Reich (1961), the concept of energy fields and energy systems are not as well developed as the work done by others (Burr, 1972; Hunt, 1996). Yet these basic ideas, developed with Pierrakos, have been connected to the concept of energy centers and energy armoring as they relate to physical development and even body shape (Brennen, 1987, 1993; Judith, 1996; Pierrakos, 1990, 1997). At the same time, the notion of energy blocks and their impact on physical development, structure, and movement add important views to the work on energy fields, especially in the development of physical and energy systems in young children. In addition, the work by Lowen and Pierrakos make connections between personality, behavior, and energy fields, suggesting that personality may in fact be the result of energy blocks and the manner in which essence is covered rather than being a basic aspect of development with children and adults. Finally, this perspective begins to clearly identify how energy blocks can cover and make it difficult to see core aspects of individuals, such as the essence (Lowen, 1990; Pierrakos, 1997).

While this perspective has been used for several decades, it does not seem to have generated much empirical support beyond the work done by the developers. By itself, such a perspective has not changed the views regarding children or had a pervasive impact on the field of child development. Yet there also are several other perspectives, which, taken collectively, begin to develop an alternative view of children and their capabilities. It is to these other views we now will turn in order to add additional perspectives to this picture.

The Enneagram and Fixations

In a similar yet separate approach, Enneagram work from Gurdjieff and Ouspensky describes another process in which protective mechanisms, called fixations, are developed (Almaas, 1999; Bennett, 1983; Blake, 1996; Ebert & Kustenmacher, 1996; Hurley & Dobson, 1993; Jaxon-Bear, 1987, 2001; Keyes, 1992; Maitri, 2001, 2005; Naranjo, 1994; Palmer, 1991; Rhodes, 2010; Riso & Hudson, 1999; Vollmar, 1997). Fixations also are designed to protect an inner or core essence and again involve physical bodies, emotions, and mental abilities. Like the work by Lowen (1990) and Pierrakos (1997), this view also suggests greater knowing and information processing than is attributed by traditional research assumptions and perspectives.

Similar in some ways to Lowen and Pierrakos' work, the Enneagram is a system of understanding character structures (or what in this vocabulary is called an Enneatype, with both a fixation and higher lesson), which distort energy of the body, emotions, and mind (Jaxon-Bear, 2001; Maitri, 2001, 2005; Naranjo, 1994; Vollmar, 1997). Just as character structures are distortions of love energy, so fixations are distortions of the energy around an individual's core essence. In this system, three core bodies are important; the physical body, the emotional body, and the mental body. When a person is balanced, energies run to all three of the bodies at approximately even rates, although the flow may vary depending on a situation or need. Most of us, however, according to this system, have an imbalance of energy with a greater flow to a particular body. This occurs because "each of us has crystallized our conception of self and the world in a way that creates an imbalance between our physical, emotional, and mental bodies. Gurdjieff describes this imbalance by saying that we 'leak energy' into one of these bodies" (Jaxon-

Bear, 1987, p. 28). This leakage of energy also is associated with a primary theme of our behavior: the physical body is related to anger, the emotional body is related to the lack of identity, and the mental body is related to fear. In most cases then, energy leakage to a body, such as the mental body, is used to ignore or deny the basic issue. For example, one may focus on mental activity and constant analysis in order to avoid facing the fear one constantly experiences in his/her life. In this way, the energy is used as a type of defense and protection to deal with the basic issue one wants to avoid and therefore distorts the energy and information coming through that energy. Typically, the chief feature of one's being is the hardest part to see and organizes how one lives and responds in a world as one defines it. Such leakages of energy may occur because of a block in some part of our energy system. For example, Sherwood (1993) suggests that a blockage in the heart chakra keeps energy from flowing properly between the physical and subtle bodies, and a person loses touch with the physical body. In such cases, the energy may then go more heavily into the mental or emotional body.

"Just as the acupuncture works to create and maintain harmonious circulation of chi [breath or life energy] by entering the being through the body, the Enneagram enters our being through the mental symbolic level to do similar work" (Jaxon-Bear, 1987, p. 28). The intent of the Enneagram is thus to free the person from the fixation to be who s/he is rather than the fixation, which is how one presents oneself (Almaas, 1998, 1999; Keyes, 1992, Maitri, 2009). People see themselves as this structure because that is where their attention goes as a basic process of their lives (Palmer, 1991). They then define who they are by these "personality" types or chief features when in fact they simply are distortions of energy (Riso & Hudson, 1999; Hurley & Dobson, 1993). In each body, when clear energy is flowing fully and in a balanced way, they see who they really are, the natural state (Jaxon-Bear, 2001). In this state, one is pure (undistorted) awareness (physical body), love (emotional body), and emptiness or silence (mental body). Such essence of the three bodies also is similar to the Buddhist view of a clear mind and open heart (Chodron, 1990).

The Enneagram outlines nine different fixations, three related to each body (Almaas, 1999; Hurley & Dobson, 1993; Maitri, 2001, 2009; Naranjo, 1995; Palmer, 1991; Riso & Hudson, 1999; Vollmar, 1997); a core point, an internalized fixation, and an externalized fixation, all developed in an attempt to avoid the related issue. Yet the fixations are not who people are but rather the presentation of distorted energy (Almaas, 1999; Maitri, 2009). An important contribution of this system is the focus on the essence of people underlying all fixations, which is awareness, love, and emptiness. In this way, the three bodies or sources of information move from protection to an undistorted way of "knowing." With a focus on the essence of people underneath the fixations, one begins to have a clearer vision of the essential nature of individuals when energies are balanced and open. This also provides a clear vision of how people might present themselves without clinging to distorted and diverted energies (Almaas, 1999; Jaxon-Bear, 2001; Maitri, 2009). In addition, this can help develop a clear vision of the possibilities of health without the layers of fixation upon which attention usually is focused. Finally, these concepts allow for a different view of children who may enter the world with fewer developments or complexities of fixations, thus knowing and expressing information from one's essence in a more direct and less distorted fashion. On the other hand, if adults view of people as their fixations and character structures, then the information that is shared in a purer form may be missed or overlooked. We see from the framework we are using. Thus, if the framework is that we are our fixations or personalities, then that is all we see. Anything else is ignored or outside our point of view.

An Evolving Perspective

The work by Lowen and Pierrakos, as well as the conceptualization of the Enneagram, only proposes the existence of an essence rather than providing clear evidence of such. One piece of interesting data, however, from the therapeutic work by Weiss (1988), provides an illustration of what people seem to be like underneath the fixations or character structures. In this case, Weiss, a psychiatrist and head of a university department with traditional training and working from a traditional perspective, began to work with a client who was experiencing difficulty overcoming her emotional problems. As Weiss continued to work with her, using hypnosis and age regression to understand the core and onset of her problems, his client moved into an altered state. This state presented a stark contrast to her personality and style in every-day life, and it illuminated a core self.

> I would become increasingly frustrated by the uncrossable gulf between Catherine's conscious, awake intellect and her trans-like superconscious mind. While she was hypnotized, I would have fascinating philosophical dialogues with her at the superconscious level. When awake, however, Catherine had no interest in philosophy or related matters. She lived in the world of everyday detail, oblivious of the genius within her (italics mine). (Weiss, 1988, p. 74)

The author later describes a wonderful metaphor about the essence of Catherine and the covering of that part of her, similar to the covering for all individuals:

> It is as if a large diamond were to be found inside each person. Picture a diamond a foot long. The diamond has a thousand facets, but the facets are covered with dirt and tar. It is the job of the soul to clean each facet until the surface is brilliant and can reflect a rainbow of colors. Now, some have cleaned many facets and gleam brightly. Others have only managed to clean a few; they do not sparkle so. Yet underneath the dirt, each person possesses within his or her breast a brilliant diamond with a thousand gleaming facets. The diamond is perfect, not one flaw. The only difference among people are the number of facets cleaned. But each diamond is the same, and each is perfect. When all the facets are cleaned and shining forth in a spectrum of lights, the diamond returns to the pure energy that it was originally. The lights remain. It is as if the process that goes into making the diamond is reversed, all that pressure is released. The pure energy exists in the rainbow of lights, and the lights possess consciousness and knowledge (italics mine). (Weiss, 1988, p. 211)

As the therapy progressed, "another layer of neurotic fears and anxieties was stripped away" (p. 115) in a rather rapid fashion when other approaches had not been successful over a longer period of time. The client was more serene, softer, and more patient. "Catherine felt more loving, and others gave love back to her. The inner diamond that was her true personality was shining brilliantly for all to see" (Weiss, 1988, p. 115). In another discussion with the client while in an altered state, her insight included the need for her father and other adults to learn to love and nurture others. "If they don't understand this...they treat children like property, instead of like people to love" (p. 177). After the therapy, when the client had found a sense of happiness and contentment she had never experienced before, she felt like life had meaning and purpose for her.

> Now that she is balanced and in harmony with herself, she radiates an inner peace that many wish for but few attain. She feels more spiritual....She has no interest in pursuing the study of psychic phenomena [which she experienced increasingly during the period of therapy and afterwards], feeling that she 'knows' in a way that cannot be learned from books or lectures" (Weiss, 1988, p. 207).

Weiss (1988, 1992, 1996, 2000, 2005) had many other clients, which have had similar experiences and similar results. While these experiences and outcomes "prove" nothing, they do demonstrate through several case studies the uncovering of an essence, which is "brilliant" and has ways of knowing from the pure energy that exists in the rainbow of lights, with the lights possessing consciousness and knowledge. This description, while quite conflictual with most theoretical traditions in the social sciences, is quite consistent with the concepts of energy fields and energy as information within physics (Brown, 1999; Burr, 1972; Hunt, 1996; Popp, 1994; Schwartz & Russek, 2001) and with Eastern views (Chodron, 1990; Yasuo, 1993).

Spectrum of Consciousness

Grof's Work

The work by Grof (1975, 1985, 1988a, 1988b, 1993, 1996, 1998; 2006; Grof & Grof, 1980, 1989, 1990) on altered states, birth experiences, consciousness, and the energy of the body adds further information and evidence for an alternative framework and a different view of children. This evidence again supports children's knowing beyond the traditional theories. Like other perspectives that challenge traditional assumptions and models, this work is not without controversy, even with people who share some similar interests and views (Wilber, 1995, 1997). Yet the concepts provide a fresh look at some old issues, with an exciting model that fits with other recent developments.

Grof's research on consciousness and altered states has been connected to many aspects of experience and psychotherapy, including the development of Holotropic Breathwork (Grof, 1985, 1988b, 1993, 1998; Grof & Grof, 1989, 1990). This thera-peutic process uses a natural altered state, achieved through deep, rapid breathing and strong music, to explore the self in a safe and non-ordinary manner (Grof, 1993). While as yet there has been little systematic research conducted on outcomes, as often occurs with new therapeutic approaches, there are some interesting case study data to support the impact of such a process. One of the experiences that often happen in this state, for example, is when adults re-experience their birth and issues or sometimes trauma associated with birth. Often times, informa-tion gained during these experiences, previously unknown to individuals, is confirmed by a parent, in some cases even reveal-ing secrets never before shared in the family (Grof, 1993). In addition, more physical evidence also has been observed, such as the exhibiting of a Babinski reflex (fanning and extending up-ward of the toes by infants when the bottom of the foot is touched rather than curling downward with adults), normally seen only during infancy, but exhibited while in an altered state by an adult re-experiencing infant states (Grof, 1993). From this work on altered states and experiences with thousands of people in the Breathwork, Grof has developed a model that connects to Bohm's (1980) notion of a holograph. From this perspective:

> energy, light, and matter are composed of interference pat-terns that carry information about all of the other waves of light, energy, and matter that they have directly or indirect-ly contacted. Thus, each part of energy and matter repre-sents a microcosm that enfolds the whole. (Grof, 1993, p. 10).

In addition, Bohm (1980) suggests that energy is informa-tion, a concept consistent with other work on energy fields (Brown, 1999; Burr, 1972; Hunt, 1996; Popp, 1994; Schwartz &

Russek, 2001), and part of that information is a memory of having made contact with other particles previously. In this way, "matter and consciousness are both aspects of the same undivided whole" (Grof, 1993, p. 10). While we often think of energy as simply a collection of particles or waves, increasingly scholars view energy as information (Schwartz & Russek, 2001), a type of knowing which we have ignored. We think of knowing as mental processing, but increasingly physicists as well as social scientists are suggesting that "knowing" is much broader and extensive that previously considered (Bohm, 1980; Grof, 1998; Hunt, 1996; Leigh, 2004; Leigh et al., 1999; Leigh et al., 2003, Metzker & Leigh, 2004; Schwartz & Russek, 2001)

The implications of these integrated ideas are tremendous. For example, the distinction between inner and outer begins to be less distinct and significant. Jung's (1959) notion of a "collective unconsciousness" and the related information becomes available to all individuals, and "the world of the psyche and the material world are not two separate entities, but that they are intimately interwoven" (Grof, 1993, p. 12).

Grof found that emotional and physical memories were stored in the body in the form of complex constellations around themes, both blissful and painful (Grof, 1988b). These constellations often seem related to aspects of the birth experiences, which seem to form foundations for later patterns of behavior. Grof (1988b) outlined four matrixes related to the birth stages. The development of these matrixes is complicated and involved, but there are several important aspects that are relevant for the current topic. First, when in these altered or regressed states, adults report actually experiencing the womb as well as things going on around them, such as emotions experienced by a mother. They also report "knowing" information about more than the mother, which later is verified by parents and others. People report feeling "absolutely convinced that he was composed of pure energy and spirit" as well as feeling "the oneness with the universe, the Tao. He had experienced his ego and a merging with all of existence" (Grof, 1993, p. 36). In a later matrix, people also indicate:

> that we may also relive the fear and confusion of an inexperienced mother or the mother's negative or strongly ambivalent attitude toward the child; these can make this phase more difficult for both mother and child. It seems

that the mother's conflicting emotions can disturb the physiological interplay between the uterine contractions and the opening of the cervix. (Grof, 1993, p. 47)

Related to this work, another scholar studying two women carrying twins from a traditional perspective posits that fears, both conscious and unconscious, may cause premature contractions (Cheek, 1995). The author hypothesizes that escalating maternal fear initiates a series of events that may end in expulsive preterm labor. The infants, he believes, then conclude that they are not wanted. Cheek notes an important feature of treatment is the re-establishment of maternal/fetal telepathic communications. If the mother loses hope of having a living child, telepathic connections are lost.

The impacts of these experiences are great. There is tremendous emotional power, authenticity, and potential for transforming views of their lives. Similar to the reports by Weiss (1988), "symptoms that had resisted months or even years of other treatment often vanished after patients had experiences such as psychological death and rebirth, feelings of cosmic unity, archetypal visions, and sequences of what clients described as past-life memories" (Grof, 1993, p. 17). Although the symptom relief is important, more interesting is the common experiences of interconnection and reflections of a cosmic intelligence that permeates the universe and all existence. People also report a sense of well-being they never thought possible. Like Lowen's work, the release of emotions and patterns of tensions held in the body appear to have immediate and strong impacts on people. Grof (1993) cannot find traditional perspectives to explain these experiences and insights, but rather feels like such perspectives represent a "conceptual straitjacket" for these unexplainable phenomena (p. 19). For example, Grof (1993) finds that the patterns developed in the body seem to occur around the sharing of the same emotional quality. In fact, this system of complex emotional constellations serves "to organize not only the individual unconsciousness, as I originally believed, but the entire human psyche itself" (Grof, 1993, p. 25). Thus, emotions may not only hold memories, but also be an organizing energy of interconnection, an idea consistent with Hunt's (1996) research. One reason a nonverbal therapeutic approach seems to be important is that these experiences developed prior to a child having language, or they are nonverbal in their very nature. In fact, what may be oc-

curring is that individuals get in touch with an energy information sharing that is difficult to translate into ordinary language,
an experience often reported by those in altered states, such as
meditation or by mystics, and apparently similar to the child's
perception of the world (Grof, 1996).

Again, Grof's work as yet does not have strong independent
support, although it is based on decades of his investigations. By
itself, it could be ignored or dismissed, but in conjunction with
other conceptual work and research, a new perspective continues
to emerge, which is important for understanding children in a
different way. This work, in conjunction with others, begins to
challenge the notion that "the newborn child lacks consciousness
and that the neonatal cortex is incapable of registering the birth
process and storing the information about it because it is not fully myelinated" (Grof, 1996, p. 16). In fact, what people re-experiencing the neonate and infant period report is similar to what
people report during anesthesia (Weiss, 1988) and during near-
death experiences (Fenwick & Fenwick, 1995; Grof & Grof,
1980; Moody, 1975, 1988, 2010; Morrissey, 1997; Morse with
Perry, 1990, 1992, 1994, 2000; Ring, 1998; Sabom, 1998;
Sutherland, 1993, Tucker, 2005). While scholars increasingly
report about the sensitivity and discrimination of infants and of
the fetus during intrauterine life (Verny, 1987), there still seems
to be denial about the registering of information around an intense and even life-threatening experience of birth and separation
from the mother (Grof, 1996). As Grof (1996) points out, the
"justification of this position by references to incomplete myeli-
nation of the cerebral cortex of the neonate can hardly be taken
seriously in light of the fact that the capacity of memory exists in
many lower organisms that do not have a cerebral cortex at
all" (p. 16), and that function in conjunction with the brain
(Myss, 1996; Pert, 1997). Children seem to have a way of knowing that is not about language, but may well be about energy as
information.

Wilber's Perspective

Wilber (1979, 1987, 1993, 1995, 1997, 2008) also has done
considerable work on the notion of consciousness, which he has
described as the spectrum of consciousness. His work is very
extensive and integrative, primarily at the theoretical level. Of

particular value is his integration of Eastern thought with Western psychology, physics, and other disciplines. The relevance to this project is his overview of the spectrum of consciousness (Wilber, 1993). Wilber (1987, 1997) has suggested a new paradigm around the idea of integration. His spectrum of consciousness is symbolized by rungs on a ladder, which represent different levels of consciousness, from the external world, through the five senses in a plural-dimensional approach. As one's own consciousness develops, Wilber suggests that the individual evolves from shadow to spirit, just as density changes from matter, body, mind, soul, and spirit. While this argument is consistent with the major religions of the world, he also suggests that different schools of psychology or psychotherapy correspond to various rungs on the ladder. This also is consistent with layers of energies or different "bodies" from an Eastern point of view (Karagulla & Kunz, 1989; Sherwood, 1993). Such notions of growth are consistent with many developmental perspectives, especially in terms of qualitative change processes (Dent-Read & Zukow-Goldring, 1997; Leigh & Loewen, 1987). Yet recent information about energy fields supports more of an integration and interaction of different frequencies rather than a layering effect most often described (Brennen, 1993; Hunt, 1996; Leigh et al., 1999; Metzker & Leigh, 2004). This integrative view is more consistent with what Grof (1993) describes in his matrix of complex constellations of patterns. In addition, when people move into the altered state and get in touch with the universal connections (Grof, 1993; Weiss, 1988), it is as if they move into at least some connection with Wilber's (1993) universal mind, Hunts' (1996) mind field, or Sheldrake's (1981) morphic field. Certainly the notion of a spectrum of consciousness is useful, especially with more of a continuum rather than discrete categories, and fits with the concept of the cleaning of the diamond described by Weiss (1988). Rather than children being at the bottom of the ladder, however, as often is assumed with "development," they may in fact be more directly connected to the mind field (Hunt, 1996) than adults who have developed blocks in energy fields and covered over the essence with "growth" in this reality. It may be this connection that is a part of children's knowing and processing of information, something that may even be natural to one who has open connections with all types of energy. This also may be the information that is recalled when people move into altered states, reconnecting through the same path to a way of knowing that is lost when the focus is pushed to verbal communication only (Leigh, 2004).

One reason for the lack of recognition of such abilities in children may have to do with the covering over and then dismissing of such aspects in adults. Thus, adults have developed physically, emotionally, and mentally, but have lost connection to the use of energy interactions and the sources of information related to such inputs for higher levels of consciousness. In contrast, children may be able to interact on the energy level and more directly from higher levels of consciousness, but they do not have the physical, emotional, or communication development to share such perspectives. Thus, where the adult is developed the child is undeveloped, and where the child is able to interact, the adult ignores the information. In this way, there is no overlap and thus little common ground between adults and infants at birth.

Inner Self Helper and Near-death Research

Two other areas of research that add additional insight and information to this perspective come from the work by Allison (Allison & Schwarz, 1998) and the research on near-death experiences (Fenwick & Fenwick, 1995; Moody, 1975, 1988; Morse & Perry, 1990, 1992, 1994; Morrissey, 1997; Ring, 1998; Sabom, 1998; Sutherland, 1993, Tucker, 2005). These two areas of work add yet further insights into the issue of the essence of individuals, especially within children.

Allison (Allison & Schwarz, 1998) has worked with multiple personality disorder for several decades. Like most psychiatrists, he approached his early work from a traditional perspective. Yet, once again, when the traditional approach was not working well, this psychiatrist happened upon an alternative approach. Using hypnosis to communicate with the "personalities" of clients, Allison discovered a unique "personality" that had a very different perspective from the others. This aspect of the individual was able to identify what was wrong with the client and how the psychiatrist could help the client. By working with this aspect of the individual, which Allison initially identified as the Inner Self Helper (ISH) and later called the essence, clients could be helped to a much greater extent and with greater sustained improvement

(Allison & Schwarz, 1998). Allison later developed training seminars to teach others how to contact and work with a client's essence, where therapy takes on a different approach and the role of the therapist changes from "expert" to facilitator.

Another area of research that lends support to the idea of something beyond the body and personality is the work on near-death experiences. Coined by the pioneering work of Moody (1975, 1988), this work has mushroomed over the past 25 years. At this point, thousands of adults and children have been interviewed from different parts of the world, with surprisingly consistent findings (Fenwick & Fenwick, 1995; Morse & Perry, 1990, 1992, 1994, 2000; Morrissey, 1997; Ring, 1998; Sabom, 1998; Sutherland, 1993, Tucker, 2005). Several significant findings are relevant to the concepts of this theoretical framework.

First, there is good documentation of information being reported by people who could not know such information unless there was some way of knowing what was occurring while the body was identified as "dead" (Fenwick & Fenwick, 1995; Ring, 1998; Sabom, 1998). These findings have been similar, whether investigated in the United States, England, Australia, or Japan (Fenwick & Fenwick, 1995; Morrissey, 1997, Ring, 1998; Sutherland, 1993). In addition, there are very similar findings with extensive research among children, where there are few cultural or religious concepts internalized to the extent we would expect with adults (Morse & Perry, 1990, 1992, 1994, 2000). There also are a few very interesting cases that suggest people report observations of things occurring during operations or interactions with others, not just a "spiritual" or other world experience. For example, Sabom (1998) reports extensively the experience of a woman who had the blood drained from her head and ears plugged during an operation where she "saw" the instruments and reported conversations during the medical procedure, which even other physicians were not able to speculate as accurately. In addition, Eadie (1996) reports a case from Russia where a man, who was thought dead, was placed in a morgue for the weekend. During that time, he visited an infant who was a neighbor and was crying constantly since birth. While out of his body, the man "communicated" with the infant, who told him "her hip had twisted during birth and was broken" (p. 198). After returning to his body, the man reported what he had learned while communicating with the infant, which proved to be correct upon x-raying the child's leg. The problem was resolved and the child quit crying. The important issue here has to do with the ability of the man to communicate with the child, and the ability of the child, just a few days old, to communicate with the man. This same communication ability is apparent when people interact with beings in psychomanteums, small dark rooms where people interact with other beings (Moody, 1993). In these cases, individuals are not in an altered state or out of their physical body, yet still frequently communicate without words. One final comment comes from the research by Sutherland (1993), who reports the experience of a "four-year-old during a tonsillectomy. She described how, while she observed the doctors during the operation, she felt much compassion for their ignorance. She felt that she, as the spirit of a four-year-old child, was so much wiser, knew so much more than they did" (p. 171).

One other important aspect of the research on near-death experiences has to do with the common description of an individual's core being or essence, usually described in some terms related to light (Brennen, 1987, 1993; Eadie, 1996; Morrissey, 1997; Ring, 1998). Such descriptions, which are common and quite consistent across many interviews, connect to the research by others on electro-dynamic field theory and energy field research.

Energy Field Research

There are two final areas of scholarship that seem to be helpful in addressing the questions raised earlier in this paper. The first is the development of electro-dynamic field theory, which provides an important framework from which to address expanded explanations for previously ignored areas of children's development and relating work previously unconnected. The second area of investigation is the literature on human energy fields, which connects to electro-dynamic field theory, but also includes work that has been viewed in isolation from the general framework. This latter work provides some specifics for an expanded view of children and of other ways of knowing that may be important for a shift from a disease or deficit approach to more of a health or strengths model.

Electro -Dynamic Field Theory

After several decades of research by Ravitz (1970), Burr and Northrop (1935, 1939), Burr (1944, 1972a, 1972b), and others, electro-dynamic field theory (EDFT) was utilized to encapsulate creative work on human energy fields (HEF). In contrast to the information about chakras and acupuncture, this area of work was based on experiments taking place primarily in the United State and England using basic scientific methods. From this perspective, each living and non-living entity is organized by a comprehensive dynamic pattern, which is both explicable and rational, based on relativity field physics (Ravitz, 1970). Such fields act as directors for chemical, metabolic, or molecular transformations and even underwrite the development of structure prior to chemical reactions occurring (Burr, 1972a), thus allowing health and disease to be measured in terms of changing intensities and directions of natural energy (Ravitz, 1970). Burr and Northrop (1935, 1939) carried out research on what they called the "life field", which they believed directed the organization of the organism, in some ways similar to the core or essence of an individual. Ravitz (1970) built upon this previous work by expanding the research and by postulating that "thought fields" interfered with the life fields to produce psychosomatic symptoms, which may possibly correspond to character structures or fixations. Ravitz further found that one could electromagnetically record the connection between hypnosis and field shifts during other state changes or related symptoms. In addition, Ravitz (1970) discovered that waking states have their own variations and fluctuations of rhythms in comparison to hypnotic or trance states, which have different rhythms. Such documentation and findings are even more impressive given the basic instruments that were far more simplistic and more difficult than current measurement devices (Hunt, 1996; Korotkov, 1998, 1999; Motoyama, 1992).
Research conducted by this team of biologists, physiologists, philosophers, and statisticians provided extensive scientific information on the subject of HEF. By finding similarities and differences connected to the human electromagnetic field, comparisons could be made with other living organisms as well as within the HEF itself. By identifying the rhythms and frequencies for the human organism, empirical verification of the HEF was provided through scientific means. Further, the rhythms of the HEF

were found to be similar and connected to other living organisms. Since 1948, evidence has been provided concerning profiles of variations in human feelings and behavior over and above that which is observable (Burr, 1972), and yet these data continue to be ignored by much of the scientific community.

Energy Fields

The concept of energy fields has a long history in Eastern cultures, where health, medicine, self-defense, and life are defined in relation to the flow of energy (Judith, 1996; Rapgay, 1996). More recently, such concepts have begun to be incorporated into theories of health and healing within medicine (Benor, 2002, 2004; Dossey, 1999; Gerber, 1988; Northrup, 1994; Orloff, 2000; Oschman, 2000; Shealy & Myss, 1993) as well as broader approaches to maintaining health and healing influences (Gresham & Nichols, 2002; Hetzel, 1994; Judith, 1994; Paulson, 1994; Sherwood, 1993; White, 1993). Human energy fields exist within the body as well as around the body, with specific energy centers called chakras (Karagulla & Kunz, 1989). Some have described several layers of energy beyond the physical body, sometimes labeled the etheric (or vital), the emotional (or astral), and the mental field. Sherwood (1993) talks about a fourth, or causal, and suggests "that the physical body is the outward manifestation of a series of subtler bodies. These subtler bodies, together with the energy of the physical body, make up a person's personal energy field" (p. 103). While all three (or four) fields are interpenetrating and synchronized such that no "physical experience is unaccompanied by emotional response and mental interpretation" (Karagulla & Kunz, 1989, p. 25), it is the etheric level which serves as the connection between the physical and other fields. This also is the field one often sees when people begin to observe the aura around the physical body. It also is the etheric field that contains what is described as the "etheric double" or counterpart to the physical particles and elements, such as organs and other body parts. Beyond these three types (sometimes referred to as the personality bodies), Paulson (1994) describes four other "spiritual" bodies: the intuitional/compassionate body, the atmic (or will/spirit) body, the monadic (or soul) body, and the divine body, each with its own function and sense of importance. While the systems are similar across traditions, names and ways of categorizing information changes from one system to another (Chogyam, 1986; Rapgay, 1996).

From this general approach, however, the physical body is vitalized by the etheric energy, which enters through the major energy centers and channels. In this way, the body receives energy from the larger environment, which helps to continue its functioning, much like the food we take in also provides us with energy as we eat and digest it. Thus, such energy is an important interplay between the physical body and the larger environment. "At the same time, the centers at the emotional and mental levels are processing energies from these fields, and these energies condition and modify the etheric energy as it flows through the network of channels in the etheric body" (Karagulla & Kunz, 1989, p. 28). In this way, energies at all levels interplay with and influence each other and also impact each other when problems or blocks occur. Such blocks inhibit and reduce the flow of energy and seem to compress and even distort or pollute the energies so that they become toxic to the individual. Karagulla & Kunz (1989) find strong connections between such blocks and physical symptoms or diseases in the body within organs or areas where the blocks occur.

The best known aspects of the energy field have been the chakra system, which is a group of "wheel-like energy centers [that are] swirling intersections of vital life forces, each chakra represent[ing] an aspect of consciousness essential to our lives....Chakras are centers of activity for the reception, assimilation and transmission of life energies" (Judith, 1994, p. 1). The chakras are not the only energy centers related to the body, but typically are identified as the "master" centers (Judith, 1994, p. 13). They connect to outer energy fields and, some suggest, supply much of the color to that field (White, 1993). In addition, each chakra (Sanskrit for 'wheel') carries a link "to specific parts of the glandular system and might therefore be described as subtle glands" (White, 1993, p. 3) or "organs of the subtle energy system" (Sherwood, 1993, p. 5). They serve as transformers for energy between the outer energy reservoirs and the physical body, transforming "the frequencies into different sensations, comprehensible to the human being, namely thought, emotions, and physical sensation" (Sherwood, 1993, p. 132).

The chakras, while having particular functions associated with each center, function as a system and must be considered as a whole (Judith, 1994). They are "energetic stepping stones" with increasing vibrational rates from the root to the crown chakra (White, 1993, p. 121). Yet the importance is for each center to spin appropriately and openly with clear connections to others (Sherwood, 1993). Thus, the chakras need to be balanced with each other, but each person has his/her own energy system with individual aspects and individual quantity flows (Judith, 1994). In terms of health and healing, "energy going in and out of the chakras affects the muscles, the nervous system and the glands. In short, it affects the entire system, and so a blocked chakra can create problems in all surrounding areas" (Paulson, 1994, p. 151). In addition, chakras can have an influence other people's chakras, especially in relationships (Leigh et al., 2010a, 2010b), and in fact can be affected by the larger culture as a whole (Judith, 1994). Thus, the energy fields, patterns, and exchanges have an influence on ourselves, those close to us in our lives, as well as those more extended in the culture itself, and are influenced by it (Wauters, 1997).

Some of the most intriguing and pioneering work over the past 25 years has been the research by Hunt (1996) on human energy fields, building on work by Burr (1972a, 1972b) and others. Hunt's studies around measuring vibrations in energy fields have led her to a collection of evidence confirming the existence of fields and implications concerning health and consciousness. For example, personal conscious awareness and health are first apparent in the field often long before any manifestation in the physical body (Karagulla & Kunz, 1989). Hunt's studies include energy field spectrums with frequencies of each color within the spectrum, and the energy field wave shapes from those spectrums. This work has focused on a shift from a chemical to an electromagnetic basis of humans and behavior. In contrast to the traditional investigation of chemical influences and basis for development, Hunt (1996) has focused on how the "…electromagnetic environments in which we live powerfully affect our biological fields" (p. 76). As a physiological psychologist, she began to address questions about muscular activity, movement, behavior, neuromuscular patterns of emotions, and health, which could not be answered by the present models. After years of research investigations, she concluded that such energy fields are critical foundations for the human condition and the environment. "It behooves us, therefore, to recognize that the health of the electromagnetic field is critical because this leads to the health or disease of the entire biological system" (Hunt, 1996, p. 68).

Hunt (1996) has focused particularly on the dynamics of such fields at they relate to health and healing. She kept looking for patterns that would help her understand how the energy field was working, but standard statistical procedures could not determine any regular patterns. Yet, "using fractal geometry, these chaotic happenings were found to have deep, profound and predictable order. With complex information, a highly-ordered pattern has emerged from beneath a superficial appearance of disorder" (Hunt, 1996, p. 35). Interestingly, such a pattern also was similar to a computer generated Rössler Chaos attractor graph pattern. From this, she proceeded to investigate relationships between the dynamics of chaos and order. What appears to be important here is not order nor chaos, but a balance or coherence that allows for a complex dynamic field to occur. It is the balance in a dynamic interaction that seems to be related to a healthy energy field. "...[T]o be healthy, an organism must exhibit dynamic flexibility in all of its systems and tissues (Hunt, 1996, p. 246). Such a complex, dynamic field allows not only for healthy functioning, but also for greater organization and creative exploration. This increases the possibilities for the organism and helps the energy system to maintain at a higher frequency or rate. Hunt also found that the strongest interaction occurs between fields when there are compatible harmonic frequencies. Such findings are consistent with energetic family interaction patterns between parents and adolescents when discussing positive and challenging issues (Leigh, 2004; Leigh et al., 2010a, 2010b).

Further, Hunt (1996) makes the connection to Sheldrake's (1981) concept of morphogenic fields. These fields occur when they are connected to behaviors and thoughts rather than substance. Such fields, which developed from past human interaction, continue to exist and influence current interactions or developments. As individuals further interact, the fields can become stronger and even facilitate learning at extended distances when people in other places tie into them and share the information contained in that field. Thus, Sheldrake (1981) argues, is how different members of the same species learn the same thing in different parts of the world at the same time. These fields, Bache (1995) argues, also work in the classroom, with the development of morphic fields from past classes as well as the current students playing a role in the learning and interaction of a group. At times, he suggests, these fields can facilitate the information exchange beyond the verbal or nonverbal levels. Such fields seem to play an important part of on-going groups, the interactions, relationships, and information exchanged. They do not seem limited to individuals, but are created at many levels, and again may help scientists understand how communication can take place between neonates and family members (Leigh, 2004).

One final aspect of the energy field has to do with emotions, which, if Grof (1993) and Hunt (1996) are correct, may be the organizing system for the field and the information contained in it. In this case, the view of emotions is not of "positive" or "negative" as historically has been the case, but rather as simply a different frequency in contrast to the physical or mental energies, working in an expansive or contractive manner, as energy tends to do. If energy is information, then emotions are simply an information system that flows in the human energy field (Leigh, 2004). Like the physical body, which provides feedback information when something is going wrong, such as pain, emotions also may provide feedback for what is occurring in the emotional field or in connection to other frequencies. While the physical body provides one type of information, and the mental frequencies provide another frequency of information, the emotional frequencies provide a third type, possibly at a frequency between the physical and mental in a range. It is not yet clear just how this organization occurs if it is the basic means for organization, but emotions may be such a frequency as to merge both the physical and mental information connectors into a complete field. The information, however, often times can be subtle, just like the beginning pains within the body. If we do not pay attention, then the pain becomes louder, not as a "punishment," but as a means of getting our attention to something that is important. It also may be a means for filing away information with a "string" or type of connector that will allow us to find it again. Finally, emotions may play a particular role of identifying discrepancies between the essence of the individual and the activities of the character structure or fixation, which we identify as "emotional reactions."

What can be especially important about the electro-dynamic field theory and energy field research in terms of children has to do with the communication of information between people. If the data by Grof (1993) and Cheek (1995) are correct, then the emotional energy is easily communicated between people who pay close attention to those frequencies. This is yet another way of communication, and possibly a very important means if the emotions are the organizing frequency. The emotions also may be a clear way of experiencing either expansive or contractive energy, both within our field as well as in fields around us. This again gives important information about what is occurring in an energy field and how it may impact us or we impact that field. Just like the knowing of children, the energy exchange in the field seems to take place whether or not people around it are aware of the information (Leigh et al., 2010a, 2010b). In fact, we would be more honest in what we share verbally if and when we realize that children already have some sense of what is occurring with us, and we only clarify or extend that information through verbal means. Finally, the emotions and feelings may provide the cleanest and most effective means of clearing away any blocks or other restrictions covering the essence. If the emotions are the common and organizing element for the complex connections, they provide the pathway for the protective elements to be released. At the same time, when we reinforce and strengthen significant aspects of one's being that are fully functioning, as with the emotional fields in children, then they do not have to deny that aspect of their life in order to function well in the reality we have created and defined. This allows children to maintain their subtle energetic skills rather than covering them up, only to work hard uncovering them at a later time. In fact, in this manner, children may well be our teachers in ways to keep the energy flow open and to process the information when it occurs in subtle forms.

Despite all the work on HEF of adults, there has been little systematic research beyond a small study of HEF in infants and young children (Leigh et al., 1997; Metzker & Leigh, 2004). White (1990) outlines some developmental issues corresponding to the seven chakras, as if children go through developmental stages consistent with the issues identified with the chakras. Kunz (1992) also discusses aspects of children's development in terms of energy fields, but in neither case are there corresponding data to support these descriptive ideas. What is needed is a large, longitudinal study to empirically document changes in the energy fields of young children in various conditions and settings. A small study has provided initial evidence of changes that take place in children's energy fields during the first four years of life (Leigh et al., 1999; Metzker & Leigh, 2004). Preliminary results of this work support many of the hypotheses outlined in this paper, but much more extensive work is needed.

Essence Theory

The integrating theme from the previous theory and research is what we call Essence Theory. From this perspective, it is hypothesized that an essence exists within each human being, lying beneath the character structure, fixation, defense mechanisms, and what commonly is called the personality, like a "diamond covered with dirt and tar" (Weiss, 1988, p. 211). Although Allison (1998) suggests it is separate, like a guide, we hypothesize it is the fundamental aspect of the human being, who we really are beneath the distortions of energy and blocks. In this way, the character structure, fixation, or even personality is simply another set of distortions in physical form. This essence not only exists, but it is capable of many different things. While there are many aspects that could be culled from all of the research reviewed here, we have tried to identify some of the key aspects that would allow for an expansion of our view of children's capabilities and begin testing some basic notions when we begin to expand our framework sufficiently to allow different research questions to be asked and addressed. Obviously such research will not be easily done, especially given the level of energetic development of most adults. At the same time, we do not develop research questions, methodologies, or instruments until our framework is expanded sufficiently to allow us to view "another dimension of reality" (Sogyal Rinpoche, 1993, p. 41).

Based on previous theories, conceptual frameworks, and research from diverse areas, there are ten ways the essence as able to perform that is different from the way we currently see children:

1. The essence is able to leave the body and observe actions, communications, or interactions while outside the physical body or even while the physical body is not functioning and may be defined as "dead." This most clearly occurs from the reports of near-death experiences, where such observations have been documented, with even greater accuracy than one could predict by adults

and children who do not have medical knowledge or who might gather the information in an ordinary manner (Fenwick & Fenwick, 1995; Moody, 1975, 1988; Morse & Perry, 1990, 1992, 1994; Morrissey, 1997; Ring, 1998, Sabom, 1998; Sutherland, 1993). There also are reports of such experiences under extremely stressful situations with children, such as when they are being abused as children by adults (DeFrain, Nelson, and Chambers, 1997). These are similar to reports of soldiers, who experience leaving the body under torture without ever learning how to do so. This seems to be an ability that people have, but we are unaware of the exact process or even awareness that it exists. Yet under such extreme circumstances, we seem to have a natural ability to do this without any prior learning. This, of course, also suggests that the essence is not synonymous with the body, but rather can function separately from the body. This would support teachers who have argued for centuries that we are not are bodies, but rather more than the physical, emotion, or mental functioning that we associate with the physical being (Jaxon-Bear, 2001; Sogyal Rinpoche, 1993).

2. The essence appears to be able to communicate without words (telepathic or thought communication). This work again comes from the near-death research (see references in #1 above) and the work with psychomanteums (Moody, 1993). This is especially clear with the infant and man in Russia, where the essence of a man outside his body communicated with an infant who was in his body (Eadie, 1996). It also occurs when people are not out of their bodies nor in an altered state, as with the work on psychomanteums. This also is supported by Grof's (1993, 1998) work with people in altered states and remembering experiences as a fetus or infant, information they report not consciously knowing at the time and later confirmed by others. Such an ability to communicate and gather information again seems to be a natural ability, exhibited at many different ages including infancy, without any need to be taught or trained. When we move into a state where we do not experience or quit thinking about our limitations, we seem to be able to carry on such communication in a very natural manner.

3. The essence seems to guide the healing process of an individual's experience. Such guidance is seen somewhat less directly with Grof's work (1975 to 2006), where the individual connects to information stored and retrieved during a healing session while in an altered state. More directly, Allison (Allison & Schwarz, 1998) identified what he initially called the ISH, although he later called it the essence. This aspect of the individual was separate from the alter-personalities, with complete knowledge of the individual as well as the implications of acts or interactions the individual had experienced. In addition, the essence knew what to do to help the individual heal, more so than the trained professional with assessments, colleagues, and research to help the psychiatrist. This also is supported by the work by Gresham and associates (Gresham & Nichols, 2002) during energy healing sessions with people. In these cases, the essence may well share information without the direct knowledge of the "personality" of the person, in part because the "communication" may not take place on the same plane as the personality. Yet once again, the essence seems able to gather, store, and share information without any "training" or "learning" taking place from infancy to elderly.

4. The essence also is able to split the main personality or character structure into alter-personalities when under stress, in order to survive the pressure of the situation (Allison & Schwartz, 1998). Such splitting would suggest that the personality is more flexible and dynamic, even separate from the one doing the splitting and developing, as seen in Lowen's (1975, 1990) and Pierrakos' (1990, 1997) notion of character structure and the perspective of the Enneagram about fixation compared to the higher lesson (Almaas, 1998,1999; Jaxon-Bear, 2001; Maitri, 2001, 2009). In a less severe form, an essence also appears to be able to help the personality move to an altered state under stress, as reported by children who were abused (DeFrain et al., 1997).

5. The essence uses multiple sources for information and ways of knowing information, including physical, emotional, mental, and spiritual (or the different energetic

frequency bands corresponding to what we call each of these elements). Such a conclusion comes from the work by Grof (1993, 1998), where people know information about their birth and prior to their birth, or other intense and stressful situations. The work on near-death experiences (Fenwick & Fenwick, 1995; Moody, 1975, 1988; Morse & Perry, 1990, 1992, 1994; Morrissey, 1997; Ring, 1998, Sabom, 1998; Sutherland, 1993) also supports the idea that people know information from many different sources, as does the work by Allison (Allison & Schwarz, 1998). In addition, work by Leigh & Metzker (Leigh et al., 1999; Metzker & Leigh, 2004) on the changes in energy fields of infants and young children provide data regarding how children use such multiple sources to gather diverse information, from changes in their auric fields to energetic connections from the 6th Chakra to people and objects, or energy rings formed with parents or caregivers. Adolescents and adults also shift their energy fields during interactions, with different forms occurring depending on how connecting or separating the interactions tend to be (Leigh et al., 2010a, 2010b). Such abilities are beyond the current scope of child development and cannot be explained with current theories, but they can be important aspects of information for parents working with their children or adolescents as well as professionals, such as teachers and therapists.

6. In addition to the multiple sources of information, the essence seems to retain and use such information for both growing and healing. Again, Grof's (1993, 1998) work identifies how memories and emotional trauma can block aspects of an individual, and the releasing of that information facilitates the healing process. At the same time, such information, once released from the emotional field, can be useful for continued development and understanding. Much of the near-death research supports the idea that learning and growing are important aspects of our experience, with many of the painful memories holding important information for our learning (Ring, 1998). In his work, Allison (Allison & Schwarz, 1998) also found that the essence held a lot of important information about learning from difficult experiences, but

such experiences also segmented the personality. With the help of the essence guide, Allison was able to help the individual integrate the different pieces back towards some type of whole, allowing for greater health and growing. Weiss (1988, 1992, 2000) also discusses how the integration and understanding of information held within the individual could facilitate growth beyond the areas where one would get "stuck," to develop greater health. This also is true when others work with people in the process of individual healing sessions (Gresham & Nichols, 2002). Again, the implications of such aspects can be very useful when parents tune into this information or professionals, such as teachers, therapists, or physicians, incorporate this information into the healing process.

7. Closely related to the previous point, the essence also seems to have an understanding of connections and the impacts our actions have on others and ourselves. Such a perspective seems automatic with many of the near-death experiences, although it also is possible here in this life as well (Ring, 1998). While such a perspective may be understandable in adults, there is evidence that such a perspective occurs in very young children who have such experiences but would not have the traditional cognitive development to explain such understandings (Morse & Perry, 1990, 1992, 1994). It also is seen in some of the explanations made by the ISH or essence in Allison's work (Allison & Schwarz, 1998). It is possible not only to see this in individuals at times, but it also includes approaches taken to teach children when we try to help them take the perspective of the other. What is particular important is that it is so easily done by the essence, even in very young children, somehow taking a larger and interconnected perspective of all our actions and deeds, both those that are helpful and those that are harmful. What is interesting about the work with children is that such a perspective occurs prior to the traditionally viewed developmental stage for taking the perspective of others and may come from a larger consciousness rather than an individual mental perspective. Again, helping children incorporate this piece rather than further separating from

it could help make shifts in their development that would be helpful not only to the child, but also to the family, school, and society.

8. Based on the pilot work by Leigh and Metzker (Leigh et al., 1999; Metzker & Leigh, 2004), young infants seem to use their energy centers (chakra centers) and fields to gather information around them. Given the lack of cognitive and physical development from a tradition point of view, it is hypothesized that the essence of the child is doing such information gathering in a very natural way. Yet this ability appears in the child before greater mental structures are formed, and may even be working underneath such structures after they are formed. In fact, the traditional perspective regarding infants not sensing any separation from a parent may be a more accurate description of the greater consciousness reality, although it is seen as a "lack of development" from traditional developmental perspectives. In this case, it may be the adult who is lacking perspective of the interconnectedness of us all, both energetically and consciously. When we take a "deficit" or "blank slate" view of children because of our own disconnection from the larger, conscious connection, we view the sense of no separation as a lack of understanding reality, and we define that as normal or the norm. In this case, it may be our infants who teach us about "reality" in the sense of a larger energetic and conscious connection even when we see the bodies as separate. Rather than one or the other being reality, it may be that both are accurate, especially when we begin to incorporate a larger perspective and possibilities of reality. When adults develop enough to connect to the larger energetic web that connects us all, we may begin to help children work with both connection and separation, rather than focusing on inaccurate dichotomy.

9. We also see that the essence develops connections that are important and helpful to others. This is seen in the work by Cheek (1995) on bonds and communication between mothers and their fetus. Such a hypothesis also develops from the NDE research and Weiss' work (1988, 1992). These connections play an important part of the

300

interactions between people, as well as the connection between the essence of an individual and the energy fields all around. This is where the essence system plays out connections with larger energy systems, whether through interactions or in the larger environment (Leigh, 2004). Again, parents and professionals who understand and begin to work with this larger perspective may begin to help children develop and maintain the energetic connections that are natural and exist, whether or not we pay attention to them. Rather than focusing children away from such connections, we might help them learn to maintain and incorporate such connections at a much more conscious level in their lives.

10. Related closely to the previous point, young children, particularly infants, literally make energy connections with others, especially caregivers. These connections can be seen in the form of energy "rings," coming out of the infant and connecting to the parent or other caregivers (Leigh et al., 1999; Metzker & Leigh, 2004). Such connections do not seem to be just about information, but rather forming a connection in a way apparently familiar to young infants. Again, given the lack of "cognitive" and physical development in infants as we know it, it is hypothesized that the essence forms such energy connections and shapes on a level that is quite natural, and probably from a larger consciousness. As children become focused more and more on verbal language and other aspects of the physical world and growth, and possibly because such forms are not initiated with them or identified as important parts of their world, they seem to quit creating such energetic forms by the ages of four or five. It very well may be that such capabilities are not lost, but rather simply are not used, as they are not seen as important. They seem to occur at certain times, such as when family members communicate (Leigh, 2004; Leigh et al., 2010a, 2010b), and they may occur during the development of "love" relationships when older, but no investigation to our knowledge has been conducted on these latter aspects of relationships and interactions.

These ten aspects are hypothesized characteristics and abilities of the essence. Beyond these and other possible aspects, the energy field of the individual and others around, including other people as well as those fields formed in the environment, also are important elements of this perspective. From this point of view, people are seen as energy beings, including the essence. In this case, energy is being viewed as information, which increasingly is being done in physics (Abraham, 1994; Bohm, 1980; Capra, 1996; Sheldrake, 1981; Schwartz & Russek, 2001) and medicine (Becker, 1990; Benor, 2004; Dossey, 1999; Gerber, 1988; Myss, 1996; Northrup, 1994; Shealy & Myss, 1993). Thus, the essence is a core aspect of the energy or information concentration, yet the connections extend in many directions with different types of energy fields, all of which are important. In this way, the extensions and connections form a "web of life," as described by Capra (1996), in important and life sustaining ways. We have focused most on the essence of children in this article, but this is just a small piece of the energy field research that has been going on for decades. Still, the essence is an important part of how each of us connects, possibly in ways we have not previously identified or seen as important, especially with infants.

When children are viewed from an Essence perspective, they are seen in a very different manner. For example, when children are conceptualized as energy beings with a dynamic essence, they are seen as open, flowing energy fields where they connect energetically to significant people in their lives, such as parents and other caregivers. They have a capable communication system within them, which we do not recognize or give any credence, quite possibly because it has been ignored, disconnected, or atrophied in most adults. For example, there is evidence that twins are able to communicate with each other without any spoken language, even at a distance (Bates et al., 1987; Playfair, 2002). If that is true for twins, it also seems likely that a mother who carries a fetus for nine months would have that same ability. This also seems to be true for fathers who are highly involved and use energy connections to interact with the fetus before being born. There certainly is a "knowing" that occurs between mothers and infants, which extends beyond language and traditional communications (Pearce, 1977). For example, heart rates and stimulation between mothers and infants parallel each other during both stressful and harmonious interactions, suggestive of physiological attunement (Field, 1987). It appears plausible that communications and attunements would occur through a harmonizing of frequencies in the energy fields. It also is suggested that infants are able to respond and participate through a type of "knowing," thereby responding to energy information within their field. It is this same manner in which an adult, while outside of a body that was lying in the morgue, was able to "communicate" with an infant and have the infant share important information with him, a "knowing" that occurred and was communicated by an infant only a few days old (Eadie, 1996).

With an awareness and reliance on such communication processes, parents, teachers, physicians, therapists, and others might influence and enhance a child's immediate post-conception communication interaction through various means. Rather than being empty vessels who need to be taught and socialized, in fact, it may be the children who will be the "teachers" of adults in ways of connecting to the heart, of communicating without words, and of "knowing" beyond the type of mental cognition we seem to value above all else. When infants and children are recognized as having an Essence with connections to all types of energy fields, including our own, a different type of relationship can be developed between adults and children where both teach and learn from each other, valuing what each has to offer without having critical aspects discounted.

We would like to provide one case example of how such a change in perspective might impact not only the way we interact and work with children, but also how they begin to change as well. The following is a true example of two very conscious parents who knew of this work and applied it to their interactions with their first child. Of course, the names and any identifying information have been changed, but nothing about the interactions have been modified. In this case, the interactions were described by one of us (JAM).

Case Example

While watching this tiny newborn human baby (we will call him Michael), I was mesmerized by the focusing and attending that went on between parents and infant. I have had several children myself, and I have worked professional with many parents and very young children. In this case, these clients intended that the infant be conceived in conscious awareness. During the pregnancy, they both energetically connected to their fetus, sang to him, talked to him out load, touched and generally sent loving energy to him from conception to birth.

At birth, the newborn was immediately drawn to the parents' voices and light from the window—natural light even though the room lights were on. Michael was a particularly focused newborn, more so than any infant I have ever seen. Although the judgment was made to perform a C-section, the parents were given equal participation in making the decision. It was a disappointment to them because the pregnancy was monitored by a midwife, where with the parents was expecting to participate in a *natural* birth. However, the inference from this decision is that the baby's awareness was not affected since both parents 'talked' him through the invasive birth. The father talked from a distance and connected energetically while the mother was open to being with the infant and focusing on him in the birth process rather than on her own discomfort or body invasion.

Currently, Michael is 9.5 months old. Since the day of the birth, the parents attend to this infant with eye contact, genuine positive regard, and, while observing small frustrations with learning, are constantly addressing him in clear verbal communications, using sign language, and including body language. They offer to help in learning particular skills and often sing with him. What all this has done is allow for the child to experience only apparent slight anxiety concerning learning tasks and to give him the ability to attempt more complex tasks, more so than any baby I have witnessed.

When attempting to mediate debilitating frustrations, the father especially has made connections at a core level, which is observed by psychic awareness and felt by the father. From his report, the baby is a willing participant energetically, and he seems to notice the energetic connections of the father. The connection seems to sooth Michael and help him relax. It also seems to encourage him in greater exploration at the time and respond energetically during the exploration. From my professional observation, the baby is more peaceful, alert, aware, and courageous when such connections are made between Michael and his father.

The case example does not prove the theory by any means. The example is intended to help parents and professionals begin to understand how they might participate with infants, children, and adolescents from a different perspective. In this case, parents and professionals not only are working with children on the physical level, but they also are including the energetic levels. In this way, development occurs by supporting physical development to occur in addition to rather than instead of the energetics that infants seem to bring into the world. Rather than boundaries between parents and children being a place of separation and protection, they work more like cell membranes that allows for an ongoing exchange, knowing what is best to allow into the organism and what should remain outside (Jordan, 2001). This seems like a much more useful metaphor, especially when we begin to see the membrane as the "brain" of the cell, rather than the nucleus, which apparently functions more like reproductive organs (Lipton, 2005). In this way, we again to move into a larger perspective that allows for more spontaneous evolution (Lipton & Bhaerman, 2009).

When children are seen from an expanded view, different research questions are asked that were never considered before, not because children are any different, but because the perspective and questions have changed. From this perspective, issues identified in the beginning of this paper, such as attachment, holding information in place, creating meaning, and transmission of values, all take on a new light, with further questions to be tested and investigated.

It has been difficult to find a means of understanding how children might exhibit such abilities or ways to see how a different knowing may occur with infants. The contribution of Essence Theory allows for such explanations to exist and expand the many new hypotheses to be tested. This theory is both old and new, and it is based on an integration of many different areas of work, including electro-dynamic field theory and the human energy field research, as well as research and other works in many different areas. Previously, such work has been ignored by much of the scientific community because we had such difficulty with a coherent perspective, measurement challenges, and confidence with the information that was obtained. More recent theoretical and empirical work has changed that, and the inclusion of this collective work begins to change the theories and research about children. Even more critically, this theory increases the way parents and professionals view and work with children, the way prospective parents consider the way children are conceived, and the way parents, teachers, and other adults interact as well as treat children. In this case, our role moves from a dependent, separated, and inferior child to an interconnected and respected child who has an essence that interconnects with and influences the energy fields of all around them.

We do not assume that all work cited here is absolutely true without question. Individually, all the work here has raised questions and been somewhat tentative in any conclusions. That seems to be characteristic of a new ways of viewing things and new perspectives. In addition, there are many more questions than answers raised here and many new hypotheses to be tested in different ways. Yet the diversity of work, both research and clinical, as well as theoretical work done in different fields, all point to new ways of looking at children that seem important and fruitful. We simply are suggesting that the collective efforts reviewed here and the ideas we have contributed to these works begins to form a picture or view of children that previous theories and research could not address. This does not discount previous theoretical and empirical work, as we said in the beginning, but expands our view of children and the possibilities for research. Certainly each child is different, which may be an "innate personality" and characteristics from genetics or learned behavior from the environment. Alternatively, it may be that each child is a unique essence with its own energy field interacting in unique ways with people and the environment around them. In addition, children may have ways of knowing and gathering information that we have only begun to explore and understand. Given that there is no real explanation for "innate" beyond genetics, which usually explains only a small portion of the variance, additional perspectives that expand possible explanations and research questions may be useful and provide other testable explanations for things occurring with children than traditional perspectives have not been able to explain. More importantly, this new perspective may help us work and be with children in ways that are more useful, integrative, and positive for their development than previous perceptions. This new theory simply adds another dimension to the approach, possibly broadening our view of who children are and how we might interact and support them in additional ways.

The focus of this perspective is not only to see infants and children in terms of their essence and energy fields or as energy beings, but also to help them hold onto their own essence as a direct guide in the development of their lives in more conscious ways. While cultural specifics vary from one group to another, this essence may help children hold a larger picture, one where we are not completely separate people, but rather individuals who also are connected in the larger whole (Capra, 1996). It may well help them keep the ways of knowing information about themselves and others at a more conscious level, where we look at how our actions and behaviors are related to others and impact others. Children still will need to develop language, cognitive skills, and social skills as part of their development, but they may hold these in a larger and more integrated environment than occurs currently. It also may help minimize the defense mechanisms that may well cutoff the connection to the essence and become so protected they do not stay aware of their body, emotions, or thoughts without distortions. Of course, as "teachers" and "guides", adults also may need to do the same thing. Such a focus on the essence also allows children to make clearer connections at multiple levels, as well as allowing adults to respond in the same manner, providing a different foundation for teaching and developing interventions with children, youth, and families.

APPENDIX B

OVERVIEW OF THE ENNEAGRAM

IMAGINING IS LIKE

Imagining is like feeling around
in a dark lane, or washing
your eyes with blood.

You *are* the truth
from foot to brow. Now,
what else would you like to know?

- Rumi[1]

The Enneagram is a tool to help people identify differences between the socialized self and the essential self or essence in nine different styles. As individuals become more familiar with the Enneatypes, they discover distortions made about reality and themselves that taint their view of the world. Unraveling those twisted perspectives allow people to increase and incorporate their own essential lesson, bringing greater peace, joy, and satisfaction to their lives.

Historical Perspective

There are two related branches of or approaches to the Enneagram. One branch was brought forth and developed by George Ivanovich Gurdjieffe, who as a young boy began asking about the essential nature of people and traveled great distances to find answers to his questions. As he grew and developed, he attracted other people because of his interesting and charismatic manner, although he also apparently could be quite rough and challenging. He ended up teaching about a model, which he called "The Fourth Way," which included an approach he reportedly received from the Sarmoung community in the Hindu Kush, [2,3] a group that Gurdjieff dates back to 2500 b.c. This model and diagram he passed on in general terms to students, such as P. D. Ouspensky[4,5] and J. G. Bennett,[6] but Gurdjieffe did not leave any written description of the Enneatypes (different styles of working with and interacting with the world) or any details of how to use the Enneatypes as a model for change. Gurdjieffe's work also impacted many other people, including these prominent leaders include (according to Speeth)[7] Rudyard Kipling, Frank Lloyd Wright, Georgia O'Keeffe, and Moshe Feldenkreis.

A second branch was developed and shared by Oscar Ichazo, who was familiar with Gurdjieffe's work. At a young age (23), Oscar Ichazo studied with mystics in Buenos Aires, who made it possible for him to continue his work with master teachers in the Middle and Far East. He then returned to Bolivia and began further developing his work and offering it to others. Claudio Naranjo heard about Ichazo's work and was excited "to find somebody who declared himself, like Gurdjieff, an emissary of the specific school towards which my search had been polarized in recent years, the school about which Gurdjieff wrote at the end of <u>Meetings With Remarkable Men</u> and Roy Davidson wrote in his traveler's report on a visit to a Sarmoung community in Hindu Kush."[8] Unlike Gurdjieff, Ichazo[9,10] went beyond a discussion of the principle of three and the diagram to describe the holy ideas, passions, and some characteristics of the fixations. But Ichazo, apparently like the Sarmoung community and Gurdjieff, kept much of the information fairly secret, limiting it to people who participated in his trainings in Bolivia and later in New York as part of his Arica System.

It was Naranjo who began teaching students in Berkeley, CA in the 1970s that made the information more available to the general public, followed by many other publications and further explanations of the systems.[11-13] Ichazo, like Gurdjieff, also included movement, in this case Arica Psychocalisthenics,[14] but it did not seem to include music as an essential aspect of the movements as did Gurdjieff. However, both approaches, as continued by Naranjo, focused on the spiritual aspect, including Ichazo's intention that this work lead towards enlightenment. In addition, Naranjo, because of his training in Psychoanalysis and his admiration for the work by Karen Horney, began to describe the development of Enneatype fixations in psychoanalytic terms, a tradition continued by Almaas[15] and Maitri.[16,17]

As more people became interested in the Enneagram, there also became a division in how this model was used. Almaas, Maitri, and Jaxon-Bear[18,19] continued the tradition of focusing on the model as a way for spiritual growth, although Jaxon-Bear incorporated more of a Hindu philosophy than has been used by other teachers. In contrast, other authors used this model as an understanding of personality.[20-27] While the holy ideas were mentioned, the primary focus was an understanding the basic personality differences of humans rather than spiritual beings. Here, I will focus on the Enneagram as a model for spiritual development without the trappings of psychoanalytic theory or the focus on the Hindu religion. This type of approach seems to be increasing in more recent publications by others as well.[28,29]

Common Features of Each Enneatype

The Enneagram model consists of three elements: the circle, the triangle, and the hexad, a figure containing six lines. The circle represents connection and unity, a line with no beginning or ending. The triangle occurs in the middle of the circle, connecting three core points on the Enneagram. The hexad is a particular combination of six lines connecting the other six points on the Enneagram in a particular fashion.

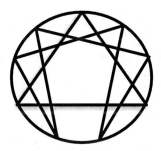

What is rather interesting about this figure is that the sequencing of these lines occurs in the same fashion as when the number 1 is divided by the number 7 (.1428571....). In fact, this same sequence of numbers occurs when the numbers 2, 3, 4, 5, and 6 are divided by 7, although the order of the numbers changes. Bennett[6] discusses some implications of the symbol as a continuation of Gurdjieff's work.

Each of the nine points where the lines and circle interconnect is a type on the Enneagram. Each point has its own characteristic, and there are some commonalities. For example, each point has both an expansive aspect, referred to by most authors as a holy idea, or what I call the essential lesson. This expansive point leads to a greater understanding of a key issue or lesson we must learn in order to unravel the distortion. The holy idea or essential lesson is some issue from which we grow and learn in our lives, an aspect that demonstrates our strengths when we are in a more expanded state, or what might be called our "strength pattern."[30] In this case, we are more aware, open-hearted, conscious, and learning. We also tend to be clearer, move more easily, and utilize our talents and skills in the most effective manner. This often can be observed during the best times in our lives, our proudest achievements, and when we are feeling most peaceful in our hearts. By incorporating this holy idea, learning this lesson, or living from the essence of our key issue, we let go of the distortion and, in the process, gain much freedom.[19]

When we do not know, understand, or learn this holy idea or understand the essential issue or lesson, we spend our time living from the distortion, illusion, and spend our lives in the more contracted aspect called fixation. The fixation typically is manifested when we are functioning more from fear, anger, or unable to feel love. It is a protected place, closed hearted, unconscious, and even asleep. This is behaving in a more "limiting pattern" as one colleague calls it.[30] This also is what more people refer to as our personality from the traditional Enneagram approach, although Riso & Hudson describe stages of development.[26] This continuum from essence to fixation has to do with where each of us is functioning within that Enneatype.

What is important to remember is that each Enneatype fixation comes from a perspective of separation, a distortion of the holy idea or essential lesson, a delusion about reality. The Enneagram is like a prism, separating out nine different objective perspectives on reality (in this case referring to a more conscious view of reality as represented in the holy ideas or essential lesson) with their nine corresponding deluded perspectives (fixations). In this case, a delusion is something which we assume to be true but which is not true. It is a twist in our minds that distort our perceptions. Its resolution is not a particular state of consciousness, but rather a corrected view of reality through which all states are experienced. Waking up to this distortion is not just a matter of confronting a lack within oneself, but rather exposing one's delusions.[15] Working with and reducing fixations is not just a matter of going into details about how each operates (treating the style like a personality and defining it as who we are), but rather seeing how a fixation core is the result of this basic delusion about reality, which can be changed or corrected through truly understanding and incorporating the essential lesson.[15] This is the fundamental difference between using the Enneagram as personality in contrast to its use as a means of increased consciousness or spiritual growth.

It also is important to keep in mind that every fixation is a style of control. It is a way of maintaining control for a desired outcome. This control is a response to living in fear and the avoidance of pain. In order to make a shift to essence and living in a more expanded state, it is important to begin to surrender both the means of control and the desired outcome. It is in this way that we begin to live from essence based on love.

There is a Sanskrit term for being, consciousness, or bliss called Satchidananda. This is a description of the subjective experience of Brahman, the sublimely blissful experience of boundless, pure consciousness, a glimpse of what the Hindu believe is ultimate reality. This term is composed of three aspects. "Sat" refers to the consciousness of being, what might be described as pure awareness of the body without distortions and judgments. "Chid" refers to the consciousness of intelligence that comes from an emptiness and silence of the mind, allowing thoughts to appear and dissolve without attachment to them. "Ananda" refers to the consciousness of love or bliss that comes from an open flowing of emotions, again without attachment or getting stuck in any one. From this perspective, Satchidananda occurs when we have a balance of expansive awareness or consciousness in body, emotions, and mind.[19] Another way to look at this is the combination of all nine essential lessons take us to a clear (undistorted) and unified view of reality, an integration of all nine lessons of essence.

Below is a figure of the Enneagram diagram with the 9 Enneatypes:

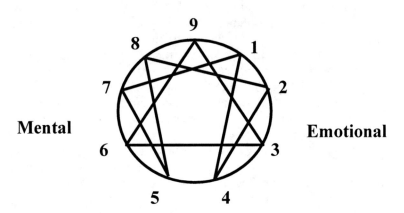

Physical

Enneatype 9: Love and the Peacemaker

The top of the triangle is Point 9 and the core point of the physical triad (Enneatypes 9, 8, and 1). This triad is composed of three lessons of essence that focus on the total view of reality or the basic principles of the reality around us (Love, Truth, and Perfection). These lessons also produce a felt sense of self and learning to trust the intelligence of the body. The fixation aspects of the physical triad tend to focus on autonomy, but they are based underneath by anger, rage, and often repression, usually resulting in physical tensions and boundaries. There typically is a resistance to the present (although not necessarily a focus on the past or future) and a formed distortion around instincts and the root of the life force.

What is very interesting is that the core point of each triad often does not look at all like the aspects described for the fixations of the triad. For example, Enneatype 9 usually looks nothing like anger, rage, or repression. This point often is called The Peacemaker. It also does not appear to be seeking autonomy, for there often is a great focus on connection and helping others by making everything peaceful and pleasant.

The essential lesson for Enneatype 9 is Love. In some ways, this is the most fundamental of all the essential lessons, and they cannot be learned without resolving the core issue of point 9. As Almaas[15] argues, this is the "heart of the truth." In this case, it is not so much a feeling of love, being in love, or the essential aspects of love. Rather, the issue is seeing existence without distortion that makes our entire existence lovable. It is the fact that objective reality has an intrinsic quality of being wonderful and pleasing, that it is intrinsically lovable. It also is understanding that everything around us and in us is composed of love, that love is the basic reality of the universe. So rather than an emotion of feeling love, it is seeing reality as composed of or comprised of being love, such that there is a sense of lovability for all aspects of our reality. When we see and understand this basic view of reality, it takes us into action that is based on love and expresses this expansive reality through all we do.

The fundamental distortion that occurs when we focus on separation rather than interconnection is that love is localized. This gets played out by the belief that love exists in some places and not others, rather than comprising all of our reality. If love is localized and exists only in some places, then the key is to understand where it exists and where it does not exist. The particular distortion and fundamental belief for Enneatype 9 is that it exists external to these people in places all around but not inside of them. It is not who they are. In this way, people in point 9 begin to feel increasingly unlovable.

The basic fear is of loss and separation from others or even of annihilation, given that there is little to love internally. The basic message they develop (even if it is never said to them out loud) is that they are OK as long as those around them are good or OK. This is the way they begin to interpret subtle messages and actions they experience in their lives. The desired outcome is to maintain their inner stability and peace of mind by focusing on where love resides, which is in others, external to those of this Enneatype.

In order to avoid such pain of feeling unlovable (given that love resides external to them), the general reaction is to fall asleep, numb themselves (drugs, alcohol, television, movies, mindless games, habitual routine) or focus on other people by making them happy, oftentimes by being very funny. So their basic nature, especially with reference to self investigation, typically is laziness and indolence. This does not apply to all aspects of their lives. They often learn to compensate by being very active and busy, through the influence of Enneatype 1, where the focus is on perfection, or Enneatype 8, where the focus is on the pursuit of truth. Because their focus is external with nothing lovable internally, they will work hard to connect with others who are smarter, funnier, better, more competent, prettier/more handsome, and more lovable. Given no internal strength, they often go to great measures to avoid conflict and therefore become very good peace makers. Internally, if a strong conflict arises, they first will disappear, either emotionally (become very flat, non-participatory), even disappearing physically or "dissolving" internally. But when pushed to the extreme, they may respond with such anger and rage that even they become concerned that such strong emotions cannot be controlled. They may experience such fits of rage that feel like they could destroy anything in front of them. Because of this core, deeply buried, internal fear of almost uncontrollable rage, they appear very pleasant and in control of such out bursts, which also would drive people away and prove their worst fear true, that they are indeed unlovable. They also are likely to give in easily to any apparent differences or conflict in order to keep people close to and loving them. They try to keep the peace at all costs and usually do not feel like they have the right to ask for anything or bother someone else. As one Enneatype 9 described it, "In the case of confrontation, I respond with indifference. That's where my power and strength lie."

When deep in fixation, these people often are quite passive, going with the flow. They are less likely to leave relationships, which could create conflicts, and often are peaceful and passive in connection with others. At the same time, they cover their feelings with humor, working to make everyone else happy, doing things for others because they are more important. In this way, their behaviors are somewhat similar and can look like Enneatype 2, where the focus is on taking care of others.

The Enneatype 9 person in fixation often appears sweet, slow, and syrupy. What is most noticeable is the absence of anger in general or the expression of anger in passive/aggressive or indirect ways (sarcasm, for example). They may "space-out," which can be seen as a blank look or clouding of the eyes. They are caught between conformist and non-conformist, compliance and rage, usually responding with non-action and a mechanization of life. Their talking style usually is a focus on endless tangents and sagas, where being listened to becomes an important unconscious issue, at times including great stories and humor. Because there is nothing lovable internally, they often merge into others, losing themselves. At the same time, they become very good at truly reflecting all points of view, typically better than any other Enneatype. This is part of the strength that develops through the fixation experience, while at the same time keeping them limited in terms of growth and expansion. They present themselves as calm and peaceful people, joining organizations that are supportive of that. They may be joyful people who love to laugh and have a good time as part of the crowd. They typically discount what they can do or what they have contributed to a group. They often defer to others in terms of making decisions and taking the lead, more likely part of a group rather than leaders with a focus on themselves. They sleep a lot, especially in times of stress, enjoying long periods of passive activity (television, movies, or computer games). They talk about fantasies around mind and emotions without experiencing either.

Every Enneatype has its essential lesson to learn and the strengths that come both from the skills that develop from the lesson as well as those that develop from the contracted fixation, the other side of the two-edged sword. At the same time, every Enneatype has a downside or problems that occur with the fixation. These aspects are more obvious in some Enneatypes than in others, but they occur in all nine points. For Enneatype 9, they often are in denial of health, financial, or personal problems. They may well have some obstinacy and resistance to getting help, in part because they do not feel worthy of assistance and support. Their general awareness and vitality may be very dampened and repressed, especially when deep in fixation. There is a general sense of inadequacy and neglectfulness, with a dependency on others that allows them to be exploited. They may experience chronic depression and emotional flatness (other than when they are up to help or entertain others). There may even be an extreme dissociation where they feel lost, confused, and deeply disconnected.

It is important to make several key shifts and changes in order to dissolve the distortion and begin to see and experience the essential lesson. With Enneatype 9, it is important to learn to recognize what they want from any given situation, beginning to value who they are internally. It is helpful to discriminate between genuine humility and the tendency to dismiss themselves and their abilities, fundamentally discounting who they are as a person. An important word for them to learn is "No." It is fine to say this to people, again gaining value for who they are internally and what they bring to the world. One way to amplify such valuing is to invest some time and energy developing themselves and their talents. At the same time, it is important to learn to recognize and process their anger, an emotion we all experience. Anger, from my perspective, is an internal response to an incongruence between two elements, such as what we want and what others may push on to us. Anger is very useful and may even motivate us into action rather than taking a more complacent response, such as depression. Yet we do not need to push our anger onto others. But, if we are not even aware of our feelings or not willing to process them, we tend to repress or dump on others these feelings that we have difficulty even understanding. Learning to accept, recognize, experience and process their own anger and feelings because they too are valued people is an important fundamental shift for this Enneatype. One of the ways others can be helpful is to assist this type to stay present with themselves and their feelings during times of stress and conflict, exploring options and possibilities, treating themselves as they would if they were helping others, because these people with the 9 Enneatype are as important and lovable as anyone. Related to this, it is helpful for them to become aware of their own needs and to express them directly rather than indirectly. Help them explore how to be empathic with others without losing themselves or dissolving. Finally, it can be useful to help them differentiate fantasy experiences from actually experiencing the present. In these ways, we begin to challenge the distortion and shift our view that love in fact is not separate and localized, but rather the foundation of our lives and of our universe, for those in this Enneatype and all of us.

Here are four examples from movies that Thomas Condon[31] and/or I think illustrate the 9 Enneatype being played on the big screen:

America's Sweethearts: Julia Roberts
Dances with Wolves: Kevin Costner & Graham Greene
Being There: Peter Sellers
Carnal Knowledge: Art Garfunkel & Ann Margret

Enneatype 8: Truth and The Boss

Like type 9, this Enneatype is part of the physical triad with an externalized focus of their energy. The emphasis of this type is on the essential lessons of reality and a fixation that is based in the body, with a foundation of anger and rage that allows for autonomy. The essential lesson here is Truth. From this perspective, truth is the awareness that undistorted reality objectively exists now and that this existence is its own definition and continues whether an individual understands it or not. When you experience pure, translucent, self-existing, boundless presence, you see that it is not only the fundamental nature of essence itself, but of everything that exists.[15] Like love, truth is experiencing an undistorted way that nature composes and experiences itself, and we are as integrated into that existence as any part of the universe. When we hold this clear view, our response is pure innocence, understanding, and working with nature in an easy and natural manner.

The distortion that occurs is a duality about life, opposition in all things because truth also is localized. This pure, boundless presence occurs in some places (heaven, certain parts of our world), but not in other places (many other parts of our earthly reality). So the focus is on the search of truth, what it is, and the defense of truth and justice. The difficulty is that when one is not in truth and the side of justice, one may feel guilty and bad, which is to be avoided at all costs. If this occurs, one becomes self-blaming, which also should be avoided, so one becomes the implementer of truth and justice. In this way, the passion may become a lust, not so much for food or even power, but a determination to be strong, right, and to implement one's understanding of truth and justice, no matter what it takes for that to happen. From this point of view, nothing should stop or get in the way of this seeking truth and justice, as everything and everyone else is less important. The basic fear is of being harmed or controlled by others, of violation. From this fear develops the basic message that you are good if you are strong and in control of the situation. The desired outcomes for these people is to protect themselves and the "deserving," determining their own course in life.

With this distortion of Truth, the Enneatype 8 searches for justice, living in the tension of self-righteousness and suppressed

319

rage. They feel OK if they are in charge and others let them be or support them having responsibility. They want to be the master of their fate, feeling the responsibility to provide, look out for those who are deserving, and present themselves as strong. They are curious what others are made of and may test them to determine their strength and grit. They view the world as a "dangerous" place, so they must be strong and are determined to get what they want and need. They often are very astute, and the end frequently justifies the means. They have little patience for incompetence (as defined by them), and they get triggered, even pushed into action by injustice (also as defined by them). They can be a bully to get their job accomplished and are quite comfortable with very large tasks (taking on a large project, planning a city, running a large corporation or organization, building an empire). They only stay if something is interesting and feel more alive when they are somewhere near an edge. They like to capture other people's attention, and the more the better.

Within the more contracted fixation, a person becomes an externalized anger point, pushing their uncomfortable feelings out on others. This is the home of the abusive character, expressed rage and blame on others, and the outlaw. This also is the home of the great warrior, afraid of nothing and taking on insurmountable tasks. They can be loud, demanding, short-tempered, and even verbally abusive. They are an innocent player within the "jungle" world. Showing weakness is avoided at all costs and appearance of competence becomes a shield to ward off attacks. They are very focused and often love to fight about justice and injustice, defending the underdog and "being right." They can defy authority and live by a personal code without regard to societal rules or regulations. They also can have paranoid feelings of being betrayed by "their people," which is a huge violation from which those who have betrayed them may never recover. In more extreme cases, they can experience increasing social isolation and bitterness, lacking both conscience and empathy. They may demonstrate episodes of rage, violence, and physical destructiveness, especially in reaction to being blamed, being betrayed, or feeling incompetent. This also may lead to plotting vengeance and retaliation against "enemies." In addition, they may see themselves as an "outlaw," even involved with criminal behavior with clear justification and exhibit episodes of striking back at society in a sociopathic manner. As this Enneatype gets into authority or responsibility mode, they tend to close their hearts in order to carry out their work.

Those with Enneatype 8 fixations may be viewed as a "bad" girl or boy, leaving their mark where ever they go. They often stand out as a "rugged individualist" and demonstrate a commanding presence, often with a steady inner drive. They typically are practical minded, usually with some type of dream for themselves. Because of the strong emphasis on self-competence, they also respect only people who are strong and can stand their ground, sometimes testing other's determination and commitment. As they can be a strong warrior, they also may well defend the "damsel in distress."

In order to loosen the fixation and distortion, people find it important to get in touch with their feelings, actually experiencing them in their body. When they are suffering, they might find constructive ways to grieve their losses and hurts rather than burying them or attacking others. It can be useful to find people they can trust and share intimate matters that may be bothering them. Incorporating some restraint in both their work and play is useful for the type. They may find it fruitful to examine their expectations for rejection and betrayal and allow themselves to be affected, again experiencing these feelings in their body. They could learn from Enneatype 9 and see the world from other people's perspective or point of view, even examining how their actions impact others. They could begin to have compassion for others (rather than simply defending an injustice), willing to help others without being responsible for them. It also would be useful to see and experience their anger, looking more inward rather than external for the triggering issue. Finally, like all fixations, yet especially with this one, opening their hearts is particularly important, living and working from this perspective in order the see and experience the natural essence of everything that exists. In this way, we begin to experience the boundless presence of the truth of the universe rather than a separation and duality imposed by our distortions.

Here are four examples from movies that Thomas Condon[31] and/or I think illustrate the 8 Enneatype being played in movies:

Meet Joe Black: Anthony Hopkins & Brad Pitt
Instinct: Anthony Hopkins
Breakfast Club: Judd Nelson
Lean On Me: Morgan Freeman

Enneatype 1: Perfection and The Perfectionist

The third Enneatype with internalized energy in the physical triad is 1, which has an essential lesson that also focuses on the general view of reality based on Perfection. In this case, the lesson is the awareness that reality is a process, moving with direction and purpose. Within this movement, each moment is connected to the process, and each moment is "perfect" in relation to the overall process. When our perception is like a clear mirror, without subjective judgment, we find reality to be just right and perfect. When we experience such a process, we also experience serenity as we relax into being in the right and perfect moment.[15]

Like other essential lessons, this type's perspective becomes distorted. In this case, the distortion occurs again with separation and the view that rightness is localized with a comparative judgment. In other words, some things are right and others are wrong. The difficulty in this case is the feeling of the person being wrong or flawed, which ends up experiencing life as "something is wrong with me." The reaction to such a feeling is to make things better, make myself better, which leads to constant improving. Given that we can never achieve "perfection" when in reality nothing is wrong with the process or us, and the distortion is based on a comparative judgment. This critical view leads to constant and insufficient improvement to remove the flawed and wrong parts of one's self, except the distortion or judgement itself. This leads to an anger that is turned inward (in contrast to the anger of Enneatype 8, that is turned outward on others) and leads to feelings of resentment. The basic fear here is of being "bad," defective, corrupt, or even "evil." The message that develops is that I am good or OK if I do what is right. So the desired outcome, which is impossible to achieve, is to be "good" in the sense of being perfect, having integrity, and being "virtuous." This again leads to a constant striving which never ends and is never sufficient or satisfied.

The basic issues for this Fixation are high standards and perfection for all. A person here feels OK only if they feel perfect and others tend to view them with perfection. They often feel like they have a mission in life with an underlying sense of knowing how things should be done, although often this knowing is not expressed out loud or shared with others. They tend to view other people as lazy and irresponsible because they do not work as hard or do things correctly (according to their internal judge). These people have a sense of what is right and what is wrong, and there are no exceptions. For them, things are done well if they are done perfectly, so nothing is quite right, always wanting to improve on everything. People here tend to be independent and try to figure things out for themselves, never losing control. Of course, no matter what they or others do, it is never going to be good enough because no one is sufficiently excellent or perfect according to their internal judgments. So an important aspect is being in "control" in order to make things perfect with their internal standards. They often suppress their own needs so they do not have to ask others, wanting to take care of themselves and not feeling like they deserve help from others. "Deep down, everyone forgets about me."

The fixation here becomes an internalized anger point. There is a strong internalization of a standard and values, where the person has their own sense of social rules and patterns. If anger occurs, the person turns it on him/herself or diverts it into work and improving, for expressed anger is not proper behavior. When anger is expressed, it shows up more often as resentment and judgment, evaluating one's own and other people's performances, or projecting it into the future as worry. The belief here is in hard work and making it through effort, feeling self-righteous and justifying their own actions through rationalization. This strong standard of values sometimes can "dissolve" through alcohol, shedding the "Puritan" role, and expression through sexuality. There may be intense feelings of disillusion and depression or outbursts of intolerance and condemnation. In the more extreme cases, there is obsessive thinking, compulsive behaviors, and periods of masochistic self-punishment.

Enneatype ones are people who would make a good "plains preacher" or small business owners, taking care of details. They are more likely to be viewed as a "good" girl or boy who would like to reform a situation or system, with a constant desire to improve it. They may leave a comfortable life to do something challenging, even extraordinary, because they felt something higher was calling them. They often try to justify their actions to themselves and others, and yet they can see some mistake or error in anything they do. They may balk at agreed-upon guidelines (usually silently), feeling like their own method would be more effective, which they will proceed to do. They typically will be at meetings on time, have things in order, and be quite consistent, even if they feel disorder internally. At the same time, they are highly sensitive to criticism from others, in part because of the constant internal criticism that goes on incessantly, which usually is more harsh than external judgments.

For people experiencing this fixation, it can be useful to get clear and well acquainted with their own inner judge. They will find it useful to become aware of their tendency to push themselves, sometimes beyond their limits of endurance. More importantly, it is very helpful to slow down and even stop their self-improvement projects, learning to just be and accept themselves as they are in the present moment. Letting others help them and understanding that contributions others make may even enhance their own perspective can be important. It is essential to become aware of their own needs and allow others to help them, as they do deserve support and assistance. Another big one, like Enneatype 9, is to recognize and process their anger through direct experiences and expression, knowing that anger sometimes is a part of the perfect moment. Building on this issue is to begin seeing the perfection in themselves, others, and nature without focusing on flaws. Related to this is to negotiate and compromise the way things are done, giving up their sense of knowing the "best" way to do things, avoiding judgment, criticism, and striving for improvement. It is helpful to encourage people in this Enneatype to celebrate accomplishments of others as well as their own, again without continual focus on flaws and improvements to what was done, even if they are not "perfect." It also is important that people here learn to relax and just play, maybe even sometimes "before work!" In these ways, again, the distortion can begin to relax and people may increasingly experience the perfection of every moment, even with the perfection of changes and the lack of change, finding the overall process to be just right.

Here are four examples from movies that Thomas Condon[31] and/or I think illustrate the 1 Enneatype being played on the big screen:

> PS, I love You: Hillary Swank
> Sleeping with the Enemy: Patrick Bergin
> Agnes of God: Anne Bancroft
> A Man for All Seasons: Paul Scofield

Enneatype 3: Law and The Achiever

Just as the physical triad includes three Enneatypes, the emotional triad includes points 3 (core), 2, and 4. In this case, the
essential lessons focus on the functioning of humanity, personal
identity, and the intelligence of the heart (Law & Harmony, Will
& Freedom, and Origin & Creation)[15]. These lessons give us a
sense of how human processes work in relation to an undistorted
view of reality. In contrast, the fixations focus on a search for
love, which feels separate and distant to these people. In response, they create an identity or image that seems like will at-
tract the love they seek. For this reason, these types sometimes
are referred to as image points. Yet there often is a feel of "need-
iness" in the search, wanting to experience the love that is sensed
and lost. The image feels like it will help them, not realizing it is
the unraveling of the distorted perspective of reality that will be
most essential for experiencing what they are seeking.

The intention of this triad is to maintain a personal identity
that will bring the attention and therefore the love they seek. The
focus in many ways is on the past, which is the history and story
of their identity. There is a concern with the love of or attachment to the socialized self, although there is not a conscious
sense that the self is false. But much of their energy has to do
with the development and maintenance of this self-image. The
underlying feeling is shame, again not usually very conscious to
these people.

The core of the emotion or feeling triad is Enneatype 3.
Here the essential lesson (Law, Harmony, Hope) is the recognition of the cosmic law of a natural order, path, and harmony of
things[15]. From this perspective, one understands that the universe
is whole, unified, and constantly changing. Everything is in motion and continuously perpetuates natural energy flows. As things
are altered, it modifies other aspects in a harmonious manner.
When one lets go into the process of natural order and harmony
around us, we do not have to take responsibility to produce to be
a part of this natural process. We can be who we are, in a state of
deep rest, which then gives us hope.[15] The distortion is that action is separate and therefore dependent on a doer, a separate
change agent. For this type, the image that develops is that if
these individuals work hard enough and achieve enough, they
will feel loved. "We become concerned about who is going to

325

take care of things and how things will be accomplished if the truth of who we are is this non-doing."[32] In this way, the 3 Enneatype is a deep exploration into connected action in contrast to separate action.

Like Enneatype 9 who rarely expresses anger, Enneatype 3 seldom shows emotion. For this image, emotions are like speed bumps that just slow them down. This type feels OK if others see them or think they are OK. They know they can accomplish something or anything if they just work hard enough. And they often do achieve many and great things, being usually quite successful in life. Of course, these are not the only people who are successful. But on the whole, this is where success is most likely to occur. This is the epitome of the American business person, Type A behavior. What they want to do is impress others, and they want to be loved for what they have done. For as they are, without work, their sense is that no one would love them. They are quite independent and even somewhat arrogant in their image, believing that "if all the world were like us, there wouldn't be any problems." They also are less likely to separate if married, for this would be an aspect of "failure" and tarnish their image. They look for quick solutions to everything, including health problems. They usually are goal oriented, even in personal development. "Just give me a list of what I need to do, and I will make the change!" On the other hand, it may be a challenge to notice any problems in their life, except as temporary behaviors or patterns for them to improve.

Their basic fear is being worthless, helpless, and having no value in life. The message that they develop for themselves is that they are good as long as they are productive, successful, and others think well of them. So their desired outcome is to feel worthwhile, accepted, and desirable. This is the place of gaining self-worth through production, cool competence, and maximum efficiency. As children, they feel loved for the product they produce rather than for themselves. Their talking style is not so much to "brag," but rather to indirectly propagandize about what they do or have done, as if that is who they are as people. They usually become very successful, obtaining financial success and considerable assets. They are constantly on the go, rarely taking time to rest or play. They often are involved in many different projects, always having things to be done and achieve success in many different arenas. They also typically are very well liked by others, although they also can be very demanding of people, imposing on others the same high standards they have for themselves.

While this type looks very positive on the surface, there are several costs to this highly developed image. People here often conceal the degree of emotional distress, may develop jealousy and unrealistic expectations of success, experience a lot of physical exhaustion and burnout from relentless workaholism, have difficulty expressing feelings and inner emptiness, and even develop severe episodes of rage and hostility when things do not go their way or work out for them.

In order to address the delusion of separation and that we only are loved by what we do, those in Enneatype 3 need to recognize when they are "turning it on" for someone. In contrast, it is useful to take time to relax, just have some fun, and let go of the list of things to do. Doing some meditation and paying attention to feelings and emotions also can be useful, even sharing their anxieties, vulnerabilities, and emptiness. They can serve more as part of a group rather than the "head," not having to be in charge and making sure things get completed. It can be useful to be creative for yourself rather than others, becoming more inner directed and authentic instead of such a strong external focus on accomplishment. Like all other Enneatypes, these changes occur best when one becomes more connected to the heart and opening the heart, separating "who we are" and "what we do." A focus on feeling and being rather than doing is important, following more of your heart's desires rather than social norms and expectations of others. Learning to do things that have no "goal" also can be useful, letting go of competition or success to focus more on fun and enjoyment. Finally, it can be useful to face and share any feelings of "worthlessness" that may be hidden deep beyond all the doing and success. Being part of the natural flow of things, in harmony and hope, helps them see this functioning of reality. "Everything that happens is part of the fabric of the universe unfurling itself. So nothing happens in isolation from the whole of that fabric, and no one initiates action of her own accord, nor do we cause things to occur separately from the momentum of that whole. It is easier to understand that we are inseparable from the oneness of the universe than it is to understand that we actually do nothing in isolation from the dynamism of the whole of reality."[33]

Here are four examples from movies that Thomas Condon[31] and/or I think illustrate the 3 Enneatype being played on the big screen:

> The Family Man: Nicolas Cage
> Rain Man: Tom Cruise
> Six Degrees of Separation: Will Smith
> Dangerous Liaisons: John Malkovich

Enneatype 2: Will and The Helper

The essential lesson we learn with this Enneatype is that the "will" is the awareness of reality, moving with direction, flowing with a force that is based on natural laws (Enneatype 3). The easiest way to deal with this force is to move with it. If you surrender to the Will, you realize that you actually are part of the flow of reality. Then it is not a matter of flowing with it, but rather realizing there is no separation, as the wave is to the ocean.[15] Moving as a part of it is both true will and true freedom. Being aware of this force, with you being a part of it, brings true humility. The delusion is that you are separate and that intention, will, and choice are localized. Thus, intention and will exist in some people, and some are more aware of it, paying more attention to it. From this delusion, people build the image that they understand and carry out intention and will better than others. The feeling by an Enneatype 2 of being loved occurs from how well they implement will and intention, which of course makes everyone like them. In this way, the 2 Enneatype is a deep exploration into connected intention in contrast to separate intention.

From this fixation, an externalized point, people try (intention) to make anyone feel close to them and like them. They will figure out what needs to be done for others before others know themselves. They are doing for others and helping others because they are the epitome of helping and serving. Giving hugs, serving things, pleasing people, and focusing on taking care of other's needs becomes their life and the image of this person. They feel good if they are flattered and focus so strongly on the needs of others that they seem to have no needs of their own. But there is a string attached to this service, which is to be viewed as the great helper who then is taken care of by others without having to be asked. They constantly want to do things for others, but there is a hurt when they are not appreciated for all they do or their own needs are not addressed by others without being expressed. From their perspectives, they have no real needs that they would verbalize. At the same time, they wanted to be cared for without having to ask, because they are so wonderful.

Their basic fear is to be unloved, unwanted for themselves alone. Rather than feeling humility by being an essential part of the natural flow and force, people inherently feel humiliated by being separate from the force, unloved and unwanted for themselves alone, unless they are doing for others. The message that develops is that they are good if they are loved by and close to others. Thus, their outcome is to feel wanted, close, and loved, which only occurs if they actively draw people in by knowing what they need and providing that for them. In contrast to feeling closeness by being interconnected with the force, they attempt to imitate that connection by creating closeness through helping. And yet, it still is an artificial interconnection, which rather than happening naturally and through awareness, occurs through manipulation. Instead of humility, there is a pride that develops because these individuals "know" others so well that they create will and intention of others through the helping and doing for others.

The fixation of this Enneatype is the epitome of the graceful, charming host/hostess. Although pride runs this fixation, they are almost never aware of this as an issue. They extract self-worth from others by giving themselves away, which often results in bitterness, resentment, and blame when they are not recognized for their great deeds. There is a frequent fantasy of being alone on an island with no one to take care of except one's self, as this is the only method for not giving up themselves. The paradox, of course, is that such circumstances would not work because they only have self-worth through other's eyes. There is considerable self-deception here, for understanding themselves may not help their image of helping others, and they sometimes will act with a sense of delusional entitlement. There may be episodes of manipulating and coercing others, especially through double binds, and even some evidence of repressed aggression. They also may show symptoms of emotional problems, usually through somatization and visiting doctor's offices with illnesses that have no clear foundation. They want to be viewed as friendly, caring, and helpful to others, even serving as the perfect martyr. They may be the friend that everyone turns to for help and seems like the only one who does so much, serving in organizations that work with those in great need. Yet all this helping comes with a string attached in terms of what they need from others (praise, admiration, care for their own unverbalized needs, and closeness) with a high cost to themselves as well, including the giving up of themselves, the heavy manipulation of others, and the accompanying resentment that develops to have their own needs addressed through indirect means.

In order to work with the delusion and shift their perspective on reality, it is helpful to begin letting go of what others think and avoid trying to win over everyone. Because they are so focused on helping other people, they often diminish the affection and helping others show them. Learning to recognize such affection and helping by others is very useful, even if these are less obvious. In addition, developing boundaries with others with others that allow them to feel without becoming entangled or responsible for helping them can be very helpful. They should be aware of using flattery to win over others, letting their pride dissolve into the essence of who they are rather than their image. It also is important for these types to be brutally honest with themselves about motives for giving and to practice giving to others without any strings, regrets, or desires to be cared for themselves. Getting in touch with their own needs, verbalizing them and asking directly for help with them is invaluable for this type. They could practice being a good receiver, such as with a surprise gift unrelated to anything they have done or any helping they have given. They also could support others in giving, praising them for their sharing without any underlying manipulation or indirect messages. In all this, people with this Enneatype can begin to see and feel the larger force that is happening, knowing they are a part of it, as we all are, and begin to flow as we all do in giving and receiving without needing praise or identity for such connection.

Here are four examples from movies that Thomas Condon[31] and/or I think illustrate the 2 Enneatype being played on the big screen:

The Birdcage: Nathan Lane
Men Don't Leave: Joan Cusack
One True Thing: Meryl Streep
Misery: Kathy Bates

Enneatype 4: Origin and The Tragic Romantic

This point is a focus on the origin of everything. The essential lesson is the perception and understanding that everything we experience (internally or externally to us) is nothing but the manifestation of Being, cosmic energy, and truth. Everything has as its inner nature cosmic energy, which appears to us in various forms. This energy is from where everything comes, no matter what the form, and all are connected.[15] In this point, we learn about manifestation from a common source and the creation of form, which, in its essence, is not separate. "Unfoldment is never disconnected from Being, since it is Being."[34] When living this lesson, people experience equanimity, for there is no separation or distance from Source, "the form and the Source are indistinguishable."[35] The delusion is that creation is unique, that the origin of things is different, and that there is not a single origin for creation. The difficulty is that people feel separate from this source, which leads to a sense of being abandoned or estranged. The response is to become controlling and feeling envious of others who feel some connection, with the sense that everyone else does better and feels less pain from this separation. In this way, Enneatype 4 is a deep exploration into connected manifestation and creation in contrast to separate manifestation and creation.

The fixation aspect of Enneatype 4, which is an internalized point, comes from a basic fear that they have no inherent identity, significance, or worth. The message that develops is that they are good if they find their significance and are true to it. Thus, the desired outcome is to find themselves and their meaning or purpose, but the distortion keeps them from finding their significance in relation to Source. So any purpose is separate from that, which never overcomes the pain that is felt from the separation. This is the classic case of the "Princess and the Pea." feeling normal when they feel pain. They have a sense of being very unique and that no one understands them or loves them adequately. They have a sense of a secret self that no one knows because fundamentally they are special and different from everyone else, or that someone special someday will discover it. They tend to do what they want to do when they want to do it, as this is part of their uniqueness and difference from others. They tend to experience others as cruel and insensitive to them, having no sense of support from the outside world. At the same time, then need to be noticed by those around them, especially for the different and unique person that they are. They also tend to be emotionally intense and can shift from one extreme to another: "I am marvelous or I am nothing." Friendships sometimes are all or nothing, with a feeling that if someone loves someone else, they must love them less. They also are likely to identify their unique talents, characteristics, and flaws.

This point is the natural home of dancers, artists, creative individuals, or people constantly working on themselves in some unique manner. They usually have a distinct style of dress that sometimes may take a while to do and yet look and act like they just threw it together. They usually live in a very well designed or at least a different type of place that has some idiosyncratic aspect to it. They may feel the loss of a parent and try to create a self that would be the person a parent would love. These types are sometimes called the natural "drama queen/king" because of their emotional volatility and touchiness. They can develop a sense of elitism and that normal rules do not apply to them. They enjoy reminiscing about the past or longing for the impossible future. There may be a constant comparison with others to deal with a deep lack of self-worth. The can experience an oppressive sense of alienation from both others and themselves, which can make relationships tenuous and unstable. At the same time, they often like to be with other people and choose being in the company of others rather than being alone. In the extreme, there can be outbursts of rage, hostility, and hatred, episodes of self-sabotage, rejection of positive influences, chronic, long-term depression and hopelessness, melancholy, along with obsessions of death, morbidity, and self-hatred.

In order to address the delusion of being separate from Source, there are several things that can be helpful for this transition. One of the first is to realize that we all have unique aspects and at the same time we are not unique. It is useful to begin to see how their perspective is like others and that holding on to a sense of uniqueness is a way of maintaining the separateness that creates their sense of abandonment and pain. It is important for them to understand that emotional volatility and moodiness are not the same as emotional sensitivity, and that emotions tell us more about ourselves than they do about others. Understanding how others are feeling and the common experiences that occur in our diverse explorations also is a useful practice. Finally, people find it important to sit with the issue of creativity and manifestation in general, exploring the connection and similarity that occurs in such processes, especially when we begin to understand that everything we experience has its origin from a source from which we are not separate and with which we create many forms, since form and source are indistinguishable.

Here are four examples from movies that Thomas Condon[31] and/or I think illustrate the 4 Enneatype being played on the big screen:

> Don Juan DeMarco: Johnny Depp
> Moonstruck: Nicolas Cage
> Roxanne: Steve Martin
> Cries and Whispers: Liv Ullmann (as mother)

Enneatype 6: Strength and The Ambivilants

The Enneatypes 6, 5, and 7 compose the mental triad within the Enneagram. The essential lessons of these three types focus on humanity in relation to Reality (Strength, Omniscience, and Wisdom).[15] These types are seeking a sense of inner guidance and support, with an emphasis on the development of a quiet mind. In the fixation aspects, lacking these lessons, they essentially begin searching for security with a focus on mental strategies and beliefs. Their focus tends to be on the future, where they spend a fair amount of their mental efforts. Their boundaries tend to be based on mental tension, in contrast to more physical or emotional separations. They have issues with insecurity and anxiety, all based on fear. While some argue that all the fixations are based on fear or a basic contraction, this is the fundamental issue for these three types in particular, in contrast to the physical and emotional triads, where the layering of emotions involves fear but may not be the layer that run the fixations themselves. The emphasis here is on the development of a quiet mind, a challenge for all three of these Enneatypes.

Enneatype 6, the core mental point, has an essential lesson that involves both strength and faith.[15] People who move from a position of strength have a foundation that helps them feel solid, even if the basis of that strength is built on an illusion. The lesson for this type is to know that the foundation of themselves is a person with a true nature that is solid and unwavering. Faith is not only the knowledge but the experience of "Essence" internally, knowing it is within all people and part of our basic nature. It is the direct experience of essence as our basic nature that is most critical.[15] The effect of such realization and experience is the strength of the essence and the human being.

> It is the recognition that who we are is not the body, our emotions, or our thoughts, but rather a presence or Beingness that has many qualities and has progressively deeper dimensions of profundity. This presence is seen here as the ground of the soul, and hence what both gives it strength and is its strength.[36]

The delusion is that there is no true nature, which creates a difficulty of feeling insecure. If one basically has nothing of value internally, similar to Enneatype 9, then the focus is to look external for their sense of self and validation. The reaction in this case, however, is to suspiciously defend. Here people use their mental powers to figure out what others are about and begin from a position of being suspicious.

From the fixation aspect, the basic fear of this type is of having no support or guidance, unable to survive on their own, and particularly of having no internal worth, similar to Enneatype 4. The basic message is that you are good or OK if you do what is expected of you, which allows them to feel external support and guidance, given that it is lacking internally. The desired outcome is to find security and support, and from that external structure a sense of internal value. This typically is done by finding some belief system as a way of avoiding their basic fear and feeling greater security. This often happens in larger institutions, such as government, the military, churches, or other sizable institutions, such as academia or medicine. This is the place of a lot of internal dialogue, generating from that self-doubt, which then gets projected out into the world. Then the environment becomes a suspicious, doubtful place while also holding on to the external structure to feel secure. This becomes the basic foundation of the push-pull, seeing both sides of an issue that is inherent in this fixation. People here have a strong loyalty to an organization or institution while also nursing serious doubts and criticism about the group. This allows people to develop strong mental skills of seeing things from opposite sides and being able to take an opposing position, often times frustrating their colleagues and supervisors. At the same time, they may come up with helpful ideas that others have missed during such a process. In this way, these people tend to live lives in this tension of holding onto security and feeling anxious doubt. They may alternate between dependency and impulsive displays of defiance. They may be the ones to question and doubt organizational procedures, even seen as nit-picking authority, and then remain with the organization, such as being the first to criticize the military and the first to re-enlist. Many of these types will have long careers in the police force, team sports, or other institutions for the sense of security. They may start educational programs without finishing or change careers in mid-stream, deciding to try something else. They also may pursue extensive athletic training (professional athlete, black belt in karate, marathon runners) because the body is an instrument of the mind. They tend to smile a lot, mainly to deflect threat. They pursue careers, even such as psychology, from a logical perspective, and they often talk in the conditional form ("if that were to happen..., if it turns out...").

In the more extreme of this type, people may experience intense anxiety and panic attacks. They often have acute inferiority feelings and bouts of depression. They have a constant fear of losing support from others and may exhibit hysterical lashing-out at perceived enemies, even if only in their own minds.

Unlike any of the other Enneatypes, this point has two basic types: the Phobic, who run, hide, or freeze when confronted or feeling strong fear (similar in some ways and sometimes confused with Enneatype 9), and the Counterphobic, who attack others when feeling insecure or fearful, even when they are not aware of such fear or insecurity (similar to and sometimes confused with Enneatype 8). Jaxon-Bear refers to this dichotomy as surrender/pushy.[19] While both of these types can do either response, they tend to have a primary pattern when their security is challenged. For example, when pushed hard enough, the Phobic may end up attacking or the Counterphobic may end up freezing or hiding. But this is not their typical response or pattern when they are challenged or deep in fear.

Like all Enneatypes, we sometimes function closer to the essential lesson at times in our lives, but we usually are not clear how to behave that way more frequently. For this Enneatype, noticing how they trusted themselves and made good decisions after the fact helps develop some sense of inner guidance that can be reliable for them. After some achievement, especially when they experienced an internal sense of a good decision or action, relaxing, breathing, and savoring the moment is very useful. They can begin to notice also all the time spent trying to figure out how to handle "possible" future problems or challenges, many of which never come to pass. Begin to take more risks, moving out of familiar patterns, and savor the exploration. It can be useful to seek out more diversity and variety to their experiences, explorations, without diving into deviant behaviors to avoid anxiety and insecurity. Spending more quiet time in meditation on a regular basis, really practicing the quiet mind may be useful. Investigating the ways to feel secure with themselves can be useful instead of focusing on an external structure that may well be a false security anyway. It can be useful to do more trusting of others, even if it does not always work out. To trust others may help to turn that inward and expand more self-trust. Playing with intuition and the way to develop trust in their own knowing, paying attention to subtler forms of information is important. In these ways, this Enneatype may begin to have greater and greater experiences of an internal, trusting Essence, realizing it is part not only of their own but of everyone's true nature.

Here are four examples from movies that Thomas Condon[31] and/or I think illustrate the 6 Enneatype being played on the big screen:

> Run Away Bride: Julia Roberts & Richard Gere
> What About Bob: Bill Murray
> Broadcast News: Albert Brooks & Holly Hunter
> Hannah And Her Sisters: Woody Allen

Enneatype 5: Omniscience and The Observer

The internal mental Enneatype is point 5. Here the essential lesson is the sense that everything is interconnected and not separate, while also seeing the differentiating elements that make up the whole. While this is similar to Enneatype 3 about Law and Enneatype 2 about Will, the focus here is on the relationship between humans and reality rather than the process or functioning. [15] It is the understanding of our place as human beings within the unity of existence. Omniscience is like looking at a whole Persian rug while also focusing on the different designs contained within it. Not only does one see the whole-body or ocean (Truth), but they also see all the separate cells, organs, and systems inside the body or the various waves and currents within the ocean.[16] In fact, we can see all of the separate people in the world and understand that we are one whole too, that the separation is not fundamental to our nature. Yet, similar to the other distortions, the twist here is on a separate existence and isolated individuals, similar to Enneatype 4. The difficulty is the feeling of isolation, cut-off from Source, and a sense of being empty inside. The reaction to this feeling is to withdraw and search for security in gathering information or other ways of feeling competent.

From the fixation perspective, the basic fear is of being helpless, useless, and incapable, in some ways similar to Enneatypes 3 and 8. Given a sense of isolation and emptiness, then one has little from which to move and interact based on a position of capability. The message that develops is that you are good or OK if you have mastered something. So the desire is to become capable and competent, looking for some set of skills and abilities to demonstrate to the world that one is capable and competent. This Enneatype avoids fear by going inside and withdrawing from contact with others, focusing instead on the gathering of information, inventions, or objects.

This type becomes the natural home of investigative reporters, eccentric inventors, scientists and researchers, fly-paper minds, and collectors who love to categorize. This type often appears with a very flat affect, sometimes with the ability to disappear into the background. In fact, many of these people feel raw from contact with the outside world, at the more extreme resulting in rashes, allergies, and phobias. Yet some of the deepest, most tender feelings can be found here, IF you are trusted and do not intrude.

Those with Enneatype 5 often participate in solitary activities, such as computer work, music composition, research projects, writing, library work, or other investigations that are done by themselves. They develop a nice, well designed living space that is small and efficient. They enjoy spending time reading, memorizing facts, and collecting information, including secrets and esoteric information. They often will come up with information that few others have even considered, let alone know the facts. They may develop elaborate and highly organized collections of objects, such as stamps, coins, baseball cards, or even tickets to concerts with all of the songs written down in order of the performance for each concert. They usually have very good memories, which is helpful to remember all the information they have collected and organized, or even being able to recite entire conversations word for word. This makes them great partners for Trivial Pursuit and undesirable opponents in an argument. At the same time, they have difficulty committing in relationships, which would give away the future and invade their privacy. They also tend to be nonconforming, at least in some quiet way.

In the more extreme form, people here can get very isolated, overly eccentric, making it difficult to live with others. They may collect so much they become hoarders, even making their living environment unhealthy or unsafe. They may develop a fear of being in public places and want to remain in their homes alone.

In order to work with this delusion and twist of reality, it becomes important to remain connected with the whole, reaching out to others, especially when feeling vulnerable and afraid. In fact, it is useful to even notice those feelings and track them in their bodies. Given the strong focus on mental energies, it also is useful to participate in physical activities and pay attention to their bodies and emotions at other times. In this way, they can become more balanced and grounded in the world and less isolated. It also would be important to risk feeling emotions, such as grief, fear, and anger. In this case, he actual experience in their bodies is important rather than spending so much time in strong mental activities. When being mental, it would be useful to identify areas that are most debilitating to their self-confidence, even allowing themselves to participate in activities they are learning with others, rather than practicing them in secret and then later demonstrating them, as if they could do them all along. Finally, as with all other Enneatypes, focusing on opening of their heart is essential, being more vulnerable, especially with people with whom they are not as close, and know they will survive the experience. As they continue to experience these things, they see the connections we have, humanity and the individuals, the ocean and the waves, the commonality and the unique aspects, the whole carpet and the patterns within it.

Here are four examples from movies that Thomas Condon[31] and/or I think illustrate the 5 Enneatype being played on the big screen:

The Edge: Anthony Hopkins
Accidental Tourist: William Hurt
Sex, Lies, & Videotape: James Spader
Another Woman: Gena Rowlands

Enneatype 7: Wisdom and The Dreamer

The issue of wisdom may seem to be essential with all of the higher lessons, and they certainly are interconnected, lessons we all could benefit from learning. But there is a special issue related to the way people experience themselves in relation to reality for this Enneatype. In this case, wisdom is realizing the need to be present to yourself and the world, then seeing the design of the personal and world evolving and transforming.[15] Related to this wisdom is the plan, which is the design process for the world that is replicated in people and vice versa. This combination of wisdom and plan results in work, which is the actual evolution and transformation, progressing form one step to another, especially within one's self.[15] "Knowing that things are unfolding according to a certain design, you do not need to have your own plans. You don't need to fantasize about how things should be."[37] When experiencing this combination of wisdom, plan, and work, one tends to experience sobriety and ease, seeing the bigger picture and interconnection, and participating in the natural transformation of self and the world. The delusion or twist, like others, is the view of separate unfoldment, separate evolving and transformation, which results in a sense of being disoriented or lost. The reaction, logically, is to create orientation, often through planning. Thus, in losing this cosmic perspective, individuals begin to focus heavily on the making of plans and planning for the future. At the same time, orientation is established through spontaneity, rationalizations, and humor. The result is gluttony, although it often has nothing to do with food. In fact, often these people often are quite thin and have strict diets while focusing on a gluttony of fun, humor, and activities.

The basic fear is of being deprived and trapped in pain. The message that develops is that you are good or OK if you get what you need. This results in a desired outcome of being happy and finding fulfillment, where ever it lies. This is the home of "Peter Pan," who is constantly happy, having fun, and finding all sorts of wonderful ways to feel satisfied. This is the externalized mental point that avoids fear by magical thinking, good thoughts that cheer everyone, and helps one to avoid pain. As Peter Pan suggests, "thinking good thoughts can make you fly away". These people usually are charmers or con people, with witty style that speaks of class and ease of life, reaching for new highs along the way. There is a fascination for new ideas and a gluttony for new experiences, which makes it difficult to stay in one place and focused on uninteresting activities, projects, and jobs. Pain is avoided by moving away and rationalized by making every move part of a larger, "divine" plan. Because of the strong focus on mental energies, they often can make brilliant connections and insights, then quickly bore with retracing steps and going deeper. One insightful respondent of this Enneatype once described herself as "deeply superficial." They often learn new skills, such as a language or playing a piano rather quickly, but they also tend to lose interest in expanding such skills. They frequently learn so many things that they do not do any very well. They may have trouble making some decision, since choosing one will eliminate other options, and yet they can be decisive when it does matter.

They may show great enthusiasm for all the different things they enjoy while they are participating in them, relishing in energizing groups and being the "life of the party." Yet they easily get bored with things, moving from one activity to another fairly quickly. They will foresee issues and generate ideas that can create wonderful events, corporations, and innovative projects with great anticipation and enthusiasm, but they usually do not want to carry out the details or actually develop any of them. They often are gifted at brainstorming and synthesizing information, preferring broad overviews and excitement of the initial stages rather than probing a single topic in depth.

In the more severe cases, there can be extreme dissipation and attempts to escape anxiety and even reality. They sometimes develop serious longstanding and debilitating addictions as another way of escaping the pain of living. They not only may exhibit impulsive behaviors, but they also can be offensive and exhibit almost infantile reactions. They can experience mania, depression, and wild mood swings, even exhibiting the more tradition manic depressive episodes, although most try to avoid long periods of depression. They also may experience periods of manic and paralyzing terror or periods of being out of control. Finally, they can get involved with compulsive activities during highly elated moods.

To address the twist in reality called the delusion, it becomes important that people with this Enneatype learn to stay present to themselves as well as others without amping up the energy. When mentally revved up, taking a moment to breathe and look at what is really going on underneath the urge to increase the energetic level is very useful. It also is important to process their feelings more completely rather than taking a look quickly and moving on to something else. This particularly would be true when dealing with fear, anxiety, and pain. It would be useful to look at their impatience, both with themselves and others, as well as their difficulty remaining with a task. Meditation could be useful for them, as with all the mental points. In this case, incorporating different types of moving meditations, such as walking, running, yoga, or cooking, may be more successful than simply sitting on a cushion, although this type of meditation also could be useful after some initial practice with others. Sharing their exuberance and genuine joy about something without pushing the energy on others or being deflated when it is not shared by others also could be a useful exercise. Another practice that could be important is to develop a plan for themselves to go into depth and detail in one area and stick with it over a period of time. This could lead to the development of a creative activity while also completing the details and enjoying the achievement that occurs. Finally, it becomes important for them to stay in touch and feel their fear that drives their reactions and pain avoiding activities or behaviors. In this way, people with this Enneatype begin to stay more present to themselves and others, participating in the natural plan and transformation that occurs with us all, even when we have difficulty identifying it at the time, and the work to progress form one step to another, remaining at peace and comfortable in the larger process.

Here are four examples from movies that Thomas Condon[31] and/or I think illustrate the 7 Enneatype being played on the big screen:

Breakfast at Tiffany's: Audrey Hepburn
Herald & Maude: Ruth Gordon
Mermaids: Cher
Patch Adams: Robin Williams

Enneatype Wings

While there are nine primary Enneatypes, we also tend to pick up an influence by those Enneatypes on one side or the other. These influences are called "wings" in the Enneagram literature. The idea is that someone with an Enneatype 9 will either be influenced by the energetics of Enneatype 8, having a stronger sense of issues around injustice, or be influenced by Enneatype 1, having a stronger need for order and striving for perfection. In this way, people begin to look a bit different within the same Enneatype when they are influenced by one wing in contrast to the other. There are a number of books who talk about this in more detail and will not be discussed further here. As those exploring an Enneatype begin to understand the essential lesson, the distortion or delusion that gets made, and how they play out their fixation aspect, it also can be useful to consider which Enneatype on either side of that point may influence the attitudes and behaviors that get exhibited and the feelings that develop internally. If you discover that you have a lot of energy in two Enneatypes next to each other (for example, types 3 and 4), it may be that you have an Enneatype in one and a wing in the other. Then, of course, the challenge is to identify which of the two is strongest (the core point) and which may be a bit secondary (the wing). Again, this can help us understand the complexity we experience and exhibit by also considering the wings of our core point.

Subtypes

Besides the core Enneatype and wing, we seem to develop different basic issues that form a subtype, which also influences us. Again, many of the Enneagram books discuss this in more detail, so a lot of space will not be spent here. Yet it is important to see some of the further complexity of this model and how we develop into very different observable forms stemming from the same source.

There are three basic subtypes that occur in all nine of the points. The first is labeled <u>Self-preservation</u>. In this case, people spend more time worrying about survival and security. This latter issue, of course, gets amplified when combined with the issue of security that is common to the mental triad. People with this subtype also appear more nervous and tightly wound. The second subtype is labeled <u>Social</u>. Here people are most interested in other people and status. They often cluster around family life, preferring groups and the social milieu. The third subtype is labeled <u>Sexual</u>. This is not just a focus on sexual behavior. But these people prefer one-on-one relationships and more emotional connection rather than larger, social groups. They tend to have more relationships with the opposite sex than their own gender group. They also tend to be more charismatic than others.

In part, what is important about the wings and subgroups is to understand the complexity of this tool for exploring ourselves. When I first heard about the Enneagram, I had little interest in it because I was not interested in another way to label people into categories. Over time, I have appreciated the many different forms that humans take and the complexity we develop. Yet it is the focus on the essential lessons and distortions or fixations we make that is most important to me. In addition, I also like the fact that rather than simply nine different points being possible, we end up with 54. If we look at the nine points, then add the wings for each type, combined with the three different subtypes within each point, we have many different ways of both creating responses to a sense of separation and ways to distort Reality. We can focus on the challenges and complexity, or we can laugh in amazement at the creativity we have developed over time.

Enneatype Examples from Movies

It may be useful to provide some more detailed discussion of Enneatype patterns that you could observe from movies. While there are many examples of people in real life, it sometimes is easier to use public examples through popular movies. So I will describe some examples from movies that I think are easy to see and enjoyable to watch. After seeing these examples, you may well begin to identify fixation and essential lesson patterns from other movies. In fact, it may be difficult for a while to watch some movies without thinking about how it may be an example of such patterns. There are many, but here are a few.

- In the movie <u>Instinct</u>, Anthony Hopkins (Enneatype 8 in this movie and quite frequently) has some fixation patterns show up in places, which at times keeps him isolated. But he shows several examples of his strength as well. For example, he is ferocious in defending another inmate, who is perceived as weak and where there is some injustice that has been done. He also has great strength in challenging the corrupt system itself. In addition, he tends to show his essential lesson pattern of Truth in his interactions and taking charge of the sessions with the psychiatrist (Cuba Gooding Jr.) doing the evaluation of Hopkins. In this latter case, he is quite clear what is most important and is determined to impart that to the psychiatrist.

• From <u>The Family Man</u>, Nicolas Cage (Enneatype 3) exhibits his essential lesson pattern near the end of the movie when the roles are reversed with his girlfriend (Tea Leoni), who wants him to stay home from England in the beginning of the movie. During the early interactions in the movie, Cage is focused on rational decisions with little emotion involved, focusing almost completely on achievement and success. This, of course, is the outcome from his efforts, even if he loses the relationship in the beginning. He also demonstrates this when he has to cancel Christmas with a relative in order to go to Colorado and close a huge deal. At the end of the movie, however, it is Nicolas who is pleading with Tea to create a different life by shifting priorities and coming from the heart with less protection, which he was unable to do when she requested it early in their relationship at a time when his heart was closed. Once his priorities shifted and his heart opened, he becomes focused on his essential lesson of recognizing the cosmic law of natural order, path, and harmony of things. And here he plays out that lesson from his heart.

• Diane Lane, in <u>Under the Tuscan Sun</u>, (Enneatype 2) gets hurt time and time again as she tried to find love by taking care of others, playing out her fixation pattern. Finally, she finds her essential lesson pattern in building a life based on satisfaction with herself rather than looking for joy in others first. She learns to see and appreciate less obvious joys and beauty, and in the process, she finds greater peace and happiness in herself and a satisfying life with the house that she remodeled for herself. Then, from this place of joy and peace, she shares her gifts with those helping her with the house, those in the community, the young couple wanting to get married, and, in the end, in a possible satisfying relationship where it is based on her moving with the flow of things in contrast to willing things into action.

• In a movie about a younger star, Christina Ricci, in Penelope, (Enneatype 6) finds that the only way to lift the curse on her and her family is by self-acceptance rather than the acceptance by others, which was the pervasive belief of herself and her extended kin. She spent years living in circumstances that were not necessary because everyone interpreted the legend of the curse as being lifted by marrying a "blue blood" man. This was living in her fear and fixation, believing that others know best about us. In the end, she had the power to change both her belief in herself and her circumstances. It is a wonderful, light hearted example of the power we all hold in relation to our own lives and the essential lesson of the 6. We all have an Essence that gives us value as ourselves.

Here is a list of other movies for each Enneatype, along with the actor playing out the particular type. It is useful to look how they play out the fixation aspects of the type as well as the essential lesson. Usually there are examples of both in a movie, and it can be useful to identify the differences. The asterisk is used here to identify the move I use to illustrate the particular fixation when teaching my Enneagram workshop.

Movies for the Enneagram:

Enneatype:	Movie & Actor's Role
9: The Peacemaker	*America's Sweethearts: Julia Roberts Dances with Wolves: Costner & Greene Being There: Peter Sellers Carnal Knowledge: Art Garfunkel
8: The Boss	*Meet Joe Black: Hopkins & Pitt Instinct: Anthony Hopkins

Breakfast Club: Judd Nelson
Lean On Me: Morgan Freeman

1: The Perfectionist
*PS, I love You: Hillary Swank
Sleeping with the Enemy: P. Bergin
Agnes of God: Anne Bancroft
A Man for All Seasons: Paul Scofield

3: The Achiever
*The Family Man: Nicolas Cage
Rain Man: Tom Cruise
Six Degrees of Separation: Will Smith
Dangerous Liaisons: John Malkovich

2: The Helper
*The Birdcage: Nathan Lane
Men Don't Leave: Joan Cusack
One True Thing: Meryl Streep
Misery: Kathy Bates

4: Tragic Romantic
*Don Juan DeMarco: Johnny Depp
Moonstruck: Nicolas Cage
Roxanne: Steve Martin
Cries and Whispers: Liv Ullmann

6: The Ambivilants
*Run Away Bride: Roberts & Gere
What About Bob: Bill Murray
Broadcast News: Brooks & Hunter
Hannah And Her Sisters: Woody Allen

5: The Observer
*The Edge: Anthony Hopkins
Accidental Tourist: William Hurt
Sex, Lies, & Videotape: James Spader
Another Woman: Gena Rowlands

7: The Dreamer
*Breakfast at Tiffany's: A. Hepburn
Herald & Maude: Ruth Gordon
Mermaids: Cher
Patch Adams: Robin Williams

Final Comment

There are just a couple of final comments I would like to make in ending this overview. The great challenge, I believe, as does one of my teachers, Eli Jaxon-Bear,[18,19] is to view Reality with "mirror like awareness," reflecting things exactly as they are with no distortions. This is to understand our true Essence as pure awareness (physical), love (emotional), and emptiness (mental), allowing us to experience Satchidananda.

There is a saying that when a pickpocket meets The Buddha, all he sees are his pockets. Unlike the pickpocket, our task is to see The Buddha inside all of us, rather than just people's pockets.

Of course, this is just one tool for changing behavior. What I like about this model is that it helps one focus on both our expansive, essential lesson aspects, as well as the contractive, fixation aspects of who we are as human beings, and the continuum between the two ends of each Enneatype. Such a continuum also allows us to see those aspects that are strengths and what we want to maintain, as well as those things that get in our way of what we want, with the possibility of shifting them more towards our expansive selves. This gives us a way incorporating more expansive aspects and Essential Lessons into our everyday behaviors and interactions. Any therapeutic or change model that assists us in those ways is very useful, I believe, for our continued conscious development.

FOOTNOTES

Front of Book

1. http://www.goodreads.com/quotes/405812-everyone-has-been-made-for-some-particular-work.

Introduction

1. Barks, C. (2006). A year with Rumi: Daily readings. New York: HarperOne, p. 313.
2. Aries, P. (1962). Centuries of childhood. New York: Vintage.
3. Boswell, J. (1988). The kindness of strangers: The abandonment of children in Western Europe from late antiquity to the Renaissance. New York: Vintage Books.
4. Greenleaf, B. K. (1978). Children through the ages. New York: McGraw-Hill, p. xiii.
5. Platt, A. M. (1977). The child savers: The invention of delinquency. Chicago: University of Chicago Press.
6. Polonko, K. A., & Lombardo, L. (2004). Enlightened witnessing: Rehumanizing through confrontation with violence. Paper presented at the annual meetings of the International Conference on New Directions in the Humanities, Prato, Italy.
7. Polonko, K. A. (2006). Exploring assumptions about child neglect in relation to the broader field of child maltreatment. Journal of Health & Human Services Administration, 29 (3), 260-284.
8. Straus, M. A., with Donnelly, D. A. (2001). Beating the devil out of them. New Brunswick, NJ: Transaction.
9. Lombardo, L, & Polonko, K. (2010). Interdisciplinary contributions to the prevention of child maltreatment. International Journal of Interdisciplinary Social Sciences, 4, 89-112.
10. Thorne, B. (1987). Re-visioning women and social change: Where are the children? Gender and Society, 1, 85-109.

11. Starck, M. (1993). <u>Woman's medicine ways: cross-cultural rites of passage</u>. Freedom, CA: Crossing Press.
12. Smith, H. (1991). <u>The world's great religions: Our great wisdom traditions</u>. San Francisco: Harper, p. 78.
13. McBrien, R. P. (1989). <u>The HarperCollins encyclopedia of Catholicism</u>. San Francisco: Harper.
14. Leigh, G. K., Metzker, J. A., & Hilton, J. M. (1999). An observational study of energy fields of infants and young children. <u>Subtle Energies and Energy Medicine, 8</u>, 1-29.
15. Metzker, J. A., & Leigh, G. K. (2004). A short-term longitudinal study of energy fields in infants and young children. <u>Subtle Energies & Energy Medicine, 15</u>, 117-145.
16. Leigh, G. K., Metzker, J. A., & Pierce, S. (2010a). Incorporating human energy research into family research and therapy. <u>Subtle Energy and Energy Medicine, 19</u>, 1-20.
17. Leigh, G. K., Metzker, J. A., & Pierce, S. (2010b). Investigating adaptability, cohesion, and human energy fields in family interactions. <u>The International Journal of Healing and Caring, 10</u>, No.1.

Chapter 1

1. Barks, C. (2006). <u>A year with Rumi: Daily readings.</u> New York: HarperOne, p. 120.
2. Burr, H. S., and Northrop, F. S. C., (1935). The electrodynamic theory of life. <u>Quarterly Review of Biology. vol. 10,</u> pp. 322-333.
3. Burr, H. S. and Northrop, F. S. C., (1939). Evidence for the existence of an electrodynamic field in living organisms. Proceedings of the National Academy of Sciences of the United States of America. Vol. 24, pp. 284-288.
4. Burr, H. S., (1944). The meaning of bioelectrical potentials. <u>Yale Journal of biology and medicine</u>. Vol. 16, pp. 353-360.
5. Burr, H. S. (1972a). <u>Blueprint for immortality: The electric patterns of life</u>. Essex England: the C.W. Daniel Company, Ltd.
6. Burr, H. S., (1972b). <u>The fields of life: our links to the universe.</u> New York: Ballantine.

7. Ravitz Leonard J. (1970) Electro-Magnetic field monitoring of changing state-function including hypnotic states. Condensed from a paper presented at 5th International Congress for Hypnosis and Psychosomatic Medicine, Johannes Gutenberg University, D6500 Mainz, Germany, May 22 1970.

8. Brennen, B. A. (1987). Hands of light: A guide to healing through the human energy field. New York: Bantam.

9. White, R. (1993). Working with your chakras: A physical, emotional, and spiritual approach. York Beach, ME: Samuel Weiser.

10. Leigh, G. K., Metzker, J. A., & Hilton, J. M. (1999). An observational study of energy fields of infants and young children. Subtle Energies and Energy Medicine, 8, 1-29.

11. Metzker, J. A., & Leigh, G. K. (2004). A short-term longitudinal study of energy fields in infants and young children. Subtle Energies & Energy Medicine, 15, 117-145.

12. Leigh, G. K., Metzker, J. A., & Pierce, S. (2010a). Incorporating human energy research into family research and therapy. Subtle Energy and Energy Medicine, 19, 1-20.

13. Leigh, G. K., Metzker, J. A., & Pierce, S. (2010b). Investigating adaptability, cohesion, and human energy fields in family interactions. The International Journal of Healing and Caring, 10, No.1.

14. Leigh, G. K., Polonko, K. A., & Leigh, C. D. (2003). A comparison of human energy fields among children, youth, adults, and Dahn masters. Subtle Energies & Energy Medicine, 14(1), 77-101.

15. Leigh, G. K., & Cendese, J. W. (2007). Investigating the impact of Integrated Awareness with breast cancer patients. Subtle Energies & Energy Medicine, 18 (3), 57-75.

16. Weiss, B. L. (1988). Many lives, many masters. New York: Fireside, p. 211.

17. Allison, R. B., with Schwarz, T. (1998). Minds in many pieces: Revealing the spiritual side of multiple personality disorder. Los Osos, CA: CIE Publishing.

18. Capra, F. (1996). The web of life. New York: Anchor Books.

19. Benor, D. J. (2004). Consciousness, bioenergy and healing: Self-healing and energy medicine for the 21st Century (Healing Research Vol. 2). Oxfordshire, UK: Helix.

20. Leigh, G. K. (2004). Using human energy fields to assess family communications. Journal of Family Communication, part of special issue, "Advancing Family Communication Theory and Research." Vol. 4 (No. 3&4), 319-335.

21. Wade, J. (2004). Transcendent sex: When lovemaking opens the veil. New York: Paraview Pocket Books.

22. Cheek, D. B. (1995). Early use of psychotherapy in prevention of preterm labor: The application of hypnosis and ideomotor techniques with women carrying twin pregnancies. The Journal of Prenatal and Perinatal Psychology and Health, 10, 5-19.

23. Chamberlain, D. (2013). Windows to the womb. Berkeley, CA: North Atlantic Books.

24. Ring, K., & Valarino, E. E. (1998). Lessons from the light. New York: Insight.

25. Ring, K. (2011). Heading toward omega. Kindle edition.

26. Weiss, B. L. (1988). Many lives, many masters. New York: Fireside.

27. Weiss, B. L. (1992). Through time into healing. New York: Fireside.

28. Weiss, B. L. (1996). Only love is real. New York: Warner Books.

29. Weiss, B. L. (2000). Messages from the masters. New York: Warner Books.

30. Ring, K., & Valarino, E. E. (1998). Lessons from the light. New York: Insight, pp. 51-53.

31. Grof, S. (1993). The holotropic mind: The three levels of human consciousness and how they shape our lives. San Francisco: Harper.

32. Grof, S. (1998). The cosmic game. Albany, NY: State University of New York.

33. Grof, S. (2000). Psychology of the future. Albany, NY: State University of New York.

34. Grof, S. (2010). The ultimate journey (2nd. Ed.). Santa Cruz, CA: MAPS.

35. Chamberlain, D. (1990). Expanding the boundaries of memory. ReVision, 12, p. 18.

36. Chamberlain, D. (2013). Windows to the womb. Berkeley, CA: North Atlantic Books, pp. 170-171.

37. Carman, E., & Carman, N. (2013). Cosmic cradle. Berkeley, CA: North Atlantic Books.

38. Dyer, W., & Garnes, D. (2015). <u>Memories of heaven</u>. Carlsbad, CA: Hay House, Inc.
39. Tucker, J. B. (2005). <u>Live before life: Children's memories of previous lives</u>. New York: St. Martin's Press, p. 229.
40. Tucker, J. B. (2013). <u>Return to life: Extraordinary cases of children who remember past lives</u>. New York: St. Martins's Griffin, pp. 218-219.
41. Weiss, B. L., & Weiss, A. E. (2012). <u>Miracles happen: The transformational healing power of past-life memories</u>. New York: HarperCollins, pp. 194.
42. Fenwick, P., & Fenwick, E. (1995). <u>The truth in the light</u>. New York: Berkley Books.
43. Moody, R. (1975). <u>Life after life</u>. New York: Bantam.
44. Moody, R. (1988). <u>The light beyond</u>. New York: Bantam.
45. Moody, R. with Perry, P. (2010). <u>Glimpses of eternity</u>. New York: Guideposts.
46. Morrissey, D. (1997). <u>You can see the light</u>. Walpole, NH: Stillpoint.
47. Morse, M., with Perry, P. (1990). <u>Closer to the light</u>. New York: Ivy Books.
48. Morse, M., with Perry, P. (1992). <u>Transformed by the light</u>. New York: Ivy Books.
49. Morse, M., with Perry, P. (1994). <u>Parting visions</u>. New York: Harper Paperbacks.
50. Sutherland, C. (1993). <u>Within the light</u>. New York: Bantam.
51. Sabom, M. (1998). <u>Light and death</u>. Zondervan Publishing House.
52. Ring, K., & Valarino, E. E. (1998). <u>Lessons from the light</u>. New York: Insight. p.245.
53. Ring, K., & Valarino, E. E. (1998). <u>Lessons from the light</u>. New York: Insight, pp. 51-53.
54. Moody, R. (1993). <u>Reunions</u>. New York: Ivy Books.
55. Weiss, B. L. (1988). <u>Many lives, many masters</u>. New York: Fireside, pp. 74.
56. Weiss, B. L. (1988). <u>Many lives, many masters</u>. New York: Fireside, pp. 207, 211 .
57. Lowen, A. (1975). <u>Bioenergetics</u>. New York: Penguin.
58. Lowen, A. (1990). <u>The spirituality of the body: Bioenergetics for grace and harmony</u>. New York: MacMillan.

59. Pierrakos, J. C. (1990). Core energetics. Mendocino, CA: LifeRhythm Publication.
60. Pierrakos, J. C. (1997). Eros, Love & Sexuality. Mendocino, CA: LifeRhythm.
61. Eadie, B. J. (1996). The awakening heart. New York: Pocket Star Books, p. 198.
62. DeFrain, J., Nelson, S., & Chambers, K. (1997, November). Investigating the long-term effects of child abuse in adults. A paper presented at the annual meetings of the National Council on Family Relations, Arlington, VA.
63. Almaas, A. H. (1998). Essence. York Beach, ME: Samuel Weiser, Inc.
64. Almaas, A. H. (1999). Facets of unity. Berkeley, CA: Diamond Books.
65. Fenwick, P. & Fenwick, E. (1995). The truth in the light. New York: Barkley Books, p. 172.
66. Long, J. with Perry, P. (2010). Evidence of the afterlife. New York: Harper One, p. 146-47.
67. Clark, A. M. (2001). Diplomacy of conscious. Princeton, NJ: Princeton University Press, p. 49.
68. OBERF, Out of Body Experience Research Foundation, http://www.oberf.org/stories_obe.htm.
69. Jaxon-Bear, E. (2001). The Enneagram of liberation: From fixation to freedom. Bolinas, CA: Leela Foundation.
70. Rinpoche, S. (1993). The Tibetan book of living and dying. San Francisco: Harper.
71. Bates, E., O'Connell, B., & Shore, C. (1987). Language and communication in infancy. In J. D. Osofsky (Ed.), Handbook of infant development (pp. 149-203). New York: John Wiley & Sons.
72. Playfair, G. L. (2002). Twin telepathy: The psychic connection. London: Chryslis Books.
73. Pearce, J. C. (1977). The magical child. New York: Plume.
74. Field, T. (1987). Affective and interactive disturbances in infants. In J. D. Osofsky (Ed.), Handbook of infant development (pp. 972-1005). New York: John Wiley.
75. Chamberlain, D. (2013). Windows to the womb. Berkeley, CA: North Atlantic Books. pp. 172-173.

Chapter 2

1. http://www.goodreads.com/quotes/78367-there-is-a-candle-in-your-heart-ready-to-be
2. Assante, J. (2012). The last frontier: Exploring the after-life and transforming our fear of death. Novato, CA: New World Library, p. 309.
3. Thomas, W. I., & Thomas, D. S. (1928). The child in America: Behavior problems and programs. New York: Knopf, 571-572.
4. Assante, J. (2012). The last frontier: Exploring the after-life and transforming our fear of death. Novato, CA: New World Library, p. 123.
5. Twain, M. (1970). The war prayer. New York: Harper-Collins.
6. Coffey, C. (2012). Growing up psychic. New York: Three Rivers Press.
7. Eason, C. (1994). Psychic power of children. London: Foulsham.
8. Bowman, C. (1998). Children's past lives. New York: Bantam Books.
9. Assante, J. (2012). The last frontier: Exploring the after-life and transforming our fear of death. Novato, CA: New World Library, p. 86.
10. Stevenson, I. (2001). Children who remember past lives. Jefferson, NC: McFarland & Company.
11. Tucker, J. B. (2005). Live before life: Children's memo-ries of previous lives. New York: St. Martin's Press.
12. Tucker, J. B. (2013). Return to life: Extraordinary cases of children who remember past lives. New York: St. Martins's Griffin.
13. Tucker, J. B. (2005). Live before life: Children's memo-ries of previous lives. New York: St. Martin's Press, p. 229.
14. Tucker, J. B. (2013). Return to life: Extraordinary cases of children who remember past lives. New York: St. Martins's Griffin, pp. 218-219.
15. Mangus, 2016 FilmRise, Moscus, and VG TV Documentary, Directed by Benjamin Ree.

Chapter 3

1. Barks, C. (2006). A year with Rumi: Daily readings. New York: HarperOne, p. 268.
2. Leigh, G. K., Metzker, J. A., & Hilton, J. M. (1999). An observational study of energy fields of infants and young children. Subtle Energies and Energy Medicine, 8, 1-29.
3. Metzker, J. A., & Leigh, G. K. (2004). A short-term longitudinal study of energy fields in infants and young children. Subtle Energies & Energy Medicine, 15, 117-145.
4. Browne, S. (2007). Psychic children. New York: Dutton.
5. Cheek, D. B. (1995). Early use of psychotherapy in prevention of preterm labor: The application of hypnosis and ideomotor techniques with women carrying twin pregnancies. Pre- and Permui-Natal Psychology Journal, 10, 5-19.
6. Playfair, G. L. (2002). Twin telepathy: The psychic connection. London: Chryslis Books.
7. Crain, W. (2011). Theories of development: Concepts and applications (6th ed.). Upper Saddle River, NJ: Pearson/ Prentice Hall.
8. Burr, H. S. (1972a). Blueprint for immortality: The electric patterns of life. Essex England: the C.W. Daniel Company, Ltd.
9. Hunt, V. V. (1996). Infinite mind: Science of the human vibrations of consciousness. Malibu, CA: Malibu Publishing Co.
10. McBrien, R. P. (1989). The HarperCollins encyclopedia of Catholicism. San Francisco: Harper.
11. Coffey, C. (2012). Growing up psychic. New York: Three Rivers Press.
12. Bowman, C. (1998). Children's past lives. New York: Bantam Books.
13. Hanh, T. N. (2007). Living Buddha, living Christ. New York: Penguin.
14. Hanh, T. N. (2015). How to love. Berkeley, CA: Parallax.
15. Doyle, B. (2012). Find your passion. Law of Attraction Magazine (pp. 6-7). Annual, 2012.
16. Cohen, A. (2011). 10 limiting beliefs to let go of. Law of Attraction Magazine (pp. 14-17). Annual, 2011.
17. Piaget, J. & Inhelder, B. (1966). The psychology of the child (H. Weaver trans.). New York: Basic Books, 1969.

18. Leigh, G. K. (1977). Language, thought, and the enhancement of self-esteem. Family Perspective, 11, 19-27.
19. Williamson, K. (2012). http://www.dailymail.co.uk/news/article-1203226/Pictured-Incredible-watercolour-paintings-boy-aged-just-SIX.html
20. Kramarik, A. (2015). www.akiane.com.
21. Crain, W. (2011). Theories of development: Concepts and applications (6th ed.). Upper Saddle River, NJ: Pearson/Prentice Hall, p. 148.
22. Crain, W. (2011). Theories of development: Concepts and applications (6th ed.). Upper Saddle River, NJ: Pearson/Prentice Hall, p. 87.
23. Steiner, R. (1995). Intuitive thinking as a spiritual path. Spring Valley, NY: Anthroposophic Press.
24. Aries, P. (1962). Centuries of childhood. New York: Vintage.
25. Greenleaf, B. K. (1978). Children through the ages. New York: McGraw-Hill.
26. Steinberg, L., Bomstein, M. H., Vandell, D. L, & Rook, K. S. (2011). Lifespan development: Infancy through adulthood. Belmont, CA: Wadsworth.
27. Erikson, E. H. (1993). Childhood and society. New York: Norton.
28. Comstock, D. L., & Qin, D. (2005). Relational-cultural theory: A framework for relational development across the life span. In D. Comstock (Ed.), Diversity and development (pp. 25-45). Belmont, CA: Brooks/Cole.
29. Gresham, L. B. (2006). Personal communication, August.
30. Kegan, R. (1994). In over our heads. Cambridge, MA: Harvard University Press.
31. Levinson, D. (1978). The seasons of a man's life. New York: Ballentine.
32. Neugarten, B. L. (1968). Adult personality: Toward a psychology of the life cycle. In B. L. Neugarten (Ed.), Middle Age and Aging. Chicago: University of Chicago Press.
33. Havighurst, R. J., Neugarten. B. L., & Tobin, S. S. (1968). Disengagement and patterns of aging. In B. L. Neugarten (Ed.), Middle Age and Aging. Chicago: University of Chicago Press.
34. Crain, W. (2011). Theories of development: Concepts and applications (6th ed.). Upper Saddle River, NJ: Pearson/Prentice Hall, p. 349.

35. Crain, W. (2011). Theories of development: Concepts and applications (6th ed.). Upper Saddle River, NJ: Pearson/ Prentice Hall, p. 350.
36. Fenwick, P., & Fenwick, E. (1995). The truth in the light. New York: Berkley Books.
37. Moody, R. (1975). Life after life. New York: Bantam.
38. Moody, R. (1988). The light beyond. New York: Bantam.
39. Morrissey, D. (1997). You can see the light. Walpole, NH: Stillpoint.
40. Morse, M., with Perry, P. (1990). Closer to the light. New York: Ivy Books.
41. Morse, M., with Perry, P. (1992). Transformed by the light. New York: Ivy Books.
42. Morse, M., with Perry, P. (1994). Parting visions. New York: Harper.
43. Sutherland, C. (1993). Within the light. New York: Bantam.
44. Ring, K., & Valarino, E. E. (1998). Lessons from the light. New York: Insight.
45. Ring, K., & Valarino, E. E. (1998). Lessons from the light. New York: Insight, pp. 177, 198.
46. Long, J. (2016). God and the afterlife. NY: Harper One.
47. Long, J. (2016). God and the afterlife. NY: Harper One, p. 98.

Chapter 4

1. Barks, C. (2006). A year with Rumi: Daily readings. New York: HarperOne, p. 234.
2. Kegan, R. (1994). In over our heads. Cambridge, MA: Harvard University Press.
3. Hanh, T. N. (2007). Living Buddha, living Christ. New York: Penguin.
4. Leigh, G. & Peterson, G. (1986) Adolescents in families. Cincinnati, OH: South-Western Publishing Co.
5. Garmezy, N. (1983). Stressors of childhood. In N. Garmezy & M. Rutter (Eds.), Stress, coping, and development in children (pp. 43-84). New York: McGraw-Hill.
6. Rutter, M. (1979). Protective factors in children's responses to stress and disadvantage. In M. W. Kent & J. E. Rolf

(Eds.), <u>Primary prevention of psychopathology: Social competence in children</u> (Vol. 3). Hanover, New Hampshire: University Press of New England.

7. Barnard, C. P. (1994). Resiliency: A shift in our perception? <u>The American Journal of Family Therapy, 22,</u> 135-144.

8. Jessor, R. (1993). Successful adolescent development among youth in high-risk settings. <u>American Psychologist, 48</u>(2), 117-126.

9. Werner, E. E., & Smith, R. S. (1992). <u>Overcoming the odds: High risk children from birth to adulthood.</u> New York: Cornell University Press.

10. Anthony, E. J. (1987). Risk, vulnerability, and resilience: An overview. In E. J. Anthony & B. Cohler (Eds.), <u>The invulnerable child.</u> New York: Guilford, p.3.

11. Rinpoche, S. (1993). <u>The Tibetan book of living and dying.</u> San Francisco: Harper, p. 41.

12. Lanza, R., & Berman, B. (2009). <u>Biocentrism: How life and consciousness are the keys to understanding the true nature of the universe.</u> Dallas, TX: Benbella Books.

13. Lanza, R., & Berman, B. (2009). <u>Biocentrism: How life and consciousness are the keys to understanding the true nature of the universe.</u> Dallas, TX: Benbella Books, p. 176.

14. Lanza, R., & Berman, B. (2009). <u>Biocentrism: How life and consciousness are the keys to understanding the true nature of the universe.</u> Dallas, TX: Benbella Books, pp. 191,196.

15. see http://www.eyetricks.com/illusions.htm.

16. Assante, J. (2012). <u>The last frontier: Exploring the afterlife and transforming our fear of death.</u> Novato, CA: New World Library, pp. 5-6.

Chapter 5

1. Barks, C. (2006). <u>A year with Rumi: Daily readings.</u> New York: HarperOne, p. 58.

2. Lipton, B. (2005). The biology of belief. Santa Rosa, CA: Mountain of Love/Elite Books.

3. Goldschmidt, P. (2008). Workshop on strength and limiting patterns. Las Vegas, NV, December.
4. Jaxon-Bear, E. (2001). <u>The Enneagram of liberation: From fixation to freedom</u>. Bolinas, CA: Leela Foundation.
5. Parti, R. with Perry, P. (2016). <u>Dying to wake up: A doctor's voyage into the afterlife and the wisdom he brought back</u>. New York: Atria Books, pp. 141,164.
6. Parti, R. with Perry, P. (2016). <u>Dying to wake up: A doctor's voyage into the afterlife and the wisdom he brought back</u>. New York: Atria Books, p. 178.
7. Ladinsky, D. (2011). <u>A year with Hafiz</u>. New York: Penguin Books, p. 356.

Chapter 6

1. Barks, C. (2006). <u>A year with Rumi: Daily readings.</u> New York: HarperOne, p. 206.
2. Levine, P. A. (1997). <u>Waking the tiger.</u> Berkeley, CA: North Atlantic Books.
3. Levine, P. A. (2010). <u>In an unspoken voice</u>. Berkeley, CA: North Atlantic Books.
4. Crain, W. (2011). <u>Theories of development: Concepts and applications </u>(6th ed.). Upper Saddle River, NJ: Pearson/ Prentice Hall.
5. Long, J. (2016). <u>God and the afterlife</u>. NY: Harper One, p. 88.
6. Grof, S. (1988a). Modern consciousness research and human survival. In S. Grof & M. L. Valier (Eds.), <u>Human survival and consciousness evolution</u> (pp. 57-79). Albany, NY: State University of New York Press.
7. Grof, S. (1993). <u>The holotropic mind: The three levels of human consciousness and how they shape our lives</u>. San Francisco: Harper.
8. Grof, S. (2006). <u>When the impossible happens: Adventures of nonordinary reality</u>. Boulder, CO: Sounds True.
9. Ring, K., & Valarino, E. E. (1998). <u>Lessons from the light</u>. New York: Insight, p. 187-188.
10. Kirtana. (1999). I Am, a song from the album, <u>This Embrace</u>. Wild Dove Music.

11. Comstock, D. L., & Qin, D. (2005). Relational-cultural theory: A framework for relational development across the life span. In D. Comstock (Ed.), Diversity and Development. Belmont, CA: Brooks/Cole, pp. 25-45.
12. Buscaglia, L. (1972a). Love. New York: Fawcett Crest.
13. Buscaglia, L. (1972b). Love: What life is all about. New York: Fawcett Columbine.
14. Buscaglia, L. (1982). Living, loving & learning. New York: Fawcett Columbine.
15. Buscaglia, L. (1992). Born for love. Therefore, NJ: SLACK.
16. Gottlieb, D. (2008). Learning from the heart. New York: Sterling.
17. Hanh, T. N. (1997). Teachings on love. Berkeley, CA: Parallax.
18. Hooks, B. (2001). All about love. New York: Perennial.
19. Jampolsky, G. G. (2000). Teach only love. Hillsboro, OR: Beyond Words.
20. Kornfield, J. (1993). A path with heart. New York: Bantam.
21. Melchizedek, D. (2003). Living in the heart. Flagstaff, AZ: Light Technology   Publishing.
22. Paddison, S. (1998). The hidden power of the heart. Boulder Creek, CA: Planetary.
23. Ruiz, D. M. (1999). The mastery of love. San Rafael, CA: Amber-Allen.
24. Williamson, M. (1992). A return to love: Reflections on the principles of A Course in Miracles. New York: Harper Collins, pp. 190-191.
25. Earthwhale, (2015). Guidance from Grandmother Whale, Channeled by Earthwhale. earthwhale.blogspot.com.
26. http://www.goodreads.com/quotes/9726-your-task-is-not-to-seek-for-love-but-mere.

Chapter 7

1. Barks, C. (2006). A year with Rumi: Daily readings. New York: HarperOne, p. 235.
2. Jampolsky, G. G. (2000). Teach only love. Hillsboro, OR: Beyond Words.

3. Walsch, N. D. (1996). <u>Conversations with God, Book 1.</u> New York: G. P. Putnam's Sons.

4. Almaas, A. H. (1999). <u>Facets of unity.</u> Berkeley, CA: Diamond Books.

5. Ruiz, D. M. (1999). <u>The mastery of love.</u> San Rafael, CA: Amber-Allen, p. 33.

6. Ring, K., & Valarino, E. E. (1998). <u>Lessons from the light.</u> New York: Insight, pp. 187-188.

7. Parti, R. with Perry, P. (2016). <u>Dying to wake up: A doctor's voyage into the afterlife and the wisdom he brought back.</u> New York: Atria Books, pp. 59, 161.

8. Long, J. (2016). <u>God and the afterlife.</u> NY: Harper One, p. 179.

9. Long, J. (2016). <u>God and the afterlife.</u> NY: Harper One, p. 195.

10. Williamson, M. (1992). <u>A return to love: Reflections on the principles of A Course in Miracles.</u> New York: Harper Collins, pp. 190-191.

11. Grof, S. (1998). <u>The cosmic game.</u> Albany, NY: State University of New York.

12. Crain, W. (2011). <u>Theories of development: Concepts and applications</u> (6th ed.). Upper Saddle River, NJ: Pearson/ Prentice Hall.

13. Freud, S. (1949). <u>Outline of Psychoanalysis.</u> New York: Norton.

14. Moody, R., & Perry, P. (2010). <u>Glimpses of eternity</u>. Harlan, IA: Guidepost Books.

15. Moody, R., & Perry, P. (2010). <u>Glimpses of eternity</u>. Harlan, IA: Guidepost Books, p. 41.

16. Moody, R., & Perry, P. (2010). <u>Glimpses of eternity</u>. Harlan, IA: Guidepost Books, p. 42.

17. Ring, K., & Valarino, E. E. (1998). <u>Lessons from the light.</u> New York: Insight, pp. 44-46.

18. Ruiz, D. M. (1999). <u>The mastery of love.</u> San Rafael, CA: Amber-Allen, p. 196.

19. Burr, H. S. (1972a). <u>Blueprint for immortality: The electric patterns of life.</u> Essex England: the C.W. Daniel Company, Ltd.

20. Burr, H. S., (1972b). <u>The fields of life: our links to the universe.</u> New York: Ballantine.

21. Barks, C. (2006). <u>A year with Rumi: Daily readings.</u> New York: HarperOne, p. 88.

22. Ladinsky, D. (2011). <u>A year with Hafiz</u>. New York: Penguin Books, p. 5.

Chapter 8

1. Barks, C. (2006). <u>A year with Rumi: Daily readings.</u> New York: HarperOne. p. 402.
2. Cozort, D. (1986). <u>Highest yoga tantra.</u> Ithaca, NY: Snow Lion.
3. Rinpoche, L. Y. (1995). <u>The tantric path of purification.</u> Boston: Wisdom.
4. Sangpo, K. (1996). <u>Tantric practice in Nying-ma.</u> Ithaca, NY: Snow Lion.
5. Chia, M. (2005). <u>Healing love through the Tao.</u> Rochester, VT: Destiny Books.
6. Chia, M. & Chia, M. (1993). <u>Awaken healing light of the Tao.</u> Huntington, NY: Healing Tao Books.
7. Feuerstein, G. (1998). <u>Tantra: The path of ecstasy.</u> Boston: Shambhala.
8. Reich, W. (1961). <u>The discovery of the orgone: The function of the orgasm.</u> New York: Noonday Press.
9. Lowen, A. (1975). <u>Bioenergetics</u>. New York: Penguin, p. 246.
10. Lowen, A. (1988). <u>Love, sex, and your heart</u>. New York: Penguin.
11. Lowen, A. (1990). <u>The spirituality of the body: Bioenergetics for grace and harmony</u>. New York: MacMillan, p. 87.
12. Pierrakos, J. C. (1997). <u>Eros, Love & Sexuality</u>. Mendocino, CA: LifeRhythm, p. 43.
13. Wade, J. (2004). <u>Transcendent sex: When lovemaking opens the veil.</u> New York: Paraview Pocket Books.
14. Wade, J. (2004). <u>Transcendent sex: When lovemaking opens the veil.</u> New York: Paraview Pocket Books, pp. 272-278.
15. Wade, J. (2004). <u>Transcendent sex: When lovemaking opens the veil.</u> New York: Paraview Pocket Books, pp. 278-280.

16. Kinsey, A. C., Pomeroy, W. E., & Martin, C. E. (1948). Sexual behavior in the human male. Bloomington, IN: Indiana University Press.
17. Kinsey, A. C., Pomeroy, W. E., Martin, C. E., & Gebhard, P. H. (1953). Sexual behavior in the human female. Philadelphis: W. B. Saunders.
18. Masters, W. & Johnson, V. P. (1966). Human sexual response. Boston: Little Brown.
19. Wade, J. (2004). Transcendent sex: When lovemaking opens the veil. New York: Paraview Pocket Books, pp. 279-280.
20. Gresham, L. B. (2005). Personal communication during workshop. Asilomar, CA.
21. Burr, W. R., Leigh, G. K., Day, R. D., & Constantine, J. (1979). Role theory-symbolic interaction and the family. In W. Burr, R. Hill, F. Nye, & I. Reiss (Eds.), Contemporary Theories About the Family, Vol. 2. New York: Free Press.
22. Brennen, B. A. (1987). Hands of light: A guide to healing through the human energy field. New York: Bantam.
23. Lombardo, L, & Polonko, K. (2010). Interdisciplinary contributions to the prevention of child maltreatment. International Journal of Interdisciplinary Social Sciences, 4, 89-112.
24. Polonko, K. A. (2006). Exploring assumptions about child neglect in relation to the broader field of child maltreatment. Journal of Health & Human Services Administration, 29 (3), 260-284.
25. Polonko, K. A., & Lombardo, L. (2004). Enlightened witnessing: Rehumanizing through confrontation with violence. Paper presented at the annual meetings of the International Conference on New Directions in the Humanities, Prato, Italy.
26. Blais, R. (2017). How to permanently reset your body weight set point. Sudbury, Ontario, Canada: The Transformation Center.
27. Burr, H. S. (1972a). Blueprint for immortality: The electric patterns of life. Essex England: the C.W. Daniel Company, Ltd.
28. Brennen, B. A. (1993). Light emerging: The journey of personal healing. New York: Bantam.

29. Anthony, E. J. (1987). Risk, vulnerability, and resilience: An overview. In E. J. Anthony & B. Cohler (Eds.), The invulnerable child. New York: Guilford, p.3.
30. Thorne, B. (1987). Re-visioning women and social change: Where are the children? Gender and Society, 1, 85-109.

Chapter 9

1. Barks, C. (2006). A year with Rumi: Daily readings. New York: HarperOne, p. 100.
2. Cheek, D. B. (1995). Early use of psychotherapy in prevention of preterm labor: The application of hypnosis and ideomotor techniques with women carrying twin pregnancies. The Journal of Prenatal and Perinatal Psychology and Health, 10, 5-19.
3. Chamberlain, D. (2013). Windows to the womb. Berkeley, CA: North Atlantic Books.
4. Jordan, J. V. (2001). A relational-cultural model: Healing through mutual empathy. Minneapolis, MN: Menninger Foundation.
5. Lipton, B. (2005). The biology of belief. Santa Rosa, CA: Mountain of Love/Elite Books.
6. Lipton, B., & Bhaerman, S. (2009). Spontaneous evolution. Carlsbad, CA: Hay House.
7. Leigh, G. K., Metzker, J. A., & Hilton, J. M. (1999). An observational study of energy fields of infants and young children. Subtle Energies and Energy Medicine, 8, 1-29.
8. Metzker, J. A., & Leigh, G. K. (2004). A short-term longitudinal study of energy fields in infants and young children. Subtle Energies & Energy Medicine, 15, 117-145.
9. Eason, C. (1994). Psychic power of children. London: Foulsham
10. Ring, K., & Valarino, E. E. (1998). Lessons from the light. New York: Insight.
11. Bowman, C. (1998). Children's past lives. New York: Bantam Books, pp. 343-344.
12. Leininger, B. & Leininger, A. (2009). Soul survivor: The reincarnation of a World War II fighter pilot. New York: Grand Central Publishing.

13. Weiss, B. L., & Weiss, A. E. (2012). <u>Miracles happen:</u>
    <u>The transformational healing power of past-life memories.</u>
    New York: HarperCollins.
14. Weiss, B. L., & Weiss, A. E. (2012). <u>Miracles happen:</u>
    <u>The transformational healing power of past-life memories.</u>
    New York: HarperCollins, pp. 306, 308.
15. Grof, S. (2006). <u>When the impossible happens: Adven-</u>
    <u>tures of nonordinary reality.</u> Boulder, CO: Sounds True.
16. Grof, S. (2006). <u>When the impossible happens: Adven-</u>
    <u>tures of nonordinary reality.</u> Boulder, CO: Sounds True, p.
    350.
17. Allison, R. B., with Schwarz, T. (1998). <u>Minds in many</u>
    <u>pieces: Revealing the spiritual side of multiple personality</u>
    <u>disorder.</u> Los Osos, CA: CIE Publishing.
18. Alexander, J. F. (1973). Defensive and supportive commu-
    nication in normal and delinquent families. <u>Journal of Con-</u>
    <u>sulting and Clinical Psychology, 40,</u> 223-31.
19. Alexander, J. F., & Parsons, B. V. (1973). Short-term be-
    havioral intervention with delinquent families: Impact on
    family process and recidivism. <u>Journal of Abnormal Psy-</u>
    <u>chology, 51,</u> 219-33.

Chapter 10

1. Barks, C. (2006). <u>A year with Rumi: Daily readings.</u> New
   York: HarperOne, p. 334.
2. Ruiz, D. M. (1997). <u>The four agreements.</u> San Rafael, CA:
   Amber-Allen.
3. Lanza, R., & Berman, B. (2009). <u>Biocentrism: How life</u>
   <u>and consciousness are the keys to understanding the true</u>
   <u>nature of the universe.</u> Dallas, TX: Benbella Books.

Chapter 11

1. Barks, C. (2006). <u>A year with Rumi: Daily readings.</u> New
   York: HarperOne, p. 174.
2. Leigh, G. K., Metzker, J. A., & Hilton, J. M. (1999). An
   observational study of energy fields of infants and young
   children. <u>Subtle Energies and Energy Medicine, 8,</u> 1-29.

3. Metzker, J. A., & Leigh, G. K. (2004). A short-term longitudinal study of energy fields in infants and young children. Subtle Energies & Energy Medicine, 15, 117-145.

4. Leigh, G. K., Metzker, J. A., & Pierce, S. (2010). Incorporating human energy research into family research and therapy. Subtle Energy and Energy Medicine, 19, 1-20.

5. Leigh, G. K., Metzker, J. A., & Pierce, S. (2010). Investigating adaptability, cohesion, and human energy fields in family interactions. The International Journal of Healing and Caring, 10, No.1.

6. Gresham, L. B. (2006). Personal communication, August.

7. Leigh, G. K. (1986). Adolescent involvement in family systems. In G. Leigh & G. Peterson (Eds.), Adolescents in families (pp. 38-72). Cincinnati, OH: South-Western Publishing Co.

8. Andrews, T. (1996). How to see and read the aura. St. Paul, MN: Llewellyn.

9. Smith, M. (1997). Auras: See them in only 60 seconds. St. Paul, MN: Llewellyn.

10. Hunt, V. V. (1996). Infinite mind: Science of the human vibrations of consciousness. Malibu, CA: Malibu Publishing Co.

11. Norcross, J. C. (2010). The therapeutic relationship. In B. L. Duncan (Ed.), The heart and soul of change: Delivering what works in therapy. Washington, DC: American Psychological Association.

12. Morse, M., with Perry, P. (2000). Where God lives. New York: HarperCollins.

13. Ring, K., & Valarino, E. E. (1998). Lessons from the light. New York: Insight.

Chapter 12

1. Barks, C. (2006). A year with Rumi: Daily readings. New York: HarperOne, p. 9.

2. Leigh, G. K., Polonko, K. A., & Leigh, C. D.(2003). A comparison of human energy fields among children, youth, adults, and Dahn Masters. Subtle Energies and Energy Medicine, 14 (1), 77-101.

3.   Weiss, B. L., & Weiss, A. E. (2012). Miracles happen: The transformational healing power of past-life memories. New York: HarperCollins, pp. 22, 23, 188, 190, 192.

4.   McKay, M. (2016). Seeking Jordan. Novato, CA: New World Library.

5.   McKay, M. (2016). Seeking Jordan. Novato, CA: New World Library, p. 71 (in ebook).

6.   Myers, I. B., & Myers, P. B. (1995). Gifts differing: Understanding personality type. Mountain View, CA: Davies-Black Publishing.

7.   Quinn, D. (1995). Ishmael. New York: Bantam.

8.   Quinn, D. (1997). The story of B. New York: Bantam.

9.   Leigh, G. K., Metzker, J. A., & Hilton, J. M. (1999). An observational study of energy fields of infants and young children. Subtle Energies and Energy Medicine, 8, 1-29.

10. Metzker, J. A., & Leigh, G. K. (2004). A short-term longitudinal study of energy fields in infants and young children. Subtle Energies & Energy Medicine, 15, 117-145.

11. Leigh, G. K., Metzker, J. A., & Pierce, S. (2010a). Incorporating human energy research into family research and therapy. Subtle Energy and Energy Medicine, 19, 1-20.

12. Leigh, G. K., Metzker, J. A., & Pierce, S. (2010b). Investigating adaptability, cohesion, and human energy fields in family interactions. The International Journal of Healing and Caring, 10, No.1.

13. Lanza, R., & Berman, B. (2009). Biocentrism: How life and consciousness are the keys to understanding the true nature of the universe. Dallas, TX: Benbella Books, p. 176.

14. Weiss, B. L., & Weiss, A. E. (2012). Miracles happen: The transformational healing power of past-life memories. New York: HarperCollins, pp. 293, 308.

15. https://en.wikiquote.org/wiki/Margaret_Mead.

16. McKay, M. (2016). Seeking Jordan. Novato, CA: New World Library, p. 127 (in ebook).

17. Barks, C. (2006). A year with Rumi: Daily readings. New York: HarperOne, p. 146.

Appendix B

1. Barks, C. (2006). A year with Rumi: Daily readings. New York: HarperOne, p. 66.
2. Naranjo, C. (1994). Character and neurosis: An integrative view. Nevada City, CA: Gateways.
3. Speeth, K. R., & Friedlander, I. (1980). Gurdjieff: Seeker of the truth. New York: Harper Colophon Books.
4. Ouspensky, P. D. (1949). In search of the miraculous. New York: Harcourt Brace & Co.
5. Ouspensky, P. D. (1949). The fourth way. New York: Vintage
6. Bennett, J. G. (1983). Enneagram studies. York Beach, MA: Samuel Weiser, Inc.
7. Speeth, K. R. (1989). The Gurdjieff work. New York: Jeremy P. Tarcher/Putnsm.
8. Naranjo, C. (1994). Character and neurosis: An integrative view. Nevada City, CA: Gateways, p. xxix.
9. Ichazo, O. (1972). The human process for enlightenment and freedom. New York: The Arica Institute, Inc.
10. Ichazo, O. (1982). Interviews with Oscar Ichazo. New York: Arica Institute Press.
11. Ichazo, O. (1976). Arica Psycho-calisthenics. New York: Simon and Schuster.
12. Naranjo, C. (1990). Ennea-type structures. Nevada City, CA: Gateways.
13. Naranjo, C. (1995). Enneatypes in psychotherapy. Prescott, AZ: Hohm Press.
14. Naranjo, C. (2004). The Enneagram of society: Healing the soul to heal the world. Nevada City, CA: Gateways Books & Tapes.
15. Almaas, A. H. (1999). Facets of unity. Berkeley, CA: Diamond Books.
16. Maitri, S. (2001). The spiritual dimension of the enneagram: Nine faces of the soul. New York: Jeremy P. Tarcher/Putnum.
17. Maitri, S. (2009). The enneagram of passions and virtues: Finding the way home. New York: Jeremy P. Tarcher/Putnum.
18. Jaxon-Bear, E. (1987). Healing the heart of suffering: Using the enneagram for spiritual growth. Self-published.

19. Jaxon-Bear, E. (2001). The Enneagram of liberation: From fixation to freedom. Bolinas, CA: Leela Foundation.
20. Coates, M., & Searle, J. (2011). Sex, love and your personality. Santa Monica, CA: Therapy Options Press.
21. Daniels, D., & Price, V. (2009). The essential Enneagram. New York: HarperOne.
22. Palmer, H. (1991). The Enneagram: Understanding yourself and others in your life. San Francisco: Harper.
23. Palmer, H. (1995). The Enneagram in love and work. New York: Harper Collins.
24. Pearce, H. (2012). Enneagram beyond the basics. Self published.
25. Rhodes, S. (2010). Archetypes of the enneagram. Seattle, WA: Geranium Press.
26. Riso, D. R., & Hudson, R. (1999). The wisdom of the enneagram. New York: Bantam Books.
27. Sheppard, L. (2000). The everyday Enneagram. Petaluma, CA: Nine Points Press.
28. Givot, I. (2012). Enneagram of healing: Exploring a process. Mercer Island, WA: ATOM Press.
29. Howell, J. B. (2012). Becoming conscious: The Enneagrams forgotten passageway. Bloomington, IN: Balboa Press.
30. Goldschmidt, P. (2008). Workshop on strength and limiting patterns. Las Vegas, NV, December.
31. Condon, T. (2011). Enneagram movie & video guide 3.0. Amazon Kindle Edition.
32. Almaas, A. H. (1999). Facets of unity. Berkeley, CA: Diamond Books, p. 257.
33. Maitri, S. (2001). The spiritual dimension of the enneagram: Nine faces of the soul. New York: Jeremy P. Tarcher/Putnum, p. 90.
34. Almaas, A. H. (1999). Facets of unity. Berkeley, CA: Diamond Books, p. 186.
35. Maitri, S. (2001). The spiritual dimension of the enneagram: Nine faces of the soul. New York: Jeremy P. Tarcher/Putnum, p. 135.
36. Maitri, S. (2001). The spiritual dimension of the enneagram: Nine faces of the soul. New York: Jeremy P. Tarcher/Putnum, p. 67.
37. Almaas, A. H. (1999). Facets of unity. Berkeley, CA: Diamond Books, p. 163.

REFERENCES

Abraham, R. (1994). <u>Chaos • Gaia • Eros</u>. San Francisco: Harper.

Alexander, J. F. (1973). Defensive and supportive communication in normal and delinquent families. <u>Journal of Consulting and Clinical Psychology</u>, <u>40</u>, 223-31.

Alexander, J. F., & Parsons, B. V. (1973). Short-term behavioral intervention with delinquent families: Impact on family process and recidivism. <u>Journal of Abnormal Psychology</u>, <u>51</u>, 219-33.

Allison, R. B., with Schwarz, T. (1998). <u>Minds in many pieces: Revealing the spiritual side of multiple personality disorder</u>. Los Osos, CA: CIE Publishing.

Almaas, A. H. (1998). <u>Essence</u>. York Beach, ME: Samuel Weiser, Inc.

Almaas, A. H. (1999). <u>Facets of unity</u>. Berkeley, CA: Diamond Books.

Andrews, T. (1996). <u>How to see and read the aura</u>. St. Paul, MN: Llewellyn.

Anka, D. & Meyers, S. (1997). <u>Quest for truth</u>. Iowa City, IA: Nobul Press.

Anthony, E. J. (1987). Risk, vulnerability, and resilience: An overview. In E. J. Anthony & B. Cohler (Eds.), <u>The invulnerable child</u>. New York: Guilford.

Aries, P. (1962). <u>Centuries of childhood</u>. New York: Vintage.

Assante, J. (2012). <u>The last frontier: Exploring the afterlife and transforming our fear of death</u>. Novato, CA: New World Library.

Atwater, P. M. H. (2003). <u>The new children and near-death experiences</u>. Rochester, VT: Bear & Company.

Bache, C. M. (1995). One mind, many pupils: Morphic fields in higher education. Paper presented at the annual meeting of the International Transpersonal Association, Palo Alto, CA, June.

Bandler, R., & Grinder, J. (1975). <u>The structure of magic: A book about language and therapy</u>. Palo Alto, CA: Science and Behavior Books.

Barks, C. (2003). <u>Rumi: The book of love</u>. New York: HarperOne.

References

Barks, C. (2006). A year with Rumi: Daily readings. New York: HarperOne.

Barnard, C. P. (1994). Resiliency: A shift in our perception? The American Journal of Family Therapy, 22, 135-144.

Bates, E., O'Connell, B., & Shore, C. (1987). Language and communication in infancy. In J. D. Osofsky (Ed.), Handbook of infant development (pp. 149-203). New York: John Wiley & Sons.

Becker, R. O. (1990). Cross currents: The promise of electro-medicine. Los Angeles, CA: J.P. Tarcher.

Becker, R. O. & Selden, G. (1985). The Body electric: Electro-magnetism and the foundation of life. New York: William Morrow & Co.

Bennett, J. G. (1983). Enneagram studies. York Beach, MA: Samuel Weiser, Inc.

Benor, D. J. (2002). Spiritual healing: Scientific validation of a healing revolution. (Healing Research Vol. 1). South-field, MI: Vision.

Benor, D. J. (2004). Consciousness, bioenergy and healing: Self-healing and energy medicine for the 21st Century (Healing Research Vol. 2). Oxfordshire, UK: Helix.

Benson, B. A., Messer, S. C., & Gross, A. M. (1992). Learning theories. In V. B. Van Hasselt & M. Hersen (Eds.), Handbook of social development: A lifespan perspective. New York: Plenum.

Benson, P. L. (1997). All kids are our kids. San Francisco: Jossey-Bass.

Blais, R. (2017). How to permanently reset your body weight set point. Sudbury, Ontario, Canada: The Transformation Center

Blake, A. G. E. (1996). The intelligent Enneagram. Boston: Shambhala.

Bohm, D. (1980). Wholeness and the implicate order. London: Routledge & Kegan Paul.

Boswell, J. (1988). The kindness of strangers: The abandonment of children in Western Europe from late antiquity to the Renaissance. New York: Vintage Books.

Bowen, M. (1978). Family therapy through clinical practice. New York: Michael Aronson, Inc.

Bowlby, J. (1969). Attachment and loss, Vol. 1: Attachment. New York: Basic Books.

Bowlby, J. (1973). <u>Attachment and loss, Vol. 2: Separation.</u> New York: Basic Books.

Bowman, C. (1998). <u>Children's past lives.</u> New York: Bantam Books.

Brennen, B. A. (1987). <u>Hands of light: A guide to healing through the human energy field.</u> New York: Bantam.

Brennen, B. A. (1993). <u>Light emerging: The journey of personal healing.</u> New York: Bantam.

Bretherton, I. (1993). Theoretical contributions from developmental psychology. In P. G. Boss, W. J. Doherty, R. LaRossa, W. R. Schumm, & S. K. Steinmetz. <u>Sourcebook of family theories and methods; A contextual approach</u> (pp. 275-297). New York: Plenum Press.

Brown, B. (2012). <u>Daring greatly.</u> New York: AVERY.

Brown, G. (1999). <u>The energy of life.</u> New York: Free Press.

Browne, S. (2007). <u>Psychic children.</u> New York: Dutton.

Burr, H. S., and Northrop, F. S. C., (1935). The electrodynamic theory of life. <u>Quarterly Review of Biology. vol. 10,</u> pp. 322-333.

Burr, H. S. and Northrop, F. S. C., (1939). Evidence for the existence of an electrodynamic field in living organisms. Proceedings of the National Academy of Sciences of the United States of America. Vol. 24, pp. 284-288.

Burr, H. S., (1944). The meaning of bioelectrical potentials. <u>Yale Journal of biology and medicine, Vol. 16,</u> pp. 353-360.

Burr, H. S. (1972a). <u>Blueprint for immortality: The electric patterns of life.</u> Essex England: the C.W. Daniel Company, Ltd.

Burr, H. S., (1972b). <u>The fields of life: our links to the universe.</u> New York: Ballantine.

Burr, W. R., Leigh, G. K., Day, R. D., & Constantine, J. (1979). Role theory-symbolic interaction and the family. In W. Burr, R. Hill, F. Nye, & I. Reiss (Eds.), <u>Contemporary Theories About the Family,</u> Vol. 2. New York: Free Press.

Buscaglia, L. (1972). <u>Love.</u>

Buscaglia, L. (1985). <u>Living, loving and learning.</u> New York: Ballantine Books.

Buscaglia, L. (1994). <u>Born for love: Reflections on loving.</u> New York: Ballantine Books.

Buscaglia, L. (1996). <u>Love: What life is all about.</u> New York: Ballantine Books.

Capra, F. (1996). The web of life. New York: Anchor Books.

Carman, E., & Carman, N. (2013). Cosmic cradle. Berkeley, CA: North Atlantic Books.

Chamberlain, D. (1990). Expanding the boundaries of memory. ReVision, 12, p. 18.

Chamberlain, D. (2013). Windows to the womb. Berkeley, CA: North Atlantic Books.

Cheek, D. B. (1995). Early use of psychotherapy in prevention of preterm labor: The application of hypnosis and ideo-motor techniques with women carrying twin pregnancies. The Journal of Prenatal and Perinatal Psychology and Health, 10, 5-19.

Chia, M. (2005). Healing love through the Tao. Rochester, VT: Destiny Books.

Chia, M. & Chia, M. (1993). Awaken healing light of the Tao. Huntington, NY: Healing Tao Books.

Chodron, T. (1990). Open heart, clear mind. Ithaca, NY: Snow Lion Publications.

Chogyam, N. (1986). Rainbow of liberated energy. Longmead, England: Element Books.

Clark, A. M. (2001). Diplomacy of conscious. Princeton, NJ: Princeton University Press, p. 49.

Coates, M., & Searle, J. (2011). Sex, love and your personality. Santa Monica, CA: Therapy Options Press.

Coffey, C. (2012). Growing up psychic. New York: Three Rivers Press.

Cohen, A. (2011). 10 limiting beliefs to let go of. Law of Attraction Magazine (pp. 14-17). Annual, 2011.

Collinge, W. (1998). Subtle energy. New York: Warner Books.

Comstock, D. L., & Qin, D. (2005). Relational-cultural theory: A framework for relational development across the life span. In D. Comstock (Ed.), Diversity and development (pp. 25-45). Belmont, CA: Brooks/Cole.

Condon, T. (2011). Enneagram movie & video guide 3.0. Amazon Kindle Edition.

Cozort, D. (1986). Highest yoga tantra. Ithaca, NY: Snow Lion.

Crain, W. (2011). Theories of development: Concepts and applications (6th ed.). Upper Saddle River, NJ: Pearson/ Prentice Hall.

Daniels, D., & Price, V. (2009). The essential Enneagram. New York: HarperOne.

References

Davis, M. (1978). Rainbows of life: The promise of Kirlian photography. New York: Harper & Row.

DeFrain, J., Nelson, S., & Chambers, K. (1997, November). Investigating the long-term effects of child abuse in adults. A paper presented at the annual meetings of the National Council on Family Relations, Arlington, VA.

Dent-Read, C., & Zukow-Goldring, P. (1997). Evolving explanations of development: Ecological approaches to organism-environment systems. Washington, DC: American Psychological Association.

Dossey, L. (1999). Reinventing medicine: Beyond mind-body to a new era of healing. San Francisco: Harper.

Doyle, B. (2012). Find your passion. Law of Attraction Magazine (pp. 6-7). Annual, 2012.

Eadie, B. J. (1996). The awakening heart. New York: Pocket Star Books.

Earthwhale, (2015). Guidance from Grandmother Whale, Channeled by Earthwhale. earthwhale.blogspot.com

Eason, C. (1994). Psychic power of children. London: Foulsham.

Ebert, A., & Kustenmacher, M. (Eds.) (1996). Experiencing the enneagram. New York: Crossroad.

Eisenstein, C. (2013). The more beautiful world our hearts know is possible. Berkeley, CA: North Atlantic Books.

Erikson, E. H. (1959). Identify and the life cycle: Selected papers. New York: International Universities Press.

Erikson, E. H. (1993). Childhood and society. New York: Norton.

Fenwick, P., & Fenwick, E. (1995). The truth in the light. New York: Berkley Books.

Feuerstein, G. (1998). Tantra: The path of ecstasy. Boston: Shambhala.

Field, T. (1987). Affective and interactive disturbances in infants. In J. D. Osofsky (Ed.), Handbook of infant development (pp. 972-1005). New York: John Wiley.

Freud, S. (1949). Outline of Psychoanalysis. New York: Norton.

Fritzlan, L. (2011). Intervention on America. Corte Madera, CA: Recovery Works.

Garmezy, N. (1983). Stressors of childhood. In N. Garmezy & M. Rutter (Eds.), Stress, coping, and development in children (pp. 43-84). New York: McGraw-Hill.

Gaydos, M. L. C. (2004). The theory of natural systems. Bloomington, IN: ArthurHouse.

Gerber, R. (1988). Vibrational medicine. Santa Fe, NM: Bear & Company.

Givot, I. (2012). Enneagram of healing: Exploring a process. Mercer Island, WA: ATOM Press.

Goldschmidt, P. (2008). Workshop on strength and limiting patterns. Las Vegas, NV, December.

Goleman, D., & Thurman, R. A. (1991). Mindscience: An East-West dialogue. Boston: Wisdom Publications.

Gottlieb, D. (2008). Learning from the heart. New York: Sterling.

Greenleaf, B. K. (1978). Children through the ages. New York: McGraw-Hill.

Gresham, L. B. (2005). Personal communication during workshop. Asilomar, CA.

Gresham, L. B. (2006). Personal communication, August.

Gresham, L. B., & Nichols, J. J. (2002). The body's map of consciousness. Salt Lake City, UT: Nonetoosoon Publishing.

Grof, S. (1975). Realms of the human unconscious: Observations from LSD research. New York: Viking Press.

Grof, S. (1985). Beyond the brain. Albany, NY: State University of New York Press.

Grof, S. (1988a). Modern consciousness research and human survival. In S. Grof & M. L. Valier (Eds.), Human survival and consciousness evolution (pp. 57-79). Albany, NY: State University of New York Press.

Grof, S. (1988b). The adventure of self-discovery. Albany, NY: State University of New York Press.

Grof, S. (1993). The holotropic mind: The three levels of human consciousness and how they shape our lives. San Francisco: Harper.

Grof, S. (1996). Ken Wilber's spectrum psychology: Observations from clinical consciousness research. ReVision, 19, 11-24.

Grof, S. (1998). The cosmic game. Albany, NY: State University of New York.

Grof, S. (2000). Psychology of the future. Albany, NY: State University of New York.

Grof, S. (2006). When the impossible happens: Adventures of nonordinary reality. Boulder, CO: Sounds True.

Grof, S. (2010). The ultimate journey (2nd. Ed.). Santa Cruz, CA: MAPS.

Grof, S., & Grof, C. (1980). Beyond death: The gates of consciousness. London: Thames and Hudson.

Grof, S., & Grof, C. (1989). Spiritual emergency. Los Angeles: Jeremy P. Tarcher.

Grof, C., & Grof, S. (1990). The stormy search for the self. Los Angeles: Jeremy P. Tarcher.

Guenther, H. V., & Kawamura, L. S. (1975). Mind in Buddhist psychology. Berkeley, CA: Dharma Publishing.

Hanh, T. N. (1997). Teachings on love. Berkeley, CA: Parallax.

Hanh, T. N. (2007). Living Buddha, living Christ. New York: Penguin.

Hanh, T. N. (2015). How to love. Berkeley, CA: Parallax.

Hartling, L. M. (2005). Fostering resilience throughout our lives. In D. Comstock, Diversity and Development, pp. 337-354).

Havighurst, R. J., Neugarten. B. L., & Tobin, S. S. (1968). Disengagement and patterns of aging. In B. L. Neugarten (Ed.), Middle Age and Aging. Chicago: University of Chicago Press.

Hetzel, R. (1994). Your life is in your chakras. Palo Alto, CA: Hetzel.

Hooks, B. (2001). All about love. New York: Perennial.

Howell, J. B. (2012). Becoming conscious: The Enneagrams forgotten passageway. Bloomington, IN: Balboa Press.

Hunt, V. V. (1996). Infinite mind: Science of the human vibrations of consciousness. Malibu, CA: Malibu Publishing Co.

Hurley, K., & Dobson, T. (1993). My best self: Using the Enneagram to free the soul. San Francisco: Harper.

Ichazo, O. (1972). The human process for enlightenment and freedom. New York: The Arica Institute, Inc.

Ichazo, O. (1976). Arica Psycho-calisthenics. New York: Simon and Schuster.

Ichazo, O. (1982). Interviews with Oscar Ichazo. New York: Arica Institute Press.

Jampolsky, G. G. (2000). Teach only love. Hillsboro, OR: Beyond Words.

Jaxon-Bear, E. (1987). Healing the heart of suffering: Using the enneagram for spiritual growth. Self-published.

Jaxon-Bear, E. (2001). The Enneagram of liberation: From fixation to freedom. Bolinas, CA: Leela Foundation.

Jessor, R. (1993). Successful adolescent development among youth in high-risk settings. American Psychologist, 48(2), 117-126.

Jordan, J. V. (2001). A relational-cultural model: Healing through mutual empathy. Minneapolis, MN: Menninger Foundation.

Judith, A. (1994). Wheels of life: A user's guide to the chakra system. St. Paul, MN: Llewellyn Publications.

Judith, A. (1996). Eastern body, Western mind: Psychology and the chakra system. Berkeley, CA: Celestial Arts.

Jung, C. G. (1959). The basic writings of C. G. Jung. Edited by V. S. Laszlo. New York: Random House.

Kramarik, A. (2015). www.akiane.com.

Karagulla, S., & Kunz, D. V. (1989). The chakras and the human energy fields. Wheaton, IL: The Theosophical Publishing House.

Kasulis, T. P., Ames, R. T., & Dissanayake, W. (1993). Self as body in Asian theory and practice. Albany, NY: State University of New York Press.

Kegan, R. (1994). In over our heads. Cambridge, MA: Harvard University Press.

Kerr, M. E., & Bowen, M. (1988). Family evaluation: An approach based on Bowen theory. New York: W. W. Norton & Co.

Keyes, M. F. (1992). Emotions and the Enneagram. Muir Beach, CA: Molysdatur.

Kinsey, A. C., Pomeroy, W. E., & Martin, C. E. (1948). Sexual behavior in the human male. Bloomington, IN: Indiana University Press.

Kinsey, A. C., Pomeroy, W. E., Martin, C. E., & Gebhard, P. H. (1953). Sexual behavior in the human female. Philadelphis: W. B. Saunders.

Kirtana. (1999). I Am, a song from the album, This Embrace. Wild Dove Music.

Kornfield, J. (1993). A path with heart. New York: Bantam.

Korotkov, K. (1998). Light after life. Fair Lawn, NJ: Backbone Publishing.

References

Korotkov, K. (1999). Aura and consciousness. Moscow: Russian Ministry of Culture.

Korotkov, K. (2002). Human energy fields: Study with GDV Bioelectrography. Fair Lawn, NJ: Backbone Publishing.

Kramarik, A. (2015). www.akiane.com.

Krippner, S., & Rubin, D. (Eds.) (1975). The energies of consciousness: Explorations in acupuncture, auras, and Kirlian photography. New York: Gordon and Breach.

Kubler-Ross, E. (1969). On death and dying. New York: Macmillan.

Kunz, D. Van Gelder. (1991). The personal aura. Wheaton, IL: Quest Books.

Ladinsky, D. (2011). A year with Hafiz. New York: Penguin Books.

Lanza, R., & Berman, B. (2009). Biocentrism: How life and consciousness are the keys to understanding the true nature of the universe. Dallas, TX: Benbella Books.

Lee, Seung-Heun (2002). Brain respiration. Las Vegas, NV: Healing Society, Inc.

Leigh, G. K. (1977). Language, thought, and the enhancement of self-esteem. Family Perspective, ll, 19-27.

Leigh, G. K. (1986). Adolescent involvement in family systems. In G. Leigh & G. Peterson (Eds.), Adolescents in families (pp. 38-72). Cincinnati, OH: South-Western Publishing Co.

Leigh, G. K. (2004). Using human energy fields to assess family communications. Journal of Family Communication, part of special issue, "Advancing Family Communication Theory and Research." Vol. 4 (No. 3&4), 319-335.

Leigh, G. K., & Cendese, J. (2008). Investigating the impact of Integrated Awareness® with breast cancer patients. Subtle Energy and Energy Medicine, Vol 18 (3), 1-15.

Leigh, G. K., & Korotkov, K. (2001, June). The GDV Measure of Energy Fields and Corresponding Data on Group Differences. Paper presented at the Annual Meetings of the International Society for the Study of Subtle Energy and Energy Medicine in Boulder, Co.

Leigh, G. K., & Loewen, I. R. (1987). Utilizing developmental perspectives in the study of adolescence. Journal of Adolescent Research, 2, 303-320.

Leigh, G. K., Metzker, J. A., & Hilton, J. M. (1999). An observational study of energy fields of infants and young children. Subtle Energies and Energy Medicine, 8, 1-29.

Leigh, G. K., Metzker, J. A., & Pierce, S. (2010a). Incorporating human energy research into family research and therapy. Subtle Energy and Energy Medicine, 19, 1-20.

Leigh, G. K., Metzker, J. A., & Pierce, S. (2010b). Investigating adaptability, cohesion, and human energy fields in family interactions. The International Journal of Healing and Caring, 10, No.1.

Leigh, G. K., Polonko, K. A., & Leigh, C. D.(2003). A comparison of human energy fields among children, youth, adults, and Dahn Masters. Subtle Energies and Energy Medicine, 14 (1), 77-101.

Lerner, H. D., & Ehrlich, J. (1992). Psychodynamic models. In V. B. Van Hasselt & M. Hersen (Eds.), Handbook of social development: A lifespan perspective. New York: Plenum.

Levine, P. A. (1997). Waking the tiger. Berkeley, CA: North Atlantic Books.

Levine, P. A. (2010). In an unspoken voice. Berkeley, CA: North Atlantic Books.

Levinson, D. (1978). The seasons of a man's life. New York: Ballentine.

Lipton, B. (2005). The biology of belief. Santa Rosa, CA: Mountain of Love/Elite Books.

Lipton, B., & Bhaerman, S. (2009). Spontaneous evolution. Carlsbad, CA: Hay House.

Lombardo, L, & Polonko, K. (2010). Interdisciplinary contributions to the prevention of child maltreatment. International Journal of Interdisciplinary Social Sciences, 4, 89-112.

Long, J. (2010). Evidence of the afterlife. New York: Harper One, p. 146-47.

Long, J. (2016). God and the afterlife. NY: Harper One.

Lowen, A. (1967). The betrayal of the body. New York: Collier Books.

Lowen, A. (1971). The language of the body. New York: Collier Books.

Lowen, A. (1975). Bioenergetics. New York: Penguin.

Lowen, A. (1988). Love, sex, and your heart. New York: Penguin.

Lowen, A. (1990). The spirituality of the body: Bioenergetics for grace and harmony. New York: MacMillan.

Lowen, A. (1995). Joy: The surrender to the body and to life. New York: Penguin.

Lowen, A. (1997). Narcissism: Denial of the True Self. New York: Touchstone.

Lowen, A. (2003). The fear of life. Alachua, FL: Bioenergetics Press.

Mangus, 2016 FilmRise, Moscus, and VG TV Documentary, Directed by Benjamin Ree.

Maitri, S. (2001). The spiritual dimension of the enneagram: Nine faces of the soul. New York: Jeremy P. Tarcher/ Putnum.

Maitri, S. (2009). The enneagram of passions and virtues: Finding the way home. New York: Jeremy P. Tarcher/ Putnum.

Martin, A. & Landrell, J. (2005). Energy psychology/energy medicine. New York: Harper Books.

Mason, J. (1993). An unnatural order. New York: Simon & Schuster.

Masters, W. & Johnson, V. P. (1966). Human sexual response. Boston: Little Brown.

McBrien, R. P. (1989). The HarperCollins encyclopedia of Catholicism. San Francisco: Harper.

McCubbin, H. I. (1997). Families under stress: What makes them resilient. Paper presented at the annual meeting of the American Association of Family and consumer Science, Washington, DC (June).

McKay, M. (2016). Seeking Jordan. Novato, CA: New World Library.

McTaggart, L. (2002). The field. New York: Harper/Perennial.

Melchizedek, D. (2003). Living in the heart. Flagstaff, AZ: Light Technology Publishing.

Metzker, J. A., & Leigh, G. K. (2004). A short-term longitudinal study of energy fields in infants and young children. Subtle Energies & Energy Medicine, 15, 117-145.

Miller, P. H. (2010). Theories of developmental psychology. New York: Worth.

Moody, R. (1975). Life after life. New York: Bantam.

Moody, R. (1988). The light beyond. New York: Bantam.

Moody, R. (1993). Reunions. New York: Ivy Books.

Moody, R., & Perry, P. (2010). Glimpses of eternity. Harlan, IA: Guidepost Books.

Moody, R. & Perry, P. (2011). The light beyond. New York: Bantam.

Morrissey, D. (1997). You can see the light. Walpole, NH: Stillpoint.

Morse, M., with Perry, P. (1990). Closer to the light. New York: Ivy Books.

Morse, M., with Perry, P. (1992). Transformed by the light. New York: Ivy Books.

Morse, M., with Perry, P. (1994). Parting visions. New York: Harper Paperbacks.

Morse, M., with Perry, P. (2000). Where God lives. New York: HarperCollins.

Moss, T. (1979). The body electric: a personal journey into the mysteries of parapsychological research, bioenergy, and Kirlian photography. Los Angeles: J. P. Tarcher.

Motoyama, H. (1979). The Functional relationship between yoga asanas and acupuncture meridians. Tokyo, Japan, I.A.R.P.

Motoyama, H. (1992). A new science of healing. Share International, 11 (7), 5-7.

Myers, I. B., & Myers, P. B. (1995). Gifts differing: Understanding personality type. Mountain View, CA: Davies-Black Publishing.

Myss, C. (1996). Anatomy of the spirit. New York: Harmony Books.

Naranjo, C. (1990). Ennea-type structures. Nevada City, CA: Gateways.

Naranjo, C. (1994). Character and neurosis: An integrative view. Nevada City, CA: Gateways.

Naranjo, C. (1995). Enneatypes in psychotherapy. Prescott, AZ: Hohm Press.

Naranjo, C. (2004). The Enneagram of society: Healing the soul to heal the world. Nevada City, CA: Gateways Books & Tapes.

Neugarten, B. L. (1968). Adult personality: Toward a psychology of the life cycle. In B. L. Neugarten (Ed.), Middle Age and Aging. Chicago: University of Chicago Press.

Noam, G. G., Higgins, R. O., & Goethals, G. W. (1982). Psychoanalytic approaches to developmental psychology. In B. B. Wolman (Ed.), Handbook of developmental psychology (pp. 23-43). Englewood Cliffs, NJ: Prentice-Hall.

Norcross, J. C. (2010). The therapeutic relationship. In B. L. Duncan (Ed.), The heart and soul of change: Delivering what works in therapy. Washington, DC: American Psychological Association.

Northrup, C. (1994). Women's bodies; women's wisdom. New York: Random House.

OBERF, Out of Body Experience Research Foundation, http://www.oberf.org/stories_obe.htm.

O'Donohue, W., & Krasner, L. (1995). Theories of behavior therapy: Exploring behavior change. Washington, DC: American Psychological Association.

Orloff, J. (2000). Intuitive healing. New York: Times Books

Oschman, J. L. (2000). Energy medicine: The scientific basis. New York: Churchill Livingston.

Ouspensky, P. D. (1949). In search of the miraculous. New York: Harcourt Brace & Co.

Ouspensky, P. D. (1949). The fourth way. New York: Vintage.

Paddison, S. (1998). The hidden power of the heart. Boulder Creek, CA: Planetary.

Palmer, H. (1991). The Enneagram: Understanding yourself and others in your life. San Francisco: Harper.

Palmer, H. (1995). The Enneagram in love and work. New York: Harper Collins.

Parti, R. with Perry, P. (2016). Dying to wake up: A doctor's voyage into the afterlife and the wisdom he brought back. New York: Atria Books.

Paulson, G. L. (1994). Kundalini and the chakras. St. Paul, MN: Llewellyn.

Pearce, H. (2012). Enneagram beyond the basics. Self published.

Pearce, J. C. (1977). The magical child. New York: Plume.

Pert, C. B. (1997). The molecules of emotion. New York: Scribner.

Piaget, J. & Inhelder, B. (1966). The psychology of the child (H. Weaver trans.). New York: Basic Books, 1969.

Pierrakos, J. C. (1990). Core energetics. Mendocino, CA: LifeRhythm Publication.

Pierrakos, J. C. (1997). Eros, Love & Sexuality. Mendocino, CA: LifeRhythm.

Platt, A. M. (1977). The child savers: The invention of delinquency. Chicago: University of Chicago Press.

383

Playfair, G. L. (2002). Twin telepathy: The psychic connection. London: Chryslis Books.

Polonko, K. A. (2006). Exploring assumptions about child neglect in relation to the broader field of child maltreatment. Journal of Health & Human Services Administration, 29 (3), 260-284.

Polonko, K. A., & Lombardo, L. (2004). Enlightened witnessing: Rehumanizing through confrontation with violence. Paper presented at the annual meetings of the International Conference on New Directions in the Humanities, Prato, Italy.

Popp, F. A. (1994). Electormagnetism and living systems. In M. W. Ho, F. A. Popp, & U. Warnke (Eds.), Bioelectrodynamics and biocommunication (pp. 33- 80). River Edge, NJ: World Scientific Publishing.

Quinn, D. (1995). Ishmael. New York: Bantam.

Quinn, D. (1997). The story of B. New York: Bantam.

Rapgay, L. (1996). The Tibetan book of healing. Salt Lake City, UT: Passage Press.

Ravitz Leonard J. (1970) Electro-Magnetic field monitoring of changing state-function including hypnotic states. Condensed from a paper presented at 5th International Congress for Hypnosis and Psychosomatic Medicine, Johannes Gutenberg University, D6500 Mainz, Germany, May 22 1970.

Reich, W. (1961). The discovery of the orgone: The function of the orgasm. New York: Noonday Press.

Rhodes, S. (2010). Archetypes of the enneagram. Seattle, WA: Geranium Press.

Ring, K., & Valarino, E. E. (1998). Lessons from the light. New York: Insight.

Rinpoche, L. Y. (1995). The tantric path of purification. Boston: Wisdom.

Rinpoche, S. (1993). The Tibetan book of living and dying. San Francisco: Harper.

Riso, D. R., & Hudson, R. (1999). The wisdom of the enneagram. New York: Bantam Books.

Ruiz, D. M. (1997). The four agreements. San Rafael, CA: Amber-Allen.

Ruiz, D. M. (1999). The mastery of love. San Rafael, CA: Amber-Allen.

Rutter, M. (1979). Protective factors in children's responses to stress and disadvantage. In M. W. Kent & J. E. Rolf (Eds.), Primary prevention of psychopathology: Social competence in children (Vol. 3). Hanover, New Hampshire: University Press of New England.

Rutter, M. (1990). Psychosocial resilience and protective mechanisms. In J. Rolf, A. Masten, D. Ciccheti, D. Neuterlein, & S. Weintraub (Eds.), Risk and protective factors in the development of psychopathology (pp. 181-214). New York: Cambridge University Press.

Sabom, M. (1998). Light and death. Zondervan Publishing House.

Sangpo, K. (1996). Tantric practice in Nying-ma. Ithaca, NY: Snow Lion.

Schwarz, G. E. R., & Russek, L. E. S. (2001). The living energy universe. New York: Harper.

Schwarz, J. (1979). Human energy systems: A way of good health using our electromagnetic fields. New York: Arkana.

Schwarz, J. M., & Begley, S. (2002). The mind and the brain: Neuroplasticity and the power of mental force. New York: Regan Books.

Searle, J. R. (1995). The construction of social reality. New York: Free Press.

Shealy, C. N., & Myss, C. M. (1993). The creation of health. Walpole, NH: Stillpoint Publishing.

Sheldrake, R. (1981). A new science of life: The hypothesis of formative causation. Los Angeles: Tarcher.

Sheppard, L. (2000). The everyday Enneagram. Petaluma, CA: Nine Points Press.

Sherwood, K. (1993). Chakra therapy: For personal growth and healing. St. Paul, MN: Llewellyn.

Smith, H. (1991). The world's great religions: Our great wisdom traditions. San Francisco: Harper.

Smith, M. (1997). Auras: See them in only 60 seconds. St. Paul, MN: Llewellyn.

Stevenson, I. (2001). Children who remember past lives. Jefferson, NC: McFarland & Company.

Speeth, K. R. (1989). The Gurdjieff work. New York: Jeremy P. Tarcher/Putnsm.

Speeth, K. R., & Friedlander, I. (1980). Gurdjieff: Seeker of the truth. New York: Harper Colophon Books.

Spiegel, M. (1988). The dreaded comparison. New York: Mirror Books.

Starck, M. (1993). Woman's medicine ways: cross-cultural rites of passage. Freedom, CA: Crossing Press.

Steinberg, L., Bomstein, M. H., Vandell, D. L, & Rook, K. S. (2011). Lifespan development: Infancy through adulthood. Belmont, CA: Wadsworth.

Steiner, R. (1983). Deeper insights in education: The Waldorf approach. Spring Valley, NY: Anthroposophic Press.

Steiner, R. (1995). Intuitive thinking as a spiritual path. Spring Valley, NY: Anthroposophic Press.

Straus, M. A., with Donnelly, D. A. (2001). Beating the devil out of them. New Brunswick, NJ: Transaction.

Stevenson, I. (2001). Children who remember past lives. Jefferson, NC: McFarland & Company.

Sullivan, H. S. (1953). The interpersonal theory of psychiatry. New York: W. W. Norton.

Sutherland, C. (1993). Within the light. New York: Bantam.

Thomas, W. I., & Thomas, D. S. (1928). The child in America: Behavior problems and programs. New York: Knopf.

Thorne, B. (1987). Re-visioning women and social change: Where are the children? Gender and Society, 1, 85-109.

Tucker, J. B. (2005). Live before life: Children's memories of previous lives. New York: St. Martin's Press.

Tucker, J. B. (2013). Return to life: Extraordinary cases of children who remember past lives. New York: St. Martins's Griffin.

Twain, M. (1970). The war prayer. New York: HarperCollins.

Verny, T. (1982). The secret life of the unborn child. New York: Delta.

Vollmar, K. (1997). The secret of Enneagrams: Mapping the personality. Rockport, MA: Element Books.

Wade, J. (2004). Transcendent sex: When lovemaking opens the veil. New York: Paraview Pocket Books.

Walker, E. H. (2000). The physics of consciousness. Cambridge, MA: Perseus Publishing.

Wallace, B. A. (1996). Choosing reality: A Buddhist view of physics and the mind. Ithaca, NY: Snow Lion Publications.

Walsch, N. D. (1996). Conversations with God, Book 1. New York: G. P. Putnam's Sons.

Wauters, A. (1997). Chakras and their archetypes. Freedom, CA: The Crossing Press.

Werner, E. E., & Smith, R. S. (1992). Overcoming the odds: High risk children from birth to adulthood. New York: Cornell University Press.

Weiss, B. L. (1988). Many lives, many masters. New York: Fireside.

Weiss, B. L. (1992). Through time into healing. New York: Fireside.

Weiss, B. L. (1996). Only love is real. New York: Warner Books.

Weiss, B. L. (2000). Messages from the masters. New York: Warner Books.

Weiss, B. L. (2005). Same soul, many bodies: Discovering the healing power of future lives through progression therapy. New York: Free Press.

Weiss, B. L., & Weiss, A. E. (2012). Miracles happen: The transformational healing power of past-life memories. New York: HarperCollins.

White, R. (1993). Working with your chakras: A physical, emotional, and spiritual approach. York Beach, ME: Samuel Weiser.

Wilbur, K. (2000). Integral psychology. Boston: Shambhala.

Wilber, K. (1997). The eye of spirit. Boston: Shambhala.

Wilber, K. (1995). Sex, ecology, spirituality: The spirit of evolution. Boston: Shambhala.

Wilber, K. (1993). The spectrum of consciousness. Wheaton, IL: Theosophical Publishing House.

Wilber, K. (1987). Eye to eye. Boston: Shambhala.

Wilber, K. (1979). No boundary: Eastern and Western approaches to spiritual growth. Boston: Shambhala.

Wilber, K. (2008). Integral life practice: A 21st century blueprint for physical health, emotional balance, and spiritual awakening. Boston: Integral Books.

Williamson, K. (2012). http://www.dailymail.co.uk/news/article-1203226/Pictured-Incredible-watercolour-paintings-boy-aged-just-SIX.html

Williamson, M. (1992). A return to love: Reflections on the principles of A Course in Miracles. New York: Harper Collins.

Yasuo, Y. (1993). The body, self-cultivation, and ki-energy. Albany, NY: State University of New York Press.

ABOUT THE AUTHOR

Geoffrey K. Leigh, Ph.D., completed his first bachelor's degree in Arabic in 1972, followed by a second degree in psychology in 1973, both at the University of Utah. He completed his master's degree in 1975 with a major in Child Development and Early Childhood Education and his doctoral degree in 1980 with a dual major in Family Studies and Sociology. Both graduate degrees were from Brigham Young University. He taught for one year at the University of Utah as a Visiting Assistant Professor, then six years at the University of Iowa as an Assistant Professor in the Department of Home Economics. He moved to a position as Associate Professor in the Department of Human Development and Family Science at The Ohio State University from 1986-1990 where he developed the marriage and family therapy component of the doctoral program. In 1990, he became Chairman of the Department of Human Development and Family Studies at the University of Nevada, Reno (UNR), where he also became a member of the Social Psychology doctoral program. He continued to teach classes and conduct research, including the investigations of children's energy fields and later the research on the energy fields of parent and adolescent interactions with Dr. Jean Metzker. In 1998, he moved to the College of Cooperative Extension to do community work as part of UNR's community outreach program in Las Vegas, NV. From 1975 until he retired in 2010, he conducted and published dozens of research papers, presented many papers at national and international conferences, and was co-editor with Dr. Gary Peterson of the book, <u>Adolescents in Families</u>. After moving to Napa, CA, he taught graduate classes part-time in the Counseling Program at St. Mary's College of CA. He currently writes, works in real estate, conducts workshops and spiritual coaching sessions, and enjoys his family and life among the vineyards in Napa Valley.

CPSIA information can be obtained
at www.ICGtesting.com
Printed in the USA
FSOW02n1313301017
40363FS